Handbook of Cross-Cultural Psychology

BASIC PROCESSES

VOLUME 3

EDITED BY

Harry C. Triandis
University of Illinois at Urbana-Champaign, USA

Walter Lonner
Western Washington University, USA

ALLYN AND BACON, INC.

Boston   London   Sydney   Toronto

Library of Congress Cataloging in Publication Data

Main entry under title:

Handbook of cross-cultural psychology.

   Includes bibliographies and index.
   CONTENTS: v. 1. Triandis, H. C. and Lambert, W. W.,
editor. Perspectives.—v. 2. Triandis, H. C. and Berry,
J. W., editors. Methodology.—v. 3. Triandis, H. C.
and Lonner, W. Basic processes.— [etc.]
   1. Ethnopsychology—Collected works. I. Triandis,
Harry Charalambos, 1926—
GN502.H36   155.8   79-15905
ISBN 0-205-06499-X (v. 3)

Printed in the United States of America.

TO

Dan Berlyne

Contents

Volume 4. DEVELOPMENTAL PSYCHOLOGY   (in press)

Preface

Cross-cultural psychology has been expanding in the past twenty years[1] to the point that there is now a need for a source book more advanced than a textbook and more focused than the periodical literature. This is the first handbook of cross-cultural psychology. It is an attempt to assemble in one place the key findings of cross-cultural psychologists. In addition to serving the needs of graduate instruction, the *Handbook* will be useful to advanced undergraduates and to professional social and behavioral scientists.

This *Handbook* will do more than summarize the state of cross-cultural psychology in the 1970s. It should provide a bridge that will allow more traffic in the direction of a new kind of psychology. One of the key facts about psychology is that most of the psychologists who have ever lived and who are now living can be found in the United States. About 50,000 psychologists live in the United States and several thousand more graduate each year. The rest of the world has only about 20 percent of the psychologists that are now or have ever been alive. Moreover, psychology as a science is so overwhelmingly the product of German, French, British, Russian, and North American efforts that it is fair to consider it an entirely European-based enterprise (with American culture considered the child of European culture). Yet, science aspires to be universal. Cross-cultural psychologists try to discover laws that will be stable over time and across cultures, but the data base excludes the great majority of mankind who live in Asia and the Southern Hemisphere. Are so-called "psychological laws" really universal? Are theories merely parochial generalizations, based on ethnocentric constructions of reality? This *Handbook* assembles reports of the methods, procedures, and findings that ultimately will give definitive answers to such questions, answers that are crucial for the development of psychology. If psychology must be changed to understand the behavior and experience of the majority of mankind, then this is a fact of profound importance. If not, it is still good to know that no changes are needed. The reality probably lies between these two extremes, and different psychological laws can be held as "true" with varying degrees of confidence.

We engage in cross-cultural psychology for many reasons, which are enumerated in the Introduction to Volume 1. Volume 1 examines the field in broad perspective and examines how it relates to some other fields. Volume 2 focuses on methodology, since the cross-cultural enterprise poses formidable methodological difficulties. The remaining volumes concentrate on basic psychological processes such as learning, motivation, and perception (Volume 3); developmental processes (Volume 4); social psychological (Volume 5); and psychopathological (Volume 6) phenomena.

One key policy decision for a handbook is whether to cover the material exhaustively, saying a word or two about every study, or in depth, saying rather more about a few key studies. Our decision for greater depth resulted in incomplete coverage. However, much of the work in cross-cultural psychology is methodologically weak. Rather than attacking such studies, we decided to de-emphasize them in favor of those studies that are methodologically defensible. However, this was not a decision that was applicable to all the methodologically weak areas. In some areas of cross-cultural psychology, there has been so *much* weak work that any student starting to work on related problems is likely to find dozens of studies and hence get the impression that this is a respectable area of inquiry. In such cases we could not ignore the weak studies. But while we had to quote them and criticize them, we could not sacrifice much space in this effort. For instance, most of the work using versions of the prisoner dilemma game in different cultures results in uninterpretable findings. In Volume 5 Leon Mann and Gergen, Morse, and Gergen discuss this work and show why it is weak.

Some work was left out simply because space limitations did not allow complete coverage. Other work was omitted on the grounds that it really is not cross-cultural psychology, and may more appropriately be included in comparative sociology, cultural anthropology, or some other field. Some of these decisions are inevitably arbitrary. Obviously, a *Handbook* like this one is likely to *define* the field, both by what it includes and by what it excludes. We are distinctly uncomfortable about some of the exclusions. For instance, our coverage of Freudian, neopsychoanalytic, and related cross-cultural studies is extremely limited. However, other theoretical systems, such as a "liberated cognitive behaviorism" (Triandis, 1977) will encompass the insights derived from this tradition. We have very little discussion of ethnoscience, ethnomusicology, and ethnolinguistics; we believe these materials now belong to other neighboring disciplines. It is of course obvious that this judgment may be wrong. A revision of this *Handbook*, which may be necessary in a decade or two, could well give a central position to one of these topics.

In writing this *Handbook* we have been very much aware of the probability that psychologists from non-European-derived cultures will find it among the most useful books that they may obtain from European-derived cultures. Much of what psychologists teach in their own cultures is based on studies done with subjects from European-derived cultures. They cannot be sure that such information is culture-general. This *Handbook* faces this question and could become a companion volume of any European-derived psychology book. Since many psychologists do not have English as their first language, we have tried to keep the language as concise as possible. If the style appears telegraphic at times, it is intentional.

We allowed the authors of the chapters considerable freedom in expressing themselves. We felt that an international enterprise such as this *Handbook*, should not impose narrow, possibly ethnocentric standards. Thus, authors have been allowed to use the style and spelling that is more appropriate in their own country. English now exists in many versions; the language of Scotland is not identical to Indian English. Rather than obliterate such differences with a heavy editorial hand, we have preserved them.

Volume 1 includes background material that any serious student of cross-cultural psychology would want to know. It examines the history, the major theoretical frameworks, and the relationship between cross-cultural psychology and some other closely related disciplines.

Volume 2 concentrates on methodological problems. Cross-cultural psychology has all the methodological problems of research done by psychologists in a homogeneous culture, plus additional ones that arise because it is cross-cultural. The authors describe the particular technique and emphasize the special difficulties—the particular methodological dilemmas that one faces in cross-cultural work—stressing those strategies developed to deal with those dilemmas. For example, since the reader is assumed to know about experimental methods, the chapters on experiments deal only with special concerns of cross-cultural psychologists doing experiments.

Volume 3 focuses on basic psychological processes—perception, learning, motivation, and so on. Here we tried to give the experimental psychologists who investigate such processes a chance to expand their perspective. We focused on what appears to be universal, but also emphasized ways in which cultural factors may intrude and change some of the processes.

Volume 4 examines developmental perspectives. Some of the key areas discussed are the development of language, personality, and cognition. Since the major effort in the past twenty years in cross-cultural developmental psychology has been on testing aspects of Piaget's theoretical system, a major focus is on this topic.

Volume 5 deals with cross-cultural social psychology. It examines the major traditional topics—attitudes, values, groups, social change—and some of the newer topics—environmental psychology and organizational psychology.

Volume 6, the last one, is of greatest interest to clinical psychologists or psychiatrists. The focus is on variations of psychopathology, on methods of clinical work, as well as on the cultural and family antecedents of psychopathology.

Our expectation is that the committed student of cross-cultural psychology will want to own all six volumes. However, in this age of specialization and high costs we know that many will buy only Volume 1 plus one other. Finally, certain specialists will want a single volume to enlarge their perspective on their own discipline, by examining the related cross-cultural work. These different patterns of acquisition produce a serious policy problem concerning coverage. A key theory or key cross-cultural finding may have to be mentioned in each volume for those who purchase only one volume, which may create considerable overlap across volumes. However, the authors have cross-referenced chapters in other volumes. Also, we have allowed minimum coverage of a particular topic that has been covered extensively in another volume, so that purchasers of only one volume will acquire some superficial familiarity with that topic.

In some cases, the topics are sufficiently large and diffuse that coverage by two different authors does not result in redundancy. When this was the case, I simply sent copies of the relevant sections of other chapters to these authors and asked them, when revising, to be fully aware of coverage in other chapters.

The idea to publish a *Handbook of Cross-Cultural Psychology* originated with Jack Peters of Allyn and Bacon, Inc. He asked me at the 1972 meetings of the American Psychological Association, in Hawaii, whether I would be interested in editing such a handbook. The idea appealed to me, but I was not sure of the need. We wrote to a sample of distinguished psychologists for their opinions. They were almost unanimous in thinking that such a handbook would be worth publishing. At the conference on "The Interface between Culture and Learning," held by the East-West Center, in Hawaii, in January 1973 we asked a distinguished, international sample of cross-cultural psychologists for their opinion. They were also supportive. By the summer of 1973 a first outline of a handbook was available, but it also became very clear that I alone could not handle the editing. The handbook should reflect all of psychology; I was not competent to deal with such a vast subject. Hence the idea emerged of having several Associate Editors, who would cover different aspects of the topic.

The Society for Cross-Cultural Research, at its 1975 Chicago meetings, heard a symposium in which G. Kelly, G. Guthrie, W. Lambert, J. Tapp, W. Goodenough, H. Barry, R. Naroll, and I presented our ideas about the shape of the *Handbook*, and we heard criticism from both anthropologists and psychologists in the audience about our plans.

In January 1976 we were fortunate to be able to hold a conference sponsored by the East-West Center, Hawaii, in which about two-thirds of the chapters were thoroughly discussed. We are most grateful to the Center for this support. The East-West Center held a course for post-doctoral level, young social scientists from Asia, the Pacific, and the United States, using the drafts of the *Handbook* chapters as a textbook. Richard Brislin, Stephen Bochner, and George Guthrie were the faculty. Fifteen outstanding young social scientists[2] were thus able to give us feedback from the point of view of the consumer, but even more important, they pointed out statements that may have been ethnocentric, incorrect, confusing, and outdated.

From the very beginning, we were committed to producing a handbook with authors from every continent. This was not possible. However, the *Handbook* includes chapters by authors from nine countries. To avoid as much ethnocentrism as possible, I appointed a board of twenty Regional Editors. These editors were asked to supply abstracts of publications not generally available in European and North American libraries. These abstracts were sent to those chapter authors who might find them useful. Thus, we increased the chapter authors' exposure to the non-English international literature. By summer 1975, fourteen of these twenty Regional Editors had supplied abstracts listed by cultural region. They were:

Africa

> R. Ogbonna Ohuche (University of Liberia, Monrovia, Liberia)
> The late M. O. Okonji (University of Lagos, Nigeria)
> Christopher Orpen (University of Cape Town, South Africa)
> Robert Serpell (University of Zambia, Lusaka, Zambia)

Circum-Mediterranean

> Yehuda Amir (Bar-Ilan University, Israel)
> Terry Prothro (American University, Beirut, Lebanon)

East-Eurasia

> S. Anandalakshmy (Lady Irwin College, New Delhi, India)
> John L. M. Dawson (University of Hong Kong)
> Wong Fong Tong (Jamaah Nazir Sekolah, Kuala Lumpur, Malaysia)
> S. M. Hafeez Zaidi (University of Karachi, Pakistan)

Insular Pacific
> Subhas Chandra (University of South Pacific, Fiji)

South America

> Eduardo Almeida (Mexico City)
> Gerardo Marin (Universidad de los Andes, Bogotá, Colombia)
> Jose Miguel Salazar (Universidad Central de Venezuela, Caracas, Venezuela)

It should be mentioned that with such an international group of authors, chapters required particularly skillful editing of the style so that all chapters would be excellent not only in content but in language. My wife, Pola, and Doris S. Bartle supplied this expertise and were among those who contributed to the realization of a truly international undertaking.

A number of colleagues functioned as special reviewers for individual chapters. Thanks are due to S. M. Berger, Charles Eriksen, Lucia French, Lloyd Humphreys, and Fred Lehman for their critical comments. In addition, the final version of each volume was read by a scholar, and I would also like to acknowledge their valuable suggestions and comments: Volume 1, Daniel Katz; Volume 2, Uriel Foa; Volume 3, Lee Sechrest; Volume 4, Barbara Lloyd and Sylvia Scribner; Volume 5, Albert Pepitone; and Volume 6, Ihsan Al-Issa.

Harry C. Triandis

NOTES

1. Documentation of this point would include noting that several journals (the *International Journal of Psychology,* the *Journal of Social Psychology* and the *Journal of Cross-Cultural Psychology*) publish almost exclusively cross-cultural papers; there is a *Newsletter,* first published in 1967, that is largely concerned with this area; there are *Directories* of the membership of cross-cultural psychologists, first published by Berry in the *International Journal of Psychology* in 1969, then revised and extended and published as a booklet by Berry and Lonner (1970) and Berry, Lonner, and Leroux (1973); and finally, there is the International Association for Cross-Cultural Psychology, which has held meetings in Hong Kong (1972), Kingston, Canada (1974), Tilburg, Holland (1976), Munich, West Germany (1978), which now has a membership of about 350 active researchers from about fifty countries. Psychology has been an international enterprise for almost a century, and the Union of Scientific Psychology, and the International Association of Applied Psychology have been meeting every two or so years, since the turn of the century. But the emphasis on collecting *comparable* data in several cultures is relatively new, and has expanded particularly after the mid 1960s. A number of regional international organizations, such as the Interamerican Society of Psychology, and the Mediterranean Society of Psychology, have become active in the last twenty years.

2. Listed by country the participants were:
   Australia: Brian Bishop (Perth, Institute of Technology), Margaret M. Brandl (Darwin, Department of Education), Betty A. Drinkwater (Townsville, James Cook University), Michael P. O'Driscoll (Adelaide, Flinders University).
   Fiji: Lavenia Kaurasi (Suva, Malhala High School)
   Indonesia: Suwarsih Warnaen (Jakarta, University of Indonesia)
   Japan: Yuriko Oshimo (University of Tokyo) and Toshio Osako (Tokyo, Sophia University)
   Pakistan: Sabeeha Hafeez (Karachi University), Abdul Haque (Hyderabad, University of Sind)

Philippines: Liwayway N. Angeles (Rizal, Teacher Education)
Thailand: Jirawat Wongswadiwat (Chaingmai University)
United States: Angela B. Ginorio (New York, Fordham University), Howard Higginbotham (University of Hawaii), Caroline F. Keating (Syracuse University), and James M. Orvik (Fairbanks, University of Alaska)

At the conference, the following authors and editors, in addition to Brislin, Bochner, and Guthrie, were also present: Altman, Barry, Berry, Ciborowski, Davidson, Deregowski, Draguns, Heron, Holtzman, Hsu, Jahoda, Klineberg, Lambert, Longabaugh, Lonner, R. and R. Munroe, Michik, Pareek, Price-Williams, Prince, Sanua, Sutton-Smith, E. Thompson, Tseng, Triandis, Warwick, Zavalloni.

Biographical Statements

HARRY C. TRIANDIS, the General Editor, was born in Greece, in 1926. During childhood he received several cross-cultural influences: German and French governesses, French and Italian high school years. After three years of engineering studies at the Polytechnic Institute of Athens, he attended McGill University in Montreal, Canada, where he graduated in Engineering. He worked in industry for three years, during which he obtained a master's degree from the University of Toronto. But engineering was not as interesting to him as studying people. He returned to McGill to learn basic psychology, and studied with Wallace E. Lambert and Don Hebb. From there he went to Cornell University, where he studied with W. W. Lambert, W. F. Whyte, T. A. Ryan, Alexander Leighton, and others. From Cornell in 1958 he went to the University of Illinois, where he is now Professor of Psychology. He conducted cross-cultural studies in Greece, Germany, Japan, and India, and worked in collaboration with black psychologists on the perceptions of the social environment among blacks and whites. His books include *Attitude and Attitude Change* (1971), *The Analysis of Subjective Culture* (1972), *Variations in Black and White Perceptions of the Social Environment* (1975), and *Interpersonal Behavior* (1977). He was Chairman of the Society of Experimental Social Psychology (1973–74), President of the International Association of Cross-Cultural Psychology (1974–76), President of the Society for the Psychological Study of Social Issues (1975–76), President of the Society of Personality and Social Psychology (1976–77), and Vice-President of the Interamerican Society of Psychology (1975–77).

WALTER J. LONNER was born in and grew up in the multi-ethnic mining city of Butte, Montana. Currently he is a professor in the Department of Psychology at Western Washington University, Bellingham, Washington. Prior to receiving his Ph.D. from the University of Minnesota in 1967, he spent two years in Europe. During a brief stay in Sweden, he translated psychological and educational research for the Royal Swedish Board of Education in Stockholm. He then worked as a school psychologist in Germany, and at the same time completed a few research projects with several European colleagues. In 1976–77, Lonner spent a sabbatical research year in Yucatan, Mexico. He is the founding editor of the *Journal of Cross-Cultural Psychology* (a role in which he continues), the co-author of *Cross-Cultural Research Methods* (1973), and has co-edited several books including *Cross-Cultural Perspectives on Learning* (1975), *Applied Cross-Cultural Psychology* (1975), and *Counseling Across-Cultures* 1976).

JAN B. DERĘGOWSKI was born in Poland. The broadening of his cultural experience began with the invasions of that country and his deportation to Siberia. These later, not entirely voluntary, travels took him to various parts of the Soviet Union, Iran, Palestine, and Egypt before he arrived in England where he graduated from the University of London in engineering and subsequently in psychology. His cross-cultural work has been done mostly in various parts of Africa. He is now a lecturer at the University of Aberdeen.

ANNE D. PICK received her Ph.D. from Cornell University in 1963 and is now professor of psychology at the Institute of Child Development at the University of Minnesota in Minneapolis. Her special interests are perception, learning, and concept and language development theory and method.

DOUGLASS PRICE-WILLIAMS received his Ph.D. in psychology from the University of London. He first taught at the London School of Economics, then emigrated to Rice University, Houston, Texas, where he was chairman of the psychology department for five years. He has been a professor in the departments of psychiatry and anthropology at University of California at Los Angeles since 1971. Professor Price-Williams has conducted cross-cultural research in different parts of Nigeria, in Mexico and Guatemala, and in the Hawaiian Islands. He has published two books of direct interest to cross-cultural psychology: *Cross-Cultural Studies* (1969), and *Explorations in Cross-Cultural Psychology* (1975). He is coeditor of *Ethos*, a journal dealing with the interrelationships between the individual and his social milieu.

CARROLL E. IZARD was born on a farm in Mississippi in 1923, when that state was so far from the mainstream of the United States that it was truly a subculture. It had been studied as such by anthropologist-psychologist John Dollard, with whom Izard studied when he made the transition to the subculture of New England. Izard's early interests were religion and philosophy, and partly because of the great gulf between the religious fundamentalism of the deep south and the liberalism of the Yale Divinity School, he remembers the adaptation to the Yale–New England subculture during his late teens and early twenties as a far more difficult one than that achieved in later years while living in Western Europe or the Soviet Union. The differences he had to confront in New England struck at his central beliefs and values and involved him personally and emotionally. The perspectives of Dollard, who introduced him to the pioneering work of Lloyd Warner and his colleagues on American subcultures, were more helpful than the liberal theology of Yale Divinity School. His appreciation of the possibilities of cross-cultural research was influenced by his experiences at Yale and his later collaboration with Silvan Tomkins, a proponent of Darwin's thesis that expressions of emotions are innate and universal. Izard has conducted cross-cultural studies in several countries of Western Europe and India. In 1974 he spent six months as a National Academy of Science research-exchange fellow with the Soviet Academy of Science in Moscow. His books include: *Affect, Cognition and Personality* (1965, with Silvan Tomkins), *The Face of Emotion* (1971), *Patterns of Emotions: A New Analysis of Anxiety and Depression* (1972), and *Human Emotions* (1977).

HANS-JOACHIM KORNADT is professor of educational psychology at the University of the Saar, Saarbrücken. A Ph.D. of the University of Marburg, he taught previously at the University of Würzburg. He is the author of several books, two of which are within the area of cross-cultural research, and of one book dealing with aggression from the viewpoint of motivation theory. In addition, he has written many articles on motivation and is editor of two volumes on aggression and frustration.

LUTZ H. ECKENSBERGER is professor of psychology at the University of the Saar, Saarbrücken where he received his diploma (1964) as well as his Ph.D. (1969). He published two books within the area of cross-cultural research (teaching problems in technical-commercial colleges in developing countries; methodological problems in cross-cultural psychology) and several articles concerning methodological problems of intercultural research, conditions of sociocultural change, the utility of a cultural perspective for ecological and environmental psychology. He is consulting editor of the *Journal of Cross-Cultural Psychology* and of *Die dritte Welt*.

WOLF BERNHARD EMMINGHAUS, Diplom-Psychologe, is a research assistant working with Hans J. Kornadt at the Institute of Educational Psychology, University of the Saar, Saarbrücken, Germany on a cross-cultural project on aggressiveness. His interests focus on motivational psychology and on learning theories, and application to educational practice.

D. E. BERLYNE was born in Salford, England in 1924. He received his B.A. and M.A. from Cambridge University and the Ph.D. from Yale University. He has taught in various universities in Scotland and the United States. For many years he was professor of psychology at the University of Toronto. A past President of the Canadian Psychological Association, and of Divisions 1 and 10 APA, and of the International Association of Empirical Aesthetics, he was also a Fellow of the Royal Society of Canada, APA, BPS, CPA and AAAS. He died in November 1976.

Handbook of Cross-Cultural Psychology

BASIC PROCESSES

VOLUME 3

1

Introduction to
Basic Processes

Walter J. Lonner
and Harry C. Triandis

Psychology is a science whose fate depends upon the stability, generalizability, and rigor of its empirical foundations. These foundations consist of certain basic processes into which can be poured (and out of which inevitably comes) everything else in the discipline. Stated simply, individuals have the capacity to perceive and to respond, to think and to learn, and their behavior, far from being a random response to stimuli, is goal-oriented. The elementary, basic processes that include perception, cognition, learning, and motivation are the concerns of this volume. The only substantial difference between the content of the chapters in this volume and psychology texts dealing with these edifices of the discipline is that culture and cultural factors are treated as coequals in this book, while in traditional coverage of these topics culture is accorded, at best, incidental status. Thus, the authors of these chapters do not present both a synopsis of the basic processes in culture-neutral terms and how they may undulate with cultural factors. Space obviously prohibits such an expansive treatment. However, some elementary knowledge of psychology's basic processes will make these chapters more vivid and understandable.

Students in beginning psychology courses are usually introduced to two of the major competing epistemological orientations. While the differences between them are often exaggerated to make a point (as they are here), the differences are evident and real, nevertheless. Specifically, on the one hand is the "hard-headed experimental" tradition, with its cherished goals of prediction, understanding, and control of psychological processes through the systematic manipulation of variables in a laboratory setting. On the other hand is the tradition, which could be called empathic understanding, phenomenology, or introspection, of clinical and social applications of personality theory. Both traditions deserve credit for their different contributions and for the ways in which each has contributed to the development of the other. In cross-cultural psychology the empirical laboratory approach has not been employed nearly as frequently as the various field and observational methods used in the broad domain of culture and personality.

In the introduction to their book on culture and cognition, Berry and Dasen (1974) pointed out a parallel imbalance in cultural investigations. They cited Bateson's (1936) use of the terms *ethos* and *eidos* to distinguish between two historical orientations in culture study by behavioral scientists. *Ethos* concerns socioemotional aspects of such studies, which have a much longer history than *eidos*, that address purely cognitive variables. Research in the *ethos* tradition usually employed "culture and personality" constructs or theoretical anchors—such as orthodox Freudianism—as starting points. The purely *cognitive* areas of psychology (sensation, perception, problem solving), which involve those domains in the tradition of *eidos*, have received until recently relatively little attention from cross-cultural researchers.

Berry and Dasen's book is one of several recent volumes that together represent a rekindled interest in if and how basic psychological processes are influenced by culture. Indeed, it has been in part a disenchantment with and gnawing distrust of the "old style" culture and personality studies that stimulated this resurgence of interest in basic processes.

A cliche of recent vintage is that cross-cultural psychology has a long history but a short past. Several publications have appeared, all within the past decade, that trace this long history (Price-Williams, 1969, 1975; Jahoda, 1970; Dawson, 1971; Lloyd, 1972; Berry & Dasen, 1974; Cole & Scribner, 1974; Serpell, 1976). The consistent theme of these surveys can be only briefly summarized here. First, homage is usually given to W. H. R. Rivers who as a psychologist-turned-anthropologist is often credited with producing the seminal cross-cultural work in basic processes (Rivers, 1901, 1905). As a member of a Cambridge team of researchers, Rivers studied such basic processes as perception and what is now called cognition using as subjects the natives who occupied the Torres Strait Islands between Australia and New Guinea as well as the Toda of Southern India. We are also told how Wilhelm Wundt (1910–1920) was evidently the only early-day psychologist who wrote extensively on cultural factors using "folk psychology" as his means to explain cultural factors in basic processes. Rivers's general conclusion was that the visual acuity of primitive peoples was not substantially different from that of Europeans, but that the former are "concrete" thinkers, while the latter have the capacity to think "abstractly." The celebrated perceptual prowess of the "savage," reported by anthropologists and ethnographers, was attributed by Rivers to be a result of his attending to minute details. Wundt's conclusions were

similar to Rivers's. For Wundt, the noble savage is not intellectually deficient; his ability, however, is restricted because he operates under more
restricted conditions. Moreover, according to Wundt, he is a rather com-
placent and happy human being who is content to live off the land in an
unhurried and unharried manner.

The writings of various influential anthropologists and sociologists are
often cited as having contributed to earlier formulations of the relationship between culture, the individual, and basic processes. Prominent
among them is Boas, who criticized the popular position of his day that
race and culture are equivalent. In his major work in this area (Boas, 1911),
he commented on observed differences between "civilized" and "primitive" man, but emphasized that these were differences in *content* and not
process. As Berry and Dasen (1974) note, Levy-Bruhl attacked the Wundt
and Boas claim of the universality of thought processes. Levy-Bruhl considered "primitive" men to be mental infants; their savage minds appeared to wander aimlessly, unable to hold the train of thought in
everyday conversation—an inaccurate and ethnocentric observation and
conclusion that was probably based largely upon poor ethnographies and
cultural insensitivities. This point of view is reminiscent of Herbert
Spencer's earlier and thoroughly criticized social Darwinist position.
Spencer's theory, as Cole and Scribner (1974, p. 15) note,

> ... led to the conclusion that nineteenth-century Englishmen were of the
> highest mentality and lived in the most advanced society, representing a
> standard against which other people could be measured. Study of existing
> races at lower social levels, Spencer then argued, could show the mental traits
> that characterized early evolutionary forms of human life.

Cole, Scribner, and their colleagues, incidentally, follow the structuralist
position of Lévi-Strauss, which is radically different from the views of
Levy-Bruhl. Lévi-Strauss believes in the "psychic unity of mankind"
(Boas, 1911) and rejects the idea that there are lower and higher, or better
and worse, levels of cognitive abilities.

This brief sampling shows some of the ideas that helped set the stage
for much work that was to follow. A more complete historical introduction is presented by Klineberg in Volume 1 of this *Handbook*. Some years
after these early theorists, the cross-cultural method in psychology was
made explicit. For the past dozen years it has enjoyed enlightened research, and theory in basic processes as they are influenced by culture has
been especially productive and often controversial.

Landmarks in the Cultural Analyses of
Basic Processes

The processes of perception (including the perception of emotions and beauty), cognition, and motivation have been placed under the cultural microscope many times and in many forms. Most of these studies are cited in this volume. There are, however, a few landmark investigations that still serve rather well not only as interesting explanations of culture-related behavior but also as perpetual research stimulators. It may be helpful at this point to summarize briefly some of these watershed studies, and introduce the central themes developed by the authors of this volume.

Perception

The publication of a book by Segall, Campbell, and Herskovits (1966) was the culmination of a project that began in 1956, half a century after Rivers had collected his venerable data on essentially the same subject matter. The project originated as a debate between Herskovits, a cultural relativist anthropologist, and Campbell, a psychologist who subscribed to a doctrine of the invariance of basic processes such as human perception. Herskovits argued that "cultural differences might well be of sufficient magnitude to influence perceptual tendencies," while Campbell thought that the "biological homogeneity of culture-learning man would preclude such an influence" (p. vi).

In the major part of the study, a total of 1,878 individuals from thirteen non-Western (primarily African) and three Western groups were administered fifty drawings, each one an example of five geometric illusions. The illusions were the Müller-Lyer (M-L), the Sander Parallelogram, two forms of the Horizontal-Vertical (H-V) illusion, and a simple perspective drawing. The results of the five-year project tended to support the empiricist position of Herskovits over the nativist leanings of Campbell. The "carpentered world" and "foreshortening" hypotheses were offered as explanations for ecocultural differences in the perception of these stimuli. Specifically, Segall et al. explain that perception depends, in part, upon "ecological cue validity," which is an aspect of Brunswik's (1956) notion of "probabilistic functionalism."

More specifically, the "carpentered world" hypothesis states that the human visual system is generally *functional* across the species, but that specific conditions affect how the visual system is utilized within different ecologies. Such tendencies within ecologies may thus be compared across ecologies. And so it is hypothesized that people who live in carpentered, right-angled environments learn quite early in their lives to make visual compensations for "reality" as it is represented by certain visual illusions. The learned habits of visual inference make the typical Western person *probabilistically* more susceptible to the M-L illusion, which has as its eco-cultural analog the frequent array of right-angled buildings and boxes. Similarly, the cultural analog of the H-V illusion is the flat cornfield, for example, with furrows (the vertical part of the illusion) retreating into the open vista. Thus for inhabitants of such terrain the vertical line would "have to be" longer, since an adjustment would have to be made for this two-dimensional depiction (foreshortening) of three-dimensional reality. There is much more by way of explanation and methodological considerations and innovation in the published study than can be given here, of course, but the impact of the study was like a dash of cold water in the faces of cloistered researchers (see Segall, *in press*, for a more current discussion of the work in which he was involved).

Another study with enduring cross-cultural virtue centered upon pictorial depth perception. Hudson (1960) used photographs as well as black and white line drawings, in which were superimposed the three depth cues of object size, superimposition, and linear perspective. Showing these materials to groups of black and white South African subjects, he found that the ability to perceive three dimensions in two-dimensional material was a learned process. Hudson tested six samples of adults differing in educational and occupational background, including a group of African teachers, and five samples of children at different educational levels. The results, while not entirely clear, showed that the five school samples and the group of African teachers responded with more three-dimensional interpretations than the remaining adult samples. This particular study also had applied implications, because it explained the tendency of black mine laborers to misinterpret mine safety posters. The results of these studies and their interpretations are still being debated. Additionally, this work, and of course that of Segall et al., has stimulated an avalanche of research on culture and perception, and several reviews in addition to the ones mentioned above (e.g., Miller, 1973; Pick and Pick, in press). Deręgowski's chapter in this volume addresses the issues raised in these debates.

Deręgowski, a leading researcher in *visual* perceptual processes as they are influenced by culture, was faced with a problem of how his chapter should be organized and of how broad its scope should be. Perception is a multifaceted domain within psychology. Lloyd (1972), for instance, partitioned work on culture and perception into two domains: work defined by the nature of the *stimulus*, and work defined *conceptually*. Strictly stimulus-defined visual perception processes include work on geometric illusions and pictorial depth perception, the seminal studies of which have already been mentioned.

Other stimulus-defined domains covered by Lloyd, and by others who have reviewed this area (e.g., Cole & Scribner, 1974; Serpell, 1976), include the perception of color and the perception of orientation. In the perception of color, the work of Lenneberg (1967) and especially Berlin and Kay (1969) stand out as basic references, with a more recent study by Rosch (1975) being an example of where research is progressing in this area and of how individuals categorize stimuli that impinge upon their senses. Berlin and Kay have shown that color naming may be a universal process, whereby eleven basic color names emerge invariantly and sequentially, depending upon where a given culture may be placed on an evolutionary phylogenetic path of development. For instance, if a culture has only two names for colors, these colors will more than likely be white and black. If there are three colors, the third will almost certainly be red, and next would come green and/or yellow, blue, etc., until a dozen or so colors are covered by a complex culture's lexicon.

In the perception of orientation, it has often been argued that cultural factors affect how an individual might perceive verticality or horizontality (e.g., Witkin & Berry, 1975; Berry 1976). It has also been argued (Wober, 1966, 1967) that European cultures "cause" their members to excel on visual cues, while traditional African cultures foster excellence on auditory or kinesthetic cues. A variable to consider here is the extent to which music and rituals associated with music affect the perception of orientation. Ethnomusicologists may argue that the cultural value placed on music, rhythm, and dance may covary with the development of such skills in the individual.

Stimulus-defined perceptual processes rely upon the extent to which individuals perceive the *objective* and *experimenter-defined* environment. The perception of the *subjective, phenomenological* world embraces research on time, space, emotion, and aesthetics (beauty). All of these processes of subjective awareness are universal properties of the human species alone, for it is inconceivable that there is much or any variation among subhuman species in these dimensions. While the reader is referred to other work on the perception of time (e.g., Doob, 1971) and space (e.g., Dasen & Heron's chapter in Volume 4 of this *Handbook*), Izard and Berlyne discuss emotion and aesthetics, respectively. Central arguments in these areas will be discussed.

Because of the breadth of research in culture and perception, and because he preferred not to be arbitrarily selective in his coverage of the area, Deręgowski had to make liberal use of notes in his chapter. Thus in the main body of his review he developed central themes around relatively few studies. In an effort to avoid an uneven expository flow, he found it necessary to note the remaining works within major sections of the chapter.

Cognition: Psychological Perspectives

As with culture and perception, much has been written in recent years on cognitive variables (e.g., memory, classification) as they are affected by culture. While Pick does not explicitly say so, these writings cover five relatively separate traditions, in addition to the related study of linguistic variables (see Bowerman's chapter in Volume 4 of this *Handbook*). These traditions are: 1) the psychometric, 2) the Piagetian, 3) the approach taken by Jerome Kagan and his associates, 4) cognitive-style research, and 5) the experimental ethnographic strategies adopted by Cole and his colleagues. A brief summary of the key tenets of each is as follows.

The psychometric tradition has its roots in the British conception of hierarchically arranged abilities, the pinnacle of which is hypothesized to be "g," or the general factor operating in intelligence (Vernon, 1969; Irvine, 1969). These investigators use multivariate techniques to ferret out general and specific factors in human attainments and abilities, which may be evident in data compiled from such tests as Raven's Matrices or Cattell's factor analytically derived Culture Fair Intelligence Test (see Brislin, Lonner, & Thorndike, 1973). The Piagetian approach has been summarized amply elsewhere (Dasen, 1972, 1977; Dasen & Heron in Volume 4 of this *Handbook*). The concept of "conservation" (e.g., of mass, volume, space, weight, and number) has been the focus of these investigations. It is axiomatic that conservation, which is synonymous with the higher type or levels of logical thought processes, is the keystone of Piaget's final stage—the stage of formal operations. Researchers typically try to identify which, if any, cultural variables affect the assumed universality of Piaget's hypothesized invariant stages of cognitive growth, and the rates that may be found within each stage.

Kagan (1975, 1976) and his associates (Kagan & Klein, 1973; Kagan, Finley, Klein, & Rogoff, 1975) use strategies that contain anthropologically sensitive blends of various approaches, including the Piagetian and psychometric. These strategies are not completely compatible, however, for Kagan has questioned the continued use of the immutability and irreversibility of the concept of developmental stages which, of course, the Piagetians and other developmental psychologists use. Cognitive competencies, they assert, should be specified according to the "class of problem in which that competence is being manifested" (Kagan, 1976, p. 192). Kagan has eschewed what he calls a "tape recorder" theory of development that assumes that from birth onward every salient experience is recorded somewhere in the brain, to be called up on demand. Arguing for great resilience in development (see especially Kagan & Klein, 1973), many of the data coming from this orientation seem to show that children who were deprived early in life in their remote villages nevertheless "caught up" with their less deprived age mates if the environments for the former become more beneficial for development. Since the data supporting this point of view have come primarily from Guatemala and used only a few tasks, it remains to be seen whether such findings are stable across cultures, situations, and time.

Cognitive-style cross-cultural research, as it has come to be known, usually is synonymous with extensions to other cultural and ecological settings of Witkin, Dyk, Faterson, Goodenough and Karp's (1962) theory of psychological differentiation (Witkin & Berry, 1975; Berry, 1976). The general framework guiding this fourth popular strategy is that a number of human ecosystems create antecedent conditions (e.g., harsh versus permissive child-rearing practices) that account for much of an individual's cognitive style. Using tasks and tests that assess the degree of an individual's differentiation in perceptual and other sensory domains, levels of "field dependence" and "field independence" can be ascertained. That is, for example, some individuals may be influenced by (or are relatively more *dependent* upon) the surrounding field or background features when judging the true upright or identifying a simple figure which is embedded in a complex figure. Conversely, some individuals may be more able, through such antecedent cultural factors as independence training and achievement striving, to perceive the true vertical or "pull out" the simple figure from the surrounding background. It has been shown in many studies, cross-cultural and otherwise, that at the extreme poles of this continuum can be found characteristic modes of functioning in such areas as pathology, defenses, learning styles, and social conformity (e.g., Witkin, Price-Williams, Bertini, Christiansen, Oltman, Ramirez, & van Meel, 1974). Jahoda (in Volume 1 of this *Handbook*) has given a cogent summary of this orientation as a major model in cross-cultural psychology.

The final—and probably the most recent as well as the most radical— of these five traditions combines the richness and fecundity of the ethnographic tradition in anthropology and the rigor of the experimental approach in psychology. Cole and his associates have thus pioneered in this area of so-called "experimental anthropology" or "unorthodox ethnography" (Cole, Gay, Glick, & Sharp, 1971; Cole & Scribner, 1974). The theme of radical cultural relativism is evident in this approach, and the notion of "cultural context" has become a byword for these researchers. They question much previous cross-cultural research, and condemn any possibly careless or overinterpreted cross-cultural "experiment" that may have led researchers to infer cognitive deficits from experimental differences (Cole & Bruner, 1971). These researchers, like most contemporary cross-culturalists, subscribe to a doctrine of "psychic unity," and have been convincing in their successful attempts to find, in the cultures they have studied, culturally relevant tasks, the strong performance on which suggests intact cognitive abilities. Again, Jahoda has considered the Cole et al. approach in Volume 1 of this *Handbook,* and Pick has drawn liberally from this strategy as a model with great virtue.

One question implicit in Pick's chapter, but not made explicit, is this: What is the better way to study human cognition across the parade of human cultures? Should the notion of "culture" stay constant (i.e., inferring psychic unity at the outset), while altering the tasks until one finds the "culturally appropriate" tasks? This is what Cole does. Or should stimuli (tests and tasks) stay constant, and with them attempt to measure how cultures may vary around such assessment devices that are as culturally "neutral" as possible? This approach is evident in the psychometric tradition, and to an extent also in the procedures of both the Piagetians and Kagan and his followers. Furthermore this approach is strongly favored and even required by those working under the Witkin differentiation hypothesis. Indeed, Berry (1976) talks of the "patterning of differentiation"—with the "patterns" developing out of variable responses to the invariant stimuli (but functionally as a consequence of ecosystem demands).

A major problem in culture and cognition involves selecting tests or other devices that are sensitive enough and relevant enough to measure adequately cognitive variables in scattered and unrelated cultures. With the Cole strategy, true comparisons may be impossible (and perhaps unnecessary), while in most of the other approaches perhaps too much is expected of relatively few devices that are treated as common yardsticks (see also Lonner, 1979). Thus, there is a manifest need to develop common ground in work on culture and cognition, so as to equilibrate these different approaches. Pick's chapter is a review headed in that direction.

An Interim Statement

Both Pick and Price-Williams implicitly equate cognition with learning, but from substantially different perspectives. What are the differences, if any, between these basic processes? Does the psychology of learning per se deserve special concentrated attention in a volume such as this?

Until fairly recently, general experimental psychology had two major subareas: the psychology of sensation and perception and the psychology of learning. These areas have faded, giving way to the emergence of the psychology of cognitive processes that is a blend of the two earlier and separate concentrations.

A major reason why this change took place is that various competing learning theories, even intraculturally, were unable to deal with specific learning issues without considering the content of what was being learned. At the same time, theories of sensation and perception lacked sufficient generality to be useful for studying more complex problems. These earlier areas dealt with *molecular* theory, the basic tenets of which were empirically demonstrated in the laboratory, where experimental conditions are often necessarily artificial. The need, then, was to combine the laboratory researcher's parsimony and formality of *how* learning takes place (that is, as a process) with a more generalizable theory that may answer "real world" questions of *what* is being learned, and *why*. Consequently, most researchers who deal with "what" and "why" questions give considerably more attention to the content as well as the context of learning than to the subtle psychophysiological principles that may be involved in the learning of cultural content.

That content has been examined cross-culturally more frequently than process can be confirmed by examining some of the recent books in cultural anthropology and cross-cultural psychology. Judging from the title of Harrington's (1973) book, *Cross-Cultural Approaches to Learning,* one might expect to read something concerning actual ethnological accounts of the theories held by members of different cultures of how people learn. This book actually contains papers about personality development and socialization processes. Similarly, a book by Brislin, Bochner, and Lonner (1975) carries approximately the same title: *Cross-Cultural Perspectives on Learning.* Again, one might have expected to read material on how different cultures approach the psychology of learning or, alternately, material about how principles of learning are influenced by different cultural conditions. In essence, the latter book intentionally uses the word "learning" in a very broad sense, and includes descriptive chapters on such topics as conflict reduction, psychopathology, initiation ceremonies, and secret societies as transmitters of cultural legacies; chapters that focus on experimental matters, such as human categorization as a basic human process, are included as well. Three other cross-cultural books, all influential and mentioned earlier in this Introduction, nearly exclusively concentrate on the results and interpretation of previous cross-cultural work (Lloyd, 1972; Berry & Dasen, 1974) or the need to reformulate experimentation on cognitive processes studied cross-culturally (Cole & Scribner, 1974).

Collectively these books support the assertion that cross-cultural researchers have shown much more interest in the *content of products* of learning rather than the documentation of the subtle and often tedious details of the *processes of learning* (e.g., Hilgard & Bower, 1975; Hergenhahn, 1976). Putting it another way, many cross-cultural researchers assume the universality of psychological process, while in fact there is yet to emerge an all-embracing theory of how people learn. The paradigms or theories of human learning that differentially guided such research are scarcely mentioned. As long as the postulate concerning the universality of principles in any learning theory is recognized as nothing more than a working assumption, and the predictions that flow from this assumption are refutable, the advances to be gained from building upon an established theoretical, empirical, and methodological foundation must outweigh the potential disadvantages in starting out with the universalist assumption. For example, it could be argued with considerable justification that commitment to any established learning principles may prolong their acceptance in the face of contradictory evidence. On the other hand, if the universality of learning principles is not assumed, and different principles of learning are identified in connection with different cultural forms, it still would be necessary to demonstrate that these culturally determined principles cannot be subsumed under more universalistic principles. In other words, to verify the cultural uniqueness of any learning principles would require the refutation of universality. Therefore, since existing principles must be dealt with at one point or another, it seems more parsimonious to start out with these principles and determine how far their usefulness can be extended before they may break down as a result of cultural factors that any particular theory simply cannot accommodate.

It is for this reason that this volume does not include a chapter on culture and learning theories per se. Any effort in this direction would necessarily result in a heavy treatment of learning theories and a thin treatment of how culture has affected them. However, cross-cultural applications of learning theory paradigms can be partitioned into two broad domains. The first concentrates on cognition as a necessary factor in determining how numbers, shapes, colors, or concepts are learned, stored, and retrieved. "Internal" operations are examined, usually using small samples of subjects while varying the conditions under which learning may take place. The second domain uses as its basic paradigm "external" (social, interpersonal) factors that influence the ways in which people behave "in the round," or how they "learn" their own cultural ways. Hence various formulations, under the popular rubric of social learning theory, seek to give an accounting of more molar approaches to learning. Dollard and Miller's (1950) attempts to unite Hullian learning theory and Freud's principles can be traced as the most systematic pioneering attempt in this area. Skinner's radical behaviorism has also been variously employed by psychologists, as well as some anthropologists, to account for behavior as a function of environmental contingencies of reinforcement, with the concept of reinforcement being nearly singular in importance in "shaping" and maintaining behavior. The most popular current social learning theories include the work of Bandura and Walters (1963) and Rotter (e.g., Rotter, Chance & Phares, 1972) and their numerous followers. For some of these researchers, cultural behavior is the sum of simple imitation learning and social reinforcement (after Tarde, 1903); for others the concepts of *behavior potential, expectancy, reinforcement value,* and the *psychological situation* are used to predict behavior. While the importance of these influential formulations should not be minimized, they belong in the province of personality development (see Volume 4 of this *Handbook*) and of social psychology (see Volume 5); this being the case, they are beyond the scope of this volume's approach to basic processes as influenced by culture.

Cognition: Anthropological Perspectives

It is evident in Pick's chapter that no contemporary cross-cultural cognitive psychologist appears to be concerned about which theory of learning is "best." Rather, experiments that are concerned with such topics as free recall, culture, and memory (Cole & Scribner, 1975b) or classification strategies (Rosch, 1975) are receiving the attention. While it is true that some sort of overall theory surely guides such workers, their real forte is the way in which they systematically conduct experiments. Recommending what they call "the method of equation," Medin and Cole (1975) believe that researchers should try to equate all relevant factors in experiments, such as attractiveness of the reward and the clarity of the stimuli and overall task, a tactic also recommended by Scribner (1976). Their advice needs to be followed critically.

The researchers to whom this methodological caution is addressed include anthropologists as well as psychologists. And therein lies the need to give a short summary of a complicated little struggle that links Pick's chapter with Price-Williams's. As mentioned earlier, Cole and his colleagues (Cole et al., 1971; Cole & Scribner, 1974, 1975a, 1975b) are among the leaders in studying the interface between psychological and anthropological approaches to cognition. The complex disagreements between these two disciplines in the way cognition is to be studied have been considered in three dichotomies by Cole and Scribner (1975a, p. 252) and in a similar way by Price-Williams (1974): (1) the psychologist's interest in process, the anthropologist's interest in content or product in defining cognition; (2) the psychologist's penchant for contrived experiments and the anthropologist's preference for naturally occurring situations for data collection; and (3) observational versus manipulative research techniques, with the psychologist preferring the latter. Believing as they do in the psychic unity of mankind theme, these researchers have searched for paths of rapprochement between the two disciplines. The issues here are far from being resolved, but encouraging progress is being made. Few are as well equipped as Price-Williams to aid in this resolution.

Price-Williams, who personifies a unique blend of anthropology and psychology, has been fatefully cast in this volume, in the role of interdisciplinary ombudsman. In one of his recent publications he wrote that "cross-cultural psychology is still at the precrystalline stage of inquiry" (1976; p. ix). Fortunately he did not shrink from the difficult task assigned him for this volume that involved making future efforts of cross-cultural psychology more crystalline through the various wide-angle lenses of anthropology. Setting to one side the "process-manipulation-contrivance" propensity of his psychological alterego, he surveyed anthropological and ethnoscientific accounts of the ways in which people think about their own personal universes without the constraining and perhaps obtrusive setting that the psychological laboratory exerts.

Context (of the experiment or of the data base in general) is the one operative word that is consistently used by those who worry about psychology's alleged artificiality and who at the same time prescribe the anthropological method as the safest antidote for such narrowness. Psychology has been criticized for its use of the "college sophomore" as its source of data and its tendency to infer universality once an experiment has been successfully replicated in another college classroom or on another campus. It is somewhat unfair that psychology has been taken to task in this way, for the context of behavior has never been overlooked by all psychologists (e.g., Brunswik, 1956; Lewin, 1951; Barker, 1968). It is to the credit of people like Campbell and Naroll (1972), Rohner (1975) as well as Price-Williams (1974) that the two disciplines are continuing to show increasing interest in each other.

The difference between the two disciplines in their respective approaches to cognition is analogous to the different types of data yielded by multiple-choice tests and essay exams. The former are indeed constraining, but results from them are easier to categorize and analyze. Moreover, responses to them over time and situations can be cumulative, forming a broadening data base. This is not the case with the essay exam that has the potential to elicit richly idiosyncratic responses of the same general character as anthropological data. The types of "folk taxonomies" people in probably any context use in structuring or coping with reality are good cases in point. As examples of cognitive strategies and operations, Price-Williams has chosen kinship systems, the Slave Indians' taxonomy of ice forms, and the category system used by skid row inhabitants to identify and code themselves and others.

Anthropology was at least a midwife in the birth of cross-cultural psychology. Its methods and ability to penetrate into the depths of culture are prerequisites for the further development of psychological contributions to cognition. The reader who is not yet familiar with the immense contributions of anthropology and its continued value to cross-cultural psychology is advised to supplement Price-Williams's chapter by reading the chapter by Munroe and Munroe in Volume 1 of this *Handbook*. A recent book of readings (Spindler, 1978) can be consulted as well.

Emotions and Their Overt Expression

With a little stretching, the content versus process distinction used in anthropological and psychological approaches in cognition can be extended to other domains of human behavior. One of these domains is the expression or display of emotions and, reciprocally, their communicative value. In his chapter, Izard summarizes three theories that have been used to explain the expression of emotions, principally via the plasticity of facial muscles. Predominant among these three theories is that of Darwin who, in 1872, was first to advance the theory that emotional patterns are largely inherited and phylogenetically linked responses that continue to have biological utility. The question has centered on whether these emotional patterns are truly innate rather than learned.

It has been fairly convincingly documented that various types of facial expressions depicted in photographs (analogous to a sort of static, frozen content) are universal, and also that there is some cultural variability in particular expressions used and the idiosyncratic cultural process that may be involved in their interpretation. In other words, facial expressions per se can be considered simple and invariant universals, while their exact meanings are variform universals requiring understanding within a particular cultural context (see Lonner's chapter in Volume 1 of this *Handbook* for a discussion of universals).

Compared to the vigor of cross-cultural research on cognitive and developmental processes, empirical research on the expression of emotions is somewhat scarce. Izard, of course, is one of the few current leaders in this area. Perhaps because of this relative scarcity of work the topic has not yet benefitted as much as it could from stimulating constructive criticism or from creative alterations of certain methods that are so frequently used that they run the risk of wallowing in their own internally consistent methodology. For example, the findings asserting the universality of emotional expression have come from research conducted largely in a fistful of Western countries, where the salience of particular emotions may largely be shared through the diffusion of expression. In this sense the argument that they are innate becomes hopelessly confounded with the position that emotions are learned.

The most thorough discussion available on the topic is Ekman's chapter, "Cross-Cultural Studies of Facial Expression," which is in his edited book, *Darwin and Facial Expression* (Ekman, 1972). Izard's chapter in this volume is an updated extension of that particular chapter that leans more in the direction of what needs to be done rather than what has been found in the past. Izard seems especially interested in tying the work on facial expressions (obviously the most important expressive component in emotions) to deeper, somatic, and affective components of emotions, and his own books reflect that tendency.

There is an interesting parallel between work on the apparent structure underlying facial expressions and Osgood's work on affective meaning (Osgood, May, & Miron, 1975). Osgood's dimensions of Evaluation, Potency, and Activity, in that order of saliency, have thus far (in the thirty-odd culture language groups that have been studied) accounted for some 60 percent of human metaphorical meaning. Beyond these dimensions are an unknown number of others that become increasingly rare because either (1) they do not carry much weight in communicating meaning or (2) they are complex component dimensions, and thus carry meaning only for the central core of a particular culture. So it is with facial expressions. The six most widely studied emotions of happiness, sadness, disgust, surprise, fear, and anger appear to carry the most communicative meaning, with other expressions becoming increasingly less salient because they either (1) do not carry much weight in communicating emotion or (2) are mixtures of the other emotions and thus are more difficult to interpret except under the rules of radical relativism.

Motivation

It was mentioned in this Introduction that psychology has yet to settle on only one learning theory. The closely related and similarly disputed area of human motivation likewise has yet to offer an unquestioned model of why people behave as they do. That being the case, Kornadt, Eckensberger, and Emminghaus were faced with a difficult selection problem when they began the task of writing their chapter on motivation as it is affected by culture (or vice versa). In what amounts to a logical compromise solution to the two alternatives of either maximizing depth (e.g., writing on only one or two motivational systems) or breadth (e.g., surveying the entire kingdom of motivational theory), they organized their chapter around competing frameworks that are exemplars of widely accepted schools of motivational theory.

Kornadt et al. first offer some preliminary thoughts on the power and pitfalls of cross-cultural research. (This brief treatment, instructive as it is, should be supplemented by the more comprehensive discussion of methodology to be found in Volume 2 of this *Handbook*.) From there they proceed to an outline of five generalizable frameworks that contain widely accepted theoretical accounts of human motivation. These are (1) the psychodynamic, with sex and aggression as central motivational constructs, (2) learning theory, which focuses on drive reduction as the prime mover, (3) cognitive systems, which return to the individual some power of choice in goal-directed behavior, (4) the ethological, which reduces man to a defender of his territorial rights, and (5) the personality/trait approach which contains the psychometric argument that test results can give a descriptive accounting of motivational tendencies whatever their origin. These five paradigms cover the majority of all cross-cultural motivational studies. The dilemma, however, is that any one of them could alone offer a plausible and even convincing rationale of the reasons why humans do what they do or even "behave" at all.

The majority of the chapter concentrates on three substantive areas that have attracted the most attention from cross-cultural researchers. In the section on dependency and attachment, the Six Cultures project is deservedly exploited as an attempt to explain how societal factors shape the behavior and henceforth motivation of its members during the human being's prolonged period of relative helplessness. Aggression, the focus of the next section, is probably the best example of how a psychological construct can be explained on various levels. For example, people may be aggressive as a result of an unsatisfied hedonistic drive (Freud), because of frustrations brought about by an unrequited drive state (experimental learning approaches), as a consequence of broad societal factors that may enhance or undermine incentive (cognitive theories), because that is the simple phylogenetic legacy that befalls the "naked ape" (ethology), or because that is the way people have been described (the trait approach).

Dependency and aggression are probably universal and, in their human form, maybe even species-specific. But even this point continues to be argued. The third and final section presented by Kornadt and his colleagues concentrates on achievement motivation. While there is some question that this motive is universal, it clearly ranks as one of the most widely studied motivational constructs in cross-cultural psychology. Unlike dependency and aggression, which transcend both cultures and various behavioral sciences, need achievement research may be a valid construct only in Western countries, and scientists using it have only occasionally been nonpsychologists.

De Gustibus Non Est Disputandum

The psychological (as opposed to the historical or sociological) study of aesthetics has a few historical landmarks, but it only recently has received new and concentrated attention. It can, at best, currently boast comparatively (and perhaps necessarily) few paths of inquiry. It follows that cross-cultural investigations of basic processes involving aesthetic tastes parallel this generally unsettled state of affairs. In his chapter covering the topic, the late Professor Berlyne implicitly acknowledged this somewhat slow accretion of evidence, but in so doing has written an exceptionally clear summary of the major historical trends and the contemporary methods used in studying aesthetics.

It was mentioned that in the cross-cultural study of visual perception, the nativist-empiricist argument has been a major stimulant. Since psychological aesthetics obviously involves perception (visual, auditory, olfactory, etc.), this nature-nurture argument can validly be used as a chief framework guiding such study. Specifically, the nativist viewpoint would suggest that for all humans there is a common thread running through all levels of the species, which would necessarily lead to the *a priori* conclusion that there is little variability in the perception of and preference for art forms. The empiricist viewpoint, conversely, would argue that cultural forms lead to culture-relative perception by individuals within each culture. This latter contention would necessarily mean, for example, that mere repeated exposure to the art forms in one's culture, at the same time associated with the reinforcement values of these forms, may account for a potentially large and expected variation in aesthetic preferences and tastes. The real state of affairs is, as Berlyne's view indicates, somewhere between these polar opposites, with the weight of the evidence leaning toward the universalist (nativist) end.

Two other points may be made as a means to introduce Berlyne's instructive chapter. The first is that few cross-cultural endeavors seem to require more liberal and creative use of the Human Relations Area Files than does the study of aesthetics. By associating research hypotheses with such indices as cultural complexity, socialization practices, or exposure to Western influences, progress can be enhanced toward the understanding of the processes underlying the acquisition and maintenance of aesthetic propensities. The horizon for hypothesis testing of this kind seems to be limitless, but also methodologically complex to carry out satisfactorily. The second point concerns methodology. As in so many cross-cultural research areas, researchers often have to choose between two general tactics. One of these would require sifting through data extracted from indigenous materials (e.g., art, song, and dance forms), while the other approach would use common yardsticks, around which may vary cultural aesthetic preferences. Berlyne has labelled these two strategies the "analytic" and the "synthetic," respectively. His own work, which is generally identifiable as the "new experimental aesthetics," clearly favors the synthetic approach. It is unfortunate that further research in the area can benefit only from his rich legacy and not from his unfolding creativity.

A Concluding Comment

This introduction summarized some historical and current trends in the study of basic psychological processes across cultures. The study and interpretation of these processes will continue to be examined and refined in their applications in substantive areas. The serious student, therefore, should consider reading the other volumes of this *Handbook*.

References

BANDURA, A., & WALTERS, R. H. *Social learning and personality development*. New York: Holt, Rinehart and Winston, 1963.

BARKER, R. G. *Ecological psychology*. Stanford, Calif.: Stanford University Press, 1968.

BATESON, G. *Naven*. Cambridge, England: Cambridge University Press, 1936.

BERLIN, B., & KAY, P. *Basic color terms: their universality and evolution*. Berkeley, Calif.: University of California Press, 1969.

BERRY, J. W. *Ecology of cognitive style: comparative studies in cultural and psychological adaptation*. Beverly Hills, Calif.: Sage/Halsted, 1976.

BERRY, J. W., & DASEN, P. R. (Eds.), *Culture and cognition: readings in cross-cultural psychology*. London: Methuen, 1974.

BOAS, F. *The mind of primitive man*. New York: Free Press, 1965. (Originally published, 1911.)

BRISLIN, R. W., BOCHNER, S., & LONNER, W. J. *Cross-cultural perspectives on learning*. Beverly Hills, Calif.: Sage/Halsted, 1975.

BRISLIN, R. W., LONNER, W. J., & THORNDIKE, R. M. *Cross-cultural research methods*. New York: Wiley, 1973.

BRUNSWIK, E. *Perception and the representative design of psychological experiments*. Berkeley, Calif.: University of California Press, 1956.

CAMPBELL, D. T., & NAROLL, R. The mutual methodological relevance of anthropology and psychology. In F. L. K. Hsu (Ed.), *Psychological anthropology*, new ed. Cambridge, Mass.: Schenkman, 1972.

COLE, M., & BRUNER, J. S. Cultural differences and inferences about psychological processes. *American Psychologist*, 1971, *26*, 867–76.

COLE, M., & SCRIBNER, S. *Culture and thought: a psychological introduction*. New York: Wiley, 1974.

————. Theorizing about socialization of cognition. *Ethos*, 1975a, *3*, 249–68.

————. Cross-cultural studies of memory and cognition. In R. V. Kail, Jr., & J. W. Hagen (Eds.), *Perspectives on the development of memory and cognition*. Hillsdale, N. J.: Erlbaum Associates, 1975b.

COLE, M., GAY, J., GLICK, J., & SHARP, D. W. *The cultural context of learning and thinking*. New York: Basic Books, 1971.

DASEN, P. R. Cross-cultural Piagetian research: a summary. *Journal of Cross-Cultural Psychology*, 1972, *3*, 23–39.

——— (Ed.), *Piagetian psychology: cross-cultural contributions*. New York: Gardner Press, 1977.

DAWSON, J. L. M. Theory and research in cross-cultural psychology. *Bulletin of the British Psychological Society*, 1971, *24*, 291–306.

DOLLARD, J., & MILLER, N. *Personality and psychotherapy: an analysis in terms of learning, thinking, and culture*. New York: McGraw-Hill, 1950.

DOOB, L. W. *Patterning of time*. New Haven: Yale University Press, 1971.

EKMAN, P. *Darwin and facial expression*. New York: Academic Press, 1973.

HARRINGTON, C. (Ed.), *Cross-cultural approaches to learning*. New York: MSS Information Corporation, 1973.

HERON, A., & DASEN, P. R. Cross-cultural tests of Piaget's theory. In H. Triandis & A. Heron (Eds.), *Handbook of cross-cultural psychology*, Vol. 4. Boston: Allyn and Bacon, 1979.

HERGENHAHN, B. R. *An introduction to theories of learning*. Englewood Cliffs, N. J.: Prentice-Hall, 1976.

HILGARD, E. R., & BOWER, G. H. *Theories of learning*. Englewood Cliffs, N. J.: Prentice-Hall, 1975.

HUDSON, W. Pictorial depth perception in sub-cultural groups in Africa. *Journal of Social Psychology*, 1960, *52*, 183–208.

IRVINE, S. H. Factor analysis of African abilities and attainments: constructs across cultures. *Psychological Bulletin*, 1969, *71*, 20–32.

JAHODA, G. A cross-cultural perspective in psychology. *The Advancement of Science* (Britain), 1970, *27*, 1–14.

KAGAN, J. Resilience in cognitive development. *Ethos*, 1975, *3*, 231–47.

———. Emergent themes in human development. *American Scientist*, 1976, *64*, 186–96.

KAGAN, J., & KLEIN, R. E. Cross-cultural perspectives on early development. *American Psychologist*, 1973, *28*, 947–61.

KAGAN, J., FINLEY, G. E., KLEIN, R. E., & ROGOFF, B. A study in cognitive development. Paper presented at the New York Academy of Sciences' Conference on Issues in Cross-Cultural Research, October, 1975. To appear in the *Annals* of the New York Academy of Sciences.

LENNEBERG, E. *Biological foundations of language*. New York: Wiley, 1967.

LEWIN, K. *Field theory in social science*. New York: Harper & Row, 1951.

LLOYD, B. B. *Perception and cognition*. Hammondsworth, England: Penguin, 1972.

LONNER, W. J. Issues in cross-cultural psychology. In A. Marsella, R. Tharp, & T. Ciborowski (Eds.), *Perspectives on cross-cultural psychology*. New York: Academic Press, 1979.

MEDIN, D., & COLE, M. Comparative psychology and human development. In W. K. Estes (Ed.), *Handbook of learning and cognitive processes*, Vol. 1. New York: L. Erlbaum Associates, 1975.

MILLER, R. J. Cross-cultural research in the perception of pictorial materials. *Psychological Bulletin*, 1973, *80*, 135–50.

OSGOOD, C. E., MAY, W. H., & MIRON, M. S. *Cross-cultural universals of affective meaning.* Champaign-Urbana, Ill.: University of Illinois Press, 1975.

PICK, H. L., & PICK, A. D. Culture and perception. In E. C. Carterette & M. P. Friedman (Eds.), *Handbook of perception.* New York: Academic Press, in press.

PRICE-WILLIAMS, D. R. (Ed.), *Cross-cultural studies.* Baltimore: Penguin, 1969.

————. Psychological experiment and anthropology: the problem of categories. *Ethos,* 1974, *2,* 95–114.

————. *Explorations in cross-cultural psychology.* San Francisco: Chandler and Sharp, 1975.

RIVERS, W. H. R. Introduction and vision. In A. C. Haddon (Ed.), *Reports of the Cambridge anthropological expedition to the Torres Straits,* Vol. II, Part 1. Cambridge, England: The University Press, 1901.

————. Observations on the senses of the Todas. *British Journal of Psychology,* 1905, *1,* 321–96.

ROHNER, R. P. *They love me, they love me not: a universalist approach to behavioral science.* New Haven, Conn.: HRAF Press, 1975.

ROSCH, E. Universals and cultural specifics in human categorization. In R. Brislin, S. Bochner, & W. Lonner (Eds.), *Cross-cultural perspectives on learning.* Beverly Hills, Calif.: Sage/Halsted, 1975.

ROTTER, J., CHANCE, J., & PHARES, E. J. *Applications of a social learning theory and personality.* New York: Holt, Rinehart and Winston, 1972.

SCRIBNER, S. Situating the experiment in cross-cultural research. In K. Riegel & J. Meacham (Eds.), *The developing individual in a changing world.* The Hague: Mouton, 1976.

SEGALL, M. *Cross-cultural psychology: human behavior in its sociocultural context.* Monterey, Calif.: Brooks/Cole, in press.

SEGALL, M., CAMPBELL, D. T., & HERSKOVITS, M. J. *The influence of culture on visual perception.* Chicago: Bobbs-Merrill, 1966.

SERPELL, R. *Culture's influence on behavior.* London: Methuen, 1976.

SPINDLER, G. D. (Ed.), *The making of psychological anthropology.* Berkeley, Calif.: University of California Press, 1978.

TARDE, G. *The laws of imitation.* New York: Henry Holt, 1903.

VERNON, P. E. *Intelligence and cultural environment.* London: Methuen, 1969.

WITKIN, H. A., & BERRY, J. W. Psychological differentiation in cross-cultural perspective. *Journal of Cross-Cultural Psychology,* 1975, *6,* 4–87.

WITKIN, H. A., DYK, R. B., FATERSON, H. P., GOODENOUGH, D. R., & KARP, S. A. *Psychological differentiation.* New York: Wiley, 1962. (Republished in 1974 by L. Erlbaum Associates, New York.)

WITKIN, H. A., PRICE-WILLIAMS, D. R., BERTINI, M., CHRISTIANSEN, B., OLTMAN, P. K., RAMIREZ, M., & VAN MEEL, J. Social conformity and psychological differentiation. *International Journal of Psychology,* 1974, *9,* 11–29.

WOBER, M. Sensotypes. *Journal of Social Psychology,* 1966, *70,* 181–89.

————. Adapting Witkin's field independence theory to accommodate new information from Africa. *British Journal of Psychology,* 1967, *58,* 29–38.

WUNDT, W. *Volkerpsychologie: Eine Untersuchung der Entwicklunge Gesetze von Sprach, Mythus, und Sitte* (Vols. 1–10). Leipzig: Engelmann, 1910–1920.

2

Perception

〜〜〜〜〜〜〜〜〜〜〜

Jan B. Deręgowski

〜〜〜〜〜〜〜〜〜〜〜

Contents

Abstract

The chapter presents a guide to the cross-cultural literature on psychological studies of perception. No specific theoretical framework is assumed, but theoretical considerations are briefly mentioned whenever the evidence reviewed adopts one of the current psychological theories.

Limitations of space made it impossible to refer to all the relevant items in the text so that some of the papers are mentioned in notes only. Such banishment does not indicate academic opprobrium.

Introduction

The central aim, albeit often unexpressed, of cross-cultural studies of perception is to investigate perceptual processes by comparing groups which differ in their cultural and ethnic characteristics or live in different environments. Such studies do not, therefore, constitute a discipline dealing with a unique subject matter, but rather an approach whereby general psychological issues can be studied. Thus, data derived from a previously untested cultural group should not be viewed in isolation from, but in juxtaposition to the appropriate established findings. This is not to imply that the data thus obtained may not cause the established scheme to be revised, quite the contrary.

The term *cross-cultural* as used here is rather inaccurate since it implies that purely cultural influences have been isolated. This is not so. The survey of the work done which follows will show that such a task has not, in general, even been attempted. The use of the term *cross-cultural* here is merely a matter of convenience and bears no closer relation to the subject matter than the term *racial* did to Thouless's (1933) studies of perception. The terms *culture* and *cultural group* will also be used in this imprecise manner in accord with the fashion of the day. For convenience, too, the term *Western* will often be used to describe those cultural groups or phenomena which have been greatly influenced by the culture grown from the Greco-Roman stock independently of their geographical location. Thus, for example, those inhabitants of Australia, Africa, or America who stem from populations which have absorbed these cultural values will be called *Western*, in contrast to Australian Aborigines, African tribes, Indian migrants, Arab nations of Africa, and Amerindian groups.

It is impossible to discuss in a single chapter all the references to the topic of culture and perception. Hence those which do not pertain directly to the problems dealt with, or are of more historical than immediate value, are omitted.[1]

A fecund field, that of Piagetian studies, will not be considered in this chapter even though some of the studies, such as those of Cowley and Murray (1962), or Dasen (1972), which this approach has fostered are of direct relevance to the studies described here. [See Dasen and Heron's chapter in Volume 4 of this *Handbook* for a review of Piagetian work.]

Those papers where perceptual measures are used to assess abilities or as an aid to personality or clinical diagnosis and the scores obtained throw but scanty light on perceptual processes per se are also omitted. These include extensive studies by Irvine of figural tests of reasoning (1969), the factorial studies of Vernon (1969) and others and much of the work discussed in the other chapters of this volume. Nor will papers concerned with the effect of social *values* on perception (such as Hallowell, 1951), or on perception in a social setting be considered.

In addition I have arbitrarily decided not to refer to work published later than the Summer of 1976, since one must draw a limit somewhere. Having done so, I have, equally arbitrarily, admitted some latecomers whenever they took my fancy and sternly resisted others.

A Cautionary Note Concerning Response Bias

Of the factors that influence the results of cross-cultural experimentation, that of *response bias* is of particular importance and will be briefly discussed here since it applies in various degrees to all experimental work and yet is seldom considered overtly. Indeed, its importance lies in the very furtive way in which it enters the experimental procedure and in the unpredictable manner in which it affects the results.

Methodologically, *response bias* presents a combination of variables which are likely to influence responses made and unlike some other uncontrolled variables cannot be relied upon to vary randomly about the mean and hence to nullify themselves, but tend to affect the magnitude of the mean. The origin of such a bias may be purely idiosyncratic. It may result from physiological or psychological causes. In both cases the effect may be considerable and *may* be related to cross-cultural differences. Thus blue-green confusion may be the effect of colour blindness (which in turn might be the effect of selective cross-breeding determined by cultural norms). It may also result from cultural usage such as the use of the same name for both colours.

These examples show that disparate cultural influences can yield superficially identical results when in fact the psychological processes involved are clearly different. In one case, subjects actually *see* the stimuli as being of the same hue, whereas the latter respond to them *as if* they were of the same hue.

Some of the studies reported do not consider the possibility of response bias where such a possibility clearly exists and hence present results that are ambiguous. The references to such studies have not been deleted, even though they *may* confound perceptual and other effects, they do present a useful, albeit slippery, stepping stone to further work.

The influences responsible for the bias are generally subtler than those given in the example above and range from the effects of experimental procedure, instructions, and language, to influences that can be postulated and that cannot be effectively disproved.[2]

The methods of controlling the effect of the bias both by adopting appropriate procedures and by statistical analysis are dealt with in Volume 2. One must, however, mention Campbell's (1964) thorough discussion of the importance of distinguishing between a failure in communication and a truly perceptual characteristic as determinants of a subject's response.

Little justification is called for in writing about perception in any setting. The processes studied are basic and important, the concepts capable of being clearly defined and open to rigorous experimentation. Even less justification is needed for writing about cross-cultural studies of perception. They have the above attributes, and by taking yet another vital factor into account—culture—they offer broader vistas and further flung horizons to those who dare.

Studies of Pictorial Perception

Although difficulties in pictorial perception which certain cultural groups experience were observed and reliably reported in the last century and were confirmed by further reports both in the nonpsychological[3] and the psychological literature (Warburton, 1951), the first systematic investigation of the problem was carried out by Hudson and was serendipitous in its origin. Hudson (1958, 1960) discovered that his subjects interpreted Thematic Apperception Test pictures as if they had lacked the ability to perceive pictorial depth—that is, the ability to "see" that a picture represents an array of three-dimensional objects distributed in space. Although Hudson's investigations were seminal to much later work, this chapter will review the problem from a perceptual rather than a historical stance, postponing detailed consideration of his findings and dealing first with more basic elements that might contribute to difficulties in pictorial perception.

To recognize a picture as such, an observer must be able to recognize that a pattern of lines and areas on a flat surface has a symbolic value. Two steps are required to do so: (1) division of the pattern into figure and background and (2) recognition of the figure as having some symbolic meaning. Thus a perceiver of the well-known Rubin's Face/Vase picture sees either the white area or the black area as background and accordingly sees the picture as either that of a vase or a face. Recognition is not, however, solely dependent upon proper division of the pattern into these two primary constituents since a degree of ambiguity may yet remain as shown, for example, by the "duck/rabbit" figure wherein the same pattern of lines offers alternative interpretations now as a duck, now as a rabbit. Pictures do not divide sharply, for observers from any culture, into those indistinguishable from the background and those which can be detected clearly by an observer. There is a zone where an observer may at one moment see a hint of a figure, but fail to do so at another. This fact must be stressed for it is apparent from some of the comments made on observations that the cross-cultural differences reported are sometimes thought of as being *qualitatively* entirely different from those present within cultures.

There are suggestions in the cross-cultural literature that some cultural groups have difficulties both with seeing that the pattern of lines represents an object and with recognizing such an object. Some of the reports at hand are unfortunately anecdotal. This is not to say that they are therefore valueless, but only that they do not describe the materials and the procedures in sufficient detail, thus obscuring the real cause and nature of the difficulty; others make such observations *passim* while dealing with different themes.[4] It should be noted that several of these authors did not maintain that the difficulty in question was in any sense absolute, but that pictorial recognition was slow and laborious (e.g. Laws, 1901; Fraser 1932). Yet others working with equally pictorially unsophisticated subjects reported no gross difficulties.[5] Doob's (1961) observations may be taken as typical of this group. He tested twenty Fulani villagers on recognition of pictures and photographs and on recall of the latter and found that a failure to identify depicted objects was rare.

> Only an occasional response seems to provide a basis for the belief that Africans sometimes experience unusual difficulty in identifying photographs or drawings. One man, for example, called an extremely clear photograph of an aeroplane "a fish" (p. 274).

These data suggest considerable intersample differences.

To a Western psychologist the difficulty of identification may at first sight appear surprising since there is evidence (Hochberg & Brooks, 1962) that a Western child of nineteen months brought up without any deliberate exposure to pictorial material and never taught to associate pictures with real objects does so spontaneously and accurately. Yet, there are situations where even highly sophisticated Western subjects have to learn how to interpret pictures. This happens, for example, to medical students learning radiography (Abercrombie, 1960). Thus the task of pictorial recognition seems to be stimulus-dependent, and the intercultural differences probably lie in the type of stimulus to which a given population is capable of responding. A careful examination of the stimuli is therefore needed. The following evidence (Deręgowski, Muldrow, & Muldrow, 1972) sustains this contention. The Mekan, a remote Ethiopian tribe, thoroughly examined pictures which were handed to them, smelling, nibbling, and flexing the paper whilst entirely ignoring the pictorial design thereon. On further investigation it was found that even this group with minimal exposure to pictorial material was, generally speaking, successful in recognizing indigenous animals in pictures printed on coarse cloth, a locally known material. If one takes even an unsuccessful recognition, such as calling a dik-dik (a type of antelope) a goat, to be an indication of pictorial perception, the number of complete failures—that is, *don't know* responses—that were observed becomes relatively low (five of sixty-eight responses). It is noteworthy, however, that when recognition occurred it was often painfully slow. Subjects seemed to piece the picture together, trying various hypotheses. They were behaving in a manner akin to that of a medical student dealing inexpertly with an X-ray plate.

Similar difficulties were observed in Kenya by Shaw (1969) and by Holmes (1963). Here subjects were found to give responses apparently derived from a single feature of the picture without considering other features. For example, a tortoise was sometimes called a *snake* because of the shape of its head and neck, sometimes an *elephant* because of the shape of its feet, and occasionally a *crocodile* because of the pattern of its shell (see Fig. 2–1).

Liddicoat and Koza (1963), on the other hand, found that urban Bantu children aged between eighteen and thirty-six months responded to pictures in accord with Gesell's norms, and sometimes surpassed these norms. A discussion of recognition difficulties in Ghanaian children responding to four of Hudson's test stimuli (*vide infra*) can be found in Mundy-Castle's (1966) paper. For an analysis of the same problem in the Baganda see Kilbride and Robbins (1969).

Reports of such difficulties have led to speculation about their origin. A widespread, but probably fallacious, argument is that based on convention.[6] It is argued that artistic styles differ and are conventional. A picture presents an amalgam of such conventions, which differ from culture to culture and have to be learned. Differences between various artistic styles both within and between cultures are adduced to sustain this argument.

Figure 2–1   A Tortoise. The figure was sometimes described as depicting a crocodile, sometimes as depicting an elephant, and sometimes as depicting a snake.[A]

And yet the deliberate distortions and drastic departures from the rules of perspective which occur in a variety of cultures can probably be explained more elegantly by an artist's desire to let the viewer know not only what the depicted object looks like (indeed this is often spurned as the purpose of a work of art) but something entirely different, often only vaguely related to the overt appearance. The painting of saints as larger than monarchs and monarchs as larger than commoners, in mediaeval art, so often given as an example of distortion of perspective, was intended to convey to viewers a conception of universal order rather than to provide them with an "identikit" for quick recognition of their betters should they ever encounter them. Similarly, such apparently bizarre styles as those of the northwestern tribes of America may have a different purpose in view than facilitation of recognition.[7] But the pictorial recognition tasks on which failures have been reported were of an "identikit" ilk. Furthermore the fact that perspective was not established in Western art until the Renaissance does not imply that it is a purely arbitrary convention with no basis in reality. Gibson (1971) argues convincingly against such a point of view. Furthermore conventions differ both in the nature and extent of their arbitrariness. Even language, sometimes considered as a convention par excellence, is not purely conventional as has been shown by Davis (1961). Similarly, various styles of depiction are not equally efficacious. Ryan and Schwarz (1956) and Fraisse and Elkin (1963) observed that speed of perception is affected by mode of representation, even in pictorially sophisticated subjects. Spencer (1963, 1965) showed that experienced engineering draughtsmen's performance on an assembly task was inferior on orthographic drawings (commonly used in engineering) than on projective drawings (isometric and perspective), which more closely approximate to the retinal patterns projected by the depicted objects. Page's (1970) comparison of Zulu children on two types of pictures presents an African analogue to these observations. His subjects found it easier to respond to photographs from life than to Hudson's drawings. Neither this nor Spencer's results are surprising. After all there is no evidence of subjects' experiencing difficulties with perception of the third dimension in the real world, and gradual modifications of the stimuli move the observer closer and closer to the point where pictures are difficult to distinguish from the objects that they depict.

Traditional oriental art whose "distortion" of perspective inspired Thouless's (1933) study of shape constancy appears to offer evidence supporting the "conventionalist" argument. However, it would be imprudent to conclude that this support is in any sense definitive. It is not known whether such style is generally found to be more comprehensible or more aesthetically pleasing to those cultures than the "correct" perspective style would be, or whether the appreciation of this style is primarily a prerogative of the artist, an instance for which analogues could readily be found in the West. Further, in this style of art some of the pictorial depth cues commonly used in the West are weaker than a Westerner would expect them to be, or even entirely absent, whereas some others (for example, position in the field) are as strong as in photographs. This leads to the baffling appearance of the style. It seems unlikely that subjects drawn from populations wherein this style prevails would be insensitive to any of the important cues in the real world. What appears more likely is that these subjects have learned to expect that some cues are weak or absent in pictures. Thus, a subject's ability to disregard the absence of such cues would decrease as the perceived reality of the stimulus increased; that is that the particular deficiency is only acceptable to the subject within certain narrow limits.

At the other end of the spectrum the effect of increase in cues available upon perception must be noted. Thus stereoscopy led to a dramatic improvement in perception by African apprentices (Dawson, 1967a), African aircraft trainees (Davies, 1973) and schoolchildren (Deręgowski, 1976).

It may be fruitful to view the problem as a failure of the perceptual mechanism to deal with an incomplete range of perceptual information and hence to investigate both the effects of such a deficiency and ways in which it can be redressed.

The failure to recognise a depicted object may lie in an inability to distinguish the background from the figures and to integrate the figures. This argument is supported by Forge's (1970) study. He reported that the Abelam of New Guinea, who were only partly familiar with photographs, could name individuals on these photographs in which they were shown standing *against a white background*, that is, in circumstances where distinction between the background and the figure is much facilitated.

But even correct recognition of a depicted object does not imply that a picture will be treated as equivalent to an object. Indeed global recognition of a face as such need not imply the same interpretation of facial expression, as Cüceloglu's (1970) study of American, Turkish, and Japanese samples has shown. A picture is often treated as if it were something of an object but not an object itself and evokes less vigorous responses than does the depicted object when either categorisation (Sigel, 1968) or mime (Klapper & Birch, 1969) are called for. In a study comparing Zambian and Scottish schoolchildren Deręgowski and Serpell (1971) found that on a sorting task Zambian children were poorer than their Scottish peers when photographs of toys were used, but the two groups did not differ when toys served as stimuli, although both groups were perfectly able to recognise the depicted objects.

This difference between objects and their portrayal is also shown by the difficulty of pictorially unsophisticated subjects in matching objects and pictures. This difficulty is greater than those which arise when matching within the same category, object to object, or picture to picture is called for (Deręgowski, 1971).

Urban Bantu children tested by Liddicoat and Koza (1963) named objects correctly more frequently than pictures of the same objects. Studies of memory also show a better recall of objects than pictures even in relatively sophisticated populations (Deręgowski & Jahoda, 1975). It may well be that in those cultures where pictures are relatively rare this gap is larger than in those where pictures abound. The development of the ability to interpret pictures is rapid in Western children, and whilst nursery children respond to all pictures as representing a static scene, by the time they reach primary school the majority are able to perceive depicted activity (Travers, 1973).

Does the recognition of a depicted object imply that it is seen as three-dimensional? Wober (1972) suggested that this is so but provided no evidence to support his view. Logically such a stance seems difficult to defend unless the rather trite criterion that correct naming implies perception of three-dimensionality is adopted. This, perceptually, is certainly not the case; a silhouette of a head is likely to be correctly named but is nonetheless seen as flat.

There is, however, little doubt that pictorial space is sometimes difficult to perceive, with drawings being interpreted as if all the depicted objects were in the same place. Systematic cross-cultural investigation of pictorial depth began with Hudson's (1960) paper. Although his results were obtained with two different types of stimuli, only the findings with the type that was later developed into a test will be treated in detail. The essence of Hudson's test consists of interpretation of simple pictures and a photograph. Each of these stimuli contains three figures so arranged and placed on such a background as to provide a combination of four of the seven pictorial depth cues listed by Blakemore (1973). Two of the cues, *familiar size* and *position in the field*, are kept approximately constant from stimulus to stimulus. The other two, *linear perspective* and *overlap*, are varied. Samples of Hudson's figures can be found in Hudson (1960) and some other studies listed in Note 11 of this chapter.[8]

Testing of pictorial depth perception with Hudson's test is preceded by testing the subject's recognition of the individual items depicted: man, elephant, spear, etc. This is necessary for labelling of an elephant as "a cat," say, shows that the familiar size cue cannot operate and such responses nullify the validity of further questions. The interpretation of a response is not, however, always easy. Some languages, as well as some respondents, have limited vocabularies and therefore terms for a word such as *horizon* may not be available. Under these circumstances the experimenter's judgement has to be invoked. But a respondent's failure to indicate recognition does not imply *absence* of pictorial depth perception. Newman (1969) has found that the corridor illusion evokes pictorial depth

Figure 2-2   One of Hudson's Stimuli Containing Both Overlap and Familiar Size Cues[B]

perception in Western children when they do not even interpret the picture as that of a three-dimensional scene. Stimuli such as the Ponzo illusion, the perspective illusion, and the "road" in Hudson's test can probably be regarded as vestigial versions of the "corridor."

Hudson (1960) showed that cultural groups and subgroups differ in the way they perceive pictures. Western children were found to have difficulties with perception of pictorial depth on their entry to school—but showed a significant improvement by the end of their primary education; but Western labourers who had rather poor schooling were poor at the task.[9] No analogous improvement was found in black schoolchildren and both they and some black graduate teachers performed badly, as did black labourers. The existence of such differences between Bantu and Western subjects was confirmed by Duncan, Gourlay, and Hudson (1973), who in addition found a significant difference between urban and rural Bantu (Zulu and Tsonga), the responses of the urban group being more akin to the Western responses.[10] Additional evidence of cross-cultural differences was obtained from a comparison of Bantu, Coloured, Western, and Indian schoolchildren on an abbreviated version of Hudson's test. The percentages of subjects capable of perceiving pictorial depth in a photograph (first bracketed entry) and of those who gave a consistent response to three line-drawings (second entry) were as follows: (1) Western (100%, 70%), (2) Coloured (78%, 48%), (3) Bantu (76%, 35%), and (4) Indian (66%, 30%). It must be noted that the Indian children had one year less education than the Bantu and Coloured children.

The report of Hudson's (1960) study evoked a number of replications and extensions. Some of these were intended to investigate the generality of the findings, others to analyse the problem further and to establish its relationship to other perceptual phenomena.[11] The criteria of three-dimensionality used in judging responses were not the same for all experimenters; the percentages of three-dimensional responders reported are not, therefore, comparable.

Another consequence of Hudson's study was a number of critical comments generally of a speculative nature and not supported by any new data. One of these, directed against Hudson's procedures, was that the responses to the stimuli might merely represent perception of a narrow and unimportant range of stimuli. This prompted Deręgowski (1968c, 1969a) and Deręgowski and Byth (1970) to conduct three experiments differing widely in the procedures used and the materials employed. In the first of these studies subjects were asked to build simple models in response to drawings which could be interpreted as portraying either plane or three-dimensional structures. (See Fig. 2-3.) The models were judged whether or not they indicated perception of pictorial depth. The same subjects were also given Hudson's test. It was found that some of the subjects who showed no evidence of pictorial depth perception on Hudson's test did so on the construction task. The converse of this did not occur. Deręgowski concluded that the two tests probably sampled the same behaviour (viz. perception of pictorial depth) but at different levels of difficulty, Hudson's test criteria being more stringent. The second study used the ability to retain and reproduce by drawing an impossible object, the two-pronged trident, as an indicator of pictorial perception, the hypothesis being that the only subjects likely to find the figure difficult to reproduce were those who could perceive pictorial depth. The construction task described above was used as a measure of pictorial depth perception and the hypothesis was

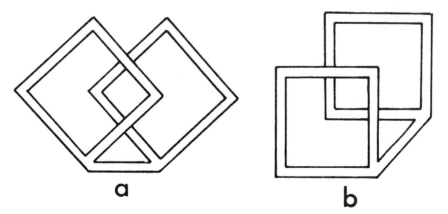

a   **b**

Figure 2-3   Stimuli Used in Construction Task (Deręgowski, 1971). Stimulus *b* was also one of the stimuli used by Deręgowski (1968) in conjunction with Hudson's test.

sustained. The third experiment presented adults drawn from a pictorially sophisticated Western population and from a pictorially unsophisticated African population with some of Hudson's pictures made into transparencies and placed in Gregory's (1966) apparatus for measuring apparent depth in pictures. In the picture having the overlap cue as well as the cues of familiar size and position, the Western sample showed perception of pictorial depth but the African sample did not. In the picture having only the latter two cues there was no difference between the samples.

Page (1970) demonstrated that subjects who showed no perception of depth on Hudson's test, showed such perception when required to judge which depicted object was nearer to them. This suggests that there may be two aspects of pictorial depth: an egocentric aspect, where distances judged are those between depicted figures and the observer, and a projective aspect, where the observer is required to place himself in the position of one of the depicted figures and make judgements from that stance. This view agrees with observations of Piaget and Inhelder (1956). The same subjects, however, occasionally failed to reproduce pictorial arrangements when asked to place tokens to indicate implied spatial relationships. (This task is similar to that used by Brown, 1969, who observed in Western children a distinctive improvement with age and schooling.) However, immediately before they performed the described tasks Page's subjects interpreted a relatively easy photograph and had undergone standard testing on Hudson's test. Both these factors could have biased the results. It may be relevant to note that Deręgowski (1968b) reported an experiment in which Zambian subjects misperceived the position from which a stimulus photograph was taken; he considered egocentricity as a possible explanation of this.

Several attempts have been made to isolate the effects of various cues to pictorial depth and to relate these to a number of variables. Kilbride and his associates (Kilbride, Robbins, & Freeman, 1968; Kilbride & Robbins, 1968) tested large samples of Buganda subjects using four of Hudson's stimuli and a somewhat modified Hudson procedure and found that the effects of familiar size, overlap and linear perspective, and perception of pictorial depth were correlated with education. The procedure that they used for assessing pictorial depth perception on the perspective drawings differed from that employed by Hudson in that it confounded recognition with perception of depth. Kilbride also found that the familiar size cue by itself is very weak but becomes considerably strengthened by the overlap cue, a result consonant with that of Deręgowski (1968c), and with Deręgowski and Byth's (1970) finding already mentioned. In Hudson's seminal paper, too, the overlap cues appear to be the strongest. Surprisingly, addition of the perspective cues to the cues of familiar size and position, which are present in all Hudson's test drawings, makes perception of pictorial depth less likely than familiar size cues alone. This suggests that linear perspective, which is weak per se (Segall et al., 1966, found the perspective illusion to be weak), does not assist the observers when presented in a rather feeble form as in the case of Hudson's drawings. Recently Duncan et al. (1973) and Sinha and Shukla (1974) have undertaken further analysis of pictorial depth cues. A developmental study of use of depth cues in drawing has been reported by Sinha and Misra (1975).

Leibowitz, Brislin, Perlmutter, & Hennessy's (1969) work provided a notion of the way in which various depth cues are used and also linked the study of pictorial perception with another much-studied topic in cross-cultural psychology: geometric illusions. They used the Ponzo figure (which may be thought of as embodying the elements of perspective) as well as pictures containing the same essential elements and a variety of other cues: a photograph portraying a texture gradient and a photograph portraying perspective as well as a texture gradient. In addition they used a monocular view of a railway track and a binocular view of a railway track. Their results showed that a summation of cues led to depth perception in their Western sample, but no such simple effect in the Guam sample.

Linguistic considerations found their expression in the work of Du Toit (1966), who, influenced by Carroll and Casagrande (1958), suggested that the differences observed by Hudson might have been due to the fact that his subjects spoke a Bantu language. There is nothing to support such a suggestion in the data since gathered. Even in Hudson's original experiment similarity of the responses made by white labourers to those of Bantu workers militated against this hypothesis. Since then the difficulty in pictorial perception has been shown to exist in such a variety of linguistic groups that it would be difficult to isolate a linguistic factor that is common to them and not present in the cultures in which the difficulty is relatively rarer. Furthermore, the difficulty has been observed when oral answers used in Hudson's test were replaced by performance of tasks.

Much of the criticism of Hudson's work is concerned with the materials and procedures used by him. Both Ferenczi (1966, p. 65) and Miller (1973) maintain that the drawings are much simplified. The same two authors criticise Hudson's questions which they think are ambiguous. In addition, Miller noted that isolation of various depth cues is not possible in Hudson's stimuli and Ferenczi pointed out the imperfect matching of samples, and advocated the desirability of an "adaptation run" with illiterate samples to enable these subjects to get used to a novel task. On the other hand, Gibson (1969, p. 403) expressed no such reservations.

Such criticisms do not invalidate Hudson's findings. The crux of these was the difference in performance between various cultural groups. That such a difference would be affected by the nature of the stimuli and by the procedure is to be expected. It would also be expected that the difference between cultural groups would decrease as pictures are enriched in cues and hence present increasingly superior (as defined by Gibson, 1954) representations of reality. Subsequent replications and extensions of Hudson's test support his findings and dispose of the above unwarranted criticisms with the exception of that of the confounding of pictorial cues (in this respect Hudson has a legitimate defence that isolation of cues was not the purpose of his experiment). The existence of the cross-cultural differences in pictorial depth perception has as a consequence been widely recognised.[12]

Jahoda and McGurk (1974a, 1974b, 1974c) and McGurk and Jahoda (1974) used a new set of stimuli in investigating the problems, in which elevation forms a major cue, and to which subjects respond by placing token figures, a procedure reminiscent of Brown's (1969). Their conclusions accord with those stated above, while their procedure offers yet another measure of the ill-defined process of pictorial perception. Their 1974c paper contains a noteworthy critique of some of the studies inspired by Hudson's test.

Practical implications of the difficulties in pictorial perception are manifold and extend from clinical and personality testing to various educational uses.[13] Doob (1961) treats the entire problem of communication in Africa, including pictorial perception. Hudson (1967) gives a general review of perception of posters and symbolic reproductions.

As one would expect from Western data (Fraisse and Elkin, 1963; Travers, 1969; Gottschalk, Bryden, & Rabinowich, 1964; Brown, 1969) there are developmental changes in individuals' ability to deal with pictorial material in non-Western cultures, too. The changes that have been observed affect all aspects of pictorial perception ranging from recognition of silhouettes (Hector, Dlodlo, & Du Plessis, 1961) to perception of pictorial depth (Dawson, Young, & Choi, 1974).

Speculations about the Cause and Nature of Findings

Findings reported by Hudson and in research reports that his work inspired lend themselves to a variety of explanations because in cross-cultural comparisons it is impossible to isolate factors such as education or literacy from exposure to Western ways, or urbanisation from loss of contact with traditional handicrafts, or from exposure to pictorial material.

Nonetheless it is probably worthwhile to examine various factors that have been suggested as influencing performance on Hudson's test and its derivatives. Hudson (1960, 1962) considers two factors to be of import in the performance of his Western subjects: educational achievement and intellectual endowment. He postulated that there is a minimum intelligence threshold below which perception of pictorial depth does not occur, even if the subjects have had full primary and even secondary education.

Since the relationship of perception of pictorial depth to educational achievement was not found in the Bantu samples, Hudson put forward a third factor in order to explain the difference between cultures: exposure to pictorial materials at preschool age. This might have played a role in influencing perception of Western labourers as well as the entire Bantu sample, since both these groups live in environments relatively impoverished in pictorial materials the impoverishment being probably more severe in the Bantu sample. As a corollary to the "deprivation effect" Hudson (1962b) put forward another effect: influence of exposure to a particular environment. He used it to explain why his Indian sample that had been exposed to the Indian artistic style performed as poorly as the Bantu sample and adduced Thouless's (1933) observations of shape constancy to sustain his claim. He further hypothesized the Bantu, as a result of environmental pressure, might have an "auditory perceptual organisation" which is "more characteristic of their culture than visual perception development" (Hudson, 1960, p. 207). Doob's (1961) and Deręgowski et al.'s (1972) data support the postulated effect of education—showing higher scores in their more educated subjects.

A study by Sinha and Shukla (1974) attempted to demonstrate that the difficulties in pictorial perception are associated with environmental deprivation. The evidence gathered shows that this *may* be so, but not that it is *necessarily* so because the samples used may have differed in genetic characteristics as well as in environment (the subjects were children from nursery schools and orphanages in India). The authors attempted to overcome this methodological difficulty by partialling out intelligence. This, however, would only have been successful if one could but assume that by partialling out intelligence one is also partialling out genetic factors. Such treatment of the data showed no significant correlation in the three- to four-year-olds whilst significant correlations obtained in older groups. These intergroup differences are interesting but do not separate the hereditary and environmental aspects of the problem.[14]

A series of studies exploring the perceptual processes of the people of Sierra Leone was conducted by Dawson (1967a; 1967b). Witkin's concept of field-dependence served as the main paradigm, and Dawson used his own and two of Hudson's pictures for measuring perception of pictorial depth. Three samples of men varying in degree of education showed concordant variation in the frequencies with which responses indicative of pictorial depth perception were made, thus supporting Hudson's thesis of the influence of education. In another sample the correlation between education and the scores on the pictorial depth perception test was $r = 0.22$. Although statistically significant this correlation is low, perhaps because the sample used was relatively homogenous. Correlation between perception of pictorial depth and field dependence was higher. Kohs' Blocks scores correlated with pictorial depth perception at $r = 0.64$ and the Embedded Figures Test did so at $r = 0.66$. This offers a suggestion that Witkin's differentiation theory may provide a definitive description of a syndrome leading to cross-cultural differences in pictorial perception.[15] A related explanation has been put forth by Barry (1957) who studied the relationship between the style of drawings characteristic in a given culture and the mode of child rearing. According to his results, cultures having above medium complexity in art tend to be above average in severity in socialization. This would suggest that subjects from such cultures should be better in analysing complex pictorial stimuli. Such a conclusion is not, however, supported by the studies of field-dependence hitherto reported. It may be that complex art forms in those severe cultures tend also to be more ritualised and that this effect overrides other influences.[16]

Biesheuvel (1972, pp. 60–61) postulates that the main cause of perceptual differences ought to be sought in environmental factors, which are impossible to disentangle. He illustrates his argument by reference to Kohs' Blocks but the argument can pari passu be applied to drawings.

> Suppose, for example, children in two ethnic groups A and B—matched in respect of age, sex, number of years of primary schooling and other environmental factors—differ on the average in an adaptability test like Kohs' Blocks, after an experimental period of individual solicitous attention and enriched tuition, applied equally to both. We can draw no conclusion about any basic, unalterable difference between them in limits of modifiability as measured by Kohs' test. We do not know whether during very early childhood or during some other significant developmental stage, the ability was irreversibly impaired by lack of appropriate stimulation or by parental attitudes adverse to the development of the skills concerned.[17]

P. E. Vernon (1969), too, points out that perhaps the major factor is the relative lack, in the upbringing of most Africans, of visual-kinaesthetic experience from infancy throughout childhood. Lack of exposure to pictorial material is also thought to be important by Mundy-Castle (1966). Munroe and Munroe's (1971) observational study of behaviour of Logoli children and Nerlove, Munroe, and Munroe's (1971) study of Gusii children could be adduced in support of Vernon's explanation; but since they are correlational, they cannot be said to provide firm support. The explanation, however, accounts for observed differences between Eskimos and Africans, both of whom lack contact with pictorial material, yet the former have considerable pictorial and mechanical aptitudes. This observation irreparably damages the argument that the learning of pictorial conventions is the essence of the problem, and suggests that early experiences in cultures where such difficulties are observed are in some other crucial way similar, and is in opposition to M.D. Vernon's (1970, p. 129) view that "concepts related to current conventions as to two-dimensional representation of space and distance" are acquired in the course of one's education.

On the other hand Kugelmass, Liebich, and Erlich (1972) show that visual perceptual exploration is affected by schooling.

Indeed the very nature of the difficulty is far from being obvious. Wober (1972) speculated that it is the space between the depicted objects which underlies the difficulties experienced by some Africans. However, responses such as those obtained by Shaw (1969) and Deręgowski et al. (1972) suggest that a difficulty of integration of pictorial elements, put forward by Deręgowski (1968c) and confirmed by Duncan et al. (1973), may offer a more apposite explanation. Logically, the arguments for recognition and integration are irresolubly linked, for integration implies that there are elements that can be integrated. Such elements, therefore, must have been recognized and their mutual relationships must presumably be such as to call for integration and hence for recognition of the new integrated entity.

This progress ad infinitum can be arrested by postulating that an organism on being stimulated generates hypotheses (Gregory, 1970, 1973) about the nature of the stimuli. These hypotheses are initially extremely vague, but by a process of iteration become clarified, the process itself consisting both of redefinition of parts and substitution of various integration schemata until a satisfactory stable state is achieved in which both aspects of the process are in concord with each other. That is, all elements perceived are defined so that their definition matches with the definition of the percept as a whole. It must be noted that while iteration is taking place any two sequential hypotheses need not necessarily lead to an increase in consonance, although in successful resolution the general trend is such that it does. There are, however, also stimuli (for example, a Necker cube) where no successful solution is possible.

It is apparent that under such circumstances a difference between responses of two groups of subjects on any perceptual task, can, when viewed in terms of this paradigm, be attributed to:

1. Difference in initial, tentative, hypotheses.
2. Ease with which a hypothesis is evaluated.
3. Ease with which a postulated hypothesis is rejected if found wanting.
4. Ease with which a new hypothesis is substituted for an abandoned hypothesis.
5. Rate at which successive hypotheses approach "correct" perception.

Deręgowski (1976a) likened this process to that employed by mathematicians in solving equations and called Newton's Approximation; such a simile describes the process well (to those familiar with rudiments of mathematics) but does not affect its hypothesized validity, which is the subject of vigorous debate extending well beyond the field of psychology and which forms a part of the nexus between psychology and epistemology of perception.

Teaching of Pictorial Depth Perception

All attempts to teach pictorial depth perception hitherto reported have one feature in common. In all of them a relatively rich source of pictorial depth cues is presented to the subject under instruction in the hope that he will subsequently be able to generalise and transfer his skills to other, poorer stimuli. Thus a group of Temne apprentices was successfully trained by Dawson (1967a) in eight weekly one-hour sessions. The training consisted of drawing and explanation of the principles involved. The results showed clear superiority of the experimental group over a carefully matched control group. The results also showed a significant positive correlation of the scores after training with field-dependence scores as measured by Kohs' Blocks. This is a fascinating but not perspicuous finding for the suggestion which it proffers—that field-dependence delimits the effect of training—cannot be readily accepted since McFie (1961) suggested that responses to a block test do improve with training (but see p. 67). It is therefore possible that Dawson observed a case of generalisation and/or transfer of learning, and hence that the two tasks share certain elements. It is, however, also possible that field-dependence defines broad frontiers within which pictorial perception, subject to training, stakes a larger or a smaller claim.

A different training technique was used by Ferenczi (1966). A special film was made and, augmented by drawings, used in instruction in perceptual and motor skills. His subjects were immigrant African workers and both literate and illiterate schoolchildren and adolescents. He tested them on a variety of tasks including two pictures inspired by Hudson's test (on which questions were asked requesting a subject to judge pictorial distance from his own position, and not between two depicted objects as is the case with Hudson's test: *L'homme que vous voyez est-il plus près de vous que la maison?* (Is the man whom you see closer to you than the house?) To evaluate the effectiveness of training, Ferenczi assessed drawings made by subjects. In addition, subjects were asked to choose a correct representation and to interpret drawings. Considerable gains were reported.

A simple but apparently effective device was developed by Priest (1966), who tried to teach a single subject using the basic elements of Hudson's drawings; he made them into a puppet peep-show with three movable figures in a cardboard box. This procedure proved efficacious, the subject responding three-dimensionally to Hudson's test "after only a few sessions of moving figures up and back." The similarity between the materials used in training and the test material makes this a questionable finding, but the method itself is worthy of further exploration.

Serpell and Deręgowski (1972) sought a method of training suitable for classroom use. They used photographs, films, and textbook pictures. A marginally significant improvement followed four hourly sessions of training on pictures. The training consisted of explanation and discussion of depth cues. A combination of elements of Hudson's test, of the construction task (Deręgowski, 1968c) and the two-pronged trident task (Deręgowski, 1969a), served as pre- and post-test measures.

Duncan et al. (1973) constructed a special apparatus for individual instruction. The method relies on a teacher explaining one by one the significance of cues. This method, like that of Serpell and Deręgowski described above, relies primarily on cognitive analysis rather than perceptual experience.

(It is interesting to note parenthetically that Haber, 1965, demonstrated that subjects' perception of the Rotating Trapezoid illusion can be destroyed by simple instruction. This illusion, it could be argued, has elements in common with illusions responsible for perception of pictorial depth.)

A brief mention of the efficacy of stereo stimuli in evoking pictorial depth perception is made by Dawson (1967a), who observed that use of such stimuli increased the proportion of three-dimensional perceivers from 47 percent to 87 percent. Later, Davies (1973) used a different technique on a group of apprentices drawn from a variety of African Air Forces sent to Britain for training hence presumably a group consisting of individuals of above average general ability. They were found to have considerable difficulties with translating from isometric to orthographic projection in engineering drawings. To remedy this, trainees were given stereoscopic drawings and asked to build models. This procedure led to an improvement in weaker students. Deręgowski (1974b) followed a similar procedure with African primary schoolboys and also found it promising. For another potentially useful approach see Leach (1975).

Illusions

Rivers (1901, 1905) was probably the first to conduct a systematic cross-cultural study of geometric illusions. Following his pioneering attempt the field lay fallow for half a century until Segall et al. (1966) renewed interest in these problems.

Rivers's samples were drawn from the Torres Straits (Papuans, New Guineans, and Murray Islanders) as well as from Southern India, which yielded a sample of Todas. The procedures used with the two geographic groups were not the same. The data reported sustain the claim that the non-Western groups were more prone to the horizontal-vertical illusion and less prone to the Müller-Lyer illusion than the Western controls. Rivers postulated that the former effect was the result of

> physiological conditions, and the effect of experience in civilised life, such experience for instance as is derived from the study of geometry and drawing, is to diminish the illusion. The Müller-Lyer illusion on the other hand is one of those of which explanation is probably more psychological. The psychological factors upon which the illusion depends are however of simple nature and affect both savage and civilised man ... the reason why the illusion is less marked to the Toda and Papuan is probably ... a difference in direction of attention, the savage attending more strictly to the two lines which he is desired to make equal while the civilised man allows the figure as a whole to exert its full influence on his mind (1905, p. 363).

In addition to the two illusions Rivers studied a wide range of other perceptual phenomena including the threshold differences in visual acuity, tactile discrimination, olfactory acuity, hearing, pain, ocular defects, colour vision, and colour and taste nomenclature.

A consideration of Rivers's reports and of Brunswick's "ecological cue validity" led Segall et al. (1966) to postulate that there are ecological and cultural factors which influence susceptibility to geometric illusions. They summarised their hypotheses thus:

> For figures constructed of lines meeting in nonrectangular junctions, there will be a learned tendency among persons dwelling in carpentered environments to rectangularise those junctions, to perceive the figures in perspective, and to interpret them as two-dimensional representations of three-dimensional objects.

Such a tendency would increase the magnitude of the Müller-Lyer and the Sander parallelogram illusions, and would be stronger in those cultures wherein carpentered objects prevail than in those where such objects are relatively scarce.

"The horizontal-vertical illusion," say Segall et al., "results from a tendency to counteract the foreshortening of lines extending into space away from a viewer," and hence leads to an overestimation of the vertical line of the illusion figure. As the higher tendency has ecological validity for subjects living in open environments, one would expect such subjects to be *more* susceptible to the illusion than their counterparts from more restricted environments. They further add that:

"Learning to interpret drawings and photographs should enhance some of these illusions, whereas learning to produce drawings representing three dimensions should reduce the illusions" (Segall et al. [1966] pp. 95-96, passim).[18]

Extensive experimentation using a specially prepared test followed. In addition to the United States sample, fourteen non-Western samples were carefully tested, largely by anthropologists. In toto nearly 1,900 subjects

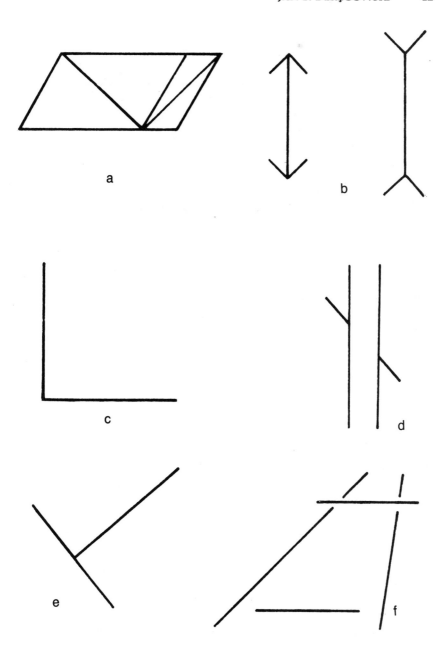

Figure 2–4   Illusion Figures: (a) Sander's Parallelogram, (b) Müller-Lyer, (c) Horizontal-Vertical (L-type), (d) Poggendorff, (e) Horizontal-Vertical in Dichosection Orientation, As Used by Jahoda and Stacey (1970), (f) Perspective, Similar to That Used by Segall et al. (1966), (g) Wundt Illusion, (h) Hering Illusion, (i) Helmholtz Square (j) Titchener Circles, (k) Boring Circles, (l) Judd Illusion.

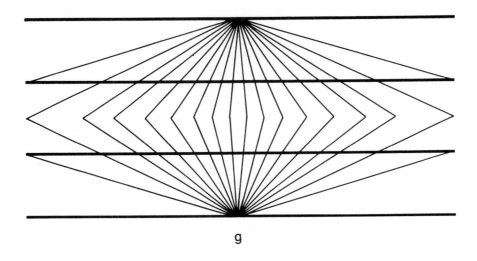

g

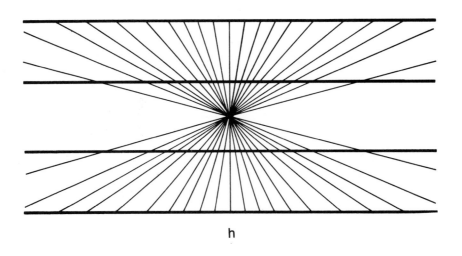

h

Figure 2-4 (*continued*)

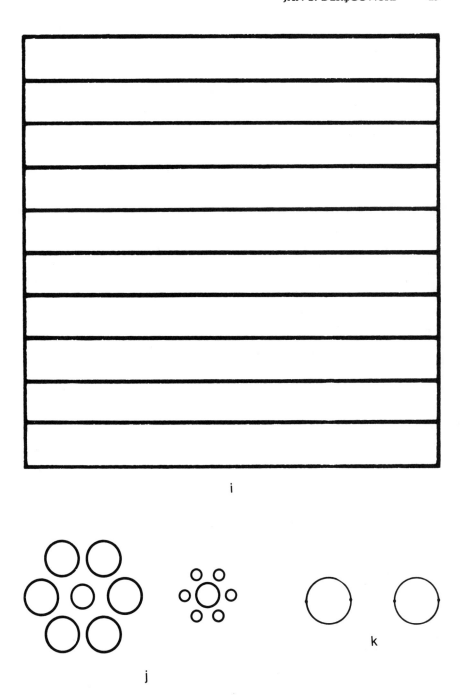

i

j

k

Figure 2-4 (continued)

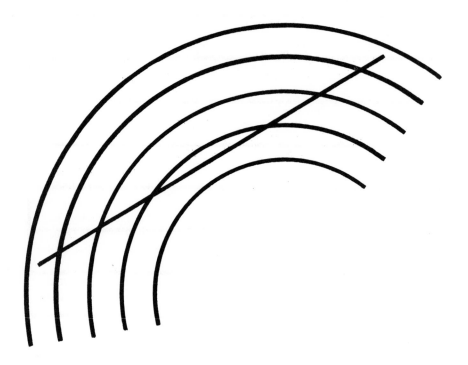

Figure 2–4 (continued)

responded to the following illusions: Poggendorf, Müller-Lyer, Sander's parallelogram, "perspective" (which could perhaps be regarded as a derivative of the Ponzo illusion) and two versions of the horizontal-vertical illusion ('L' and 'T'). No reliable data could be obtained on the Poggendorf. Of the data obtained with the other stimuli the "perspective" effect was rather weak, but the remaining four stimuli yielded strong evidence of cultural difference, which on the whole tended to support the empiricist hypotheses. Samples drawn from more carpentered environments showed more susceptibility to the Müller-Lyer and Sander's parallelogram illusions than did samples drawn from less carpentered backgrounds. Samples drawn from populations exposed to open vistas were found (but here the effect was relatively weaker) to be more prone to the horizontal-vertical illusions than the samples drawn from areas (such as dense forests) where open vistas are rare. It was also found that on the whole children were more prone to the Müller-Lyer illusion than were the adults drawn from the sample population. (The authors explain this difference, which is contrary to the carpentered world hypothesis, by offering a post facto hypothesis that adults tend to compensate for errors which exposure to the carpentered environment causes whereas children have not yet gained this ability.) The horizontal-vertical illusion presented no clear trend in this respect.

This extensive study proved to be as inceptive in the area of illusions as Hudson's work was in the area of pictorial perception. A review of some of the studies which followed is presented below.

Beyond Rivers and Segall et al.

Notwithstanding the close connection between Segall et al. (1966) and Heuse's (1957a) study, the finding of the two studies cannot be compared directly because the measures of illusion susceptibility are not stated. Heuse merely quotes the frequencies with which illusions were perceived by soldiers of many African tribes, but mostly from Sudan and Guinea, and by a Western control group. Six types of illusion were used within a battery testing various cognitive and intellectual skills. The results show greater inconsistency within the African group than within the Western group, which might have arisen, as the author points out, because the subjects did not understand the instructions or were suggestible. The

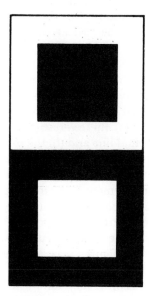

Figure 2-5   Irradiation Illusion Stimulus.

finding to which the author draws special attention is that of the greater susceptibility of the Western subjects to the irradiation illusion. (See Fig. 2–5). This phenomenon was subsequently investigated on United States whites and blacks (Pettigrew and Nuttall, 1963). The difference in susceptibility to the illusion was found to be present, but only when a black and white version of stimuli (similar to that used by Heuse) was employed. This fact seems to argue against visual acuity being a plausible explanation, yet this is the explanation that the authors advance. They also present several other hypotheses involving social and personality constructs, but none of these has as yet received support. It is noteworthy that Rivers (1901) observed the absence of the phenomenon in question in his Torres Straits study.

Other studies of illusions that followed can be conveniently divided into those which refine Segall et al.'s work and those which introduce new elements by trying to establish how perception of illusions relates to perception in general.

Jahoda's (1966) paper falls in the former category. Three samples were used, one British and two Ghanaian. The latter differed from each other in both the carpenteredness and openness of their environment. The Müller-Lyer and the T-type horizontal-vertical illusion figures were used. It was found that in the M-L illusion Segall et al.'s prediction was fulfilled as far as the relationship of the British sample to the two African samples was concerned, but the expected difference between the two African groups was not observed. On the horizontal-vertical illusion, the British sample, which scored within the range of the African samples, behaved in accordance with the expectations derivable from Segall et al.'s data, but again, the data derived from the African samples did not support the hypothesis. Indeed two of the African groups that were judged to have "closely similar cultural and ecological characteristics" obtained entirely different scores. An unfortunate choice of the horizontal-vertical stimulus might, in some measure, have been responsible for this effect. Kunnapas (1955) has demonstrated that the T-type stimulus evokes an illusion which consists of two elements: (a) the overestimation of the vertical line as compared with the horizontal line and (b) the overestimation of the dividing line. Deręgowski (1967) reanalysed both Segall et al.'s and Rivers' (1905) data, showing that the L-figure which, unlike the T-figure, does not contain the "dichosection" element is the more appropriate tool for investigation of the ecological hypothesis. Moreover, Segall et al.'s data obtained with this figure lend stronger support to their original hypothesis than the data obtained with the T-figure. Further empirical support for the distinction between the two figures was adduced by Jahoda and Stacey (1970).

Mundy-Castle and Nelson (1962) administered the Müller-Lyer illusion, the "perspective" illusion and two versions of the horizontal-vertical

illusion to a group of inbred and culturally isolated Western forest workers. They found that the responses of this group were more similar to that
of black and Bushman groups than to that of westernized whites. The data
for the non-Western groups used in this comparison were those of Morgan (1959). Since Bushmen live in a desert and have a noncarpentered
culture, they contrast in these respects with the forest workers, and the
results run contrary to both major hypotheses of Segall and his associates.

Morgan's (1959) study, which was carried out using Segall et al.'s materials, also failed to support the hypotheses. The populations sampled
were (a) illiterate black labourers (b) white students and graduates (c) Kalahari Bushmen. Both black miners and Bushmen were found as previously to be less affected by the M-L illusion than the white group; but,
contrary to the hypothesis, there was no significant difference between the
response of the white and Bushmen groups to both types of the horizontal-vertical illusion. Moreover, the black labourers differed significantly
from those two groups, being more prone to illusion. Morgan suggested
that the effect of education upon perception of illusion in black populations ought to be studied, thus echoing Rivers's suspicions. She also suggested that a tachistoscope be used to standardize the time for which
stimuli are shown to the subjects.

In none of these studies has an attempt been made to control for genetic differences between samples. Gregor and McPherson (1965) tried to
do so using two samples of Australian aborigines. The support obtained
for Segall et al.'s hypothesis is rather tenuous, there being considerable
within-sample differences between men and women and between types of
illusion figures. As far as the "carpentered environments" hypothesis is
concerned, only women's responses to Sander's parallelogram support it
whilst their responses to the Müller-Lyer figure yield no significant results. The ecological hypothesis receives no direct support, there being no
significant differences, but the authors suggested that the performance on
this task yielded such high scores (the two groups used here gained higher
scores than any reported by Segall et al.) that the subjects from both
groups might have been responding, as a result of their exposure to open
vistas, at about the highest attainable levels.

Richardson, Lock, Lee, and Tee (1971) compared Chinese and Western residents of Singapore on the Müller-Lyer illusion and found the former group far more susceptible. Since environmentally the two groups
were matched, both were urban, the authors attribute the effect to the effort of Chinese script on the Chinese sample. This appears prima facie
rather a remote possibility, even more so than the possibility of the effect
of the preferred artistic style. Furthermore, Dawson, Young, and Choi's
(1973) results are contradictory to those of Richardson et al., as they show
Hong Kong Chinese to be *less* susceptible to the Müller-Lyer illusion than
an American sample and obtain a consonant result on Sander's parallelo-

gram. This large study of developmental trends of susceptibility to four illusions (Müller-Lyer, Sander's parallelogram, horizontal-vertical "L," horizontal-vertical "T") within a Chinese sample was supportive of both hypotheses of Segall et al. The authors also investigated the relationship between illusion susceptibility and scores attained on the (a) Kohs' Blocks test, (b) Embedded Figures Test, (c) Rod-and-Frame Test, (d) 3D Pictorial Perception Test, and (e) the Traditional-Modern scale. The correlation coefficients obtained clearly showed complex relationships among various parameters. The most noteworthy features were the highly significant (but not high) correlations between two measures of field dependence (Embedded Figures Test and Kohs' Blocks) and the two versions of the horizontal-vertical illusion. There were no significant correlations involving either the Müller-Lyer illusion or the 3D Pictorial Perception test, but there was a relatively high significant correlation of Sander's parallelogram scores with the traditional-modern scale. A decrease of illusion susceptibility with age (age range: three to seventeen years) was also confirmed by this study. These observations indicate only one rather dispiriting conclusion; that studies of illusions do not give easy access to the perceptual differences between cultures.

Bonte (1962) used two methods for measuring the Müller-Lyer illusion: a preliminary version of Segall et al.'s apparatus and a slide based upon Rivers's design. She found that whereas results obtained with the latter showed no difference in illusion susceptibility of the Bashi and the M'buti of the Congo and the European control group, such a difference was obtained when Europeans and the Bashi were compared using Segall's method; the Europeans, as expected, showed greater susceptibility to the illusion. Segall et al. discussed Bonte's findings at some length and suggested that the discrepancies between her results and their own results were probably due to the imperfections of Bonte's apparatus and her experimental procedure.

Several important experiments on illusions have been carried out by Berry. In one of these, using Kohs' Blocks as a measure of development, Berry (1968) showed that the negative results reported on testing the carpentered world hypothesis might be a result of the confounding of two factors: carpenteredness of the environment and perceptual development (the increasing carpenteredness fostering increases in the Müller-Lyer illusion, but the increasing perceptual development hindering such an increase). The samples of Eskimo and Temne used by Berry did not permit a perfectly balanced analysis. Nonetheless, the results show clearly that whereas no significant differences on the illusion were observed within total samples between the "urban/traditional" and "rural/traditional" groups, such differences did occur when the Eskimo subsamples were matched on Kohs' Blocks. When the scores of the "high-carpentered" and "low-carpentered" groups were compared, higher scores, as expected, obtained in the group coming from the urban/transitional and highly car-pentered environment. A parallel comparison within the Temne group on subsamples matched on their exposure to "carpenteredness" yielded a higher illusion score in the group having lower Kohs scores, thus recon-firming Berry's hypothesis. It will be noticed that on both these compari-sons the ethnic factor was kept constant and that no direct cross-cultural comparisons were made. The obtained result, as Berry points out, does not provide a satisfactory overall explanation of the illusion, for a com-parison of his Eskimo and Temne rural groups coming from a similar moderately carpentered environment and having about the same illusion scores shows a large difference on their Kohs' scores, the Eskimos' score being considerably higher. This suggests that cross-cultural matching on Kohs' Blocks would not in this case produce samples with equal propen-sity to the Müller-Lyer illusion. A question of the universality of the cor-relation between responses to this illusion and the scores on Kohs' Blocks needs to be considered.

In another experiment, Berry (1971a) considered, in addition to the above factors, the effect of the pigmentation of the *fundus oculi*. Here a positive rank correlation (reverse of the expected correlation) between Kohs scores and Müller-Lyer scores was obtained. Partialling out carpen-teredness reduced, but did not eliminate the effect. Thus doubts about the generality of the Kohs' Blocks–Müller-Lyer illusion correlation are strengthened. On the other hand the data obtained support the carpen-tered world hypothesis by yielding a strong correlation between the illu-sion scores and the carpenteredness rankings. The strength of this effect is moderated by the pigmentation, a factor which will be considered more fully.

A paper by Jahoda and Stacey (1970) incorporated several elements which were not previously investigated in a cross-cultural context. The number of illusion figures used was large and included the Helmholtz square, Sander's parallelogram, Müller-Lyer, dichosection, horizontal-vertical (L-type), Poggendorf, Boring circles, Titchener circles, Judd 1, Judd 2, Wundt, and Hering. (See Fig. 2–4.) Samples of subjects were drawn from institutions of higher learning in Scotland and Ghana. Each sample contained two subsamples, one having at least two years of sys-tematic training in drawing and the other having no such training. The most important findings obtained were: (1) The illusions formed clusters which were not the same for both groups: The Helmholtz square and horizontal-vertical illusions formed one cluster, and the Sander's parallel-ogram, Müller-Lyer and Titchener circles formed a second cluster in the case of the Scottish sample. In the case of the Ghanaian sample the Helm-holtz circles, horizontal-vertical, Müller-Lyer and Sander's parallelogram formed a general cluster; (2) The data showed a significant culture effect on all but the Müller-Lyer and dichosection. Scots were more illusion-prone in all cases except the Helmholtz square and the horizontal-vertical; (3) The effect of specialist training was found to be moderate, just as in Carlson (1966). As far as the carpentered-world hypothesis is concerned the data offer a weak support: untrained Ghanaians showed lower susceptibility than untrained Scots to Sander's parallelogram. There were no other significant differences. Remember, however, that the two samples were drawn from educationally similar environments. The *ecological* hypothesis on the other hand is sustained by the results; the Ghanaian sample showed greater susceptibility to the horizontal-vertical (L-type) illusion. No hypothesis was offered by the authors for the greater susceptibility of the Scottish sample to a large proportion of illusions. Post facto, it may be noted that greater susceptibility is a sui generis index of the magnitude of influences which various elements of a figure exert upon each other, a situation analogous to that which arises when various elements of meaningful pictorial display are being integrated in the course of perception of a picture. The dichosection effect investigated in the paper is of special importance to Piaget's (1969) theory of perception of the horizontal-vertical illusion. The findings obtained are difficult to reconcile with the postulated attentional effects. If the effects of dichosection and the horizontal-vertical illusion were, as Piaget suggests, both due to the same attentional factor they should be equally affected by Jahoda and Stacey's experimental manipulation. This clearly is not the case.

Another noteworthy finding of this study is the absence of support for the hypothesis that susceptibility to illusions is related to field-dependence as measured by the Embedded Figures Test in a sample of untrained Ghanaians. An important distinction is clearly made in the paper between (1) universal determinants of a particular illusion and (2) factors responsible for the strength of an illusion in a particular culture. Mercado, Ribes, and Barrera (1967) have shown the applicability of such a distinction to the Müller-Lyer illusion. When semicircular or rectangular lines are used instead of the usual "arrowhead" the illusion persists, albeit in decreased intensity. If the carpentered-world hypothesis is valid, this difference between responses to two types of stimuli should show cross-cultural variations compatible with the nature of the environment. The same argument can be applied to other variants of the illusion (Robinson, 1972, p. 20) as well as to other illusion figures. Cross-cultural differences should affect the form of the regression equation connecting responses made to variants of the illusion figure.

Robinson (1972) wrote a brief review of the cross-cultural studies of illusions. Unfortunately, it obscures the essential difference between the two hypotheses presented by Segall et al. and fails to note that the *relative* differences in the environment are postulated to influence the illusions. Robinson claims that Segall et al. have taken insufficient account of differences between "Africans and Europeans." "Chiefly these are educational differences, particularly differences in experience with drawings on paper, and physiological differences between races themselves" (p. 10). The first of these points appears to ignore the fact that Segall et al. ranked their samples on the intensity of variables that they hypothesised should influence perception. The second postulates the existence of physiological differences which may influence perception without specifying what such physiological differences could be, and hence is not helpful. One such difference arising from a difference in pigmentation of the *fundus oculi* has, however, been advanced as a possible reason for differences in perception of illusions.

A recent study of illusions, their relationship to field-dependence and factor structure (Taylor, 1974) offers an exhaustive factor analysis of illusions. Findings obtained from 274 white men showed weak relationships between illusions and field-dependence. Factor analysis of illusions showed that twenty-one types of illusions formed groups subject to different factors, the two main being distortion of the length of the line and distortion of line direction. These two factors appear, according to Taylor, to agree well with the two classes of illusions suggested by Robinson (1968). Furthermore, the Poggendorff illusion appeared to have unique qualities. (Two similar main factors are suggested by a later study of several illusions (Coren, Girgus, Erlichman, & Hakstian, 1976)).

Although Taylor's study is not cross-cultural, its findings are of immediate importance to the subject matter of this chapter, and it is a cause for regret that Taylor did not use all the illusion figures used by Segall et al. (1966) and by Jahoda and Stacey (1970), especially that the various versions of the horizontal-vertical illusion were not tested.

Davis and Carlson (1970) investigated the role of attentional factors in cross-cultural differences in perception of the Müller-Lyer illusion. Such a possibility had been considered by Rivers (as shown in the quotation at the beginning of this section) and was revived by Doob (1966). Doob wondered whether the more analytic (a term which is perhaps synonymous with nonsynthetic, i.e., failing to integrate) attitude the non-Western populations have may be responsible for their lesser susceptibility to illusions. Segall et al. (1966, p. 184) made little of this suggestion since for them it lacked support of a plausible ecological condition which would provide a functional hypothesis. The procedure used by Davis and Carlson consisted of two variants of instructions that differed in the extent to which they drew the subject's attention to the lines that had to be compared. The results obtained were inconclusive. The strongest, and in a way most surprising, effect is the significantly lower susceptibility to illusions observed in the Ugandan students than in both Western groups *and* in a sample of rural Banyakole adults. Another noteworthy finding is that the magnitude of the effect varies with types of stimuli used, an observation already reported by Bonte (1962). Davis and Carlson regard the difference between their two African samples as being confirmatory of Davis's (1970) earlier report that more sophisticated subjects make more discriminating judgments and hence are less prone to the illusion. Granted that this is so, the reported finding was in agreement with Segall et al.'s hypothesis, provided the lesser potency of such sophistication in the West can be justified and thus explain the yawning gap between the results obtained with Ugandan and American university samples. Yet it does not seem that the educational hypothesis is readily acceptable. Davis derived this hypothesis from Segall et al.'s attempt to explain the lesser susceptibility of adults than of children to illusions. The argument is that the perceptual habit learned as a result of exposure to certain ecological phenomena is moderated later in life by acquisition of more analytical perceptual skills. Davis attempted to evaluate this hypothesis by considering correlations between numbers of years of formal education and susceptibility to the illusion. The data obtained were ambiguous, offering but a suggestion of a negative correlation.

It is apposite to contrast Davis's suggestion with Jahoda's (1966) more specific suggestion of a relationship between perception of pictorial depth and susceptibility to illusion; Jahoda postulates that these two effects correlate positively. Thus the effects put forward by Davis and Jahoda oppose each other. Jahoda's suggestions of both educational and pictorial sophistication can be questioned, as Davis does, by using Jahoda's own results and pointing out that Jahoda's samples, which were less susceptible to illusions, *were* nevertheless susceptible. This argument seems to lack validity. The question under consideration is not the presence of susceptibility to the illusions, but the differences in magnitude of such susceptibility and its determinants. All Segall et al.'s samples, with the sole exception of Suku children, were susceptible to the Müller-Lyer illusion. In the case of Sander's parallelogram the effect was even stronger; there were no exceptions. Thus, minimal susceptibility is probably present throughout the human species, but that its observed magnitude depends largely on as yet ill-defined factors. This general statement may also be applied to the observations of the horizontal-vertical illusions.

The effect of the specific type of illusion figure must not pass unnoted. There is no ground for believing that the traditional descriptive taxonomy corresponds closely to the modus operandi of the perceptual mechanism. It has been shown (see e.g. Robinson, 1972) that by appropriate modification of figures a "Müller-Lyer" figure can be made to evoke the reverse of the commonly encountered illusion. Such observations suggest that different mechanisms may be triggered by different illusions and suggest that great care be exercised in responding to Davis's (1970) call that several samples within each culture be tested on several different instruments.[18]

Wober (1972) argued that susceptibility to the horizontal-vertical illusion, according to Segall and his associates, should be less when the figure is presented in an L-orientation than when it is rotated to orientation ⊥ Wober's data showed an absence of the expected difference and hence he questioned the value of his own interpretation of the Segall et al. hypothesis. The element of interpretation needs to be stressed for such a finding does not appear on a closer examination to be inconsistent with Segall et al.'s thesis. Wober based his interpretation on the illustrative example given by Segall et al., which happens to be a description of a pavement. Had they, instead, chosen a coffered ceiling, which they well might have done, the predictions derived by Wober would have been just as irrelevant to the theory, the implications of which are clearly apparent from the stimuli used by Segall et al.; one of these, "the inverted T," is in the "pavement" orientation, whilst the other, "the inverted L," is in the coffered ceiling orientation. Furthermore, Wober's contention—that of two equal lines, parallel and normal to the observer's line of sight, the line further away from the observer appears smaller—is palpably false as shown by Leibowitz et al.'s (1969) study of the Ponzo illusion. Wober's experimental procedure, too, lacks refinement. Specifically, the sequence of orientations is constant and the colours of the two lines of the figure differ, with the line of the same colour always being used as a standard.

Valentine (1912) and more recently Finger and Spelt (1947), and Avery and Day (1969) have carefully demonstrated that in fact the inverted-L illusion is stronger than upright L. Contradictory evidence was obtained in a recent study by Schiffman and Thompson (1975). Their stimuli were exposed in a tachistoscope for 100 milliseconds, and yielded results contradictory to both those of Segall et al. and of Wober. The sense of illusion was found to reverse with the inversion of the figure. The vertical member was seen as longer in the L orientation but the horizontal member was seen as longer in the ⊥ orientation. Thus the effect may well be related to the interaction between elevation within the plane of the stimuli and the duration of exposure. It is not surprising that relative elevation should affect responses since it constitutes one of the basic monocular cues (Blakemore, 1973), and has been shown to be of import in studies of pictorial perception (McGurk & Jahoda, 1974). The effect of duration which these results suggest and its interaction with elevation are less expected. There appear to be no cross-cultural data on this issue.

Further supportive evidence for the perspective effect of the illusion is provided by Cormack and Cormack (1974), who measured the effect of the inclination to the "vertical" upon the magnitude of the illusion. This study supported the suggestion offered by Hochberg and Brooks (1960) that asymmetry is an important determinant in perception of pictorial depth. It also sustains the notion that angles made by linear elements influence perception greatly (Parker, 1974). Dawson (1973) found that the susceptibility to the horizontal-vertical illusions was lower in the right-eye dominant observers and suggested that apart from superior spatial skills, culturally determined glance curves affect the illusion. The latter effect is not convincingly demonstrated in Dawson's paper and even he suggests that it calls for a thorough investigation.

An important variant of illusory experience is evoked by three-dimensional stimuli. Its importance has two roots: (1) Some theories [e.g., those invoking constancy scaling mechanisms (Gregory, 1966)] explain illusions evoked by pictorial stimuli as related to perception of three-dimensional objects; hence, circumstances under which illusions can be evoked by three-dimensional objects are of theoretical interest, and (2) presentation of three-dimensional stimuli obviates objections which are advanced whenever drawings are used in pictureless cultures, viz. that drawings constitute a culturally unacceptable medium of testing. Extension of the traditional testing procedures by incorporation of this variant by Leibowitz et al. (1969) has already been mentioned and will be discussed further.

Allport and Pettigrew (1957) used a different experimental procedure. They tested groups of Zulus differing in urbanisation on Ames's rotating window and found, as expected, that the tendency to see the model as oscillating rather than rotating depended on the conditions under which it was viewed. This conclusion was based upon the absence of a noticeable difference in the effect when optimal conditions were used with urban and rural samples. Allport and Pettigrew suggested that their results offered no firm support to either nativist or empiricist theories. Slack (1959) placed greater stress on the significant differences of performance in suboptimal conditions. He suggested, as a contrary interpretation, that since rural scores of the Zulu were less similar to the Western scores than the urban scores, the results support the empiricist approach. Segall et al. (1966) agree with this conclusion.

Illusions and Pictorial Perception

Figures which evoke illusions can be regarded as abstract pictures whose elements influence each other in a rather unusual way. The existence of such a relationship is implicit in Rivers's postulated effect of the study of geometry upon susceptibility to illusions and is reflected in Segall et al.'s rationale. Attempts can be made therefore to establish to what extent illusions can be found in ordinary pictures or to what extent experience with pictorial material affects perception of illusions, as suggested by Jahoda (1966).

Wober (1970) carried out an experiment aimed at evaluating directly the relationship postulated by Jahoda and reports no significant correlation between the responses obtained to a pictorial perception test and those to the horizontal-vertical illusion. Hence, it would appear that an explanation of susceptibility to the horizontal-vertical illusion in terms of pictorial perception may not be valid. Unfortunately it is not plain in Wober's report whether he used a "T" or an "L" form of the illusion figure, a fact of consequence in view of Jahoda and Stacey's finding. However, even if the "T" figure had been used it could be claimed that it represents, to some extent, a valid measure of the relevant phenomenon. This can scarcely be said of the modified version of Hudson's and Dawson's tests that Wober employed, for whereas the illusion figure allowed subjects to explore the entire spectrum of possible responses, a pictorial perception test must have explored but narrow segments of the corresponding spectrum. (The same criticism may apply to Dawson et al.'s 1973, study of correlations between susceptibility of illusions and 3D pictorial perception scores already discussed.) This effect can be readily seen in Leibowitz et al.'s (1969) and Brislin's (1974) results, wherein the same population is seen to yield different scores depending on the richness of the stimuli in depth cues. It is interesting to note here that Wober found a positive correlation between the horizontal-vertical illusion and the perspective illusion. The perspective illusion according to Leibowitz et al., and Brislin and in an intensified form according to Newman, 1969, carries a clear implication of depth. Furthermore, Stacey (1969) showed, on a Western sample at least, that the horizontal-vertical illusion contains an implicit depth cue.

Leibowitz et al. (1969), Leibowitz and Pick (1972), and Kilbride and Leibowitz (1975) conducted a series of studies on the Ponzo illusion. Their stimuli were similar to those that were regarded by Segall et al. as evoking the perspective illusion. The chief difference was that whilst Leibowitz's figures were symmetrical about the vertical axis of the stimulus, Segall et al.'s figures were asymmetrical, one of the two slanting lines being inclined at a much greater angle to the vertical than the other (as in Fig. 2–4). Although according to Hochberg and Brooks (1960) asymmetrical patterns foster perception of pictorial depth, Segall et al. found this illusion to be relatively weak, none of the samples showing more than 8 percent discrepancy. The sample rank scores did, however, correlate with those obtained by using other illusions including the horizontal-vertical. Yet such a correlation was not found when individual scores were considered. Likewise, Rivers (1901) found an elaborated version of this illusion to be weak. On the other hand, Smith (1973), using the same illusion with a Xhosa sample, obtained data that supported the carpentered world hypothesis.

Leibowitz et al. (1969) used three pictures showing the Ponzo figure, as well as a control figure, and found that in the case of his American (Western) sample from Pennsylvania the magnitude of the illusion increased with the number of pictorial depth cues.[20] This was not so in the case of the Guam sample, where little difference obtained between the responses made to the simple illusion figure and the figures that presented additional cues. This absence of an expected increase is even more surprising when data from the Ugandan sample (Leibowitz & Pick, 1972) are considered. The Ugandan students, it seems, responded similarly to the Pennsylvania students and unlike their Guam peers. Ugandan villagers, on the other hand, showed scarcely any perception of the illusion. The authors did not consider the ambiguous position of the Guam sample but attempted to explain the discrepancy between the two Ugandan samples (which obviously cannot be explained on ecological grounds) by suggesting that Ugandan villagers, being relatively unfamiliar with pictorial material, were greatly influenced by the physical flatness of the stimuli and thus did not respond to perspective cues—another echo of Rivers's speculations—present, but not investigated in Segall et al.'s book.

An important extension of this study using the Ponzo as well as some other stimuli is reported by Brislin (1974). This study, in addition to the cultural variable, investigated the effects of the age of subjects and of the orientation of the stimuli. The finding that the figures with their point of convergence at the top evoke a stronger illusion than those with their point of convergence to the left, is of importance to the considerations of the influence of symmetry upon the perception of depth. Another interesting finding is that the observed age trends are ambiguous. The failure of the Guam sample to show an age trend on their responses to the stimuli involving linear perspective can be understood in terms of the ecological hypothesis. It is, however, difficult to invoke this hypothesis to explain the failure of this sample to take into account the cues present in the density gradients, which are present in all environments.

The explanation based on the inability to see pictorial depth gains support from Kilbride and Leibowitz's (1975) paper. The same paper suggests, however, that suppression of surface cues is not a satisfactory remedy for failure to see depth. Such a finding is contrary to expectations, for Boring (1964) has pointed out that a mere interposition of a lens or even of a mirror affects the constancy scaling mechanism by suppressing surface cues in a picture.

The Effect of Retinal Pigmentation

Pollack (1963) demonstrated that whilst visual brightness and contrast threshold increased with age (in the range eight to fourteen years) the Müller-Lyer illusion decreased. He suggested that such a result showed that "there is little ground for arguing . . . (that) decreasing magnitude of illusion is due to . . . learning." This judgment seems to be somewhat rash. Since the rationale behind the argument was that both these phenomena are due to a decrease of sensitivity "of the human visual apparatus to light stimulation" one would expect similar results to obtain had subjects been asked to judge illusion figures in Pollack's apparatus at various intensities of illumination. Pollack did not use such a control procedure but relied in his argument on Oyama's (1960) study. It is noteworthy that such a peripheral effect, if it exists, could merely moderate the process which has been shown to be probably central in its nature (Julesz, 1971); it could not be responsible for its very existence. Unfortunately the operation of the putative moderating mechanism is not clearly described by Pollack. Why should a judgment of an illusion figure be more affected than the judgment of ordinary rectilinear segments? If the effect of increasing density is to obfuscate the figure, should not such a change be reflected in the larger variance of the judgments made rather than in the lowering of the mean? A subsequent study by Silvar and Pollack (1967) showed that there is a significant difference in ratings of pigmentation of *fundus oculi* of American Negro and Caucasian subjects, the latter being more often classified as lightly pigmented. In another study (Pollack & Silvar, 1967), a group of subjects (thirteen blacks and two whites) with darkly pigmented *fundus* was compared with a group of subjects with a lightly pigmented *fundus* (nineteen whites and one black) on their scores on the Müller-Lyer illusion. It was found that the former group experienced illusion to a lesser extent. Since each of the groups was ethnically (culturally) almost homogeneous, the results are ambiguous and it is impossible to say whether the result obtained is indicative of an ethnic (cultural) difference or merely of a difference in pigmentation.

This ambiguity and other considerations induced Bayer and Pressey (1972) to replicate and extend Pollack's experiments. Both the Müller-Lyer and the horizontal-vertical (probably the "T" type) illusions were used. The procedure differed greatly from that used by Pollack, but the control stimuli show that the observed data are not artifacts. Young Caucasians, who served as subjects, were allocated on the basis of optometric rating into five categories differing in *fundus* pigmentation. No support for the relationship between the pigmentation of the *fundus* in either of the illusions was found. In a similar unpublished study Robinson and Reece (1975) failed to find support for the pigmentation effect in a Welsh sample and concluded that "either there is a racial difference in extent of illusions which is nothing to do with retinal pigmentation or ... there is some threshold level of pigmentation, darker than any encountered here, at which the extent of illusion suddenly changes." Intuitively such a discontinuity in the phenomenon seems unlikely. Additional evidence supportive of this view can be found in Dwyer and Stanton (1975). Furthermore, Weaver (1974) found in Ghana that perception of the Müller-Lyer figure and of Sander's parallelogram was affected by the ecological experience of subjects whose pigmentations did not differ. Yet further questions can be raised when Jahoda and Stacey's (1970) observations are considered. They found, as already stated, that the Ghanaian and Scottish subjects did not differ on the dichosection element but did differ on the horizontal-vertical element of the horizontal-vertical illusion. There seem to be no obvious grounds for thinking that the former should be affected less by the pigmentation whereas the ecological hypothesis does argue in favour of the observed difference.

However, the evidence is not entirely one-sided. Berry (1971a) and Jahoda (1971) obtained data supporting the pigmentation hypothesis. Berry (1971a) reanalysed his cross-cultural data (Berry, 1966, 1969) by taking into account the skin pigmentation and hence, by implication, the macular pigmentation of his ten samples. Calculation of coefficients of concordance yielded a surprising result in view of Berry's own previous work: Kohs' Blocks scores correlated positively with susceptibility to the Müller-Lyer illusion. Correlation between carpenteredness and Müller-Lyer illusion scores was positive albeit rather small so that "the only conclusion possible from the data was that pigmentation is the best prediction of Müller-Lyer susceptibility" (p. 196). This conclusion implies that a physiological and an innate factor has a stronger correlation with susceptibility than any of the variables hitherto considered. Before such a conclusion is espoused, however, certain weaknesses in the study must be considered. First, as mentioned above Silvar and Pollack (1967) demonstrated the correlation between skin pigmentation and pigmentation of the *fundus* on an American sample; however, there is no certainty that such a relationship can be extrapolated to the populations used by Berry. Second and equally importantly, this study, just as Pollack's original study, confounds ethnicity, culture, and pigmentation. Third, although ranking of carpenteredness enables partialling out of this effect, there are other cultural aspects which are left uncontrolled and hence may also be confounded with pigmentation. Much of the critique that has been evoked by Segall et al.'s study (e.g., that it omits consideration of literacy) can also *mutatis mutandis* be applied here. It follows that such control paradigms as those applied by Berry (1968) to the problem of carpenteredness could fruitfully be extended to the problem of pigmentation. If within-culture comparisons and comparisons of groups of equal pigmentation were to support the reported findings, then this genetic effect would emerge as of considerable consequence, not only because of its correlation with susceptibility to the Müller-Lyer illusion, but also because of its correlation with Kohs' Blocks scores, which Berry reports. Thus a peripheral effect possibly offering a certain attraction, which can be placed under the label "differences are only skin deep" (see discussion of "compensatory" hypotheses), might derive a profound meaning from the latter correlation and through it with a number of functions with which Kohs' Blocks scores correlate.

A further piece of supportive evidence comes from Jahoda's (1971) Malawian study. He replicated and extended Pollack's work by testing samples of subjects in Malawi and Scotland. He used blue and red illusion figures since these were found (Pollack, 1970) not to evoke different responses in white American subjects, but were expected to be perceived differently by the African samples: susceptibility to the blue figures was expected to be less than to the red figures. Analogously Jahoda expected Africans to perform less well on the colour recognition task presented under the guise of matching of geographical profiles when purple/blue stimuli were used than when yellow/red stimuli were used. Furthermore, a positive correlation between the relative illusion susceptibility on the two figures and the performance on the recognition task was anticipated. No such effects were hypothesised to arise in the Scottish sample. The results obtained confirmed the hypotheses. The only significant difference observed in response to the Müller-Lyer figure was the higher susceptibility of the Malawi sample to the red figure than to the blue one. There was no difference between the two samples on either of the figures; this does not, however, affect the carpentered world hypothesis to any extent since both samples consisted of highly sophisticated subjects. The result, however, is not consistent with Davis's (1970) findings of the significant differences between American and Ugandan students already described. The Malawi subjects were worse on colour matching than the Scottish subjects on both segments of the spectrum. More importantly they were, as anticipated, more successful with the yellow/red shadings than with the purple/blue ones. (This effect is probably analogous to that observed by Rivers [1905].) Thus this hypothesis is also sustained; the anticipated correlation was also obtained.

These findings offer a prima facie support for Pollack's pigmentation hypothesis. Unfortunately the design employed confounded cultural group with pigmentation and it cannot therefore be claimed that such support is definitive. Responses of the Malawi sample seem, however, worthy of more detailed consideration. For example, the two tasks used differed considerably, the Müller-Lyer task calling for quick judgment of a briefly exposed stimulus (the method used was a derivative of the method used by Pollack and Silvar (1967), whilst on the "geographical test" short-term memory was involved as the subject had to identify a cross-profile of shading identical with that which he had been shown immediately before. The reported data do not allow one to judge whether the results were obtained because subjects were less certain of their judgments when responding to one of the purple/blue figures, or, alternatively, whether the subjects showed a systematic bias. It is also noteworthy that the observed differences in illusion susceptibility, although obviously systematic, are very small (about 1.2 percent; the magnitude of the illusion being about 10 percent). Furthermore, the correlation of 0.38 between the two tasks (Müller-Lyer and Geographical), although significant, is probably too small to imply that a single mechanism controlling both processes is equally involved in both of them.

Stewart (1973) conducted an extensive study of samples drawn from the United States and various environments in Zambia, especially designed to contrast Pollack's physiological hypothesis with the ecological hypothesis of Segall et al. Her comparison of United States blacks and United States whites showed no difference between the two groups in their susceptibility to illusions. This is interpreted as supporting the environmental hypothesis. Unfortunately, although a four-point scale was used to rate some of the subjects on pigmentation, there is no report of the use of such ratings in analysing the data. The table of results contrasts simply whites and blacks on their responses to two illusions, Müller-Lyer and Sander's parallelogram. The result, as presented, is therefore reconcilable with those of Pollack and Silvar (1967) and Bayer and Pressey (1972), for it is possible for the following state to prevail: $\underline{WL \quad WD}$ B; where $\underline{W}$ = whites, $\underline{L}$ = light pigmented, $\underline{D}$ = dark pigmented, $\underline{B}$ = blacks, and symbols underscored by a common line do not differ significantly. Hence Stewart's analysis of the pigmentation effect does not resolve the issue.

Her data, however, are somewhat more definitive in their support of the ecological hypothesis. They show a steady increase of susceptibility of illusion with exposure to carpentered environment, and would have been convincing if only the suspicion of selective migration could have been eliminated. This suspicion is reinforced by the absence of difference in overall susceptibility to illusions in most carpentered samples, and a very pronounced change between rural and urban samples and within the urban sample (Township versus middle class groups) that the data suggest. Stewart followed the Allport and Pettigrew (1957) tradition of using three-dimensional stimuli for investigation of illusions by adapting Ames's distorting room and using it to test United States white, United States black, and Zambian samples. No differences between the two United States samples were observed, thus casting doubt on the pigmentation hypothesis. No significant trend was observed in Zambian samples ranked on their carpenteredness. If the United States black sample is added to those at the extreme of the scale sequence as being most carpentered, the trend reaches significance. However, one can reasonably question, as Stewart herself points out, the pure "blackness" of the Evanston blacks. It is also difficult to see why the two samples from the most carpentered environments are thought to differ in the extent of their environmental experience, as the Zambian sample is described as "Lusaka Middle Class."

A further study of Jahoda (1975) failed to confirm his earlier findings. The samples used here were derived from Scotland and Ghana and were required to identify portions of rectangular solids which were depicted in either red or blue, in block line drawings. In addition to this novel task they were also given the Paper Folding Test derived from the Educational Testing Service Kit for cognitive tests (Buros, 1965). The findings were that both samples performed less well on the blue stimuli than on the red stimuli; the greater disparity between the two colours of the stimuli, which was expected to be found in the case of the Ghanaian group, was not observed. Moreover, the scores on the Paper Folding Test did not correlate with the differences between the scores obtained on the two hues in either of the samples. It was also found that Ghanaians scored significantly lower than the Scots on the identification task.[19]

The experimental procedures used contain an implicit assumption that the spatial tasks of the type used are prone to the same manner of influence as the illusion figures. This need not necessarily be the case although such a connection is clearly put forward in the carpentered world hypothesis. One could argue in defence of the pigmentation hypothesis that the mechanism postulated therein is essentially perceptual and that the task used by Jahoda of such a complexity that it is likely to involve a higher mechanism. The validity of such an argument rests upon the precise nature of the "pigmentation mechanism" which, as has been said, has not been defined. In addition, the significantly lower scores of the Ghanaian samples and the significantly lower scores of girls within the Scottish sample suggest that the identification task contained an important spatial component, whereas lack of correlations between the scores on the two tasks observed shows that the two tests did not in fact measure the same variable. This unexpectedly complex relationship hinders deduction of any unambiguous conclusion from the results.

A cross-cultural review of colour vision and colour nomenclature, impressive in its breadth of scope, has been published by Bornstein (1973b). He concluded from an examination of linguistic, psychological, and physiological criteria that increased yellow pigmentation leads to increased absorption of short wavelength radiation. This results in (a) depression of spectral sensitivity for short wavelengths; (b) confusion of short wavelength stimuli in colour matching and colour naming; and (c) increase of visual acuity. It is suggested that the evidence presented accounts for both environmental and cultural influences since the density of the yellow pigment is affected by both exposure to sunlight and by dietary habits. Such results as presented in Jahoda's (1971) cartographic study can therefore be accounted for. On the other hand, Bolton, Michelson, Wilde, and Bolton's (1975) results are contrary to those that Bornstein would expect, both in so far as the perception of the Sander parallelogram, the Müller-Lyer, and the Horizontal-Vertical illusions, and the perception of colour are concerned. In the case of the Horizontal-Vertical illusion the results support the ecological hypothesis. However, since no direct measures of retinal pigmentation were taken by Bolton and his colleagues, the results are not entirely convincing, for it is possible that there was a negligible difference between the two groups of subjects in this respect. The study therefore questions somewhat hesitatingly, Bornstein's observations. This is not to say that the search for such physiological factors should not continue. As Bornstein's earlier version of the paper (Bornstein 1973a) suggests, quite the opposite holds.

It might be that the issue of retinal pigmentation offers an empirical watershed between culture and race and that pigmentation tends to attenuate cultural experiences. However, evidence now in hand is not convincing that the effect of pigmentation is likely to affect more complex cognitive functions than simple perception of colour.[20]

Studies of Constancies

The studies of illusions and studies of constancy are linked not only by the fact that the processes involved in the former phenomenon are suggested to be responsible for the latter (see e.g. Segall et al., 1966; Gregory, 1966) but also because in both cases the perceptual mechanism blends the data from the environment and its past experience in such a manner as to question the naive assumption that the size of the retinal projection alone determines the percept. Therefore one would expect cross-cultural studies to show differences in perception of constancies just as differences were found in perception of illusions. Thouless (1933) compared responses of British and Indian students on two tests. One of these measured "a tendency to see the real shape of a circle inclined to the eye at such an angle" as to yield a perspective ellipse, and the other "the tendency to see the 'real' relative sizes of two circular discs." A combined measure on these two tasks yielded higher scores in the Indian group showing their greater tendency to phenomenal regression to the real object. This tendency, it was thought, was responsible for the absence of perspective and shadows in Oriental art. In short: Indians draw as they see and they see differently than Westerners do.

Piotrowski (1935) discussed Thouless's findings and concluded that vision in true perspective is not a natural phenomenon but that it depends largely on education, environment, maturity, and intelligence, on the nature of the task and on "conscious attitude." He suggested further that the difference in phenomenal regression between Indian and British students was a result rather than a cause of the differences between Oriental and Western art. The relationship between art and perception has also been speculated upon by Porkas (see Gaddes, McKenzie, and Barnsley, 1968) whose comparison of Northwestern Indian and white groups showed no such effect.

Beveridge (1935) extended Thouless's (1932) Glaswegian studies by testing students from West Africa. Both shape and size constancy were tested and it was found that the mean phenomenal character for the African lies between that for the European and the true character. Thouless, when commenting on Beveridge's paper, pointed out that in his earlier paper (1933) he demonstrated a parallel difference on these variables between Indian and British subjects.

Bush and Culwick (no date) compared Europeans, Tanganyikan petty officials and domestic servants, and a group of subjects of mixed Arab-African descent on a shape constancy task and found a significantly higher coefficient in the African group than in the two other groups. They found the discrepancy between the Arab-African and the African group particularly interesting since the former were not exposed to much pictorial material in the course of their education, yet, unlike the African group, had no difficulties with pictorial perception and even preferred those pictures which were drawn in perspective. They have thus put forward a link between perceptual constancy and pictorial perception. It is possible to extend this by postulating that the same mechanism that is responsible for constancy is also responsible for the magnitude of the Ames's room illusion investigated by Stewart (1973) in Zambia. Testing of shape constancy in Europeans, educated and uneducated Senas, and in Mang'anja schoolchildren (Myambo, 1972) supports these findings. African constancy scores were generally higher and were higher still in the uneducated Senas. An analysis of the Mang'anja sample and comparison of their scores with those of Europeans yielded the surprising result that shape constancy tends to decrease with age in the latter but not in the former group. Barring the possibility of differential interpretation one is faced with a puzzling contrast between the Sena and Mang'anja results from which it appears that the influence of education is ambiguous.

Perhaps the least Westernised population whose perception of size constancy has been studied were samples of Kalahari-Bushmen (Reuning & Wortley, 1973) and BaMbuti Pygmies (Turnbull, 1961). Comparisons of the data gathered in the Kalahari with those from other groups rank them (from most to least constancy) in the following order: Bushmen, South African whites and Bantu, Bantu locomotive drivers, and white students of optometry. That is, Bushmen are least influenced by the size of the retinal image. The high scores of Bushmen are thought to have been a result of experience in estimating distances whilst hunting or a result of natural selection imposed by the stringency of the environment. Winter (1967) discussed these results at length. Reuning and Wortley pointed out that E.E.G. measurements taken by Nelson (1964) and Van Wyk (1964) suggested that Bushmen have a higher "psychic tempo" and are usually more active or alert than whites or the illiterate blacks tested, and stress the importance of this finding. They further pointed out that the Bushmen had difficulties in isolating test stimuli from other environmental cues, and hence that their high scores "could well suggest strong field-dependence."[21] Turnbull's observations are less systematic and merely suggested that the BaMbuti, who inhabit dense forests, are very prone to experience a breakdown of the constancy scaling process when viewing an open vista similar to that experienced by Western subjects over much larger distances.

A connection between pictorial perception and constancy is also suggested by Mundy-Castle and Nelson (1962), who found that white forest workers, nursery children, and black workers all overestimated the size (i.e. showed underconstancy) when tested on size constancy. All three groups differed significantly from a group of white research workers. Mundy-Castle and Nelson thought that this was a result of relatively smaller conceptual influence upon perception in the former three groups.

The role of constancies in perception of illusion figures has already been mentioned. It should be noted, however, that recently the concept of constancy has been discussed by Thouless (1972) who suggested that the phenomenal characteristics perceived are a result of a compromise between the characteristics of the retinal projection of a shape and cues derived from the information about slope, distance, illumination and other factors. However, in the case of implicit-shape constancy (Derę-gowski, 1976b) and some of the illusions (Gregory, 1966) strong constancy effects occur in spite of great paucity of cues other than the retinal projection.

Perception of Other Geometrical Patterns

Most geometric stimuli do not evoke illusions and there is no a priori reason to postulate that responses to such stimuli would differ among cultures. In fact they do differ, as the data will show. Much of the data in question have been obtained incidentally by experimenters concerned with some more general purpose, such as measurement of intelligence. Nevertheless, they offer an important insight into perceptual phenomena.

The Pattern Completion Test (PATCO) (see Figure 2–6) developed by Hector (1958, 1959) requires subjects to complete a pattern of three rectangles by addition of another identical rectangle in such a manner as to render the final pattern symmetrical either about an axis in its plane (bilateral or mirror symmetry) or about an axis perpendicular to its plane (skew symmetry). In the original version of the test (Hector, 1958), the stimulus rectangles as well as the rectangle with which the response is made are black. In the modified version of the test (Hector, 1959), the symmetrical pair of the stimuli is printed in a different colour than the odd stimulus to

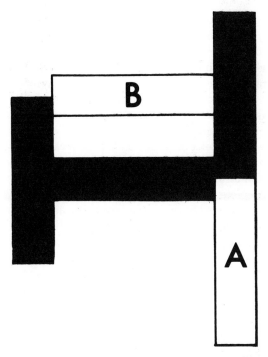

Figure 2-6   Two Possible Responses to the Same Stimulus (Black Oblongs) on PATCO Test. Response A renders the pattern symmetrical. Response B renders it skew symmetrical.[c]

which subjects have to provide an enantiomorph (i.e., a similar figure so placed that the entire arrangement becomes symmetrical). The test was intended to sample the same ability as Raven's Matrices but perhaps also involved the Gestalt or closure principle. Von Mayer (1963) took up Hector's speculation that the test measures closure and tested the same subjects on the PATCO and the Street Gestalt Test, but obtained no supportive evidence for the hypothesis. It is nonetheless apposite to examine some of the findings about perception which the PATCO test yielded.[22]

The natural errors made by testees are of interest in the present context as they probably provide information about the perceptual difficulties that the test presents. That is, they are at least of equal value to the information provided by correlations of the scores obtained with those obtained on other tests. Fridjohn (1961) reported Reuning's (1960) finding that the test items can be divided into three categories depending upon the spatial relationship between the axis of symmetry and the orientation of the longer axis of the missing enantiomorph (parallel to such axis, at 45˚ to such axis, and at 90˚ to such axis). In considering the results obtained by various experimenters, Fridjohn made the important point that certain populations are likely to be more exacting in their performance, i.e., that they are likely to be precise in making their responses. Tekane's (1961) analysis of errors supports Fridjohn's contention, as does Crawford-Nutt's (1974) analysis of responses of African policemen. The latter also shows that entirely random responses are relatively infrequent. It therefore appears that when cross-cultural differences on this and allied tests are considered, at least two factors, accuracy and precision, are involved. These may need to be taken account of separately.[23]

In another study Tekane (1963) used a new variant of the test, all the items being so designed that they could be completed either by introduction of a bilateral or a rotational enantiomorph. The subjects were merely enjoined to complete the patterns in any way they liked. It was thought that the test would reveal both the tendency to make symmetrical patterns and a higher frequency of bilaterally symmetrical patterns than of the rotationally symmetrical ones. Illiterate black miners were found to make fewer symmetrical responses than black schoolchildren from a high school. In addition, the latter made bilateral responses about as frequently as rotational responses, whereas the miners favoured the former. Simple translation occurred in both groups, but although it is said to be common in African indigenous art it was not as frequent as the total of the other type of responses. Tekane points out that 97 percent of his subjects made regular responses, i.e., responses that were either symmetrical, translational, or asymmetrical, but with the response rectangle so placed that its sides were parallel to those of other rectangles and presumably so that it was abutting to one of them.[24]

A study by Reuning and Wittman (1963) takes the above issues further and offers some noteworthy observations derived from analysis of their own and of previously published data by Roberts, MacQuarrie, & Shepherd (1959), Mundy-Castle and Nelson (1962), Hector (1959), Fridjohn (1961), and Tekane (1963). The same version of the test as used by Tekane (1963) was used here, subjects being allocated to three groups matched on their Progressive Matrices scores. One group was instructed to seek bilateral symmetry, the second rotational symmetry and the third either of these two forms. The subjects were Western students of a college of education. It was found that this sample found rotational symmetry easier. Analysis of these data in conjunction with other data mentioned above yields two important observations:

> (1) Bilateral symmetry is fundamental in human cognition and thus a test principle, less dependent on educational achievement and cultural-technological advancement; [and] (2) Rotational symmetry, as an essentially man-made phenomenon, is less familiar—and as a test principle, more difficult—to people living in a natural (i.e. not much altered by man) and technologically simple environment. (Reuning and Wittman, 1963, p. 89)

It is noteworthy that the bilateral symmetry which, as the authors point out, is abundant in the environment, prevails there mostly in the form of symmetry about the vertical plane. There is evidence (e.g. Paraskevopoulos, 1968) which suggests that the plane of symmetry affects the ease with which symmetry is perceived. It would therefore be interesting to distinguish among those responses obtained on the PATCO test items that differ in orientation of their implicit axes of symmetry. If the orientation of the axis is of consequence then an essential difference between responses made to the two types of symmetry may well lie in the assumptions subjects make about this orientation when attempting bilateral responses and the absence (of necessity) of such assumptions when rotational responses are made.

Cross-cultural observations of differences in perception of orientation are not new. Laws (1886) noted that Malawi housemaids found it hard to learn in what orientation objects ought to be placed. Subsequently, similar difficulties were noted under more rigorous experimental conditions. Nissen, Machover, and Kinder (1935) found that Sousou children living in a culture isolated from literate cultures experienced difficulties with reproduction (by drawing) of abstract designs, and in several cases the reproduced designs were rotated relative to the models. These difficulties however, as suggested by the authors, might have been caused by the subjects' inexperience in drawing. Biesheuvel (1949) comments about pattern reproduction difficulties, especially those of orientation among South African mine workers. McFie reported orientation difficulties in both Ugandan student nurses (1954) and in Ugandan technical school entrants (1961), when he tested them using Wechsler's Block Design test. Similar difficulties were also observed in the responses to the Terman-Merrill Memory for Designs test, which was used only with the latter of the two groups of subjects. McFie proposed that the essence of the difficulties lies in the cultural background of the subjects (a suggestion which has also been put forward by Jahoda (1956), and that the difficulty is that of correct comparison. His 1961 study suggests, but does not demonstrate (Derȩgowski, 1972a), that the difficulty may decrease if the subjects are given general technical training. Unfortunately McFie did not have a control group and his findings are weakened by the lack of evidence for a consistent relationship between correlations of Kohs' Blocks scores and scores on other tests that he used.

Such difficulties with spatial relations have also been reported by Fowler (1940) and, Jahoda (1956) who studied a sample of Ghanaian children and noted that on the Goldstein-Scheerer Cube Test the subjects paid little attention to the spatial arrangement of the blocks on the table. Furthermore, Jahoda observed that the spatial position "errors" could easily be remedied by direct and emphatic instructions, whereas the accuracy of pattern reproduction was not easily improved. Shapiro's (1960) study provides yet more data on this issue. His samples consisted of illiterate, mostly immigrant, African street sweepers in a Rhodesian town and educated Africans. The latter were on the staffs of elementary schools. The subjects were requested to copy Kohs-type designs on a piece of paper. The differences between the orientation of the scorable drawings thus obtained and the models were measured. The angles of rotation obtained from the two groups were compared and found to differ significantly, the illiterate group rotating more. Shapiro suggested that the rotations produced were lawful and were influenced by two factors: (1) the orientation of the axis of symmetry of the design; and (2) the orientation of the pattern as a whole; that is, whether the square was presented in the "square" or in the "diamond" orientation.

There appeared, therefore, a divergence of opinion about the nature of the observed rotations. Some of the researchers maintained that the rotations were probably unsystematic, a result of lack of attention to the problem of orientation (Nissen et al., 1935; Biesheuvel, 1952a; Jahoda, 1956; McFie, 1961), whilst others notably Shapiro (1960), and Maistriaux (1955, and undated), thought that the rotations were lawful. These contrary opinions led Deręgowski (1972a) to compare Icelandic and Zambian schoolchildren, who were asked to reproduce simple Kohs-type patterns using wooden chips. Two types of patterns were used, one forming traditional squares, the other, circles. It was found that the rotations observed were lawful and resulted from two tendencies: (1) a stronger tendency to render stimuli presented in "diamond" orientation as squares and (2) a weaker tendency to render the patterns presented symmetrical about the subjects' median plane. The Zambian subjects rotated their reproductions in such a way as to render them symmetrical about the median plane significantly more often than the Icelandic subjects. A similar tendency to rotate was also observed in a sample of unsophisticated Zambian labourers. This finding, which confirms that the orientation of the axis of symmetry is probably of consequence, is in turn sustained by Serpell's (1971b) observation of Zambian children engaged in discrimination learning of simple geometric forms, since the difficulty of discrimination can be defined (Deręgowski and Ellis, 1974) in terms of the subject's ability to handle symmetrical configurations.

Two recent studies by Jahoda (1976b, 1977) and two by Deręgowski, show a continued interest in these phenomena. Jahoda's work explores the relationship between the functionally defined difficulty of patterns and the extent to which they are rotated, and offers a suggestion that the concept of *sameness* entertained by subjects may influence the manner in which they perceive and execute the experimental task. Deręgowski, on the other hand, argues that a drift to perceptual stability (Deręgowski, 1977a) is responsible (Derĕgowski, 1977b) for cross-cultural differences on responses made to Kohs-type patterns.

The paradigm used by Serpell in his discrimination studies was derived from a study by Rudel and Teuber (1963), which was concerned with discrimination learning of American children. The urban data obtained in Zambia were compared with Rudel and Teuber's data and the trend of the developmental curve was found to be similar as was the order of difficulty of the stimuli used. The Zambian children did, however, lag behind their American counterparts. Consideration of responses falling well outside the chance response zone, i.e., those responses made by children six and one-half years old and older, as plotted by Serpell, suggests a lag of about three years. A comparison of the two Zambian samples shows a similar lag between them and the rural children responding in a manner similar to that of their counterparts of the same number of years of schooling but one to two years younger. These findings prompted Serpell (1971b) to suggest that the lag is probably due to large differences in the intellectual stimulation provided to the two groups (i.e., American and Zambian) by their home and nursery school environments. The strength of such a suggestion depends on the relative position of the environments on the "stimulation" continuum which unfortunately is not assessed in the paper. Indeed the notion is so vaguely specified that it escapes immediate empirical verification. It must be noted, however, that similar consistent differences between cultural groups were observed by Cowley and Murray (1962) who compared white and Zulu children on a variety of Piagetian tasks.

Hochberg and Brooks (1960) showed that an asymmetrical figure is more likely to be perceived as three-dimensional than a symmetrical figure of the same family. This finding with its obvious relevance to both perception of symmetry and perception of pictorial depth—phenomena much studied in a cross-cultural context—induced Derĕgowski (1971) to compare Scottish and Zambian schoolboys on a task involving construction of a model in response to a stimulus figure that was presented in two orientations: (1) with its axis of symmetry inclined, and (2) vertical. Zambian schoolboys did not differ in their responses to the two figures, but Scottish schoolboys responded three-dimensionally significantly more often to the figure with an inclined axis of symmetry. This result may appear to be contradictory to Derĕgowski's (1972a) own finding that when building patterns, subjects from the same population were found to use symmetry. Derĕgowski suggested that subjects responded to figures as if they were symmetrical about their median plane, and therefore that the contradiction is only apparent. Some support for such dominance of symmetry is provided by his 1974a study. This study, using similar materials to those used by Derĕgowski (1972a), suggested that African subjects tend to build symmetrical responses to both symmetrical and asymmetrical stimuli, and explored further difficulties that subjects encounter when requested to reproduce a simple geometric Kohs-type pattern.[25]

Problems of pattern perception were also investigated using techniques derived from information theory studies (Attneave, 1955), wherein a pattern of dots within a matrix had to be reproduced. Cole, Gay, and Glick (1968a) investigated these phenomena in the general context of quantitative behaviour (see also Gay & Cole, 1967). The subjects, Kpelle schoolchildren of Liberia and American students, were asked to tell how many spots they saw on a card that was shown to them in a tachistoscope. The authors observed differences both between and within cultures. The sophisticated American subjects responded correctly more often than the Kpelle. More interestingly, perhaps, Kpelle children made relatively less use than Americans of the patterning of the stimuli. The authors (Cole, Gay, & Glick, 1968b) suggested that these cultural differences are nontrivial. Since the nature of patterning used by Cole et al. is not clearly defined it is difficult to say how the present results relate to a Zambian study (Deręgowski, 1972b) in which schoolchildren were required to reproduce patterns that were either symmetrical or asymmetrical. The asymmetrical patterns either contained two identical elements or were random. In the symmetrical patterns the axis of symmetry was either vertical or horizontal. The results were largely inconclusive perhaps because of the difficulty of the patterns used, the matrices being rather large (6 x 6 cells). An analogous Western study has been published by Paraskevopoulos (1968). Possible relationships between symmetry of figures and social structure are discussed by Fisher (1961) and by Levi-Strauss (1963).

Although a report by Clement, Sistrunk, and Guenther (1970) is mainly concerned with aesthetics—dealing as it does with pattern preferences—it is so closely related to the problem discussed above that it merits a mention here, as does its extension to Japanese subjects (Iwawaki & Clement, 1972) because it is possible to advance an argument that some of the "errors" observed in a variety of perceptual tasks may be of aesthetic origin. In the case of Kohs' Blocks, for example, a rotation can perhaps be interpreted as the subject's attempt to improve upon the model with which he is provided.

An interesting study involving extrapolation of a position of a dot and subsequent feedback of a correct response was carried out by Mundy-Castle (1967) on Ghanaian children. Since the task involves the ability to note the pattern, it probably shares some attributes of the "information theory" tasks described above. It also may have an element in common with the Gestalt continuation task since there, too, the pattern has to be extrapolated. Indeed the errors made by children (spatial inversions, rotations, and reflection) are similar to those made by Ghanaian children responding to the Gestalt continuation test (Mundy-Castle, 1968). On both tasks, performance improves with age, the improvement being more rapid between age groups five to six and seven to eight years, than between the latter group and the group aged nine to ten years. An extension of this study has been carried out by Snelbecker, Fullard, and Gallaher (1971).

An extensive study of acquisiton of diagonality in children (Olson, 1970) has the relatively rare distinction of including nonwestern samples. It shows performance of children from two Kenyan tribes (Logoli and Kipsigis) to be worse than that of their Canadian counterparts on a task of arranging pegs in a diagonal row as shown in a model. Performance appeared to be affected by schooling and to some extent by age, tribal allegiance, and sex of subjects. These data thus confirm, but do not clarify, the difficulties observed on other perceptual tasks. The general inference drawn by Olson that the poor performance was due to lack of elaboration of general cognitive development lacks convincing empirical support, since the evidence is only correlational.

The problems of shape and orientation are related. Not only are there "preferred orientations" associated with particular shapes (Braine, 1973) but the same geometrical shapes in different orientations are perceived as being different. The former phenomenon in a cross-cultural context was investigated by Antonovsky and Ghent (1964), who compared Iranian and American children; and by Serpell (1971a), who also investigated the problem of discrimination between geometrical figures (Serpell, 1971b). The study of orientation preference is a further development of Ghent's (1961) work and concerns itself with the effect of location of "focal feature" and familiarity upon orientation preference.

It is noteworthy, however, that although Antonovsky and Ghent's paper showed that the orientation preferences of Iranian children were identical with those of their American counterparts the scores of the former were lower on all of the thirteen stimuli used. Thus notwithstanding an identical tendency cross-cultural effects may be present. Such a possibility receives further support from Serpell's (1971a) observations which, in spite of the large cross-cultural similarities, which he rightly stresses, also contain a number of striking differences.

Barabasz, Dodd, Smith, and Carter (1970) investigated perception of the "focal" point in two Caucasian and black samples in the United States. One of the Caucasian groups and the black group were described by the authors as deprived. No differences were found between the two Caucasian groups but both groups differed significantly from the black group, which gave fewer responses contrary to those expected from the position of a "focal point." The lack of differences between the "deprived" groups led the authors to suggest that the difference is not a result of education. Unfortunately, the authors did not analyse the responses in sufficient detail and it is impossible to say whether the intercultural differences were systematic or whether they were a result of random responding. If they were, in fact, systematic then the discrepancy gains a specific psychological meaning, and might help to elucidate which of the two possible effects suggested by the authors—genetic or cultural—led to the response observed. Such attributive analysis is, however, fraught with dangers because of the large number of factors involved and the temptation to arrive at "definitive" conclusions. Thus a slight correlation of scores with age on a perceptual test was observed in Kenya among African and European children (Bowden, 1969a). The expected difference between the sexes was also noted, as was the almost significant superiority of the Europeans. Bowden uses these data to argue that, given identical environments, the differences between the two populations tend to disappear. Such argument entirely ignores the selective sampling which immigration imposed upon both populations and that probably invalidates the conclusions reached.

It is possible that the responses obtained to Kohs' patterns, already discussed, were also influenced by the "focal point" effect. However, the nature of the data at hand and the difficulty of deriving conclusions from the data obtained in experiments concerned with "focal points" renders discussion of the two sets of phenomena entirely speculative.

Relatively long response times found in some cultures have been commented upon by several researchers (e.g. Jahoda, 1956; Hudson, 1960). Ombredane, Bertelson, & Beniest-Noirot (1958), using a simple pencil-and-paper test, found that such slackness (relative to a European sample) was not a function of the difficulty of the task but could more plausibly be explained "by a general lack of interest in speed performance than by slower operations of mental functions" (p. 336). Unfortunately, this conclusion has not been explored further by other workers, in spite of its importance, as shown by a variety of studies where the time factor has probably been responsible for cultural differences in scores. Thus, for example, Clinton (1931) found that American blacks and whites differed more on their scores on the mirror-drawing and writing subtests of the Otis scale than on simple letter marking; scores on these tasks vary among themselves in respect of the time factor.

Perception of Colour and Form

Two papers by Serpell (1969a, 1969b) compared cultural differences in responses to colour and to form. The latter of these reviews the area and presents experimental evidence showing that neither absolute values of brightness and saturation nor the forms used influence the frequency of form-responses either in the Zambian or the English samples used. The English subjects were found to respond to form rather than colour more frequently than the Zambian subjects. The results are in agreement with those of Suchmann (1966), who observed analogous differences between Nigerian and American children and with Kellaghan's (1968) observation of Irish and Yoruba children. They can also be seen as similar to Carroll and Casagrande's (1958) observations of Navaho Indians and white Americans. In the other study Serpell (1969a) found that attention to form increased with education and age of his Zambian subjects and concluded that that trend was primarily educational. This view is also expressed by Schmidt and Nzimande (1970), who studied schooled and unschooled Zulu children. Such agreement beteeen studies is gratifying, especially since it is also concordant with observations of Greenfield, Reich, and Olver (1966). The possibility of self-selection in such studies as that of Smith and Nzimande must however be borne in mind. It may be that those subjects who are relatively unschooled are such not as a result of choice (as methodology would demand) but as a result of a complex selection. It is also noteworthy that Suchmann's (1966) results show no change of preference with age and education and in this respect they differ from Serpell's results.

Serpell (1970) further advanced the view that educational influence on attentional preference for form arises from perceptual familiarization with the geometrical forms themselves, quite independently of the ease with which they are named. The role of linguistic labelling is also questioned by the work of Deręgowski and Serpell (1971). In their comparison of Scottish and Zambian schoolboys on a sorting task they found that Zambian boys sorted models of cars and animals, which they could label correctly by colour significantly more often than did their Scottish peers. No analogous difference was observed when pictures were used in place of models. As one would expect from studies of pictorial perception, the Zambian subjects performed less well on pictures than on models whilst no such difference was observed in the case of the Scots.

A study of card-sorting by Irwin and McLaughlin (1970) yielded results compatible with Serpell's. In the former study it was reported that Mano pupils of Liberia and Liberian adults tended to sort by colour or number rather than by form. Schooling was found to increase the ability to sort by form but not the preference for form. Cultural familiarity was also shown to affect sorting. The authors interpret the latter results as showing that interest leads to formation and use of an abstract (functional) classification. (Their results can be compared with those of Price-Williams, 1962; Greenfield et al., 1966; and Evans and Segall, 1969.)

The effect of cultural familiarity on sorting can be used to sustain the argument that such familiarity is also likely to influence other responses, wherein coding of the stimuli influences responses and hence furthers both the carpentered-world and ecological hypotheses whose influence upon studies of illusions has already been discussed. The evidence for cultural familiarity is also important for entirely different, methodological reasons, for it provides an illustration par excellence of the possibility of response bias, and the theoretical complications to which such a bias is likely to lead. In this respect these studies share a characteristic ambiguity with those of binocular rivalry, where, too, it is sometimes difficult to isolate the effect of a manipulated variable from that of the response bias.

Data obtained from a sample of Ibo children (Okonji, 1970) suggested that a transfer of training occurs when subjects are taught to define categories on a complex form-colour-size sorting task and then tested on sorting of models of familiar objects. Such transfer is not accompanied by a similar transfer on the Kohs' Blocks. Even so, the sorting tasks described above are highly cognitive and there is no evidence about the facilitation that such training may provide for more perceptual activities. A paper by Irwin, Schafer, and Feiden (1974), whilst confirming most of the findings described in the literature, also demonstrates a distinct superiority of educated American subjects over unschooled Mano subjects in their ability to describe actions. The authors suggested that the use of language in problem solving and learning increases with education.

Thus the role of language which appears to be less than previously thought in the simple tasks of colour discrimination may be considerable when more complex tasks are involved.

Cross-cultural studies of perception of colour fall into two domains: (1) the domain of studies deriving from a physiological tradition, which includes studies of colour blindness and its determinants and distribution; and (2) the domain of studies in which perception of colour is merely used as a convenient phenomenon providing a measure for such cultural artifacts as language. Recent research (Berlin & Kay, 1969) has suggested, however, that these approaches are not as divergent as was once thought.

A short historical summary of cross-cultural studies of colour appears in Chapanis (1965) and in Segall et al. (1966). The topic had its origins in the study of ancient writers' descriptions of colours, by scholars who were puzzled by their terminology (Gladstone, 1858; Geiger, 1880; Magnus, 1880 and 1883). Literary speculation soon advanced into empirical investigation, spurred perhaps in part, by false assumptions of ancients' misperceptions, for as Pickford (1972) reported off the Grecian isles the sea may indeed be wine red. Rivers (1901) examined *in extenso* work that preceded and was contemporaneous with his own foray in the area. His paper on the Toda (1905) (see also Titchener, 1916) devotes an entire section to the results obtained in India. His conclusions were unambiguous as exemplified by his comparison of the Todas' responses to the responses of other groups: "They all show a tendency to discriminate greens, blues and violets less definitely than reds and yellows, and show that the deficiencies in nomenclature for the former group of colours are accompanied by a certain degree of deficiency in their discrimination" (p. 328). He adds that it is open to question whether this is due to actual insensitiveness or merely to lack of interest, but he favours the former. This work was subsequently criticised by others, the opinion turning towards a "cultural" explanation and culminating in a belief that there is no such thing as a "natural" division of the spectrum.

The visible colour spectrum has, therefore, for some time been considered a continuum suitable for any and all modes of arbitrary divisions. These assumptions made perception of colour an ideal subject matter for cross-cultural comparisons intended to test the effect of language upon perception.

Thus Brown and Lenneberg (1954) tested codability of colours and found it to correlate with accuracy of recognition of colours. However, Lenneberg (1961) failed to confirm such a relationship, thereby throwing doubt upon the claim that language arbitrarily partitions perceptually isotropic and homogeneous colour solids. This doubt is also expressed in Pickford's (1972) monograph on psychology and aesthetics. Berlin and Kay (1969) asked their informants drawn from twenty different linguistic groups to choose exemplars of basic colour terms present in their respective languages. They found that the same "focal" colours tended to be chosen independently of the language of the subjects. This experiment, which questioned even more seriously than Lenneberg's later observations the dominance of linguistic categories, led to a revival of research in the area. Notably, Heider (1971, 1972) Heider and Olivier (1972); (see also Rosch (Heider) [1975]) carried out a cross-cultural investigation into perception of colour and memory for colour. Her results, obtained from the Dani of New Guinea, English-speaking Americans, and speakers of other languages, both children and adults, suggest that the same colours tend to be treated as "focal" in all these groups. It appears that the linguistic cause is in disarray. This is not, however, as complete as Heider's (1971) speculations would imply. She states that colour space is not a domain well suited to the study of the effects of language on thought as suggested by Lenneberg (1967), but that, on the contrary, it furnished an excellent example of the influence of underlying perceptual-cognitive factors on the formation and reference of linguistic categories. Granted the role of the "focal" peaks, there are still regions in between these peaks, and in these valleys of ill-defined hues language may still hold sway. It is noteworthy that Heider's work has been done with little coloured (Munsell) chips serving as stimuli. Since colour is but one of the attributes of such chips, one may well ask to what extent, if any, it has been influenced by other attributes. Would the focal point for green remain unchanged if the subjects were, say, to choose their response from a set of grasses, or cows, rather than from the set of chips? This question may be important because Olmsted and Sigel (1970) have shown that colour/form preferences are not independent of the experimental task. Murube and

Da La Fuente's (1975) observations that, given a complete spectrum, their Saharan subjects divided it in a manner showing cultural influences, also argue for caution in evaluation of linguistic effects.[26]

Harkness (1973), in a paper more properly falling within the domain of linguistics than perception, investigated the development of colour terms in two Guatemalan societies, one Spanish- and the other Mam-[27] speaking, and found that the basic colour terms evolved similarly in both languages.

The studies of colour defects have attracted a modicum of attention, especially in the context of development of colour vision in man (Rivers, 1901). The evidence at hand (e.g., Geddes, 1947; Pickford, 1972) shows considerable differences between ethnic groups in this respect. Certain cultures on account of their isolation offer excellent possibilities of investigating the genetic aspects of the problem (e.g., Ichikawa, 1973). Those and other studies of a "physiological" ilk are not discussed in this chapter.

Two recent papers by Bornstein (1973a, 1973b), already referred to in the section in illusions, are pertinent to the issues just discussed. So are Serpell's (1969a, 1969b) papers concerned with attentional preference for colour. An interesting example of such studies, undertaken in a South African industrial setting, is provided by Wyndham (1975).

Binocular Disparity

To assess the salience of stimulus characteristics researchers can use either a single stimulus possessing two stimulus characteristics, as has been done in the studies of colour/form dominance, or present two stimuli, each displaying one of the characteristics, but in mutual conflict. The latter paradigm is used in the studies of binocular disparity which, according to Levelt (1968), are incorrectly labelled as studies of binocular rivalry. A well-known example of such a study is that of Bagby (1957). He presented Mexican and American subjects with stereogram slides and found that subjects within each group perceived more readily stimuli derived from their own culture. Later Pettigrew, Allport, and Barnett (1958) used the same technique to investigate the effect of membership of a cultural group upon perception of photographs of members of other cultural groups. Recently, Lent (1970), inspired by Pettigrew et al.'s (1958) study, carried out a series of experiments on white Americans, Mexicans and light- and dark-skinned American blacks. Bagby's work was extended by Berry (1969), who applied the same method to Scottish, Eskimo, and Temne subjects. His hypotheses were that: (a) subjects will tend to report that they see stimuli from their own culture more readily than stimuli from an alien culture, and (b) that such a tendency will be greater in the perceptually (visually) poorly developed and more field-dependent Temne than in the perceptually well developed and self-reliant Eskimos. Both these hypotheses were confirmed. An alternative measure which involved drawing of tachistoscopically-presented stimuli supported this conclusion. It thus elucidated the performance of the perceptual mechanism when it is required to process ill-defined stimuli and demonstrated (if one disregards for a moment the absence of genetic controls) the effects of ecology and culture. It is noteworthy that on both the measures Scottish scores fell between those of the Temne and Eskimo groups.

In so far as all work involving presentation of disparate stimuli to two eyes can be said to involve binocular disparity, the use of Pandora's box (Deręgowski and Byth, 1970) ought again to be mentioned, although the method they used did not investigate rivalry but relied on subjects' ability to combine binocular and monocular information. Gregory and Harris (1975) investigated the problem of constancy scaling using binocular disparities and their findings suggested that the method could almost certainly be used with more imagination than has hitherto been the case, the disparate stimuli used differing not simply, and grossly, in their culture origin but also along more subtle perceptual continua.

Researchers must however, be aware of the possibility of response biases in all the studies which present ambiguous stimuli. It is possible to postulate that Bagby's Mexican subjects confronted with slides presenting two different sports chose as a response the sport more familiar to them, and that the American subjects did the same. The result, which is perfectly valid, may therefore not indicate a clearer perception of the Mexican slide in the former and of the American slide in the latter group, but rather the fact that different responses were available to the two groups or that different perceptual organization was imposed upon confusing perceptual data. A variety of factors might influence such organization, some of these reflecting emotional states and personality characteristics rather than purely perceptual processes.

Eidetic Imagery

Although cross-cultural differences in eidetic imagery have been speculated upon in the first quarter of the century and later by Husén (1945), systematic cross-cultural investigations of the phenomenon are rare. Peck and Hodges (1937), inspired by Jaensch's (1930) suggestion that there should be ethnic differences, reviewed early investigations into quality and frequency of *eidetikers*. Finding the data unconvincing, they tested samples drawn from white, Mexican, and black children living in Texas. Of the three samples blacks were by far the best *eidetikers* (persons prone to eidetic imagery) as measured both by the frequency with which the phenomenon occurred and its richness. Mexican children were found to be on the whole better *eidetikers* than white children, but this global observation needs to be qualified by pointing out large changes of the percentage of *eidetikers* with age, which was a characteristic of the Mexican sample only. Recently Doob (1946, 1965b, 1966, 1970) carried out studies of this phenomenon, one of which will be briefly summarised here. The tripartite object of the study was to investigate cultural variability, functions, and correlational-causal factors of eidetic imagery. Samples were drawn from five African societies: Ibo, Kemba, Somali, Masai, and a mixed Swahili-speaking group from Tanzania. Haber and Haber's (1964) and Siipola and Hayden's (1965) Western groups provided the baseline. A considerable variation in the frequency with which the images occurred in various groups was observed; their nature did not, however, appear to vary greatly. The tentative conclusion that Doob derived from this observation was that the eidetic images "may represent a survival from an earlier stage in the development of man and that normally they may be, but need not be, activated when the individual is experiencing some special difficulty in coping with the environment" (p. 33).

An extension of Doob's work was undertaken by Levak (1969) who tested the Bororo of Brazil. She found no evidence of a strong form of eidetic imagery. In the rural (nonaccultured) setting women were found to experience eidetic imagery more often than men. A very tenuous support for the hypothesis that unacculturated groups are more prone to images was also observed. This elusiveness of eidetic imagery has also been reported by Feldman (1968) who worked in Ghana. Subsequently, Sheehan and Stewart (1972) attempted to assess frequencies of imagery in samples of aboriginal children differing in the extent of their contact with the European community and found that the group with least contact had a higher incidence of imagery. A further study (Sheehan, 1973) involving very remote communities showed no such distinct trend.

Unfortunately these studies have not been followed by further work in the area in spite of Doob's suggestion of several inviting hypotheses. This is probably so because the *eidetikers* are difficult to find, their responses are often unstable, and the experiments call for considerable experimental expertise, which may yet provide only unconvincing results; prospective experimenters are thus greatly discouraged. This seems a pity. Cross-cultural differences of such purely perceptual processes as differences in constancies or differences in pattern perception and their relationship to eidetic imagery would seem particularly worthy of further attention.

Meanwhile such isolated and contradictory findings as have hitherto been reported and the absence of a solid theoretical schema do nothing to dispose of Doob's (1966) description of the phenomenon as "will-o'-the-wisp."

Perception of Time

Anecdotal evidence suggests that perception of time differs from society to society, and that in some societies less attention is paid to time than in others. Bache's (1895) study of reaction times of whites, Indians, and blacks, presents some such speculations. There is, however, little empirical evidence pertaining to this problem. Myers (1903) was probably the first to research systematically into cross-cultural differences in the perception of time. His sole predecessor, whom he briefly mentions, was Herzen, who studied reaction time in Japanese conjurors and Europeans. Unfortunately, details of that tantalizing juxtaposition are not available. Lambeth and Lanier (1933) review early work on the topic. More recently, Doob's work has dominated the field (for an exhaustive survey of his work, see Doob [1971]). Schwitzgebel (1962) compared Dutch and Zulu subjects on their ability to estimate one minute and found that the latter made larger underestimates. Unfortunately, a precise interpretation of data obtained in the course of estimation experiments is difficult. A cross-cultural difference might under such circumstances arise out of any one or more of the following: (1) different attitude to time, (2) difference in familiarity with units of time (e.g., a minute may not have any specific meaning to the subject), and (3) differences in familiarity with numbers (e.g., a subject may say "100" whenever he means a large number). In a more searching study, Doob (1960) elicited response by using a measure of awareness of subjective time. Jamaican rural subjects of little education were found to have less awareness of distinction between subjective and objective times than did their urban counterparts. The same rural subjects, however, were better than the town subjects at estimating the length of the interview. These results led Doob to suggest that increased contact with civilization might produce not greater efficiency in judging temporal intervals, but greater awareness of time. This process may be analogous to differential perception of shape and colour already discussed.

Robbins, Kilbridge, and Bukenya (1968) also compared rural and urban Baganda samples on time estimates. The mean time estimates of the rural sample were consistently larger than those of the urban sample, both samples overestimating the temporal intervals used (15 seconds, 30 seconds and 60 seconds). Bowden's (1969b) criticism of the way Robbins et al.'s data were analysed (that comparing sample means does not yield a complete picture) is valid, but he is in error in thinking that considerations of variances brings the question of accuracy "down to the individual level." Applications of t and F tests at each temporal interval using data reported by Robbins et al. yield a significant difference of variance at all levels, the rural sample being consistently less homogenous. No significant differences were found between the two samples in their accuracy at any of the three levels and, rather inconsistently, there was no significant overestimation of the interval by the rural group at the 15 seconds and 60 seconds level and by the urban group at the 30 seconds and 60 seconds level.

The difference between the samples therefore lies primarily in the homogeneity of the estimates. The data unfortunately do not answer the question of whether such a difference arises because of greater interindividual differences in the rural sample or because individual rural subjects are less precise than the town dwellers, or both.

Deregowski (1970a) investigated cultural influence in Zambia upon recall of time and other data. He found that there was no significant difference between rural women and urban schoolboys in recall of numbers (other than price) not relating to temporal phenomena. On the other hand, rural women were inferior to schoolboys when recalling temporal items. This, he argued, showed more clearly than time-estimate experiments the effect of differing cultural values of time. Evidence supportive of this interpretation is provided by Price and Tare (1975).

The last two experiments link the present chapter with the studies of value of time and time perspective (e.g., Melikian, 1969; Meade and Singh, 1970; Holm and McConnachie, 1976). They also bring to attention the cross-cultural studies of measurement, a strangely neglected area in which Hallowell (1942), Gay and Cole (1967), Cole et al. (1968a), and Cole, Gay, Glick, and Sharp (1971) present major findings.[28]

Visual, Olfactory, and Auditory Acuity

Although studies of visual and olfactory acuity have as long a tradition in intercultural comparisons as those of illusions (Rivers, 1901 and 1905), recent studies in these areas are relatively rare.[29] Chandra (1972) compared Fijians and Indians on Gough and McGurk's (1967) Perceptual Acuity Test, and in accord with earlier findings on French, Italian, Swiss, and American samples found an expected age gradient (for a description of an application of the test to Western samples see Gough & Delcourt 1969; Gough & Meschieri, 1971). More specific tests of visual acuity were carried out jointly by Humphries and Wortley (1971) and Wortley and Humphries (1972) in South Africa. Myers (1903) returned from Torres

Straits according to his own admission just as he went there; that is, without a wholly satisfactory method of investigation into olfaction. This state of affairs still prevails; Worms (1942) obtained descriptions of various odours from Australian aborigines. His conclusion, as far as perception is concerned, is rather global: *"De gustibus non est disputandum."*

The story of auditory acuity is similar. Here, too, intensive cross-cultural work was done at the beginning of this century (Bruner, 1908). Since then no systematic large scale testing has been attempted, although tests of musical ability have occasionally been used. Early research into gustatory perception is reported by Myers (1904).

Cutaneous Sensation

Little work has been done in this area, which in common with the corresponding area of general psychology has been largely neglected. McDougall's (1903) studies carried out under the auspices of the Torres Straits expedition are probably the oldest systematic investigation in a cross-cultural setting. A discussion of these findings will be found in Titchener (1916). Grover's (1970) study of haptic perception of urban African children falls outside the scope of the present review being "Piagetian" in its origins. However, lack of such studies of this topic is surprising especially since some of the "compensatory hypotheses" (q.v.) advocated would lead one to expect considerable cross-cultural differences.

In an interesting but isolated study of symmetry and asymmetry of hand movements, Jahoda (1976a) observed striking differences in the developmental trends between Scottish and Ghanaian schoolchildren.

Maze Tests

Porteus's Maze was one of the earliest psychological tests to be used cross-culturally. The data that it yielded are summarized in Porteus (1965), Porteus and Gregor (1963), and in articles listed therein. A recent historical review of the test (David, 1974) provides further background material.

The test has been extensively rather than intensively used. The studies it inspired were carried out in a variety of cultures and on a range of subcultural groups (e.g., delinquents and various psychiatric patients). The widest uses were probably those for assessment of intelligence (see, e.g., Vernon, 1969; MacArthur, 1967); and in general research (e.g., MacCrone,

1928; Nissen et al., 1935; Ibarrola, 1951). It was regarded by most of the workers as a measure of intelligence (just as Kohs' patterns were) and hence its perceptual components have not been extensively evaluated. The present state of data suggests that valuable results could be obtained from a systematic cross-cultural evaluation of its perceptual characteristics.

Porteus's Maze was probably the earliest test used to study perception of African Bushmen. The work was carried out by Porteus himself (Porteus, 1937) and later by MacCrone (Minde, 1937). However, Reuning (1971) and Reuning and Wortley (1973) (whose monograph on testing of the Bushmen deserves especial attention) did not consider the maze an appropriate instrument to use with the Bushmen mainly because they thought (1) the idea of a maze test of the Porteus type to be entirely alien to Kalahari dwellers, and (2) because use of the mazes would call for a very competent interpreter. They therefore introduced solid mazes through which a cylinder had to be rolled by tilting a plexiglass-covered box. Subjects had no apparent difficulties comprehending the nature of the task. The maze test scores obtained correlated markedly with the Gestalt Continuation Test and with the test requiring the subject to detect four dots forming the corners of a square identical with the stimulus square.

Jahoda (1969) administered the Perceptual Maze Test (Elithorn, 1955) in Ghana. This maze, in which the subject always moves in essentially the same direction, has yielded promising results in spite of certain difficulties of administration. The scores of a subsample of subjects, who in addition to the maze were given the Block Design Test and an abbreviated version of the Embedded Figures Test, correlated (at about 0.50) with the scores on these tests. This confirmed similar observations made earlier in Europe. A significant correlation (0.73) between Porteus's Maze scores and scores on the Gestalt Continuation Test was also obtained from a sample of Australian aborigines by Gregor and McPherson (1963).

While the maze tasks are concerned with the subjects' ability to find their way through the maze in spite of many false cues that the stimulus provides, the studies of closure are said to test the extent to which relatively simple data are transformed by the perceiver contrary to the overt experimental instructions.

Closure

Thus Michael (1953), in order to evaluate the Gestalt claim that "sensory organization . . . arises from dynamics of the nervous system," compared Western subjects with Navaho who had a "fear of closure," and in whose culture "as a spirit outlet a basketmaker leaves an opening in the design; the weaver leaves a small slit between threads" (Kluckhohn & Leighton, 1946). Split rings are characteristic of Navaho art and Michael used these in his investigation. The subjects were required to copy such designs which were exposed for short intervals. No significant differences between the two groups were obtained. The results therefore fail to repudiate the *Gestalten*. Berry (1966) used the closure phenomenon to compare three samples: Temne of Africa, Eskimo, and Scotsmen (see Jahoda's chapter in Volume I of this *Handbook*). The findings were that at all ages Temne proved less aware of the presence of a gap in the geometrical figures presented tachistoscopically. The scores of the Scottish sample fell between the Eskimos' and the Temne's. This result was interpreted as demonstrating that ecological necessity for detailed discriminations augmented by a long experience of their relatively barren visual environment, has increased the Eskimos' awareness of minute cues so that it is greater than that of the Temne.

There is no immediately apparent reason for supposing that procedural differences are responsible for the presence of the effect in Berry's data and its absence in Michael's results. This discrepancy is probably due to the differences between the samples. The effect taken in isolation can be said to support either "the field dependence hypothesis" or to be a finding relevant to the "compensatory hypothesis." It is noteworthy that if it is taken as supportive of the compensatory hypothesis it appears to run contrary to Biesheuvel's critique of Poortinga's study (Poortinga, 1971), since it deals with visual acuity rather than with visual percepts.

Theories of Perceptual Organization

Witkin's theory of field-dependence (Witkin & Berry, 1975) is, with the possible exception of Piaget's theory, the most influential of the theories of perceptual organization in contemporary cross-cultural studies. Since it is extensively discussed by Jahoda in Volume 1 of the *Handbook* it will not be discussed here.[30] Other approaches will, however, be briefly mentioned.

The scientific search for a systematic relationship between perceptual variables and culture was reported in 1937 when Nadel inspired by Bartlett's (1932) work, compared two Nigerian tribes—Yoruba and Nupe—which lived in the same environment and belonged to the same linguistic group. Furthermore their economic and social systems were essentially similar. However, according to Nadel, the tribes differed greatly in other cultural respects, the Yoruba having elaborate cosmology, vigorous representational art, and a "strong sense for pantomime;" the Nupe lacking all these attributes, being vague in their beliefs, imageless in art, and having no parallel to the Yoruba sense of drama. Reproduction of a narrative and description of pictures were used as experimental tests.

> The results showed a marked difference in the story experiment; the Yoruba laid stress on logical and rational elements while the Nupe showed distinct appreciation of situational facts and connections of time and place. In the picture experiment the response of the first group was meaning-oriented, the response of the second enumerative and appreciative of spatial arrangements.

It was concluded that: "Between cultural differentiation and the psychological differentiation there exists close correspondence" (1937b, p. 211).

These conclusions have much in common with recent discussions of cross-cultural differences. The three basic types that Nadel described are: (1) The dominant type ... rational, logical, and intent on meaning-oriented interpretation (Yoruba); (2) The type combining an enumerative approach to observational data with a stress on spatial and temporal arrangement (Nupe); (3) A secondary type among the Nupe characterised by an emotional impressionate disposition.

A study by Beveridge (1939) should also be mentioned in this context. He compared African and European subjects, bodily tilted in a huge box, on their ability to adjust a rod to a horizontal position. The tilt was about an axis in the subjects' fronto-parallel plane. The subjects were thus forced to respond when presented with two sets of contradictory cues, those visually derivable from the walls, roof, and floor of the box which they would see, and those of proprioception. He found that Africans were more accurate in their adjustments, their perception being guided "less by visual and more by other cues" than that of Europeans. Thus Beveridge can perhaps be said to have anticipated both Witkin's studies and the possibility of cultural differences in sensory profiles. The differences in procedure between Beveridge's and Witkin's tilted body experiments must be stressed here because interpretations of results which these experiments have yielded have led to a minor controversy (Dawson, 1971; Wober, 1972). Under both conditions the subject experiences proprioceptive stimulus of the body tilt but in Beveridge's case the stimulus is more complex since the subject has to manipulate a hinged rod which he adjusts to the horizontal plane. Visual stimulation also differs; in Beveridge's case a subject gains his information from two sources: position of the box and position of the rod, i.e., from the same sources as his proprioceptive information; in Witkin's case no such matching of information can occur, the visible stimuli not being immediately linked with proprioceptive stimuli. It must also be noted that the axes of tilt of the body used in the two procedures are mutually orthogonal.

Not all roads lead to Witkin's theory, however, and an assortment of other formulations grouped under the convenient heading of Compensatory Hypotheses will be considered next.

"Compensatory" Hypotheses

A certain sense of fairness, one suspects, is responsible for the popularity of compensatory theories of perception (Lloyd, 1972, p. 144) both within and outside psychological circles; so much so, that hypotheses such as Biesheuvel's (1943, 1952a) that Africans may be more tolerant of the monotony of the machine operative work than Europeans because of their gift of rhythmic motion became accepted as a fact (e.g. Kilby, 1961; Rollings, 1961). A sentiment similar to Biesheuvel's can be found in Hudson (1960), who suggested that auditory perception may be more characteristic of Bantu cultures than visual perception. Musical talent is thought by Biesheuvel to be a distinguishing mark of Africans. He supports this argument with Oliver's (1932a) studies, which showed that African children had greater musical talent than their Western counterparts.[31]

Ombredane (1954, 1967), Rollings (1961) and McLuhan (1962, p. 43) put forward the notion of such differences in perceptual profiles between cultures and later Wober (1966) suggested a term "sensotype"—the pattern of relative importance of the different senses by which children learn to perceive the world and in which patterns they develop their abilities. These patterns may be predominantly visual in one culture, while in another culture, auditory or proprioceptive senses may have much higher relative importance. A similar suggestion, also derived from McLuhan, is made by Carothers (1972), a psychiatrist of considerable African experience. Wober (1966) provided supportive evidence for his argument by considering data from a series of tests that he administered to a group of Nigerian workers. These data were gathered in order to see whether various tests of field dependence yielded commensurate scores in all cultures. Wober's data showed that on a version of the Rod and Frame Test (R.F.T.) responses of his Nigerian subjects were not influenced by the tilt of the chair in which they sat but were affected by the tilt of the frame; apparently they were relatively more sensitive to proprioceptive than to visual cues. A confirmation of this finding was derived from another experiment in which responses of Nigerian subjects to the Embedded Figures Test (E.F.T.) and R.F.T. were compared with published responses of an American sample. (In the latter population high correlation of scores on the two tests normally prevails, the notable exception being scores of professional dancers, who score better on the proprioceptive test without a corresponding improvement of "visual" scores). Wober found that his Nigerian subjects' responses were similar to those of the American dancers studied by Witkin and Asch (1948). Unfortunately his procedure differed greatly from that normally used for testing in America. The illustration of the apparatus published (Wober, 1967) suggests that either the subjects were bodily tilted by a muscular research assistant or had to get up from the chair whenever their body tilt had to be changed. Such large doses of proprioceptive feedback as these two processes involve are unlikely to have occurred in the American sample. There were, in addition, several other methodological discrepancies between the studies, which Serpell (1976) lists and with which Witkin and Berry (1975) show some concern. In view of these discrepancies it is doubtful whether the results obtained from the two samples can be meaningfully compared.[32]

Poortinga (1971, 1972) conducted a thorough investigation into fundamental abilities of simple stimulus processing in the visual and auditory modalities. African and Western students were required to make judgments of loudness and brightness. No significant differences between the two groups were found on judgments of brightness; on judgments of loudness the Europeans performed "somewhat better than the Africans." In another experiment on choice reaction-time to various kinds of sound and clearly discriminable visual stimuli, Africans were found to be considerably slower than Europeans. For both groups there was a considerable improvement with training but with little tendency to converge. Thus no support was found for the hypothesis that the superiority of responses under auditory conditions over those under visual conditions will be greater in an African than a European sample.

Biesheuvel (Poortinga, 1971, p. 75), commenting upon these results, pointed out that they may not be relevant to his hypothesis. "Africans may perceive . . . more readily through the auditory than through the visual sense modality. Preference does not necessarily depend on or lead to greater acuity or differential capacity with regard to basic sense data as distinguished from percepts." The crux of this comment probably lies in the suggestion that the data used by Poortinga are too basic to evaluate the hypothesis. The phenomenon is postulated to lie towards the cognitive rather than the sensory end of the perceptual spectrum. If this is so, the phenomenon is of necessity more "cultural" in its contents; careful matching achieved by Poortinga is therefore difficult to replicate and so is convincing demonstration of its existence. Poortinga's experiment does, however, put in question the more restricted idea of sensotype. Research into cross-cultural differences in sensory integration done in Zambia (Okonji, 1974) was inspired by the Birch and Belmont (1965b) study. This shows significant differences between Caucasian and Zambian (African) children both when the latter are drawn from a school serving the local elite (and attend the same school as the Caucasian children) and when they come from a school serving poorer parts of the community. Caucasians are better at recognizing sound patterns than their African counterparts. An Asian sample (drawn from the same elite school) obtained higher scores than the African sample and lower than the Caucasian sample. The result is puzzling not only in view of the widespread claims of higher sense of rhythm in African populations but also in its origin and its relationship to the sensory specialization.

Okonji (1974) considers briefly the possibility of nutritional effects, but adduces no evidence of their presence in either of the African groups, and they are not likely to be widespread in the elite group. The question of origin is thus open.

Sensory specialization does not predict the ease of sensory transfer; hence, it is possible that the Caucasian sample, although inferior at perception of auditory input, was so superior at matching it to the visual input that this more than compensated for the reverse relationships between the two inputs in the African sample. This too, however, remains an open question.

An experiment by Kershner (1972) investigated the applicability of the compensatory hypothesis to the relationship between language and spatial perception. Bilingual Spanish-American and American children were used to determine whether spatial ability in some children may not compensate for linguistic deficiencies. As expected, the former group was found to be more "analytic-spatial" and the latter more "global." These findings suggest a central rather than peripheral "compensation," and point to the possible differences in the laterality of the brain. In their turn they suggest the possibility that in polyglotic cultures the effects observed may prevail. One must, however, beware of the assumption that polyglotism occurs wherever a multiplicity of language is to be found (as is the case in many African states). A monograph by Serpell (1968) shows the immense complexity of the linguistic issue under such circumstances.[33]

Concluding Remarks

Of many traits of the cross-cultural approach to perception, two general characteristics are outstanding: rapid and uneven growth.

The first of these calls for no further comment while the latter does. The nature of the distortion in growth is of interest as are the causes responsible for it. The first can be briefly described thus: cross-cultural studies of perception are a caricature of Western studies. That is, in the non-Western studies the trends and tendencies present in the studies in the West are accentuated and exaggerated and the elements that are "secondary" in the West are muted and sometimes entirely ignored. This does not mean that the cross-cultural studies are a pathetic parody of Western studies, but it does indicate cross-cultural workers' intense desire to remain within the mainstream of experimental psychology whilst gathering cross-cultural data. Few, like Doob (1966), dare to choose a will-o'-the-wisp. This aspect is likely to change as the value of cross-cultural work becomes more widely recognized.

Three general factors have contributed to these distortions:

1. Most studies have been carried out in areas that are easily accessible geographically and culturally. Since most of this work has been done in the anglophone areas (with the francophone areas very much the second group in size), there is a regrettable paucity of evidence from other parts of the world. There is, too, a distressingly modest number of studies from truly remote areas.

2. Visual perception has traditionally occupied, and for good reasons, the pride of place in Western studies, but other perceptual modalities have also been studied. In cross-cultural work, in spite of claims that modality profiles differ from culture to culture, little has been done in modalities other than vision.

3. Most of the work reported has been inspired by Western theories using Western methods. But theories are selective and so are data collected under their influence. Granted that "local" theoretical schemata are unobtainable, it is obviously worthwhile (as Hudson [1960] has done) to keep one's eyes open for "unusual" behaviour. A large lacuna in cross-cultural studies, as Lippert (1967) has pointed out, is that of applied aspects of perception.[34]

Notes

1. The reader may wish to trace such works by referring to one of the following bibliographies: Andor (1966) (an annotated bibliography; a new edition is forthcoming), Klingelhoffer (1967), Hoorweg and Marais (1969), Irvine, Sanders, and Klingelhofer (1972). All these relate to Africa where, more by accident than design, most of the studies described were carried out. There are also several noteworthy reviews. These include articles by Triandis, (1964), Doob (1965), Tajfel (1969), Dawson (1971), Triandis, Malpass, and Davidson (1972), and Ord (1972); a monograph by Lloyd (1972), a book by Cole and Scribner (1974), and Serpell (1976), and another, concerned with methodology, by Brislin, Lonner, and Thorndike (1973). Segall, Campbell, and Herskovits's (1966) now classic text provides a useful historical review. Further relevant information can also be found in various chapters of this *Handbook* whose content overlaps with or complements the content of the present chapter.

2. It is particularly unfortunate when unsubstantial imputations are made that the subjects were terrorized. (For an example of an exchange relevant to this issue see Bradley [1960], Dana and Voigt [1962], and Bradley [1964].) In cross-cultural psychology as elsewhere one must assume the basic honesty and common sense of the experimenters unless there are clear indications to the contrary.

3. Examples of such reports, which are primarily of a historical value, can be found in Laws (1901), Kidd (1904), Fraser (1932), Herskovits (1948 and 1959), and Davies (1957).

4. Reports of Laws (1901), Kidd (1905 and 1906), Larken (1927), Fraser (1932), Nadel (1939), Herskovits (1948, p. 281; 1959, p. 56), Warburton (1951), Biesheuvel (1952a), Davies (1957), Unesco (1963), Forge (1970), Guthrie, Brislin, and Sinaiko (1970). Bitsch (1972), and Cole and Scribner (1974) belong to these categories. For a recent study of pictorial recognition by Caucasian children see Berry, Judah, and Duncan (1974).

5. To this group belong: Thomson (1885), Lloyd (1904), Mead (1961), Brimble (1963), Holmes (1963), Hutton and Ellison (1970), and Deręgowski (1968a and 1971a).
   An utter failure of an adult, who had been functionally blind until the age of fifty-two at which age he had corneal transplants, to recognize depicted objects although able to recognize the magazine in which the picture appeared, is reported by Gregory and Wallace (1963). This suggests that pictorial perception was not, in this case, acquired simultaneously with the stereognostic perception.

6. For discussions of the role of convention in pictures see Thouless (1933), Herskovits (1959), Gombrich (1962) and Tajfel (1969) and the references given therein. The findings that certain patterns evoke spontaneous responses in subhuman species, for example that a bird is frightened by the eye-spots of a butterfly, (Cott [1969], Hinton [1973]), suggest that, in a sense, pictorial perception occurs in such species. For an extension of this idea into the realms of art, see Coss (1968).

7. See Boas (1927), Levi-Strauss (1963), and Deręgowski (1970b).

8. *The figures intended to illustrate the test as reproduced by Lloyd (1972, p. 63) are incorrect. In all of them, the essential feature of Hudson's stimuli, alignment of the spear with both the animals, is absent.*

9. This sample which contained ten illiterate workers in a total of sixty can scarcely be thought of as representative of the population, even though fifty-seven of the workers were unskilled.

10. This result is reminiscent of Allport and Pettigrew's (1957) study of Ames's rotating window. For a study of the relationship between the rotating trapezoid and perspective using an ingenious adaptation of Gregory's (1966) Pandora's box see Olson (1974).

11. The list of cross-cultural studies is too long for inclusion in the body of the text. A comprehensive, but not exhaustive, list follows: Nadel (1937a, 1937b); Hudson (1958, 1960, 1962a, 1962b, 1967); MacLean (1960); Fonseca and Kearl (1960); Doob (1961); Brimble (1963); Holmes (1963, 1964); Du Toit (1966); Abiola (1966); Mundy-Castle (1966); Ferenczi (1966); Dawson (1967b); Deręgowski (1968a, 1968b, 1968c, 1969a, 1970, 1971a, 1971b, 1973, 1974b, 1976a, 1976b), Kilbride and Robbins (1968, 1969); Kilbride, Robbins, and Freeman (1968); Jahoda (1968, 1970); Poole (1968); Fuglesang (1970); Shaw (1969); Elkind (1969); Wober (1970, 1974); Guthrie, Brislin, and Sinaiko (1970); Grant (1970); Forge (1970); Hutton and Ellison (1970); Deręgowski and Byth (1970); Omari and Cook (1972); Deręgowski and Serpell (1971); Guthrie, Sinaiko, and Brislin (1971); Deręgowski, Muldrow, and Muldrow (1972); Dun-

can, Gourlay and Hudson (1973); Waldron and Gallimore (1973); Davies (1973); Omari and MacGinitie (1974); Jahoda and McGurk (1974a, 1974b, 1974c); McGurk and Jahoda (1974); Kennedy (1974, 1975); Cole and Scribner (1974); Sinaiko (1975); Deręgowski (1976); Opolot (1976); Leach (1977); Hagen and Johnson (1977).

Of the recent papers Miller (1973) and Jahoda and McGurk (1974c) are of especial methodological interest for they present a critique of other studies. Olson's (1975) results are not comparable to Jahoda and McGurk because he used photographic slides.

Deręgowski's (1976b) paper concerns itself with an experimental investigation of the relationship between shape constancy and pictorial perception, a topic not previously tackled in cross-cultural work, but which patently relates to the relationships among illusions, constancy, and pictorial perception. A related study, unfortunately confounding an established illusory effect with implicit-shape effect, was reported by Olson (1976).

A related phenomenon of interpretation of a single picture as if it were a cartoon strip (i.e. as if it portrayed a temporal sequence) was inconclusively pursued by Wober (1974), Deręgowski and Munro (1974), and Munro and Deręgowski (1976).

Studies of preference for 'split-representation' drawings which according to Levi-Strauss (1963) are of social significance were conducted by Hudson (1962a), Mundy-Castle (1968), and Deręgowski (1970b, 1973).

12. Jahoda (1968, 1970); Lloyd (1972); Miller (1973); Cole and Scribner (1974).

13. Fonseca and Kearl (1960); MacLean (1960); Hector and Hudson (1962); Winter (1963); Jahoda (1968); Shaw (1969); Fuglesang (1970); Agbasiere and Chukwujekwu (1972); Davies (1973); Serpell (1974); Jahoda, Cheyne, Deręgowski, Sinha, and Collingbourne (1976).

14. On the other hand, if the intelligence scores were primarily determined by the environment, then the effect of partialling out of intelligence would be similar to partialling out of the environment and should lead to reduced correlations. (See section on "compensatory" hypotheses.)

15. See Witkin and Berry (1975).

16. There are aesthetic aspects of Barry's work also.

17. To such a comment of bleak despair one can perhaps answer by pointing out that although neither frictionless surfaces nor perfect vacuum can be achieved in nature, this does not prevent one from attempting to approximate to such states and deriving laws from observations obtained whilst such approximations apply.

18. The same results were published earlier in an abbreviated form (Segall, Campbell, & Herskovits, 1963) and evoked a critical comment from Spitz (1963), which was in turn rejoined (Segall & Campbell, 1963).

19. A noteworthy series consisting of thirty geometrical figures and illusion stimuli (the Perceptual Acuity Test) was developed and used by Gough and Hug (1968) for comparison of American and French schoolchildren and appears to be a useful general tool.

Even a thorough investigation of a single illusion can reveal considerable complexity of the processes involved. Thus Weale (1975) has shown that the irradiation illusion is greatly influenced by the contrast effects and that the classical illusion (light figure on a dark background appearing larger) is reversed at low contrasts. Furthermore, masking and blurring of the target contours were observed by Weale, which suggested involvement of the edge detectors *under the new but not necessarily under classical conditions.* These conclusions strengthen the caveat appended to Pettigrew and Nuttall's (1963) conclusions.

In addition to a variety of stimuli, use of a wide variety of methods for studying illusions would appear advisable, for example use of Julesz's (1971) "cyclopean" methods would help to define the extent to which peripheral factors (such as pigmentation of the *fundus oculi*) affect these phenomena.

Similarly the effects of visual acuity could be investigated by using figures either with variable back illumination or by interposing filters between the observers and the stimuli; however, although suggestions of involvement of visual acuity in such phenomena as the Müller-Lyer illusion and the Irradiation illusion have been made, no such simple and direct devices have been used.

Evidence supporting the basic assumption of Segall et al. (1966) that ecological visual experience affects perception can also be found in a paper by Annis and Frost (1973), who compared Western subjects with Cree Indians and found differences in anisotropies of acuity consistent with differences in environmental experience. These findings have, however, been questioned by Timney and Muir (1976) who observed differences in anisotropy between Western and Chinese subjects living in the same carpentered environment.

Ward and Coren (1976) found that the Müller-Lyer illusion increased under high blur conditions. This result is concordant with the expectations of Einthoven's theory, but difficult to reconcile with the postulated effects of pigmentation. Location of the point containing the most important information may be of consequence. Cohen's (1976) study of Israeli and Austrian responses to pictures suggesting the influence of "writing and reading" habits and Braine's (1965) observations on location of the point and mode of scanning are of interest.

20. The conclusions reached in this study have been questioned by Schiff (1970). Leibowitz, Brislin, Perlmutter, and Hennessy (1970), whilst admitting that there are difficulties in cross-cultural experimentation, dealt with the main points of Schiff's critique in their rejoinder. Recently Brislin and Keating (1976) extended the cross-cultural studies of the Ponzo illusion to the "real world" and obtained results agreeing with the carpentered-world hypothesis and Liebowitz's observations. Taylor (1976) extended his earlier (Taylor, 1974) analysis of illusions, obtaining concordant evidence.

21. However, such interpretation taken in extreme would suggest that the Bushmen also find it difficult to detect their prey, especially so since many animals have protective colouring. Since the Bushmen are excellent hunters this is unlikely to be the case.

22. For evaluation of the original version of the PATCO test as a substitute for Raven's Progressive Matrices see Roberts, Macquarrie and Shepherd (1959); Fridjohn (1961); Mundy-Castle and Nelson (1962); and Reuning and Wortley (1973).

23. Here, as well as elsewhere, a clear distinction between *precision* and *accuracy* is of importance. Precision is taken to reflect exactness but not necessarily correctness of response. Accuracy, on the other hand, reflects correctness. These terms derived from engineering have been used in preference to their close an-

alogues *reliability* and *validity*, because they are intended to describe the nature of responses in a much narrower spectrum than the more widely known psychological counterparts. The validity of a test, such as that of manual dexterity, indicates the extent to which the performance on the test correlates with the performance on some industrial task, whereas accuracy merely relates to the optimal performance on the task itself. The analogy between precision and reliability is somewhat closer; here again, the former term is used in a rather narrower sense pertaining to responses to a specific task.

24. It would be interesting to compare responses made to this test with those of the same population made to the seven-squares projective test (Hector & Hudson, 1959; Bradley, 1960), which gives the subject a free hand in constructing a pattern.

25. Difficulties with application of the related tests as a psychological measure are fully discussed by Ord (1971, 1972). The latter paper contains an extensive bibliography of special relevance to occupational psychology. Bhatia's (1955) Indian study relating Block test measures to the subjective level of intelligence as perceived in the population tested ought also to be mentioned in this context. Degallier (1904) reports an early finding of rotation of letters and digits in a Congolese sample. This contrasts, prima facie, with Chou's (1935) observation that Americans were capable of deciding upon the correct orientation of Chinese characters with which they were not familiar. The two tasks concerned do, however, differ greatly.

26. A girl may choose a Munsell chip of a colour she would not choose to be buried in, let alone wear. A brief discussion of the issue of the cultural relevance of tasks will be found in Brislin, Lonner, and Thorndike (1973). The related problem of comprehension and communication of units of measurement by Sesotho is briefly and anecdotally discussed by Wallman (1965). Davidoff (1972) investigates and discusses briefly the effect of induced bias upon colour/form responses.

27. Mam is a Mayan language.

28. This neglect is surprising because recognition of commensurability of different objects can be said to be symptomatic of abstraction of the measured feature in a given culture.

29. An early Brasilian study by Ranke (1897) who on finding "a group of natives popularly known for their keeness of sight gave tests to some of them" is noted by Garth (1931). Ranke found that the visual powers of Brazilians were within the range of those of the Europeans. Garth adds that "similar results were obtained when small groups of Arabs, Egyptians and other people were tested for visual acuity" (p. 43). Hints of possible superiority of "primitive" races in this respect can however be found in reports of some very skilled observers, e.g. in Darwin's (1892, p. 209) comments upon Fuegians and Humbold's observations at Quito. Rivers (1905) reviews other early studies.

   Both Van Graan (1974) (on industrial studies) and Bornstein (1973a) (on general issues) offer some useful comments upon the topic of this section.

   There is a body of literature on taste blindness (see Boyd and Boyd, 1937; Allison, 1951) that is not considered here.

30. Some work inspired by Witkin's concepts of field-dependence and field-independence has, however, been done. This work falls outside the scope of this chapter.

31. Turnbull's (1961) informal observations also support this view. Birch and Belmont's (1965a) study, on the other hand, does little to elucidate the issue.

32. In addition, as Lloyd (1972) points out, the effect of training might have influenced correlations; it is also possible to postulate that an element of selection biased the result, because only those people took up skilled dancing whose proprioceptive skills were so high that they would not be accurately measured on the same scale as these skills in the rest of the population. It is impossible to tell whether either or both of the above effects applied. One can, however, question the validity of the conclusions reached, especially since the precision of responses may vary from culture to culture. (A finer method of scoring such as that proposed by Nyborg (1974) would under such circumstances seem apposite.)

33. It has also been said that certain cultures may foster greater attention to the social environment (Rollings, 1961). To investigate this claim, in the realm of perception and memory, Deręgowski, Shepherd and Ellis (1973) tested Scots and Bantu Rhodesians on recognition of photographs of mugs and faces. They found no significant interaction between the groups of subjects and type of stimulus. The result is contrary to the expectation derived from considerations of social values and hence bears upon the field-dependence theory. The authors point out, however, that this may be due to the fact that pictures rather than depicted objects were used, and pictures are known to be less efficacious than the objects they portray in evoking responses.

One ought to note in this context recent cross-cultural studies of facial recognition (Shepherd, Deręgowski, and Ellis [1974], and Ellis, Deręgowski, and Shepherd [1975].) In both these studies photographs were used as stimuli. These studies relate to earlier interracial comparisons (e.g. Malpass & Kravitz, 1969). Ellis (1975) has recently reviewed the entire area of facial recognition. See also Cüceloglu (1970).

34. An interesting and perhaps precursory study of the relationship between lateralisation and field-dependence is reported by Dawson (1972). It combines the analysis of the effects of social pressure towards conformity and performance on a variety of measures of spatial perception. The results showed that the more conforming population (Temne) had a lower incidence of left-handedness than the more permissive Arunta and Eskimo. Subjects with mixed dominance (right hand/left hand) were found to be more field-dependent. The possibility of an interaction between social and biological factors is thus foreshadowed. Jones (1974) also considered the impact of socialization on the development of spatial ability. Gaddes et al. (1968) observed a slight superiority in spatial imagery of Amerindian schoolchildren over their white counterparts, on a series of standard tests (Cattell Culture Fair, Goodenough Draw-a-Man, Block Design, and Porteus Maze). On development of laterality in Nigerian children, see Bakare (1974).

A. Reproduced by permission of the African Medical and Research Foundation of London.

B. Reproduced by permission of Dr. W. Hudson, of Johannesburg, South Africa.

C. Reproduced by permission of Dr. H. Reuning and of *Psychologia Africana*.

References

ABERCROMBIE, M. L. J. *The anatomy of judgment.* London: Hutchinson, 1960.

ABIOLA, E. T. *The intelligent behaviour of Nigerian children.* Ibadan: Ibadan University Press, 1966.

AGBASIERE, J. A., & CHUKWUJEKWU, S. E. Teaching mechanical engineering design in Africa. *Chartered Mechanical Engineer,* 1972, *19,* 62–64.

ALLISON, A. C. A note on taste blindness in Kenya Africans and Arabs. *Man,* 1951, *51,* 119–20.

ALLPORT, G. W., & PETTIGREW, T. F. Cultural influence on perception of movement: the trapezoidal illusion among Zulus. *Journal of Abnormal and Social Psychology,* 1957, *55,* 104–13.

ANDOR, L. E. *Aptitudes and abilities of the black man in Sub-Saharan Africa (1784–1963).* Johannesburg: South African Council for Scientific and Industrial Research, 1966.

ANNIS, R. C., & FROST, B. Human visual ecology and orientation anisotropies in acuity. *Science,* 1973, *182,* 729–31.

ANTONOVSKY, H. F., & GHENT, L. Cross-cultural consistency of children's preferences for orientation of figures. *American Journal of Psychology,* 1964, *77,* 295–97.

ATTNEAVE, F. Symmetry, information, and memory for patterns. *American Journal of Psychology,* 1955, *63,* 209–22.

AVERY, G. C., & DAY, R. N. Basis of the horizontal-vertical illusion. *Journal of Experimental Psychology,* 1969, *81,* 376–86.

BACHE, M. R. Reaction time with reference to race. *Psychological Review,* 1895, *2,* 475–86.

BAGBY, J. W. A cross-cultural study of perceptual predominance in binocular rivalry. *Journal of Abnormal and Social Psychology,* 1957, *54,* 331–34.

BAKARE, C. G. M. The development of laterality and right-left discrimination in Nigerian children. In J. L. M. Dawson & W. J. Lonner (Eds.), *Readings in cross-cultural psychology.* Hong Kong: Hong Kong University Press, 1974.

BARABASZ, A. F., DODD, J. M., SMITH, M., & CARTER, P. E. Focal point dependency in inversion perception among Negro, urban Caucasian, and rural Caucasian children. *Perceptual and Motor Skills,* 1970, *31,* 136–38.

BARDET, C., MOREIGNE, F., & SENECAL, J. Le test du dessin Goodenough appliqué à des ecolieres Africains. *Bulletin de la société medicale d'afrique noire,* 1959, *4,* 225–70.

———. Application de test de Goodenough à des ecolieres Africains de 7 à 14 ans. *Enfance,* 1960, *1,* 199–208.

BARRY, H. Relationship between child training and the pictorial arts. *Journal of Abnormal Psychology,* 1957, *54,* 380–83.

BARTLETT, F. C. *Remembering: a study in experimental psychology.* Cambridge, England: Cambridge University Press, 1932.

BAYER, C. A., & PRESSEY, A. W. Geometric illusions as a function of pigmentation of the fundus oculi and target size. *Psychonomic Science,* 1972, *26,* 77–79.

BELOFF, H., & COUPAR, S. Some transactional perceptions of African faces. *British Journal of Social and Clinical Psychology*, 1968, 7, 169–75.

BERLIN, B., & KAY, P. *Basic colour terms: their universality and evolution.* Berkeley: University of California Press, 1969.

BERRY, F. M., JUDAH, R., & DUNCAN, E. M. Picture recognition by pre-school children. *The Journal of Psychology*, 1974, 86, 137–38.

BERRY, J. W. Temne and Eskimo perceptual skills. *International Journal of Psychology*, 1966, 1, 207–29.

——. Ecology, perceptual development, and Müller-Lyer illusion. *British Journal of Psychology*, 1968, 59, 205–10.

——. Ecology and socialization as factors in figural assimilation and binocular rivalry. *International Journal of Psychology*, 1969, 4, 271–80.

——. Müller-Lyer susceptibility: culture, ecology, and race. *International Journal of Psychology*, 1971a, 6, 193–97.

——. Psychological research in the North. *Anthropologica*, 1971b, 13, 143–57.

BEVERIDGE, W. M. Racial difference in phenomenal regression. *British Journal of Psychology*, 1935, 26, 59–62.

——. Some racial differences in perception. *British Journal of Psychology*, 1939, 30, 57–64.

BHATIA, C. M. *Performance on intelligence test under Indian conditions.* Madras: Oxford University Press, 1955.

BIESHEUVEL, S. *African intelligence.* Johannesburg: South African Institute of Race Relations, 1943.

——. Psychological tests and their application to non-European people. In G. B. Jeffrey (Ed.), *The yearbook of education.* London: Evans, 1949.

——. The study of African ability, Part 1: the intellectual potentialities of Africans. *African Studies*, 1952a, 11, 45–48.

——. The study of African ability, Part 2: a survey of some research problems. *African Studies*, 1952b, 11, 105–17.

——. The nation's intelligence and its measurement. *South African Journal of Science*, 1952c, 49, 120–38.

——. The occupational abilities of Africans. *Optima*, 1952d, 2, 18–22.

——. Adaptability: its measurement and determinants. In L. J. Cronbach & P. J. O. Drenth (Eds.), *Mental tests and cultural adaptation.* The Hague: Mouton, 1972.

BIRCH, H. G., & BELMONT, I. Social differences in auditory perception. *Perceptual and Motor Skills*, 1965a, 20, 861–70.

——. Auditory-visual integration intelligence and reading ability in school children. *Perceptual and Motor Skills*, 1965b, 20, 295–305.

BITSCH, J. Personal communication, 1972.

BLAKEMORE, C. The baffled brain. In R. L. Gregory & E. H. Gombrich (Eds.), *Illusion in nature and art.* London: Duckworth, 1973.

BOAS, F. *Primitive art.* Oslo: Instituttet for Sammenlignende Kulturforskning, 1927.

BOLTON, R., MICHELSON, C., WILDE, J., & BOLTON, C. The heights of illusion: on the relationship between altitude and perception. *Ethos*, 1975, 3, 403–24.

BONTE, M. The reaction of two African societies to the Müller-Lyer illusion. *Journal of Social Psychology*, 1962, *58*, 265–68.

BORNSTEIN, M. H. Colour vision and colour naming: a psychophysiological hypothesis of cultural difference. *Psychological Bulletin*, 1973a, *80*, 257–85.

————. The psychophysical component of cultural difference in colour naming and illusion susceptibility. *Behaviour Science Notes*, 1973b, *8*, 41–101.

BORING, E. B. Size constancy in a picture. *American Journal of Psychology*, 1964, *77*, 494–98.

BOWDEN, E. A. F. Perceptual abilities of African and European children educated together. *Journal of Social Psychology*, 1969a, *79*, 149–54.

————. Accuracy of time estimation among rural and urban Baganda: a reinterpretation. *Perceptual and Motor Skills*, 1969b, *28*, 54.

BOYD, W. C., & BOYD, L. G. Sexual and racial variations in ability to taste phenyl-tio-carbamide with some data on the inheritance. *Annals of Eugenics*, 1937, *8*, 46–51.

BRADLEY, D. J. Ability of black groups to produce recognizable patterns on the Seven Squares test. *Journal of the National Institute for Personnel Research*, 1960, *8*, 142–44.

————. Problems of recognition in Bantu testing. *Perceptual and Motor Skills*, 1964, *19*, 718.

BRAINE, L. G. Age changes in mode of perceiving geometric forms. *Psychonomic Science*, 1965, *2*, 155–56.

————. Asymmetrics of pattern perception observed in Israelis. *Neuropsychologia*, 1968, *6*, 73–88.

————. Perceiving and copying the orientation of geometric shapes. *Journal of Research and Development in Education.* 1973, *6*, 44–55.

BRIMBLE, A. R. The construction of a non-verbal intelligence test in Northern Rhodesia. *Rhodes-Livingstone Journal*, 1963, *34*, 23–25.

BRISLIN, R. The Ponzo illusion: additional cues, age, orientation, and culture. *Journal of Cross-Cultural Psychology*, 1974, *5*, 139–61.

BRISLIN, R. W., & KEATING, C. F. Cultural differences in perception of the three-dimensional Ponzo illusion. *Journal of Cross-Cultural Psychology*, 1976, *7*, 397–411.

BRISLIN, R., & LEIBOWITZ, H. W. The effect of separation between test and comparison objects in size constancy at various age levels. *American Journal of Psychology*, 1970, *83*, 372–76.

BRISLIN, R. L., LONNER, W. J., & THORNDIKE, R. M. *Cross-cultural research methods.* New York: Wiley, 1973.

BROWN, L. B. The 3D reconstruction of a 2D visual display. *Journal of Genetic Psychology*, 1969, *115*, 257–62.

BROWN, R. W., & LENNEBERG, E. H. A study of language and cognition. *Journal of Abnormal and Social Psychology*, 1954, *49*, 454–62.

BRUNER, F. G. The hearing of primitive peoples. *Archives of Psychology*, 1908, *11*, 1–113.

BUROS, O. K. (Ed.), *The sixth mental measurement yearbook.* New York: Gryphon Press, 1965.

BUSH, R. E., & CULWICK, A. T. *Illustration for Africans.* Undated report.

CAMERON, N. Functional immaturity of the symbolization of scientifically trained adults. *Journal of Psychology*, 1938, *6*, 161–75.

CAMPBELL, D. T. Distinguishing differences of perception from failures of communication in cross-cultural studies. In F. S. C. Northrop & H. H. Livingston (Eds.), *Cross-cultural understanding: epistemology and anthropology.* New York: Harper & Row, 1964.

CARLSON, J. A. Effect of instructions and perspective drawing ability on perceptual constancies and geometric illusions. *Journal of Experimental Psychology*, 1966, *72*, 874–79.

CARROLL, J. B., & CASAGRANDE, J. B. The function of language classification in behaviour. In E. E. Maccoby, T. M. Newcombe, & E. L. Hartley (Eds.), *Readings in social psychology.* New York: Holt, Rinehart and Winston, 1958.

CAROTHERS, J. C. *The mind of man in Africa.* London: Tom Stacey, 1972.

CHANDRA, S. An assessment of perceptual acuity in Fiji: A cross-cultural study with Indians and Fijians. *Journal of Cross-Cultural Psychology*, 1972, *3*, 401–06.

CHAPANIS, A. Colour names for colour space. *American Scientist*, 1965, *53*, 327–46.

CHIANG, C. A new theory to explain geometrical illusions produced by crossing lines. *Perception and Psychophysics*, 1968, *3*, 174–76.

CHILCOTT, M. Two studies in visual perception and appreciation. *OVAC Bulletin*, April, 1967, 14–17.

CHOU, S. K. Reading and legibility of Chinese characters. An analysis of judgments of Chinese characters by American subjects. *Journal of Experimental Psychology*, 1935, *18*, 318–47.

CLEMENS, E. Racial differences in colour-blindness. *American Journal of Physical Anthropology*, 1930, *14*, 417–32.

CLEMENT, D. E., SISTRUNK, F., & GUENTHER, Z. Pattern perception among Brazilians as a function of pattern uncertainty and age. *Journal of Cross-Cultural Psychology*, 1970, *1*, 305–14.

CLINTON, R. J. A comparison of white and Negro children: norms on mirror drawing for Negro children by age and sex. *Educational Psychology*, 1931, *22*, 186–90.

COHEN, A. S. Einfluss von Schriebund Lesegewohnheiten auf die Asymmetrie der oplischen Wahrnehmung. *Zeitschrift fur Sozialpsychologie*, 1976, *7*, 59–68.

COLE, M. An ethnographic psychology of cognition. In R. Brislin, S. Bochner, & W. Lonner (Eds.), *Cross-cultural perspectives on learning.* Beverly Hills: Sage/Halsted, 1975.

COLE, M., GAY, J., & GLICK, J. Some experimental studies of Kpelle quantitative behaviour. *Psychonomic Monograph Supplements*, 1968a, *2*, 173–90.

———. A cross-cultural investigation into information processing. *International Journal of Psychology*, 1968b, *3*, 93–102.

COLE, M., GAY, J., GLICK, J. A., & SHARP, D. W. *The cultural context of learning and thinking.* New York; Basic Books, 1971.

COLE, M., & SCRIBNER, S. *Culture and thought: a psychological introduction.* New York: Wiley, 1974.

COREN, S., GIRGUS, J. S., ERLICHMAN, H., & HAKSTIAN, A. R. An empirical taxonomy of visual illusions. *Perception and Psychophysics*, 1976, *20*, 129–37.

CORMACK, E. O., & CORMACK, R. H. Stimulus configuration and line orientation in the horizontal-vertical illusion. *Perception and Psychophysics*, 1974, *16*, 208–12.

COSS, R. G. The ethological command in art. *Leonardo*, 1968, *1*, 273–87.

COTT, H. B. Animal form in relation to appearance. In L. L. Whyte (Ed.), *Aspects of form*. London: Lund Humphries, 1969.

COWLEY, J. J., & MURRAY, M. Some aspects of the development of spatial concepts in Zulu children. *Journal of Social Research*, 1962, *13*, 1–18.

CRAWFORD-NUTT, D. H. Symmetry completion test (SYMCO): development of a scoring method. *Psychologia Africana*, 1974, *15*, 191–202.

CÜCELOGLU, D. M. Perception of facial expressions in three different cultures. *Ergonomics*, 1970, *13*, 93–100.

DANA, R. H., & VOIGT, W. H. The Seven Squares test. *Perceptual and Motor Skills*, 1962, *15*, 751–53.

DARWIN, C. *Journal of researches into natural history and geology of the countries visited during the voyage of H. M. S. "Beagle" round the world, under the command of Capt. Fitzroy, R. N.* London: Ward, Lock and Bowden, 1892.

DASEN, P. R. Cross-cultural Piagetian research: a summary. *Journal of Cross-Cultural Psychology*, 1972, *3*, 23–39.

DAVID, K. H. Cross-cultural uses of the Porteus maze. *Journal of Social Psychology*, 1974, *92*, 11–18.

DAVIDOFF, J. The effect of colour distraction on a matching task in Ghanaian children. *International Journal of Psychology*, 1972, *7*, 141–44.

DAVIES, R. *The camel's back service in the rural Sudan*. London: John Murray, 1957.

DAVIES, T. N. Visual perception of engineering drawings. *Engineering Designer*, 1973, *4*, 22–31.

DAVIS, C. M. Education and susceptibility of the Müller-Lyer illusion among the Banyakole. *Journal of Social Psychology*, 1970, *82*, 25–34.

DAVIS, C. M., & CARLSON, J. A. A cross-cultural study of the strength of the Müller-Lyer illusion as a function of attentional factors. *Journal of Personality and Social Psychology*, 1970, *16*, 403–10.

DAVIS, R. The fitness of names to drawings: a cross-cultural study in Tanganyika. *British Journal of Psychology*, 1961, *2*, 115–28.

DAWSON, J. L. M. Traditional values of work efficiency in a West African mine labour force. *Occupational Psychology*, 1963, *37*, 209–18.

———. Cultural and physiological influences upon spatial-perceptual processes in West Africa, Part I. *International Journal of Psychology*, 1967a, *2*, 115–28.

———. Cultural and physiological influences upon spatial perceptual processes in West Africa, Part II. *International Journal of Psychology*, 1967b, *2*, 171–85.

———. Theory and research in cross-cultural psychology. *Bulletin of British Psychological Society*, 1971, *24*, 291–306.

———. Temne-Arunta hand-eye dominance and cognitive style. *International Journal of Psychology*, 1972, *7*, 219–33.

———. Temne-Arunta hand-eye dominance and susceptibility to geometric illusions. *Perceptual and Motor Skills*, 1973, *37*, 659–67.

DAWSON, J. L. M., YOUNG, B. M., & CHOI, P. C. C. Developmental influences on geometric illusion susceptibility among Hong Kong Chinese children. *Journal of Cross-Cultural Psychology*, 1973, *4*, 49–74.

————. Developmental influences in partial depth perception among Hong Kong Chinese school-children. *Journal of Cross-Cultural Psychology*, 1974, 5, 3–22.

DEGALLIER, A. Notes psychologiques sur les Nègres pahouins. *Archives de Psychologie*, 1904, 4, 362–68.

DENNIS, W. Handwriting conventions as determinants of human figure drawing. *Journal of Social Psychology*, 1958, 22, 293–95.

DERĘGOWSKI, J. B. The horizontal-vertical illusion and the ecological hypothesis. *International Journal of Psychology*, 1967, 2, 269–73.

————. Pictorial recognition in subjects from a relatively pictureless environment. *African Social Research*, 1968a, 5, 356–64.

————. On perception of depicted orientation. *International Journal of Psychology*, 1968b, 3, 149–56.

————. Difficulties in pictorial depth perception in Africa. *British Journal of Psychology*, 1968c, 59, 195–204.

————. Perception of the two-pronged trident by two- or three-dimensional perceivers. *Journal of Experimental Psychology*, 1969a, 82, 9–13.

————. Preference for chain-type drawings in Zambian domestic servants and primary schoolchildren. *Psychologia Africana*, 1969b, 12, 172–80.

————. Effect of cultural value of time upon recall. *British Journal of Social and Clinical Psychology*, 1970a, 9, 37–41.

————. Note on the possible determinants of "split-representation" as an artistic style. *International Journal of Psychology*, 1970b, 5, 21–26.

————. Orientation and perception of pictorial depth. *International Journal of Psychology*, 1971a, 6, 111–14.

————. Responses mediating pictorial recognition. *Journal of Social Psychology*, 1971b, 84, 27–33.

————. Reproduction of orientation of Kohs-type figures: a cross-cultural study. *British Journal of Psychology*, 1972a, 63, 283–96.

————. The role of symmetry in pattern reproduction by Zambian children. *Journal of Cross-Cultural Psychology*, 1972b, 3, 303–07.

————. Drawing ability of Soli rural children: a note. *Journal of Social Psychology*. 1972c, 86, 311–12.

————. Illusion and culture. In R. L. Gregory & E. H. Gombrich (Eds.), *Illusion in Nature and Art*. London: Duckworth, 1973.

————. Effect of symmetry upon reproduction of Kohs-type figures: an African study. *British Journal of Psychology*, 1974a, 65, 93–102.

————. Teaching African children pictorial depth perception: in search of a method. *Perception*, 1974b, 3, 309–12.

————. On seeing a picture for the first time. *Leonardo*, 1976a, 9, 19–23.

————. Implicit-shape constancy as a factor in pictorial perception. *British Journal of Psychology*, 1976b, 67, 23–29.

————. "Principle of economy" and perception of pictorial depth: a cross-cultural comparison. *International Journal of Psychology*, 1976c, 11, 15–22.

————. Some cross-cultural thoughts on perceptual continua. In Y. H. Poortinga (Ed.), *Basic problems in cross-cultural psychology*. Amsterdam: Swets & Zeitlinger, 1977a.

————. A study of orientation errors in response to Kohs-type figures. *International Journal of Psychology*, 1977b, *12*, 183–91.

DERĘGOWSKI, J. B., & BYTH, W. Hudson's pictures in Pandora's box. *Journal of Cross-Cultural Psychology*, 1970, *1*, 315–23.

DERĘGOWSKI, J. B., & ELLIS, D. Symmetry and discrimination learning. *Acta Psychologica*, 1974, *38*, 81–91.

DERĘGOWSKI, J. B., & JAHODA, G. Efficacy of objects, pictures, and words in a simple learning task. *International Journal of Psychology*, 1975, *10*, 19–25.

DERĘGOWSKI, J. B., & MUNRO, D. An analysis of "polyphasic pictorial perception." *Journal of Cross-Cultural Psychology*, 1974, *5*, 329–43.

DERĘGOWSKI, J. B., & SERPELL, R. Performance on a sorting task: a cross-cultural experiment. *International Journal of Psychology*, 1971, *6*, 273–81.

DERĘGOWSKI, J. B., MULDROW, E. S., & MULDROW, W. F. Pictorial recognition in a remote Ethiopian population. *Perception*, 1972, *1*, 417–25.

DERĘGOWSKI, J. B., SHEPHERD, J. W., & ELLIS, H. D. A cross-cultural study of recognition of pictures of faces and cups. *International Journal of Psychology*, 1973, *8*, 269–73.

DODD, J., & BARABASZ, A. A cross-cultural comparison of inversion perception at three age levels. *Journal of Educational Research*, 1968, *62*, 34–36.

DOOB, L. W. *Becoming more civilized: a psychological exploration.* New Haven: Yale University Press, 1960.

————. *Communication in Africa: a search for boundaries.* New Haven: Yale University Press, 1961.

————. Eidetic images among Ibo. *Ethnology*, 1964, *3*, 357–63.

————. Psychology. In R. A. Lystad (Ed.), *The African world: a survey of social research.* New York: Praeger, 1965a, pp. 373–415.

————. Exploring eidetic imagery among the Kamba of Central Kenya. *Journal of Social Psychology*, 1965b, *67*, 3–22.

————. Eidetic imagery: a cross-cultural will-o'-the-wisp? *Journal of Psychology*, 1966, *63*, 13–34.

————. Correlates of eidetic imagery. *Journal of Psychology*, 1970, *76*, 223–30.

————. *Patterning of time.* New Haven: Yale University Press, 1971.

DUNCAN, H. F., GOURLAY, N., & HUDSON, W. *A study of pictorial perception among Bantu and white primary school children in South Africa.* Johannesburg: Witwatersrand University Press, 1973.

DU TOIT, B. M. Pictorial depth perception and linguistic relativity. *Psychologia Africana*, 1966, *11*, 51–63.

DWYER, W. O., & STANTON, L. Racial differences in colour vision: do they exist? *American Journal of Optometry*, 1975, *52*, 224–29.

EINTHOVEN, W. Eine einfache physiologische Erklarung für verschiedene geometrisch—optisch Tauschungen. *Pfluger's Archiv für Physiologie*, 1898, *71*, 1–43. (See Chiang [1968] for a recent representation of this theory.)

ELITHORN, A. A preliminary report on a perceptual maze test sensitive to brain damage. *Journal of Neurology, Neurosurgery and Psychiatry*, 1955, *18*, 287–92.

ELKIND, D. Developmental studies of figurative perception. In L. P. Lipsitt & H. W.

Reese (Eds.), *Advances in child development and behaviour.* New York: Academic Press, 1969.

ELLIS, H. D. Recognizing faces. *British Journal of Psychology,* 1975, *66,* 409–26.

ELLIS, H. D., DERĘGOWSKI, J. B., & SHEPHERD, J. W. Descriptions of white and black by white and black subjects. *International Journal of Psychology,* 1975, *10,* 119–23.

EVANS, J. L., & SEGALL, M. H. Learning to classify by colour and function: a study of concept discovery by Ganda children. *Journal of Social Psychology,* 1969, *77,* 35–53.

FELDMAN, M. Eidetic imagery in Ghana: a cross-cultural will-o'-the-wisp? *Journal of Psychology,* 1968, *69,* 259–69.

FELLOWS, B. *The discrimination process and development.* Oxford: Pergamon Press, 1968.

FERENCZI, V. *La perception de l'espace projectif.* Paris: Didier, 1966.

FINGER, F. W., & SPELT, D. K. The illustration of horizontal-vertical illusion. *Journal of Experimental Psychology,* 1947, *37,* 243–50.

FISHER, J. L. Art styles as cultural cognitive maps. *American Anthropologist,* 1961, *63,* 79–93.

FONSECA, L., & KEARL, B. Comprehension of pictorial symbols: an experiment in rural Brazil. *Department of Agricultural Journalism Bulletin, University of Wisconsin,* 1960, *30* (entire issue).

FORGE, A. Learning to see in New Guinea. In P. Mayer (Ed.), *Socialization.* London: Tavistock, 1970.

FOWLER, H. L. Report on psychological tests on natives in the Northwest of Western Australia. *Australian Journal of Science,* 1940, *2,* 124–27.

FRAISSE, P., & ELKIN, E. H. Etude genetique de l'influence des modes de presentation sur le seuil de reconnisance d'objets familiers. *L'Anne psychologique,* 1963, *63,* 1–12.

FRASER, A. K. *Teaching healthcraft to African women.* London: Longmans, Green & Co., 1932.

FRIDJOHN, S. H. The PATCO test, symmetry, and intelligence. *Journal of the National Institute for Personnel Research,* 1961, *8,* 180–88.

FUGLESANG, A. Picture style preference. *OVAC Bulletin,* 1970, No. 22, 46–48.

GADDES, W. H., McKENZIE, A., & BARNSLEY, R. Psychometric intelligence and spatial imagery in two Northwestern Indian and two white groups of children. *Journal of Social Psychology,* 1968, *75,* 35–42.

GARTH, R. T. *Race psychology: a study of racial mental differences.* New York: McGraw-Hill, 1931.

GAY, J., & COLE, M. *The new mathematics in an old culture.* New York: Holt, Rinehart and Winston, 1967.

GEDDES, W. R. The colour sense of the Fijian natives. *British Journal of Psychology,* 1947, *37,* 30–36.

GEIGER, L. *Contributions to the history and development of the human race.* (A. Geiger, ed.) London: English and Foreign Philosophical Library, 1880.

GHENT, L. Form and its orientation, a child's eye view. *American Journal of Psychology,* 1961, *74,* 177–90.

GIBSON, E. J. *Principles of perceptual learning and development.* New York: Appleton-Century-Crofts, 1969.

GIBSON, J. J. A theory of pictorial perception. *AV Communication Review,* 1954, 2, 3–23.

———. The information available in pictures. *Leonardo,* 1971, 4, 27–35.

GLADSTONE, W. E. *Studies on Homer and Homeric age,* Vol. III. Oxford: Oxford University Press, 1858.

GOMBRICH, E. H. *Art and illusion.* London: Phaidon Press, 1962.

GOTTSCHALK, J., BRYDEN, M. P., & RABINOWICH, M. S. Spatial organisation of children's responses to pictorial display. *Child Development,* 1964, 35, 811–15.

GOUGH, H. G., & HUG, C. Perception de formes geometriques et d' illusions chez des enfants français et americains. *International Journal of Psychology,* 1968, 3, 183–90.

GOUGH, H. G., & DELCOURT, M. J. Developmental increments in perceptual acuity among Swiss and American school-children. *Developmental Psychology,* 1969, 1, 260–64.

GOUGH, H. G., & McGURK, E. A group test of perceptual acuity. *Perceptual and Motor Skills,* 1967, 24, 1107–15.

GOUGH, H. G., & MESCHIERI, L. Cross-cultural study of age-related differences in perceptual acuity. *Journal of Consulting and Clinical Psychology,* 1971, 37, 135–40.

GRANT, G. V. Spatial thinking: a dimension in African intellect. *Psychologia Africana,* 1970, 13, 222–39.

GRAY, C. R., & GUMMERMAN, K. The enigmatic eidetic image: a critical examination of methods, data, and theories. *Psychological Bulletin,* 1975, 82, 383–407.

GREENFIELD, P. M., REICH, L. C., & OLVER, R. R. On culture and equivalence. In J. S. Bruner, R. R. Olver, & P. M. Greenfield (Eds.), *Studies in cognitive growth.* New York: Wiley, 1966.

GREGOR, A. J., & McPHERSON, A. Personnel selection tests and nonliterate peoples. *Mankind Quarterly,* 1963, 3, 151–58.

GREGOR, A. J., & McPHERSON, D. A. A study of susceptibility to geometric illusion among cultural subgroups of Australian aborigines. *Psychologia Africana,* 1965, 11, 1–13.

GREGORY, R. L. *Eye and brain.* London: World University Library, 1966.

———. *The intelligent eye.* London: Weidenfeld and Nicolson, 1970.

———. Illusion in nature and art. In R. L. Gregory & E. H. Gombrich (Eds.), *Illusion in nature and art.* London: Duckworth, 1973.

GREGORY, R. L., & HARRIS, J. P. Illusion destruction by appropriate scaling. *Perception,* 1975, 4, 203–20.

GREGORY, R. L., & WALLACE, J. G. Recovery from early blindness. *Experimental Psychology Monograph,* 1963, No. 2.

GROVER, V. M. Haptic perception of young urbanised African children. *South African Journal of Psychology,* 1970, 1, 49–55.

GUTHRIE, G. M., BRISLIN, R., & SINAIKO, H. W. *Some aptitudes and abilities of Vietnamese technicians: implications for training.* Arlington: Institute for Defence Analyses, Science and Technology Division, 1970.

GUTHRIE, G. M., SINAIKO, H. W., & BRISLIN, R. Non-verbal abilities of Americans and Vietnamese. *Journal of Social Psychology,* 1971, 84, 183–90.

HABER, R. N. Limited modification of the trapezoidal illusion with experience. *American Journal of Psychology*, 1965, *78*, 651–55.

HABER, R. N., & HABER, R. B. Eidetic imagery: one frequency. *Perceptual and Motor Skills*, 1964, *19*, 131–38.

HAGEN, M. A., & JOHNSON, M. M. Hudson pictorial depth perception test: cultural content and question with Western sample. *Journal of Social Psychology*, 1977, *101*, 3–11.

HALLOWELL, A. I. Some psychological aspects of measurement among the Saulteaux. *American Anthropologist*, 1942, *44*, 62–77.

———. Cultural factors in structuralisation of perception. In J. H. Rohrer & M. Sherif, *Social psychology on the cross-roads*. New York: Books for Libraries Press, 1951.

HARRIS, D. B. *Children's drawings as measures of intellectual maturity*. New York: Harcourt, Brace and World, 1963.

HARKNESS, S. Universal aspects of learning colour codes: a study of two cultures. *Ethos*, 1973, *1*, 175–200.

HAVIGHURST, R. J., GUNTHER, M. K., & PRATT, J. E. Environment and the Draw-a-Man test: the performance of Indian children. *Journal of Abnormal Psychology*, 1946, *41*, 50–63.

HAWARD, L. C. R., & ROLAND, W. A. Some inter-cultural differences in the Draw-a-Man test: Goodenough scores. *Man*, 1954, *54*, 86–88.

———. Some inter-cultural differences on the Draw-a-Man test, Part 2: Machover scores. *Man*, 1955a, *55*, 27–29.

———. Some inter-cultural differences on the Draw-a-Man test, Part 3: conclusion. *Man*, 1955b, *55*, 40–42.

HECTOR, H. A new pattern completion test. *Journal of the National Institute for Personnel Research*, 1958, *1*, 132–34.

———. A coloured version of the Pattern Completion test. *Journal of the National Institute for Personnel Research*, 1959, *7*, 204–05.

HECTOR H., DLODLO, M. S., & DU PLESSIS, C. E. An experiment on silhouette recognition and projection with Bantu children of different ages. *Journal of the National Institute for Personnel Research*, 1961, *8*, 195–98.

HECTOR, H., & HUDSON, W. Pattern specificity in a sample of Mozambique tribesmen on the Seven Squares test. *Journal of the National Institute for Personnel Research*, 1959, *7*, 156–61.

———. *An investigation into the usefulness of safety posters designed for Bantu industrial workers by the National Occupational Association*. Johannesburg: National Institute for Personnel Research, 1962.

HEIDER, E. R. "Focal" colour areas and the development of colour names. *Developmental Psychology*, 1971, *4*, 447–55.

———. Universals in colour naming and memory. *Journal of Experimental Psychology*, 1972, *93*, 10–20.

——— & OLIVIER, D. C. Structure of the color space in naming and memory for two languages. *Cognitive Psychology*, 1972, *3*, 337–54.

HERSKOVITS, M. J. *Man and his works*. New York: Knopf, 1948.

———. *A cross-cultural view of bias and values*. Lecture delivered under the auspices of the Danforth College, Greenville, North Carolina, 1959.

HEUSE, G. A. *Biologie du noir.* Bruxelles: Edition d'Afrique Centrale, 1957b.

———. Études psychologiques sur les noirs Soudanais et Guinéens. *Revue de Psychologie des Peuples,* 1957a, *12,* 35–68.

HILL, A. L. Perception of constancy or perceptual compromise. *Bulletin of the British Psychological Society,* 1973, *26,* 2.

HINTON, H. E. Natural deception. In R. L. Gregory & E. H. Gombrich (Eds.), *Illusion in nature and art.* London: Duckworth, 1973.

HOCHBERG, J., & BROOKS, V. The psychophysics of form: reversible perspective drawings of spatial objects. *American Journal of Psychology,* 1960, *73,* 337–54.

———. Pictorial recognition as an unlearned ability: a study of one child's performance. *American Journal of Psychology,* 1962, *75,* 624–28.

HOLM, N., & McCONNACHIE, K. R. Time perspective in Aboriginal children. In G. E. Kearney & D. W. McElwain (Eds.), *Aboriginal cognition: retrospect and prospect.* New Jersey: Humanities Press, 1976.

HOLMES, A. C. *A study of understanding of visual symbols in Kenya.* London: Overseas Visual Aids Centre, 1963.

———. *Health education in developing countries.* London: Nelson, 1964.

HOORWEG, J. C., & MARAIS, H. C. *Psychology in Africa: a bibliography.* Leyden: Africa-Studiecentrum, 1969.

HUDSON, W. The African in industry. *Engineer and Foundryman,* December 1958, 39–40.

———. Pictorial depth perception in sub-cultural groups in Africa. *Journal of Social Psychology,* 1960, *52,* 183–208.

———. Pictorial perception and educational adaptation in Africa. *Psychologia Africana,* 1962a, *9,* 226–39.

———. Cultural problems in pictorial perception. *South African Journal of Science,* 1962b, *58,* 189–95.

———. The study of the problem of pictorial perception among unacculturated groups. *International Journal of Psychology,* 1967, *2,* 89–107.

HUMPHRIES, D., & WORTLEY, W. Visual acuity: an attempt at the accurate measurement of visual acuity of illiterates and an evaluation of accepted norms. *Psychologia Africana,* 1971, *14,* 1–11.

HUSÉN, T. Studier rorande de eidetiska fenomenon. *Lunds Universitets Arsskrift,* 1945, *41,* 1–128.

HUTTON, M. A., & ELLISON A. *Some aspects of pictorial perception amongst Niuginians.* Konedob: Psychological Services Section, Department of the Public Service Board, Territory of Papua and New Guinea, 1970.

IBARROLA, R. Aportacion al estudio del rivel mental de los indigenas de Guinea. *Archives del Instituto de Estudios Africanos,* 1951, *5,* 7–29.

ICHIKAWA, K. Genetic studies of colour blindness on the schoolchildren in the perfectly isolated tribe: Yami (Formosa). *Acta Societatis Optamologicae Japonicae (Nippon Ganka Gakkai Zasshi),* 1973, *77,* 1908–15.

IRVINE, S. H. Figural tests of reasoning in Africa. *International Journal of Psychology,* 1969, *4,* 217–28.

IRVINE, S. H., SANDERS, J. T., & KLINGELHOFER, E. L. *Human behaviour in Africa: a bibliography of psychological and related writings,* Westport, Conn.: Greenwood Press, 1972.

IRWIN, M. H., & McLAUGHLIN, D. H. Ability and performance in category sorting of Mano children and adults. *Journal of Social Psychology*, 1970, *82*, 15–24.

IRWIN, M. H., SCHAFER, G. N., & FEIDEN, C. P. Emic and unfamiliar category sorting of Mano farmers and United States undergraduates. *Journal of Cross-Cultural Psychology*, 1974, *5*, 407–23.

IWAWAKI, S., & CLEMENT, D. E. Pattern perception among Japanese as a function of pattern uncertainty and age. *Psychologia*, 1972, *15*, 207–12.

JAENSCH, E. R. *Eidetic Imagery*. New York: Harcourt Brace, 1930.

JAHODA, G. Assessment of abstract behaviour in a non-Western culture. *Journal of Abnormal and Social Psychology*, 1956, *53*, 237–43.

————. Geometric illusions and environment: a study in Ghana. *British Journal of Psychology*, 1966, *57*, 193–99.

————. Some research problems in African education. *Journal of Social Issues*, 1968, *24*, 161–75.

————. Cross-cultural use of the perceptual maze test. *British Journal of Psychology*, 1969, *39*, 82–86.

————. A cross-cultural perspective in psychology. *The Advancement of Science*, 1970, *27*, 57–70.

————. Retinal pigmentation, illusion susceptibility, and space perception. *International Journal of Psychology*, 1971, *6*, 199–208.

————. Retinal pigmentation and space perception: a failure to replicate. *Journal of Social Psychology*, 1975, *97*, 133–34.

————. Rapidity of bilateral arm movements: a cross-cultural study. *Psychologia Africana*, 1976a, *16*, 207–14.

————. Reproduction of Kohs-type drawings by Ghanaian children: orientation error revisited. *British Journal of Psychology*, 1976b, *67*, 203–11.

————. Cross-cultural study of factors influencing orientation errors in reproduction of Kohs-type figures. *British Journal of Psychology*, 1977, *69*, 45–57.

JAHODA, G., & McGURK, H. Pictorial depth perception: a developmental study. *British Journal of Psychology*, 1974a, *65*, 141–49.

————. Development of pictorial depth perception in cross-cultural replications. *Child Development*, 1974b, *45*, 1042–47.

————. Pictorial depth perception in Scottish and Ghanaian children: a critique of some findings with Hudson's test. *International Journal of Psychology*, 1974c, *9*, 255–67.

JAHODA, G., & STACEY, B. Susceptibility to geometrical illusions according to culture and professional training. *Perception and Psychophysics*, 1970, *7*, 179–84.

JAHODA, G., CHEYNE, W. B., DERĘGOWSKI, J. B., SINHA, D., & COLLINGBOURNE, R. Utilisation of pictorial information in classroom learning: a cross-cultural study. *AV Communication Review*, 1976, *24*, 295–315.

JOHNSON, D. L. The Draw-a-Man test and Raven's Progressive Matrices: performance of Guatemalan boys and Ladino children. *Revista interamericana de psicologia*, 1967, *1*, 143–57.

JONES, P. A. Intra-cultural differences in susceptibility to geometric illusions and in pictorial depth perception. *Perceptual and Motor Skills*, 1974, *38*, 188–90.

JULESZ, B. *Foundations of Cyclopean perception*. Chicago: University of Chicago Press, 1971.

KELLAGHAN, T. Abstraction and categorization in African children. *International Journal of Psychology*, 1968, 3, 115–20.

KENNEDY, J. M. Is gradual pattern recognition of pictures by Ethiopian subjects a differentiation process? *Perception*, 1974, 3, 29–31.

———. Outline picture perception by the Songe of Papua. *Perception*, 1975, 4, 391–406.

KERSHNER, J. R. Ethnic group differences in children's ability to reproduce direction and orientation. *Journal of Social Psychology*, 1972, 88, 3–13.

KIDD, D. *The essential Kafir*. London: A. and C. Black, 1905.

———. *Savage childhood: a study of Kafir children*. London: A. and C. Black, 1906.

KILBRIDE, P. L., & LEIBOWITZ, H. Factors affecting the magnitude of the Ponzo illusion among the Baganda. *Perception and Psychophysics*, 1975, 17, 543–48.

KILBRIDE, P. L., & ROBBINS, M. C. Linear perspective, pictorial depth perception and education among the Baganda. *Perceptual and Motor Skills*, 1968, 27, 601–02.

———. Pictorial depth perception and acculturation among the Baganda. *American Anthropologist*, 1969, 71, 293–301.

KILBRIDE, P. L., ROBBINS, M. C., & FREEMAN, R. B. Pictorial depth perception and education among Baganda schoolchildren. *Perceptual and Motor Skills*, 1968, 26, 1116–18.

KILBY, P. African labour productivity reconsidered. *Economic Journal*, 1961, 71, 273–91.

KLAPPER, Z. S., & BIRCH, H. G. Perceptual and action equivalence of photographs in children. *Perceptual and Motor Skills*, 1969, 29, 763–71.

KLEINFELD, J. Cognitive strengths of Eskimos and implications for education. *Institute of Social and Government Research Occasional Paper No. 3*. Fairbanks: University of Alaska, 1970.

KLINGELHOFER, E. L. *A bibliography of psychological research and writing in Africa*. Uppsala: Scandinavian Institute of African Studies, 1967.

KLUCKHOHN, C., & LEIGHTON, D. *The Navaho*. Cambridge, Mass.: Harvard University Press, 1946.

KUNNAPAS, T. M. An analysis of the vertical-horizontal illusion. *Journal of Experimental Psychology*, 1955, 49, 134–40.

KUGELMASS, S., LIEBLICH, A., & ERLICH, C. Perceptual exploration in Israeli and Bedouin children. *Journal of Cross-Cultural Psychology*, 1972, 3, 345–52.

LAMBETH, M., & LANIER, L. H. Race difference in speed of reaction. *Journal of Genetic Psychology*, 1933, 42, 255–97.

LARKEN, P. M. Impressions of the Azande. *Sudan Notes and Records*, 1927, 10, 85–134.

LAWS, R. *Women's work in heathen lands*. Paisley: Parlane, 1886.

———. Quoted in H. P. Beach, *Geography and atlas of Protestant missions*. New York: Student Volunteer Movement for Foreign Missions, 1901.

LEACH, M. L. The effect of training on the pictorial perception of Shona children. *Journal of Cross-Cultural Psychology*, 1975, 6, 457–70.

———. Pictorial depth perception: task levels imposed by testing instruments. *International Journal of Psychology*, 1977, 12, 51–56.

LEIBOWITZ, H., BRISLIN, R., PERLMUTTER, L., & HENNESSY, R. Ponzo perspective as a manifestation of space perception. *Science*, 1969, *166*, 1174–76.

———. A rejoinder to: Illusions and sampling environmental cues by W. Schiff. *Science*, 1970, *3*, 395.

LEIBOWITZ, H., & PICK, H. L. Jr. Cross-cultural and educational aspects of the Ponzo perspective illusion. *Perception and Psychophysics*, 1972, *12*, 430–32.

LENNEBERG, E. Colour naming, colour recognition, colour discrimination: a re-appraisal. *Perceptual and Motor Skills*, 1961, *12*, 375–82.

———. *Biological foundations of language.* New York: Wiley, 1967.

LENT, R. H. Binocular rivalry and the perception of race in United States. *British Journal of Psychology*, 1970, *61*, 521–33.

LEVAK, M. D. Eidetic images among the Bororo of Brazil, *Journal of Social Psychology*, 1969, *79*, 135–37.

LEVELT, W. J. M. *On binocular rivalry.* The Hague: Mouton, 1968.

LEVI-STRAUSS, C. *Structural anthropology.* New York: Basic Books, 1963.

LIDDICOAT, R., & KOZA, C. Language development in African infants. *Psychologia Africana*, 1963, *10*, 108–16.

LIPPERT, S. Ergonomics needs in developing countries. *Ergonomics*, 1967, *10*, 617–26.

LLOYD, A. B. Acholi country, Part II. *Uganda Notes*, 1904, *5*, 18–22.

LLOYD, B. *Perception and cognition.* Harmondsworth: Penguin, 1972.

MACARTHUR, R. S. Sex difference in field dependence for the Eskimo: replication of Berry's findings. *International Journal of Psychology*, 1967, *2*, 139–40.

MACCRONE, I. D. Preliminary results from the Porteus Maze tests applied to native schoolchildren. *South African Journal of Science*, 1928, *25*, 481–84.

———. *Race attitudes in South Africa: historical, experimental, and psychological studies.* London: Oxford University Press, 1937.

McDOUGALL, W. Cutaneous sensations. In *Reports of the Cambridge Anthropological Expedition to Torres Strait*, 1903, *2*, 189–95.

McFIE, J. African performance on an intelligence test. *Uganda Journal*, 1954, *18*, 33–43.

———. The effect of education on African performance on a group of intellectual tests. *British Journal of Educational Psychology*, 1961, *31*, 232–40.

McGURK, H., & JAHODA, G. Developments of pictorial depth perception: role of figural elevation. *British Journal of Psychology*, 1974, *65*, 367–76.

MACKINNON, A. A. Eskimo and Caucasian: a discordant note on cognitive perceptual abilities. *Proceedings of the Annual Convention of the American Psychological Association*, 1972, *7*, 307–08.

McLUHAN, M. *Gutenberg galaxy.* London: Routledge and Kegan Paul, 1962.

MACLEAN, U. Blood donors for Ibadan. *Community Development Bulletin*, 1960, *11*, 26–31.

MAGNUS, H. F. Untersuchungen Über den Farbensinn der Naturvolken. *Physiologische Abhandlungen*, 1880, Ser. 2, No. 7.

———. Über ethnologische Untersuchungen des Farbensinnes. In R. Virchow & F. Holtzendorff-Vietmansdorff (Eds.), *Sammlung gemeinverstandlicher wissenschaftliechter Vortrage.* Breslau, 1883.

MAISTRAUX, R. *L'intelligence noire el Sondestin.* Les Éditions de Problèmes d'Afrique Centrale. Bruxelles (no date).

———. La revolution des noirs d'Afrique. Sa nature, ses causes, ses remèdes. *Revue de psychologie des peuples,* 1955, *10,* 167–89; 1956, *11,* 397–456.

MALPASS, R. S., & KRAVITZ, J. Recognition of faces of our own and other races. *Journal of Personality and Social Psychology,* 1969, *13,* 330–35.

MALPASS, R. S., LAVIGNEUR, H., & WELDON, D. Verbal and visual training in race recognition. *Perception and Psychophysics,* 1973, *14,* 285–92.

MEAD, M. *Coming of age in Samoa.* Harmondsworth: Penguin, 1961.

MEADE, R. D., & SINGH, L. Motivation and progress effects on psychological time in sub-cultures of India. *Journal of Social Psychology,* 1970, *80,* 3–10.

MELIKIAN, L. Acculturation time perspective and feeling tone: a cross-cultural study of perception of the days. *Journal of Social Psychology,* 1969, *79,* 273–98.

MERCADO, S. J., RIBES, I. E., & BARRERA, R. F. Depth cues effect in the perception of visual illusions. *Revista interamericana de psicologia,* 1967, *1,* 137–42.

MICHAEL, D. N. A cross-cultural investigation of closure. *Journal of Abnormal and Social Psychology,* 1953, *48,* 225–30.

MILLER, R. J. Cross-cultural research in the perception of pictorial materials. *Psychological Bulletin,* 1973, *80,* 135–50.

MINDE, M. *In search of happiness.* London: Frederick Muller, 1937.

MITCHELL, N. B., & POLLACK, R. H. Block design performance as a function of hue and race. *Journal of Experimental Child Psychology,* 1974, *17,* 377–82.

MORGAN, P. A study of perceptual differences among cultural groups in Southern Africa, using tests of geometric illusions. *Journal of the National Institute of Personnel Research,* 1959, *8,* 39–43.

MUNDY-CASTLE, A. C. Pictorial depth perception in Ghanaian children. *International Journal of Psychology,* 1966, *1,* 290–300.

———. An experimental study of prediction among Ghanaian children. *Journal of Social Psychology,* 1967, *73,* 161–68.

———. Gestalt continuation and design copying in Ghanaian children. *Ghana Journal of Child Development,* 1968, *1,* 40–63.

MUNDY-CASTLE, A. C., & NELSON, G. K. A neuropsychological study of the Knysna forest workers. *Psychologia Africana,* 1962, *9,* 240–72.

MUNRO, D., & DEREGOWSKI, J. B. Polyphasic pictorial perception: failure to confirm the effect of language. *Journal of Cross-Cultural Psychology,* 1976, *7,* 111–16.

MUNROE, R. L., & MUNROE, R. H. Effect of environmental experience on spatial ability in East African Society. *Journal of Social Psychology,* 1971, *83,* 15–22.

MUNROE, R. L., MUNROE, R. H., NERLOVE, S. B., & DANIELS, R. E. Effects of population density on food concerns in three East African societies. *Journal of Health and Social Behaviour,* 1969, *10,* 161–71.

MURUBE, J., & DA LA FUENTE, J. La identificacion de los colores ente les Saharaliis. *Achivos sociedad espanola de oftamologia,* 1975, *35,* 863–72.

MYAMBO, K. Shape constancy as influenced by culture, western education, and age. *Journal of Cross-Cultural Psychology,* 1972, *3,* 221–31.

MYERS, C. S. Smell. In *Reports of the Cambridge Anthropological Expedition to Torres Strait,* 1903, *2,* 169–85.

————. The taste names of primitive peoples. *British Journal of Psychology*, 1904, *1*, 117–26.

NADEL, S. F. A field experiment in racial psychology. *British Journal of Psychology*. 1937b, *28*, 195–211.

————. Experiment on culture psychology. *Africa*, 1937a, *10*, 421–35.

————. An application of intelligence tests in the anthropological field. In F. C. Bartlett, M. Ginsberg, E. J. Lindgren, & R. H. Thouless (Eds.), *The study of society*. London: Kegan Paul, 1939.

NELSON, G. K. *Race, culture, and brain function*. Johannesburg: Institute of the Study of Man in Africa, 1964.

NERLOVE, S. B., MUNROE, R. H., & MUNROE, R. L. Effect of environmental experiments on spatial ability: a replication. *Journal of Social Psychology*, 1971, *84*, 3–10.

NEWMAN, C. V. Children's size judgments in a picture with suggested depth. *Nature*, 1969, *223*, 418–20.

NICHOLSON, J. R., & SEDDON, G. M. The influence of secondary depth cues on the understanding by Nigerian schoolboys of spatial relationships in pictures. *British Journal of Psychology*, 1977, *68*, 327–33.

NISSEN, H. W., MACHOVER, S., & KINDER, E. F. A study of performance tests given to a group of native African Negro children. *British Journal of Psychology*, 1935, *25*, 308–55.

NYBORG, H. A method for analysis of performance in the Rod-and-Frame Test, I and II. *Scandinavian Journal of Psychology*, 1974, *15*, 119–23; 124–26.

OKONJI, M. O. The differential effects of rural and urban upbringing on the development of cognitive styles. *International Journal of Psychology*, 1969, *4*, 193–205.

————. The effect of special training on the classificatory behaviour of some Nigerian Ibo children. *British Journal of Educational Psychology*, 1970, *40*, 21–26.

————. Socio-economic background, race, and auditory-visual integration in children. In J. L. M. Dawson & W. J. Lonner (Eds.), *Readings in Cross-Cultural Psychology*. Hong Kong: Hong Kong University Press, 1974.

OLIVER, R. A. C. The musical talent of natives of East Africa. *British Journal of Psychology*, 1932a, *22*, 33–343.

————. The adaptation of intelligence tests to tropical Africa, I and II. *Overseas Education*, 1932b, *4*, 186–91; *5*, 8–13.

OLMSTED, P. D., & SIGEL, I. E. The generality of colour-form preference as a function of materials and task requirements among lower-class Negro children. *Child Development*, 1970, *41*, 1025–32.

OLSON, D. R. *Cognitive development: the child's acquisition of diagonality*. New York: Academic Press, 1970.

OLSON, R. K. Slant judgments from static and rotating trapezoids correspond to rules of perspective geometry. *Perception and Psychophysics*, 1974, *15*, 509–16.

————. Children's sensitivity to pictorial depth information. *Perception and Psychophysics*, 1975, *17*, 59–64.

————. Sensitivity to pictorial shape perspective in five-year-old children and adults. *Perception and Psychophysics*, 1976, *20*, 173–78.

OMARI, I. M., & COOK, H. Differential cognitive cues in pictorial depth perception. *Journal of Cross-Cultural Psychology*, 1972, *3*, 321–25.

OMARI, I. M., & MACGINITIE, W. H. Some pictorial artifacts in studies of African children's pictorial depth perception. *Child Development*, 1974, 45, 535–39.

OMBREDANE, A. *L'exploration de la mentalité des noirs au moyen d'une éprenue projective: Le Congo T.A.T.* Bruxelles: Institut Royal Colonial Belge, 1954.

———. Points of view for psychologists working with Africans. In R. Wickert (Ed.), *Readings in African psychology from French language sources.* East Lansing: Michigan State University, 1967.

OMBREDANE, A., BERTELSON, P., & BENIEST-NOIROT, E. Speed and accuracy of performance of an African native population and of Belgian children on a paper-and-pencil perceptual task. *Journal of Social Psychology*, 1958, 47, 327–37.

ONO, H. Apparent distance as a function of familiar size. *Journal of Experimental Psychology*, 1969, 79, 109–15.

OPOLOT, J. A. Differential cognitive cues in pictorial depth perception in Ugandan children. *International Journal of Psychology*, 1976, 11, 81–88.

ORD, I. G. *Mental tests for pre-literates.* London: Ginn, 1971.

———. Testing for educational and occupational selection in developing countries. *Occupational Psychology*, 1972, 46, No. 3, Monograph Issue.

OYAMA, T. Japanese studies on the so-called geometrical optical illusion. *Psychologia*, 1960, 3, 7–20.

PAGE, H. W. Pictorial depth perception: a note. *South African Journal of Psychology*, 1970, 1, 45–48.

PARASKEVOPOULOS, I. Symmetry recall and preference in relation to chronological age. *Journal of Experimental Child Psychology*, 1968, 6, 254–64.

PARKER, D. M. Evidence for the inhibition hypothesis in expanded angle illusion. *Nature*, 1974, 250, 265–66.

PECK, L., & HODGES, A. B. A study of racial differences in eidetic imagery of pre-school children. *Journal of Genetic Psychology*, 1937, 51, 141–61.

PETTIGREW, T. F., ALLPORT, G. W., & BARNETT, E. O. Binocular resolution and perception of race in Africa. *British Journal of Psychology*, 1958, 49, 265–78.

PETTIGREW, T. F., & NUTTALL, R. L. Negro American perception of the irradiation illusion. *Perceptual and Motor Skills*, 1963, 17, 98.

PIAGET, J. *The mechanisms of perception.* London: Routledge and Kegan Paul, 1969.

PIAGET, J., & INHELDER, B. *The child's conception of space.* London: Routledge and Kegan Paul, 1956.

PICKFORD, R. W. *Individual differences in colour vision.* London: Routledge and Kegan Paul, 1951.

———. *Psychology and visual aesthetics.* London: Hutchinson, 1972.

PIOTROWSKI, Z. Racial differences in linear perspective. *Journal of Social Psychology*, 1935, 6, 479–85.

POLLACK, R. H. Contour detectability threshold as a function of chronological age. *Perceptual and Motor Skills*, 1963, 17, 411–17.

———. Müller-Lyer illusion: effect of age, lightness contrast, and line. *Science*, 1970, 170, 93–94.

POLLACK, R. H., & SILVAR, S. D. Magnitude of Müller-Lyer illusion as a function of the pigmentation of the fundus oculi. *Psychonomic Science*, 1967, 8, 83–84.

POOLE, H. E. The effect of urbanization upon scientific concept attainment among

Hausa children in northern Nigeria. *British Journal of Educational Psychology,* 1968, *38,* 57–63.

POOLE, H. Restructuring the perceptual world of African children. *Teacher Education in New Countries,* 1969, *10,* 165–72.

POORTINGA, Y. H. Cross-cultural comparison of maximum performance tests: some methodological aspects and some experiments with simple auditory and visual stimuli. *Psychologia Africana, Monograph Supplement No. 6,* 1971.

———. A comparison of African and European students in simple auditory and visual tasks. In L. J. Cronbach & P. J. D. Drenth (Eds.), *Mental tests and cultural adaptation.* The Hague: Mouton, 1972.

PORTEUS, S. D. *The maze test and mental differences.* Vineland: Smith Printing and Publishing House, 1933.

———. *Primitive intelligence and environment.* New York: Macmillan, 1937.

———. *Porteus maze tests: fifty years of application.* Palo Alto: Pacific Books, 1965.

———. Ethnic groups and the maze test. In R. E. Kutner (Ed.), *Race and modern science: a collection of essays.* New York: Social Science Press, 1967.

PORTEUS, S. D., & GREGOR, J. Studies in intercultural testing. *Perception and Motor Skills,* 1963, *16,* 705–24.

PRICE, J. R., & TARE, W. A cross-cultural study of recall of time-related and non-time-related verbal material. *International Journal of Psychology,* 1975, *10,* 247–54.

PRICE-WILLIAMS, D. R. Abstract and concrete modes of classification in a primitive society. *British Journal of Educational Psychology,* 1962, *32,* 50–61.

PRIEST, R. H. Personal communication, 1966.

REUNING, H. An experimental psychological contribution to our knowledge of the Bushmen. Paper delivered at the Annual Congress of South African Association of Advanced Science, Johannesburg, 1960.

———. Experimentell-Psychologische Buschmann-Studies in der zentralen Kalahari. *S. W. A. Wissenschaftliche Gesellschaft Journal,* 1971, *26,* 17–43.

REUNING, H., & WITTMAN, G. Relative difficulty of two kinds of symmetry in the PATCO test. *Psychologia Africana,* 1963, *10,* 89–107.

REUNING, H., & WORTLEY, W. Psychological studies of the Bushmen. *Psychologia Africana, Monograph Supplement No. 7,* 1973.

RICHARDSON, S., LOCK, C. H., LEE, A., & TEE, T. S. The Müller-Lyer illusion: a cross-cultural study in Singapore. *Ergonomics,* 1971, *13,* 526.

RIVERS, W. H. R Vision. In *Reports of the Cambridge Anthropological Expedition to Torres Strait.* Cambridge University Press, 1901, 2; 1–132.

———. Observations on the senses of the Todas. *British Journal of Psychology,* 1905, *1,* 321–96.

ROBBINS, M. C., KILBRIDE, P. L., & BUKENYA, J. M. Time estimation and acculturation among the Baganda. *Perceptual and Motor Skills,* 1968, *26,* 1010.

ROBERTS, A. O. M., MACQUARRIE, M. E., & SHEPHERD, J. M. Some aspects of the pattern completion test. *Journal of the National Institute for Personnel Research,* 1959, *8,* 59–64.

ROBINSON, J. O. Retinal inhibition and visual distortion. *British Journal of Psychology,* 1968, *59,* 29–36.

————. *The psychology of visual illusion.* London: Hutchinson University Press, 1972.

ROBINSON, J. O., & REECE, I. P. F. Retinal pigmentation and visual illusion. Unpublished report, 1975.

ROLLINGS, P. J. A note on the cultural direction of perceptual selectivity. *Acta Psychologica*, 1961, *19*, 669–700.

ROSCH, E. *Universals and cultural specifics in human categorisation.* In R. W. Brislin, S. Bochner, & W. J. Lonner (Eds.), *Cross-cultural perspectives on learning.* New York: Halsted, 1975.

RUDEL, R. G., & TEUBER, H. L. Discrimination of direction of line of children. *Journal of Comparative and Physiological Psychology*, 1963, *56*, 892.

RYAN, I. A., & SCHWARTZ, C. B. Speed of perception as a function of mode of representation. *American Journal of Psychology*, 1956, *70*, 60–69.

SCHIFF, W. Illusion and sampling environmental cues. *Science*, 1970, *168*, 395.

SCHIFFMAN, H. R., & THOMPSON, J. G. The role of figure orientation and apparent depth in the perception of the horizontal-vertical illusion. *Perception*, 1975, *4*, 79–83.

SCHMIDT, W. H. O., & NZIMANDE, A. Cultural differences in colour/form preference and classificatory behaviour. *Human Development*, 1970, *13*, 140–48.

SCHLOSBERG, H. Stereoscopic depth from single pictures. *American Journal of Psychology*, 1941, *54*, 601–05.

SCHWITZGEBEL, R. The performance of Dutch and Zulu adults on selected perceptual tests. *Journal of Social Psychology*, 1962, *57*, 73–77.

SEGALL, M. H., & CAMPBELL, D. T. Reply to Spitz. *Science*, 1963, *140*, 422–24.

SEGALL, M. H., CAMPBELL, D. T., & HERSKOVITS, M. J. Cultural differences in perception of geometric illusions. *Science*, 1963, *139*, 769–71.

————. *Influence of culture on visual perception.* Indianapolis: Bobbs-Merrill, 1966.

SERPELL, R. Selective attention and interference between first and second languages. *University of Zambia Institute for Social Research Communication*, No. 4, 1968.

————. Cultural differences in attentional preference for colour over form. *International Journal of Psychology*, 1969, *4*, 1–8.

————. The influence of language, education, and culture on attentional preference between colour and form. *International Journal of Psychology*, 1969b, *4*, 183–94.

————. Attention theory, colour-form preference, second language learning, and copying orientation. *African Social Research*, 1970, *9*, 660–68.

————. Preference for specific orientation of abstract shapes among Zambian children. *Journal of Cross-Cultural Psychology*, 1971a, *2*, 225–39.

————. Discrimination of orientation by Zambian children. *Journal of Comparative and Physiological Psychology*, 1971b, *75*, 312–16.

————. How perception differs among cultures. *New Society*, 1972, *20*, 620–23.

————. Can pictures teach? *Science and Education in Zambia*, 1974, *5*, 11–18.

————. *Culture's influence on behaviour.* London: Methuen, 1976.

SERPELL, R., & DERĘGOWSKI, J. B. *Teaching pictorial depth perception: a classroom experience.* University of Zambia, H. R. D. U. Report, 1972.

SHAPIRO, M. B. Rotation of drawing by illiterate Africans. *Journal of Social Psychology*, 1960, 52, 17–30.

SHAW, B. *Visual symbols survey*. London: Centre for Educational Development Overseas, 1969.

SHEEHAN, P. W. The variability of eidetic imagery among Australian aboriginal children. *Journal of Social Psychology*, 1973, 91, 29–36.

SHEEHAN, P. W., & STEWART, S. J. A cross-cultural study of eidetic imagery among Australian aboriginal children. *Journal of Social Psychology*, 1972, 87, 179–88.

SHEPHERD, J. W., DEREGOWSKI, J. B., & ELLIS, H. D. A cross-cultural study of recognition memory for faces. *International Journal of Psychology*, 1974, 9, 205–11.

SIGEL, I. E. *The distancing hypothesis: a causal hypothesis for the acquisition of representational thought*. Paper delivered at University of Miami symposium on the effects of early experience, 1968.

SIIPOLA, E. M., & HAYDEN, S. D. Exploring eidetic imagery among the retarded. *Perceptual and Motor Skills*, 1965, 21, 275–86.

SILVAR, S. O., & POLLACK, R. H. Racial differences in pigmentation of the *fundus oculi*. *Psychonomic Science*, 1967, 7, 159–60.

SINAIKO, H. W. Verbal factors in human engineering: some cultural and psychological data. In A. Chapanis (Ed.), *Ethnic variables in human factors engineering*. Baltimore: Johns Hopkins University Press, 1975.

SINHA, D., & MISRA, P. Use of pictorial depth cues in children's paintings: a developmental study. *Indian Journal of Psychology*, 1975, 50, 222–31.

SINHA, D., & SHUKLA, P. Deprivation and development of skill for pictorial depth perception. *Journal of Cross-Cultural Psychology*, 1974, 5, 434–51.

SLACK, C. Critique of the interpretation of cultural differences in the perception of motion in Ames's trapezoidal window. *American Journal of Psychology*, 1959, 72, 127–31.

SMITH, T. The susceptibility of Xhosa groups to a perspective illusion. *Journal of Social Psychology*, 1973, 90, 331–32.

SNELBECKER, G. E., FULLARD, W., & GALLAHER, G. M. Age-related changes in pattern prediction: a cross-cultural comparison. *Journal of Social Psychology*, 1971, 84, 191–96.

SPENCER, J. A preliminary enquiry into engineering drawing comprehension. *Occupational Psychology*, 1963, 37, 181–95.

———. Experiments in engineering drawing comprehension. *Ergonomics*, 1965, 8, 93–110.

SPITZ, H. H. Cross-cultural differences. *Science*, 1963, 140, 422.

SPOERL, D. T. A note on the Anastasi-Foley cultural interpretation of children's drawings. *Journal of Social Psychology*, 1941, 13, 187–92.

STACEY, B. Explanations of the H-V illusion and the foreshortening of receding line. *Life Science*, 1969, 8, 1237–46.

STEWART, M. V. Tests of the "carpentered world" hypothesis by race and environment in America and Zambia. *International Journal of Psychology*, 1973, 8, 83–94.

SUCHMANN, R. G. Cultural differences in children's colour and form preferences. *Journal of Social Psychology*, 1966, 70, 3–10.

TAJFEL, H. Social and cultural factors in perception. In G. Lindzey & E. Aronson

(Eds.), *The handbook of social psychology*, Vol. 3. Reading, Mass.: Addison-Wesley, 1969, 315–94.

TAYLOR, T. R. Optical illusions: their relationship to field dependence, their theory, and their factor structure. Johannesburg: National Institute for Personnel Research, Report No. 177, 1972.

———. A factor analysis of 21 illusions: the implications for theory. *Psychologia Africana*, 1974, *15*, 137–48.

———. The factor structure of geometric illusions: a second study. *Psychologia Africana*, 1976, *16*, 177–200.

TEKANE, I. An error analysis of responses to PATCO test by Bantu industrial workers. *Journal of the National Institute for Personnel Research*, 1961, *8*, 189–94.

———. Symmetrical pattern completion by illiterate and literate Bantu. *Psychologia Africana*, 1963, *10*, 63–68.

THOMSON, J. *Through Masailand: a journey of exploration.* London: Sampson Low, Marston, Searle and Rivington, 1885.

THOULESS, R. H. Individual differences in phenomenal regression. *British Journal of Psychology*, 1932, *22*, 217–41.

———. A racial difference in perception. *Journal of Social Psychology*, 1933, *4*, 330–39.

———. Perception constancy or perceptual compromise? *Australian Journal of Psychology*, 1972, *22*, 133–40.

TIMNEY, B. N., & MUIR, D. W. Orientation anisotropy: incidence and magnitude in Caucasian and Chinese subjects. *Science*, 1976, *193*, 699–701.

TITCHENER, E. B. On ethnological tests of sensation and perception. *Proceedings of American Philosophical Society*, 1916, *55*, 204–36.

TRAVERS. R. M. W. *A study of the advantages and disadvantages of using simplified visual representation in instructional materials.* Washington, D. C.: United States Office of Education, Department of Health, Education and Welfare, 1969.

———. Age and levels of picture interpretation. *Perceptual and Motor Skills*, 1973, *36*, 210.

TRIANDIS, H. C. Cultural influences upon cognitive processes. In L. Berkowitz (Ed.), *Advances in experimental social psychology.* New York: Academic Press, 1964.

TRIANDIS, H. C., MALPASS, R. S., & DAVIDSON, A. R. Cross-cultural psychology. *Biennial Review of Anthropology*, 1972.

———. Psychology and culture. In *Annual Review of Psychology*, 1973, *24*, 355–78.

TURNBULL, C. M. Some observations regarding the experiences and behaviour of the BaMbuti Pygmies. *American Journal of Psychology*, 1961, *74*, 304–08.

UNESCO. *Simple reading material for adults: its preparation and use.* Paris: UNESCO, 1963.

VALENTINE, C. W. Psychological theories of the horizontal-vertical illusion. *British Journal of Psychology*, 1912, *5*, 8–35.

VAN GRAAN, C. H. Some applications of ergonomics in the South African Mining Industry. *South African Mining Engineer*, 1974, *24*, 282–89.

VAN WYK, I. EEG in Kalahari. *Psygrams*, 1964, *6*, 17–22.

VERNON, M. D. *Perception through experience.* London: Methuen, 1970.

VERNON, P. E. *Intelligence and cultural environment.* London: Methuen, 1969.

VON MAYER, B. The PATCO test, intelligence, and closure. *Perceptual and Motor Skills*, 1963, *17*, 890.

WARBURTON, F. W. The ability of Gurkha recruits. *British Journal of Psychology*, 1951, *42*, 123–133.

WALDRON, L. A., & GALLIMORE, A. J. Pictorial depth perception in Papua, New Guinea, Torres Strait, and Australia. *Australian Journal of Psychology*, 1973, *25*, 89–92.

WALLMAN, S. Communication of measurement in Basutoland. *Human Organization*, 1965, *24*, 236–43.

WARD, L. M., & COREN, S. The effect of optically induced blur on the magnitude of the Müller-Lyer illusion. *Perception and Psychophysics*, 1976, *7*, 483–84.

WEALE, R. A. Apparent size and contrast. *Vision Research*, 1975, *15*, 949–55.

WEAVER, D. B. *Intra-cultural test of empiristic vs. physiological explanations for cross-cultural differences in geometric illusion susceptibility using two illusions in Ghana.* Doctoral dissertation, Northwestern University, 1974.

WINTER, W. The perception of safety posters by Bantu industrial workers. *Psychologia Africana*, 1963, *10*, 127–35.

————. Size constancy, relative size estimation, and background: a cross-cultural study. *Psychologia Africana*, 1967, *12*, 42–58.

WITKIN, H. A. A cognitive-style approach to cross-cultural research. *International Journal of Psychology*, 1967, *2*, 233–50.

WITKIN, H. A., & ASCH, S. E. Studies in space perception, IV. Further experiments on perception of upright with displaced visual fields. *Journal of Experimental Psychology*, 1948, *38*, 762–82.

WITKIN, H. A., & BERRY, J. W. Psychological differentiation in cross-cultural perspective. *Journal of Cross-Cultural Psychology*, 1975, *6*, 4–87.

WITKIN, H. A., DYK, R. B., FATERSON, H. F., GOODENOUGH, D. R., & KARP, S. A. *Psychological differentiation: studies of development.* New York: Wiley, 1962.

WOBER, M. Sensotypes. *Journal of Social Psychology*, 1966, *70*, 181–89.

————. Adapting Witkin's field independence theory to accommodate new information from Africa. *British Journal of Psychology*, 1967, *58*, 29–38.

————. Confrontation of the H-V illusion and a test of three-dimensional picture perception in Nigeria. *Perceptual and Motor Skills*, 1970, *31*, 105–06.

————. On cross-cultural psychology. *Bulletin of the British Psychological Society*, 1972, *25*, 203–05.

————. Polyphasic picture perception: a phenomenon demonstrated in Africa. In J. Dawson & W. Lonner (Eds.), *Readings in Cross-cultural Psychology. Proceedings of the Inaugural Meeting of the International Association for Cross-Cultural Psychology.* Hong Kong: Hong Kong University Press, 1974.

WOODWORTH, R. J. Racial differences in mental traits. *Science*, 1910, *31*, 171–86.

WORMS, E. Sense of smell in Australian aborigines. *Oceania*, 1942, *13*, 107–30.

WORTLEY, W., & HUMPHRIES, D. Visual acuity, II. Study of acuity of vision of South African Whites, Bantu, and Bushmen. *Psychologia Africana*, 1971, *14*, 11–19.

WYNDHAM, C. H. Ergonomic problems in the transition from peasant to industrial life in South Africa. In A. Chapanis (Ed.), *Ethnic variables in human factors engineering.* Baltimore: The Johns Hopkins University Press, 1975.

3

Cognition: Psychological Perspectives[1]

Anne D. Pick

Contents

Abstract

The study of human cognition is the study of how people learn and think. Many different experimental tasks have been used to assess cognitive functioning in members of different cultures. Most such tasks are intended either to reflect how people's knowledge of objects and concepts is organized, or to reflect how people's knowledge of space and of objects in space is organized. Several issues of procedure and methodology must be considered in evaluating observations about cognitive functioning in people from different cultures. Among these issues are the validity of the experimental tasks, ambiguity of communication, and the representativeness of samples of subjects.

Familiarity with the relevant objects and with the type of task to be performed, and formal education are associated with apparent cultural differences in how people represent objects. The effect of these factors is primarily on the magnitude of the observed cultural differences. When people know about the objects they are doing something with, and when formal education is equivalent, cultural differences in how people represent objects are minimal or absent. On the other hand, when variations in the cultural context are associated with variations in schooling or knowledge of the objects, then cultural differences have been more often observed.

How people represent knowledge about space is another aspect of cognitive functioning that psychologists and anthropologists have studied cross-culturally. Members of different cultures use complex spatial reference systems. The hypothesis is intriguing that early socialization experiences and typical styles of living foster certain ways of thinking about and representing spatial relations. However, the hypothesis remains to be supported since there are especially serious problems posed by unrepresentative groups of subjects and by the use of tasks unfamiliar to or inappropriate for some of the subjects.

The goal of some research projects has been to identify possible cultural bases for variations in general intelligence. Three culture-related factors have been identified as potentially relevant for understanding such variations: early social and cognitive stimulation, early nutrition, and education. Clear interpretation of apparent cultural differences in general intellectual functioning is virtually impossible because of the culture-specific nature of tests of intelligence and because of the difficulty of ensuring the representativeness of samples of subjects' tests.

For both logical and methodological reasons, general questions about cultural universality of relativity of cognition may be unanswerable. Significant relations between facts of culture and cognitive development can be identified by observing patterns of performance in conditions in which both tasks and settings vary systematically and specifiably and in which subjects' assumptions about appropriate behavior are clear.

Introduction

The study of human cognition is the study of how people learn and think. Psychologists who study cognition have long been interested in the cross-cultural study of cognition. At least one reviewer has suggested that cross-cultural study is a strategy for investigating individual differences in development (LeVine, 1970, p. 559). It has also been argued that in order to establish generality of findings, it is necessary to do cross-cultural studies (Jahoda, 1970, p. 58). An immediate purpose of psychologists who venture into a new culture to conduct a cross-cultural investigation may be to determine whether different groups of people perform a particular set of tasks similarly. However, the more general purpose of the investigation is not the observation of performance on a particular set of experimental tasks. The experimental tasks are usually constructed with the assumption that to perform them requires certain cognitive skills. It is the effect of culture-related variables on these cognitive skills that psychologists want to study. For example, they may want to identify the effects of particular interventions or experiences such as malnutrition on cognitive development. Or, they may be interested in the effects of school attendance, or of growing up in a rural or an urban milieu on some aspect of cognitive development. Most generally, the purpose of the cross-cultural study of cognition is to identify the intellectual outcomes of growing up in one culture instead of another.

Can this purpose of the cross-cultural study of cognition be fulfilled? What can be learned about human cognition by identifying cultural differences and similarities? When cultural differences are attributable to experience, they are like the results of natural experiments demonstrating the flexibility of the human mind. The theoretical task is to specify the essential nature of the relevant experience and its mechanism for operation. When cultural differences in cognition can be attributed to physiological or biological differences among people, they may provide clues for investigating the mechanisms of cognition and its development. Where there are important similarities in the cognitive functioning of diverse groups of people, these similarities may help identify aspects of cognition that are universal. In short, cross-cultural study is a strategy for acquiring knowledge about human cognition.

The successful identification of cultural differences and similarities in cognition rests heavily on the experimental tasks and how they are presented. Obviously, they are appropriate to the extent that they do engage the intended cognitive skills. The criterion for assessing the effects of cultural variables is how members of different cultures perform the tasks, and a major problem and pitfall for researchers is to establish the validity of that criterion. It is especially crucial in cross-cultural studies to know the cognitive requirements of experimental tasks since cultures vary in so many ways that identifying the critical variation is often logically or practically impossible.

A topic that illustrates this point clearly is the cross-cultural study of visual illusions in which the magnitude of various illusions is assessed in members of different cultural groups. (See Deręgowski's chapter in this volume for a review of this topic.) There are many potentially relevant differences among a set of cultures, and in order to identify the important one(s) relevant for the illusion, one must have prior knowledge about why the illusion occurs. Goodnow (1969) described some conditions that must be met in order to make useful interpretations of apparent differences in cognitive activity in culturally diverse groups of people. These conditions have to do with the context in which differences and similarities in the behavior of people in different cultures can be interpreted.

> When we consider intellectual growth or style in different cultures, we are confronted by three requirements. We need to obtain . . . some picture of skills common to people from many backgrounds, as well as skills that differentiate among them. At the same time, we need to find the features of milieu that may account for the similarities and differences in skills. And finally, . . . we have to ask as we transpose a task from one culture to another, whether the same answer means the same thing in both worlds. (Goodnow, 1969, p. 439)

Goodnow's third requirement especially implies methodological standards that must be conformed to before inferences can be made about cultural variables and cognition. When apparent cultural differences or similarities have been identified and the validity of the experimental task established, or presumed, there are two additional questions that can be asked to help determine whether Goodnow's requirements have been met.

The first question is whether there is unambiguous communication between the people performing the experimental tasks and the inventors of the tasks. The observations made from cross-cultural studies of pictorial perception (see Deręgowski's chapter in this volume; also see Pick & Pick, in press) are a demonstration of the potential effects of ambiguous communication. In the most typical procedure for studying how members of different cultures interpret representational pictures, people are shown a set of line drawings and asked a few standard questions about what they see. If they answer in terms of the lines on the paper, i.e., in terms of the two-dimensional information in the picture, the usual interpretation is that they cannot accurately interpret the representational information. On the other hand, if they answer in terms of the representational information, the usual interpretation is that they can accurately interpret representation of depth and distance relations in pictures. The problem with the first interpretation is that it may not be clear to the respondents that the questions refer to the representational information in the pictures instead of the two-dimensional information. If the people performing the experimental tasks do not understand their requirements as being those that the inventor of the tasks has in mind, then differences in the way people perform the task do not necessarily reflect differences in their cognitive functioning.

The effect of ambiguous communication can be discrepant rather than shared meaning between the respondents and the investigator—discrepancies about what the task means and how it should be performed. Such discrepancies may be related to observed differences in performing the task. Thus, when aspects of the procedure are ambiguous, observations about differences in performance can be misleading.

The second question is whether the groups of people whose cognitive functioning is assessed are appropriately representative of their respective cultures. Often investigators working in foreign cultures for limited periods of time will select groups of subjects because they are easily available. Obviously such groups may or may not be typical of the larger population from which they are selected or representative of the diversity of that population. Many interpretations and assertions about relations between culture and cognition have been based on small samples of individuals who may or may not be representative of the cultural group from which they come (e.g., Berry, 1966; Brazelton, 1972; Brazelton, Robey, & Collier, 1969; Greenfield, 1966; Greenfield, Reich, & Olver, 1966; Landauer & Whiting, 1964; Tronick, Koslowski, & Brazelton, 1971).

Many different experimental tasks have been used to assess cognitive functioning in members of different cultures. Most such tasks are intended either to reflect how people's knowledge of objects and concepts is organized, or to reflect how people's knowledge of space and of objects in space is organized. Cross-cultural studies of these topics will be considered first, and then the cross-cultural study of intelligence will be discussed. Finally, some concluding comments will be made about strategies and current trends in the cross-cultural study of cognition. The issues raised earlier in this chapter are relevant for each of these topics in assessing the evidence and rationale by which cultural variables are related to aspects of cognitive functioning.

Object Representation

Are there cognitive strategies or ways of thinking that characterize people who grow up in different cultural environments? Do people in different cultures organize and represent information about objects in similar ways? Or are there aspects of one's cultural environment that determine what features of objects are important or useful? The physical environment and the objects in it have many more features than people can attend to, think about, and remember. What factors determine those features that are attended to and used, and those that are ignored? An adequate account of human cognitive functioning will include answers to these questions, and the purpose of some cross-cultural studies of cognition has been to help provide those answers.

Classification

It has frequently been asked whether people in different cultures classify objects in the same way, i.e., according to the same attributes. Finding out why some objects are judged similar to each other and why others are not can help people understand how they represent information about objects when they think.

A task typically used to study classification is to present a small collection of objects or shapes and to ask people to group together those that are alike. The results of studies in the United States have shown a developmental trend toward the use of form rather than color as a basis for grouping the shapes (see Suchman & Trabasso, 1966). Such a trend is not always observed among children in other cultures (e.g., Suchman, 1966) and this cultural difference may be attributable to differences in education. Zambians, for example, are more likely to use form for classification as the number of years of their schooling increases (Serpell, 1969a), and young British children—who have attended nursery school—are more likely to use form than are young Zambian children who have not attended nursery school (Serpell, 1969b).

All shapes used in these studies were two-dimensional and geometric, and the relation between education and the use of form rather than color as a basis for judging the shapes may have to do with their familiarity and with the habitual use of labels for shapes that are drawn on paper. Triangles, squares, and circles acquire their identity by virtue of their form and not their color, and children may learn this by being told the names of the shapes by their parents or teachers.

When photographs of objects rather than geometric shapes are the items to be classified, schoolchildren in Senegal, in Zambia, and in Scotland tend to classify by form rather than by color (Deręgowski & Serpell, 1971; Greenfield et al., 1966). Early education may not have such a clear relation to how children classify three-dimensional objects however. Okonji (1974) asked young preschool aged Zambian children to classify three-dimensional geometric shapes and he found few differences between the children in nursery school and the children not attending school in how they sorted the objects.

In some classification tasks, people are asked to identify differences among shapes or objects rather than similarities. Lloyd (1971) used such a task with Nigerian children from three to eight years of age, some from "elite" homes in which the mothers were educated and the children in school, and some from "traditional" homes, in which the mothers were uneducated and most children were not in school. She reported that performance improved with age, and that children from "elite" homes performed better than children from "traditional" homes. These findings are in accord with those of an earlier study in which older "westernized" Nigerian boys performed "better" on a sorting task than did "nonwester-nized" Nigerian boys (Kellaghan, 1968). In discussing the findings from this study it was suggested that the two groups of boys may have differed in their familiarity with the test materials and that unfamiliarity, in turn, limits the level of abstraction available to the subjects. In this case, level of abstraction was determined by a boy's explanation of the basis for his classifications.

It is possible that familiarity with the items to be classified is relevant also for interpreting some apparent educational differences in classifica-tion skills. Price-Williams (1962) tested Nigerian schoolchildren and nonschool-going children six and one-half to eleven years in age with ma-terials that were quite familiar to both groups. He used two collections of objects for sorting tasks. One collection contained toy animals, two dead beetles, and a fish. A second collection contained plants from the local area. The children were asked to gather together those items that belonged together, and to make groups in as many different ways as possible. In a second task, items were presented in sets of three and the child was asked to identify the one of the three that was not like the others. The sets of three items were constructed *not* by the experimenter, but by selecting from the groups formed by the children in the first task. Testing was done in the local language and the results were similar for both collections of objects and for both tasks. Age, and not education, was related to the children's performance. The older children made more sorts in the first task, and made more correct identifications in the second task than the younger children did. Also, children who had never attended school per-formed similarly to the schoolchildren.

The suggestion that familiarity with the relevant material may help people understand apparent educational differences in classification skills is supported by observations made when familiarity is manipulated directly. Uneducated Liberian adults do not sort colored geometric shapes on the basis of form, although Liberian schoolchildren do (Irwin & McLaughlin, 1970). However, the uneducated adults sort bowls of rice in terms of features such as cleanliness, polish, and type of grain—all fea-tures requiring careful analysis of the material. American college students, however, sort the bowls of rice primarily in terms of quantity (Irwin, Schafer, & Feiden, 1974). Also, when Nigerian children sorted items that were generally more familiar to them than to a comparison group of Scot-tish children, the oldest Nigerian children performed better than the old-est Scottish children did (Okonji, 1971). With items equally familiar to the two groups, performance of the two groups was similar.

Why does familiarity with items facilitate classifying them in more complex or sophisticated ways? Possibly it is because people already know about more of the features of familiar items, instead of having to discover them when they first encounter the items. This possibility fits some observations of classification of items differing in familiarity but having similar features. Greenfield (1974) asked educated and uneducated Mexican children to classify familiar flowers and then to classify unfamiliar objects—rods—that varied in some of the same ways, e.g., length and color, as the flowers. Children over eight years of age could easily classify and reclassify both types of items. Further, even the youngest children (four to five years of age) could classify the unfamiliar items at least as easily as they could classify the familiar items that they had previously sorted.

Claims of apparent cultural differences in ability to abstract or to think in generalities have been made on the basis of findings from a number of studies in which sorting tasks have been used. Schoolchildren from Kansas have been said to show a higher level of abstract ability than schoolchildren in Guadalajara, Mexico (Mercado, Guerrero, & Gardner, 1963). Schoolchildren in Boston and in Mexico City have been said to show a higher level of abstract ability than rural Mexican schoolchildren (Maccoby & Modiano, 1966). And white schoolchildren in Anchorage showed more sophisticated classification skills than Eskimo children in Anchorage—some of whom attended the same school (Greenfield et al., 1966).

Several questions of procedure have to be answered in order to interpret claims of cultural differences in abstraction abilities. When differences are found between rural and urban schoolchildren in the same grade, is the quality of education similar in the two milieus? If not, education is not really controlled. When cultural differences are found, to what extent are those differences related to the languages of testing and answering? Often, the subjects' own descriptions of their categorizations are assessed for the degree of abstractedness of conceptualization reflected. But such assessment may be unreliable if descriptions must be translated into the tester's language or even interpreted for the tester before they can be evaluated; also, the assessment may be unreliable if the subjects must make their descriptions in a language that is not their primary language of communication. Collison (1974) found that Ghanaian schoolchildren performed at a higher conceptual level in their primary language than in English—the language they used in school. Greenfield et al. (1966) reported the opposite pattern for children in Senegal using their primary language and their school language, which was French.

In the types of sorting tasks that have just been discussed, the respondents classify the items according to their own rules, and the investigator infers what those rules are. A related task is one in which the investigator defines the classification rules, and the respondent has to learn them. The familiar concept learning tasks fit this description. The respondent has to learn to identify objects consistently on the basis of some feature. The investigators do not tell the respondent what that feature is; they only say whether each choice is right or wrong and the respondent has to infer what the relevant feature is. Such constrained classification tasks have been used in a number of cross-cultural studies. Skill in performing such tasks increases with age (Mundy-Castle, 1967) and especially with education. Cole, Gay, and Glick (1968) observed uneducated Liberian children and adults to be less skilled than Liberian schoolchildren, and they observed American and Liberian schoolchildren to perform similarly.

The relation between preference for a feature and ease of learning to use that feature for classification was studied by Evans and Segall (1969). They tested rural and urban primary schoolchildren in Uganda. The task required learning to classify sets of pictured objects by color and by function. Nearly all the children required fewer trials to use color consistently than to use function. Rural schoolchildren required more trials to learn to use function consistently than did urban schoolchildren, and a group of uneducated adults required most trials of all. Subsequently, it was established that the relative discriminability of the two features did not determine the differential ease of learning to use them. Education was the variable most clearly related to ease of learning to use function; it would be interesting to determine whether the effect of education is specifically to facilitate using function, or more generally, to facilitate inducing rules for classification. The investigators pointed out that the uneducated adults obviously attend to objects routinely and are perfectly aware of their identities and functions. They also point out that the word "alike" in Luganda as in English has a primary connotation of physical appearance. Possibly, uneducated subjects may simply have interpreted their instructions quite literally and directed their attention accordingly.

Cole, Gay, Glick, and Sharp (1969) studied the relation between another aspect of language and the ease of learning to use size as a feature for classification. They noted that in Kpelle, a language spoken in Liberia, an equivalent of "smaller than" is rarely used whereas an equivalent of "bigger than" is common. They asked whether for young speakers of Kpelle—in comparison to young Americans—it would be easier to identify consistently the larger of two objects than to identify the smaller of two objects. The American children were three to five years old; the Liberian children were four to eight years old.

At the very beginning of the task, when the children could only guess (i.e., before the tester has said whether the choice is correct) the Liberian children tended to choose the larger item, but the American children showed no such bias. After the first choice, though, there was no apparent relation between the children's learning to select the larger as compared to the smaller item and the language they spoke. The very youngest Liberian children could explain the choice of the larger item better than they could explain the choice of the smaller item. However, no group of children, either Liberian or American, provided more than a minority of explanations that were generally regarded as adequate. These observations may reflect a general imprecision in young children's descriptions, regardless of what language they speak.

The educational differences that have been observed in these tasks may reflect differences in difficulty of learning to use one or another feature, or they may reflect differences in initial attention to features. The latter suggestion is supported by some observations made by Ciborowski and Cole (1971, 1972, 1973). They used some complicated classification tasks that were more accurately solved by educated Americans than by uneducated Liberians. However, when additional information (besides the tester's indication of correctness) was provided, nearly all of the subjects could solve all of the problems. In other words, when attention is directed explicitly and appropriately, subsequent performance from disparate groups is sometimes equivalent.

What can be learned about cognitive functioning from these many observations about how people from different cultures classify things? For one thing, education seems to reduce apparent cultural differences in object classification. Schoolchildren and educated adults from many locales use similar features to classify objects, and they sort objects in similar ways. Familiarity with the relevant objects is also related to how people from different cultures classify things. When people are familiar with the objects they are asked to manipulate and to sort, they have knowledge about many features of those objects, and this knowledge may expedite classifying the objects in varied and complicated ways.

Memory

What people remember about arrays of items helps investigators understand how people organize and represent information about objects in the world around us. Many investigators have been interested in cultural differences in what people remember, and in how people go about trying to recall information about things seen previously. Often the tasks used to study such memory strategies require children to identify objects or pictures seen previously for a brief time. Both age and education are related to how well people from different cultures perform experimental tasks designed to assess their memory (Wagner, 1974; Scribner, 1974). In one such study Guatemalan children five to twelve years of age were shown a collection of familiar objects, given an opportunity to study them, and then, with the objects occluded, were asked to recall the objects by name (Kagan, 1972). The number of objects recalled increased with age as did a tendency to report together objects belonging to the same category (e.g., articles of clothing, animals, etc.). Subsequently urban American children five, eight, and eleven years of age, and rural Guatemalan children of the same ages were shown a collection of pictures; their memory for the pictures was tested immediately or after varying periods of delay (Kagan, Klein, Haith, & Morrison, 1973). The pictures, sixty in all, were taken from American magazines. Correct identifications increased with age for both groups. Delaying the memory test had no effect on the Guatemalan children, and a negligible effect on the Americans.

The differences between the children's performance in the two locales were greater for the younger children than for the older children and the oldest children from the two cultures were assumed to be performing at the same high level. However, there was a clear ceiling effect in the memory task for the American children and even these children, like the Guatemalans, might have shown continued improvement had the task been more difficult for them. The materials were certainly more familiar to the Americans, and familiarity did affect the Guatemalans' recognition memory.

A predicted effect on memory of familiarity was found in another comparison of Guatemalan and American children. Meacham (1975) thought that children growing up in a Guatemalan village might have less need to discriminate and remember objects than would children growing up in an urban American environment. However both groups of children, he thought, would learn to remember locations. He designed an experimental task that required children to answer questions about *where* items were hidden, i.e., the location of items, or about *what* items were hidden, i.e., the identity of the items themselves. The Guatemalan children found the questions about location easier to answer than the questions about the objects, whereas the American children found the two types of questions equally easy to answer.

Some investigators have used tasks in which people are asked to estimate the amount or quantity of items in a briefly presented array. Though different from the tasks just described, these estimation tasks reflect a type of memory functioning. In order to make accurate estimates, subjects must be able to use an accurate representation of the units in which the estimate is made. The effects of familiarity with the relevant materials are clearly apparent in such tasks. For example, in one series of comparisons of Liberians and Americans (Cole et al., 1968), one task was used in which people estimated the number of pint size cans of rice contained in comparison cans of differing sizes. Uneducated Liberian adults were somewhat more accurate than Liberian and American schoolchildren, and a great deal more accurate than American adults.

In another task estimates were made of the number of stones contained in a briefly viewed pile. Again, uneducated Liberian adults performed the task most accurately, and American adults least accurately. American university students improved with practice, but they still were not significantly more accurate than the Liberians who only performed the task once. In still another number-judgment task (reported in Cole et al.,

1968) subjects estimated the number of dots presented tachistoscopically in two-dimensional arrays. In this task, unlike the previous one, American schoolchildren and university students were more accurate than the Liberians. Other tasks required estimates of time, e.g., matching the time interval required to pace off a certain distance, and once again, Liberians were more accurate than Americans. When estimates were made of the lengths of sticks, in handspans, American as well as Liberian adults were more accurate than American and Liberian schoolchildren. In other distance-estimation tasks Liberian schoolchildren tended to be more accurate than Liberian adults.

In summary, these findings suggest that when judgments are required about features of real objects, uneducated adults who are familiar with the objects are at least as accurate and are sometimes more accurate than are people who have had formal education. When the judgment required is artificial, e.g., the number of dots in a tachistoscopically presented array rather than the number of stones in a briefly viewed pile, educated people are more accurate. An instance that seems to contradict this interpretation is one in which Dutch adults were found to be more accurate than Zulu adults in a number of estimation tasks (Schwitzgebel, 1962). However, the judgments were made in absolute units like inches and minutes, units with which the Dutch may have been more familiar than were the Zulus. So, it can be suggested that when the units of judgment are known, and the materials and features to be judged are familiar, accuracy of estimation judgments does not depend on formal education. In general, the observation from cross-cultural studies of memory has revealed few if any relations between cultural variables and how people remember. Most of the cultural effects have to do with how much or how accurately people remember, and the most apparent basis for these effects is whether people are familiar with the material they are trying to remember.

Conservation

The concept of conservation has been the topic of many cross-cultural studies. This concept, from Piaget's theory of intellectual development, refers to the ability to recognize the identity of objects or substances in spite of changes in their appearance. Conservation requires people to make judgments about objects on the basis of some features rather than other features. Cross-cultural investigators have been interested in conservation, because the way people perform conservation tasks is presumed to reflect how they think about objects.

Piaget's theory has had an important influence on the study of culture and cognition. However, since it is the subject of a separate chapter (see Dasen and Heron's chapter in Volume 4 of this *Handbook*) neither the theory nor the specific topic of conservation will be discussed fully here. Several authors have evaluated the cross-cultural observations about conservation (e.g., Brislin, Lonner, & Thorndike, 1973, pp. 170 ff; Cole & Scribner, 1974, pp. 146 ff). An important issue is the criteria for verifying different aspects of Piaget's theory cross-culturally. Dasen (1972a) and Goodnow (1969), among others, have discussed criteria for evaluating reported results from tasks such as conservation tasks when they have been conducted in different cultural contexts. Some obvious common problems are differences in testing and scoring methods, in age range of subjects, in amount and kind of verbalizations elicited from subjects, and in language of testing (local or foreign).

A common report is that of a similar sequence of conservation development across cultures, but of a "lag" in development of conservation for members of some cultures in comparison to others (e.g., Dasen, 1972a, 1974, 1975; Feldman, 1974; Goldschmid, Bentler, Debus, Rawlinson, Kohnstamm, Modgil, Nicholls, Reykowski, Strupczewska, & Warren, 1973; Heron & Dowel, 1973; de Lemos, 1974). One investigator (de Lemos, 1969) suggested a genetic basis for such effects after finding differences in performance on conservation tasks between children in Australia who were full and who were part Aboriginal. However, an attempt to replicate these findings was unsuccessful (Dasen, 1972b) and the original findings are called into question by a reanalysis of the data (Vetta, 1972).

Education has been cited as a specific experience important to the development of conservation. When the conservation performance of schoolchildren in Senegal and in Nigeria was compared with the performance of children in those countries not attending school, the former groups performed at a higher level (Greenfield, 1966; Owoc, 1973). Even the quality of early education has been suggested as a factor important in the differences in conservation performance, at least among Zambian and European schoolchildren (Heron & Simonsson, 1969). Okonji (1971), who found differences on Piagetian tasks between Ugandan schoolchildren and Ugandan children not in school, suggested that the relation between education and conservation may be partly a function of relevant extracurricular activities such as games involving numbers.

It is difficult to identify the source of observed differences between children attending school and those not in school. Nearly all such comparisons favor schoolchildren, but do the differences reflect the effects of schooling on cognitive functioning, or do they reflect the selection of brighter children to attend and remain in school? Also, it is especially important, in assessing the effects of such a general cultural variable as schooling, to ensure that an adequate sample of subjects has been obtained. In one case it was concluded that only about half of the children not attending school achieve conservation by the age of thirteen or so, but that all schoolchildren do. The children not in school on which this conclusion was based numbered only twelve (of whom six demonstrated an understanding of conservation by the age of about thirteen and of whom six did not) (Greenfield, 1966, pp. 233–34).

Formal education apparently is not an absolute prerequisite for some successful conservation performance since young Nigerian children not attending school show a regular progression with age in successful performance (Price-Williams, 1961). Also, among schoolchildren between five and nine years of age in Beirut, age, but not school grade or mother's literacy, was related to understanding of conservation tasks (Za'rour, 1971). Likewise Ohuche (1971) found that age and not type of school predicted conservation performance among schoolchildren in Sierra Leone.

Goodnow (1962) found conservation performance to be comparable and successful among boys representing four ethnic-cultural milieus in Hong Kong; European middle class, Chinese middle class (boys attending Anglo-Chinese schools), Chinese low socioeconomic class attending school, and Chinese low socioeconomic class not attending school. She suggested that an important milieu effect on conservation task performance is not education per se, but rather the general information that is provided by one's environment. For example, the Europeans provided fuller explanations for their judgments than did the low socioeconomic status Chinese boys; one reason might be not that the Europeans were better able to make the judgment, but that they had available more detailed information. Similarly, she suggested that there are environmental determinants of how a problem or task gets defined. For example, for schoolboys, the conservation task involving liquid may be an intellectual exercise; for the nonschoolboys, it may be a situation raising concern about spilled water (Goodnow, 1962, p. 11).

In a follow-up study, Goodnow and Bethon (1966) asked whether differences in performance on conservation tasks might be unrelated to school attendance per se, but instead might be a function of general differences in intelligence. American children judged "average" and "dull" in intelligence, and matched in pairs for chronological age were tested. The children judged "dull" performed less successfully on the conservation tasks than did children judged "average" in intelligence who, in turn, performed quite like the children tested earlier in Hong Kong, both European and Chinese, educated and uneducated. DeLacey (1972) also found performance on Piagetian tasks related to assessed level of intellectual functioning in several cultural groups in Australia.

One noncurricular factor that may be related to conservation is manual experience (Furby, 1971; Price-Williams, Gordon, & Ramirez, 1969). Price-Williams et al. (1969) selected Mexican boys who were sons of potters and boys matched in age and education who were sons of fathers engaged in other jobs. In general, the potters' sons performed better on conservation tasks, and the presumption is that manipulating and judging pliable objects was an important specific experience distinguishing the two groups of boys.

Familiarity with the test materials themselves is another factor associated with differences in conservation performance. Lester and Klein (1973) found that Guatemalan children performed at a higher level in a conservation task when the materials were familiar. These children also increased their level of performance from a first to a second testing time. Thus, both the degree of familiarity with the testing materials and with the nature of the task affected their apparent understanding of the concept of conservation. A point made by Cole and Scribner (1974, pp. 155–56) is relevant for interpreting such effects. They noted, as has Goodnow that in interpreting cultural differences in conservation performance, it is important to know that the task means the same thing in different cultures, and also to know what the implications are of how one performs it for cognitive functioning.

Generalizations about relations between culture and how or what people think or remember about objects generally are limited by the types of objects that have been used in the studies reviewed, and by the restricted range of experimental tasks. Familiarity with the relevant objects and with the type of task to be performed, and formal education emerge as clear factors associated with apparent cultural differences in how people represent objects. The effect of these factors is primarily on the magnitude of the observed cultural differences. When people know about the objects they are doing something with, and when they have equivalent experience with formal education, apparent cultural differences in how they represent objects are minimal or absent. On the other hand, when variations in the cultural context are associated with variations in schooling or knowledge of the objects, then cultural differences have been more often observed. Educational effects on how people think about and use objects are not limited by any means to knowledge formally taught in school. The consistency with which one's physical and social context facilitates certain ways of thinking about and using objects may influence how one performs a particular experimental task.

Spatial Representation

How people represent knowledge about space is another aspect of cognitive functioning that psychologists and anthropologists have studied cross-culturally. They have asked whether people who live in different social and physical environments develop different ways of organizing and using spatial information. Do they develop different ways of learning and thinking about space and about objects in space? In short, do they develop different spatial reference systems?

The most detailed description of spatial reference systems is Gladwin's (1970) description of the system used by sailors from Puluwat to navigate among islands in the Western Pacific. Distances among the islands are great enough that voyages often last many days and frequently there are no visible landmarks. However, the sailors do not depend on obvious navigation aids like charts and radios and only recently have begun to use compasses.

The reference system contains information about many relevant features of the sky and of the sea. For example, information about the habits of local sea birds is used to provide information about one's location. Changes in the color of the water and in wave formations are used to identify coral reefs around the islands. The variations in those changes that depend on the conditions of weather, sea, and sky are also specified. Changes in the "feel" of a boat as it moves through the waves are used to detect changes in the course, and to help maintain a particular course. The reference system also includes detailed information about the positions and patterns of stars in the night sky. These star patterns and reference islands are used to specify rules for navigating between particular islands. Parallax information also is explicitly described in terms of the patterns of apparent movement of islands as boats pass on one or another side of them at a particular angle.

An important aspect of Gladwin's description is the method he used to study the navigation system. It is a method that can be used by other investigators who want to study systematic but unfamiliar behavior patterns. Gladwin engaged a master navigator to teach him the system so that he could acquire the information on which the system is based and the rules for using that information. He discussed the rules of the system with his teacher, and so gradually constructed a description of the conceptual basis for the navigation system. By asking his teacher questions about the system, he could correct inaccuracies in his model of it.

Another spatial reference system—that of the Temne in West Africa—has been described by Littlejohn (1963) though in much less detail than Gladwin's description of the Puluwat system. The Temne system, together with the concepts of field-dependence and field-independence, has been the basis for most cross-cultural studies of spatial representation.

The concepts of field-dependence and field-independence refer to how people rely on visual and other information in making judgments about their own orientations and the orientations of objects in space. Since personality characteristics are thought to underlie the extent of one's field-independence, one purpose of the cross-cultural studies has been to test hypotheses about child rearing and other socialization practices as predictors of personality characteristics and thus of degree of field-dependence (Dawson, 1967; A. Pick & H. Pick, in press; H. Pick & A. Pick, 1970; Witkin, 1967; Witkin, Dyk, Faterson, Goodenough, & Karp, 1962; Witkin, Lewis, Hertzman, Machover, Meissner, & Wapner, 1954). Although such hypotheses are intriguing and influential (e.g., Lloyd, 1972; MacArthur, 1967; Witkin & Berry, 1975; Wober, 1967), their validity is difficult to determine because of methodological problems in most of the studies that have been conducted. For example, groups of people who vary in the relevant socialization practices frequently vary in the extent to which they are familiar with the types of tasks used to assess their spatial skills and degree of field-dependence (e.g., Berry, 1966; Dawson, 1967). Since familiarity with the tasks does affect performance (Okonji, 1969; Siann, 1972), it is not clear that early socialization experiences also have a role in determining that performance. Also, an issue referred to earlier—that of ensuring the representativeness of groups of subjects—is especially apparent in the studies of socialization practices and spatial skills. Some investigators have used different methods of subject recruitment for groups that vary in the supposedly relevant socialization practices and styles of life. In one extreme instance, one group of people—a more "westernized" group—was recruited from the contacts of a local bar owner (Berry, 1966, p. 209) and another group consisted of all the people available in a hunting camp at the time the testing team visited the camp (Berry, 1966, p. 210). Such different methods of subject recruitment may produce groups of people who are not equally representative of their respective cultural groups—again making it difficult to identify important relations between socialization experiences and spatial skills.

One early experience that might be related to the development of spatial skills is the opportunity to explore the environment. Such a possibility was investigated in studies done in Kenya (Munroe & Munroe, 1971; Nerlove, Munroe, & Munroe, 1971). Children were observed to see how far from home they typically wandered and they were also asked to perform tests of spatial ability. Each child was paired with another of the same age and, as it turned out, the children from each pair who wandered farther from home were also the children who performed better on most of the tests. Thus, the children's skill at performing the spatial tasks was related directly to their spatial experience in the environment.

Many tasks used to assess people's spatial skills require them to build a model, copy a form, or to make some other type of production (Deręgowski, 1968, 1971, 1972a, 1972b; Tekane, 1963). If the people whose spatial skills are being assessed have varying or little actual experience drawing or copying, then such tasks are inappropriate. For example, if people have never before held pencils (Shapiro, 1960), then their spatial skills may not be assessed adequately via a paper and pencil task. A typical criterion for scoring the copies people make is whether they are oriented in the same way as the model; however the instructions are often inexplicit about whether one should take orientation into account in making a copy. There is evidence from studies with children in Ghana (Jahoda, 1956) and in Zambia (Serpell, 1971a, 1971b) that when instructions are explicit about the relevance of orientation for a task, young children can notice and use orientations of shapes.

In sum, members of different cultures use complex spatial reference systems. The hypothesis is intriguing that early socialization experiences and typical styles of living foster certain ways of thinking about and representing spatial relations. However, the evidence for the hypothesis is tenuous at best because of especially serious problems introduced by unrepresentative groups of subjects and by the use of tasks unfamiliar to, or inappropriate for, some of the subjects.

Cross-Cultural Study of Intelligence

Up to now, the discussion has focussed on the relation of cultural variables to how people think about objects and to spatial representation. The goal of some research projects has been to identify possible cultural bases for variations in general intelligence. Several issues are relevant to evaluating evidence in pursuit of that goal. The first is that most tests of intelligence are culture-specific; thus, when non-Westerners do not score well on Western tests of intelligence (Haward & Roland, 1954, 1955a, 1955b; Nissen, Machover, & Kinder, 1935) their performance is obviously not properly interpreted as an index of their intelligence. But it is not just the tests themselves that are culture-specific. Lloyd distinguishes two issues for the cross-cultural study of intelligence: the "culture-bound nature of definitions of intelligence," and "the biological or genetic basis of intelligence" (1972, p. 110). However, these issues may not be separable; if the first is a matter of fact, then the second may be impractical if not impossible to study cross-culturally. The acknowledgement of the culture-bound nature of definitions of intelligence has taken several forms.

Wober (1972) attempted to study directly and to describe the Ugandans' concept of intelligence. He showed adults and schoolchildren pictures of pairs of men. In each pair, one man was drawn taller than the other. He asked of each pair such questions as: Which man is wiser, more intelligent, faster, slower; and he observed which adjectives and adverbs were associated with the concept of intelligence. Primary schoolchildren associated slowness and swiftness equally often with intelligence and wisdom; secondary schoolchildren less frequently than other groups associated slowness with intelligence. In interpreting the findings, it is difficult to distinguish between associations of characteristics with the concept intelligence and age differences in understanding connotations of specific words such as slow, swift, etc. Nonetheless, this seems to be the only report of how intelligence is defined by members of a culture different from the ones in which tests of intelligence were constructed and standardized.

One recurring thesis is that there are cultural differences in abilities, e.g., that Africans think concretely and Europeans abstractly and conceptually, and that European experimenters are to be criticized for considering conceptual abilities as the skills to be assessed as intelligence (Cryns, 1962, p. 296). Many years ago, however, the point was made by Biesheuvel (1949) that using the same assessment measure in different cultures does not ensure that similar abilities are being assessed in members of different cultures; that, in Goodnow's (1969) terms, the same response does not mean the same thing in different places.

Many investigators have noted that test items or tasks used to assess some aspect of intellectual functioning in people from different cultures must adequately reflect that aspect of intellectual functioning in the relevant cultures (e.g., Berry, 1974; David, 1974; Smith, 1974; Wieman & Guthrie, 1972). Some tasks, for example nonverbal tests, are constructed so as to be relatively less culture-specific. The cultural neutrality of such tests, however, may be more apparent than real since scoring categories and their interpretation still may be highly culture-specific (Laosa, Swartz, & Diaz-Guerrero, 1974).

Biesheuvel conducted an extensive testing program in South Africa (Biesheuvel, 1949, 1952, 1958; Biesheuvel & Liddicoat, 1959, 1960; Langenhoven, 1960). He noted that the poor performance of black South Africans on intelligence tests is not a valid assessment of their abilities to think abstractly and conceptually because "there is ample evidence that within their own cultural context they are able to do all these things" (Biesheuvel, 1949, p. 98). He also anticipated current controversy when he argued that if environmental conditions are not identical for two groups, differences between those groups cannot be ascribed to genetic variation.

> There are, to be sure, many common elements that can be varied within each culture in a near-identical manner (such as nutrition and education) but there are other features that are unique to and non-variable within a culture (such as climate or kinship systems). There may even be subtler influences at work, pertaining to the values, the internal tensions, the cosmology of a culture which, as a field within which all other variations take place, could affect the outcome of any experimental manipulation. As the limits of modifiability would therefore be set with reference to noncomparable environmental circumstances, the difference between these limits could not be looked upon as residual. (Biesheuvel, 1958, pp. 166–67)

Biesheuvel discussed many problems of comparing test scores of people from different cultures. The tests are not culturally neutral; even when test procedures are equated for different groups, motivation and attitudes toward test taking are not. He does not argue that there are no cultural differences in abilities and that the only measurable performance differences arise from culture bias of tests, familiarity with test-taking, with pencils, etc. (Langenhoven, 1960). Rather, he argues there are cultural differences in abilities; they are difficult to measure, and their genesis cannot be identified at present (Biesheuvel, 1952, 1972; Biesheuvel & Liddicoat, 1960).

Attempts have been made to identify variables within a culture that are associated with group variations in test scores, i.e., to identify the basis for culture bias of tests. Contact with Western culture is one such variable (Abiola, 1965; Hudson, Roberts, van Heerden, & Mbau, 1962). Porteus and Gregor (1963), for example, attributed test score differences between two groups of adults in South Africa to the extensive contact one of the groups had had with whites. However, thirty-three years intervened between testing the two groups, and a number of factors besides contact with Western culture may have influenced test performance during that time.

Other factors associated with group differences in test scores are familiarity with test materials (Faverge & Falmagne, 1962) and conditions of testing. Vernon (1967) tested groups of schoolchildren in East Africa with a standard intelligence measure under several different conditions: oral or written instructions in English or Swahili. The children were then retested either under the same conditions, or with instructions given in a different language, or with coaching about how to do well on the test. In general, the scores on the second test were higher than those on the first and there were clear motivational effects; the scores of the children who were urged to try hard and to do well increased a great deal from the first to the second testing. Since all of the children were in school and had taken exams, it is possible that effects of practice, motivation, language, etc. would be even more dramatic for less sophisticated subjects.

Cognitive and social stimulation provided to infants has also been cited as relevant to cultural differences in intelligence. In some cases, observations are made of infants in one culture, and then the observations are compared with norms for American infants (e.g., Goldberg, 1972). In other investigations of the relation between child care practices, social stimulation, and early intellectual development, direct observations—both cross-sectional and longitudinal—have been made of infants in the relevant cultures. However, the numbers of infants tested has been small, and the sample selection haphazard. For example, in one case, the performance of ten first-born infants in Boston was compared with the performance of ten later-born infants in Zambia (Tronick, Koslowski, & Brazelton, 1971). In another, three American infants were observed for the first week of life, and the observations compared with those of a few Mayan infants in Mexico (Brazelton, 1972). In an earlier study (Brazelton et al., 1969) Zinacanteco infants in Mexico were observed periodically during the first year of life, and their development seemed to lag in comparison to American infants. However, only one or two Zinacanteco infants were observed at a given age, American infants were not tested, and the largest differences in scores occurred between experimenters (Brazelton et al., 1969, pp. 283, 288).

Three other variables have been identified as affecting general intellectual development: rural versus urban environment, education, and early nutrition. The variable of rural versus urban environment is probably the least precise of the three, and its importance may be in the extent to which it covaries with such experiences as education and with socioeconomic differences in opportunities available for relevant experiences (e.g., Schmidt & Nzimande, 1970). It has been argued that "an under-developed milieu does not stimulate a dynamic reasoning" (Peluffo, 1967, p. 195), but the basis for describing a rural environment as under-developed is not explicit.

The effects of education on general intellectual development have been assessed with several measures in addition to standardized intelligence tests. Deręgowski (1970), for example, predicted that uneducated Zambian women would not perform as well as schoolboys on a task requiring recall of details of a story. The prediction was confirmed, but since the stories were presented in different languages to the two groups, and there are differences in addition to school attendance distinguishing between the uneducated rural dwelling women and the schoolboys, it is difficult to ascribe the results unambiguously to the effects of education. Other evidence for the importance of education in intellectual development is similarity in test performance by students in schools in different cultures (McFie, 1961).

How does education exert an effect on intellectual development and functioning? One reason the question is so difficult to answer is the problem of sample selection encountered previously. It is rare to find groups of children who differ only in whether or not they attend school. When education is not universal within a culture as, for example, in northern Nigeria where children are not selected for schooling haphazardly (F. C. Alozie, personal communication), any systematic selection may allow apparent effects of "schooling" to be reflected on tests given as early as the first week or month of school (e.g., Fahrmeier, 1975). In short, the separation of schooling effects from differences in the samples of children selected for study is difficult when the test performance of educated and uneducated people from the same culture is compared.

To answer the question about how education exerts its effect, Goodnow (1969) pointed out (1) that the distinction between education and absence of school attendance summarizes sets of experiences, and (2) that the distinction refers to different sets of experiences.

> In reality, all environments make demands, present problems, and reward particular ways of coping. And these ways of coping limit or open up other ways of coping. In other words, "no schooling" is not a baseline of untroubled nature, but the result itself of an active, even if different, form of training (Goodnow, 1969, p. 456).

She urged that more systematic attempts be made to specify the skills included in tasks that reflect the effects of schooling. For example, she suggested that one skill learned early by the schoolchild is to combine different types of material. She suggested that in assessing and comparing skills of schoolchildren and skills of children not in school:

> If we do not use material that has already some past significance in relation to this task, we may never know what the unschooled child can do. But if we stop with this material, we may never know how much of his thought is replication rather than extension of past experiences (Goodnow, 1969, p. 459).

In short, she suggested that an important apparent effect of education on intellectual development is learning flexibility, learning to use alternative strategies. Similarly, Cole et al. (1971, p. 224) suggested that children in school learn new skills, and they learn to apply skills in situations other than those in which they were applied previously. Scribner and Cole (1973) concluded that a theory of formal education is required in order to identify important relations between particular aspects of education and intellectual functioning in people from different cultures.

The third variable identified as exerting an effect on general intellectual development is early nutrition. Several investigations completed or under way have as their goal the understanding of the effect of early malnutrition, especially insufficient protein, on cognitive development. The effect may be direct, e.g., on brain development, or it may be indirect via such characteristics as passivity that accompany malnutrition and may reduce receptivity to important new stimulation and information. Klein, Habicht, and Yarbrough (1971) reviewed many studies of this problem. One that is most widely cited was conducted in a rural Guatemalan village by Cravioto, DeLicardie, and Birch (1966). They asked whether malnutrition in early childhood would be related to intersensory integration as an index of intellectual development. Attained height was the index of prior nutritional status. The performance of the tallest 25 percent of the children in the village was compared with that of the shortest 25 percent of the children on a task requiring matching of objects presented to different modalities. The shorter group made more errors for some types of judgment than did the taller group. The results of this study as well as those of studies of animals (Barnes, Moore, Reid, & Pond, 1968; Cowley, 1968) and observations of children hospitalized for malnutrition for varying time periods (e.g., Champakan, Srikantia, & Gopalan, 1968; Cravioto & DeLicardie, 1970; Cravioto & Robles, 1965; Witkop, Baldizon, Castro, & Umana, 1970) provide the information about the adverse effect of early malnutrition on cognitive development. Klein, Freeman, Kagan, Yarbrough, and Habicht (1972) attempted to assess separately the relation to intellectual development of the social environment and of nutrition among children from three to six years of age in Guatemala. The children's nutritional status was rated by head circumference as well as by attained height. In general, the relations between the measures of cognitive functioning and of physical growth were low; so also were the relations between the measures of social environment and of cognitive functioning low (Klein et al., 1972, pp. 222–23). The results were interpreted as reflecting the influence of both social environment and of early nutrition on cognitive development.

Richardson (1968) noted that many factors besides nutrition are associated with physical growth and attained height at a given age. The problem of establishing a good index of nutritional status is especially difficult in retrospective studies of malnutrition and cognitive development, since the nutrition event occurs at an early age, since the status of intellectual development cannot be assessed until a much later age, and since many important events and conditions intervene. In short, the evidence currently available is equivocal about the magnitude of the specific contributions of early nutrition and of the early social environment to general intellectual development.

Strategies and Trends in
Cross-Cultural Study of Cognitive
Development

One method of cross-cultural study has not been discussed here only because the topics investigated with the method have had more to do with personality development than with cognitive development (see chapter by Tapp in Volume 4 of this *Handbook*). However, as a strategy, it is as appropriate to use to study one type of process cross-culturally as to study another. This strategy consists of describing and rating many variables in many cultures and then using the resulting patterns of correlations to identify factors that may affect development (Whiting, 1961; Whiting & Child, 1953). Typically, each culture is rated for the presence or absence of each of several characteristics or variables, and then the relations among the variables are assessed across all the cultures. For example,

Landauer and Whiting (1964) observed a relation between the presence or absence in cultures of practices of piercing infants, i.e., inoculation, circumcision, etc., and the average height of samples of at least twenty-five adult men from those cultures. The relation was interpreted in terms of the stimulating effect of early stress on subsequent physical development (Landauer and Whiting, 1964, p. 1018).

This strategy is similar to that used by Segall, Campbell, and Herskovits (1966) to study cultural differences in the magnitude of various visual illusions in that samples of individuals from many different cultures were observed (see Pick & Pick, in press; Deręgowski's chapter in this volume). It is different from that of Segall et al. in that each culture is considered as an individual case.

There are three points to note about the use of this strategy for studying cultural effects on cognitive functioning. First, as with any retrospective method, many conditions and events intervene between the event whose effect is being assessed and its supposed outcome. Hence, it is difficult to identify the crucial antecedent event. In the study of stress and development, for example, it is not even known whether the adult men from the cultures in which piercing is practiced were themselves inoculated or circumcised as infants. A second point, obviously related to the first, is that it seems especially important when observations are made in so many cultures, to know that the sample of subjects from each culture is adequately representative of the members of that culture. Naroll (1973) provides a detailed discussion of sampling in cross-cultural studies. Third, it is both an advantage and a disadvantage of this strategy that many observations are made about each culture. An advantage, of course, is that a great deal of information is obtained about a culture. A disadvantage, for documenting a particular hypothesized relation, is that the antecedent event or condition may be more highly related to a variable irrelevant to the hypothesis being tested than to the supposed consequent variable. One critic of this method has questioned whether the relations identified with this strategy reside in the patterns of observations from different cultures, or whether the relations reside in the investigator's head (Guthrie, 1971).

Feldman and Hass (1970) have suggested that it is necessary to use complementary correlational and experimental methods in identifying culture-related effects on development. When an important difference among cultures is observed, and its effects tentatively identified, then the relation can be confirmed either by manipulating the crucial condition or by observing it across a range of values within a culture. Cole and Bruner (1971, p. 873) have similarly argued

> If we accept the idea that situational factors are often important determinants of psychological performance, and if we also accept the idea that different

cultural groups are likely to respond differently to any given situation, there seems to be no reasonable alternative to psychological experimentation that bases its inferences on data from comparisons of both experimental and situational variations.

One or the other of two general hypotheses about culture and cognition provides the context for most contemporary psychological cross-cultural research on cognitive functioning. One is that cognitive processes are similar in individuals in different cultures, the other is that cognitive processes are dissimilar in individuals in different cultures and depend upon cultural variables. (See Cole et al., 1971, Chapter 1; and Lloyd, 1972, for discussions of the history of the two positions.) Support for both positions is claimed from concurrent evidence (Triandis, Malpass, & Davidson, 1973, p. 356; Kagan et al., 1973, p. 223).

An hypothesis occasionally described as a third alternative (see Lloyd, 1972, p. 148) is that of Cole et al. (1971) who interpreted the findings from their studies of Liberian children and adults as showing that "cultural differences in cognition reside more in the situations to which particular cognitive processes are applied than in the existence of a process in one cultural group and its absence in another" (p. 233). In fact this hypothesis is a variant of the more general position that the cognitive processes of individuals in different cultural groups are similar. Cole and Bruner (1971, p. 868) make explicit the view "that different groups (defined in terms of cultural, linguistic, and ethnic criteria) do not differ intellectually from each other in any important way."

Throughout this discussion we have seen instances in which apparent cultural differences in cognitive functioning are potentially attributable to such factors as education, familiarity with test materials and test-taking, or inadequate and incomplete communication (Sechrest, Fay, & Zaidi, 1972). Obviously there are additional factors, such as motivation, which might produce differences in performance that do not reflect differences in basic skills. In fact, it may be improbable that clear support could be provided for the general hypothesis of cultural relativity in fundamental cognitive processes. The problem of obtaining adequate samples of subjects from several cultures may simply be too great. Only if the cognitive skill in question has minimal intracultural variation could one be sure that variation in performance among subject groups from different cultures is based on factors inherent in the cultures—either genetic or experiential.

If a general hypothesis about the cultural differences in basic cognitive processes cannot be supported unequivocally, i.e., if such differences cannot be identified clearly, then the alternative that cognitive processes are similar across cultures cannot be tested and disproven, and then it will not be a useful hypothesis for guiding research. It may be more practical to retain as an assumption the universality of cognitive functioning (or to reject it as irrelevant) than to attempt to obtain direct empirical support for it.

One strategy proposed for the study of culture and cognition is to observe the types of intellectual activities engaged in by members of different cultures and then to relate those activities to patterns of performance on experimental tasks requiring the use of specific intellectual skills (Cole, et al., 1971, p. 217). An emphasis on the patterns of performance observed in different settings may circumvent the problems of interpreting findings from simple comparisons among cultures. This strategy, which Goodnow also has proposed (Goodnow, 1970, pp. 246–247), may prove to be a useful approach for identifying relations between cultural conditions and cognitive activity.

Cole (1972) has suggested that initial observations of discrepant task performance by members of different groups be followed by manipulations of the relevant conditions until similar performance is obtained from the different groups. Campbell (1964), and Segall et al. (1966, p. 176) argued that such a baseline of similar performance is not only desirable but also necessary when comparisons are to be made of the performance of members of different cultures. For example, if cultural differences in perception are being studied, unless experimenter and subjects perceive similarly in most situations, then discrepant performance cannot be attributed to differences in perception rather than to ambiguous communication. Only because differences in perception among different groups are small, can they be identified; if such differences appeared large, then they would more likely be failures of communication (Campbell, 1964, p. 325). When comparable performance from different groups can be achieved, then differences in performance from those same groups can be more sensibly interpreted.

One trend is discernible in how investigators conceptualize the problems to be studied. Specifically, there seems to be less current interest in studying dissimilar cognitive development in different cultures and more interest in confirming the universality of cognitive functioning. This trend, if verified, may illustrate two general points about the cross-cultural study of cognition. First, it may be unproductive to continue to try to support empirically one or the other general hypotheses of the relativity or universality of cognitive functioning. Second, there is a close relation between the rules communicated to a subject about how to perform a task and the investigator's conclusion about which of the two general hypotheses is supported. A slight change in the rules also changes the conclusion.

The trend toward hypothesizing cognitive universals is illustrated in the chronology of the study of the relation between the color terms of a language and how speakers of a language use colors. In early studies a procedure was used in which speakers of several languages were shown colors and asked to name them. The results supported the view that there is neither similarity across languages in the number of color terms commonly used nor in the portions of the spectrum that are referents for color names (Ray, 1952, 1953). Speakers of different languages performed differently on a variety of tasks requiring color judgments (Brown & Lenneberg, 1954; Lantz & Stefflre, 1964; Lenneberg & Roberts, 1956; Stefflre, Vales, & Morley, 1966).

Beginning in the late 1960s, a different interpretation was made of evidence about the relation between color terms and use of colors. A procedure was used by which speakers of different languages were shown color samples and first asked to indicate all the samples that could be referred to with a given color term, e.g., red. Then, they were asked to select one sample as the "best example" of that term. Colors selected as best examples of color terms turned out to be similar across languages (Berlin & Kay, 1969). Further, speakers of different languages performed similarly on several tasks requiring judgments of these best example, or "focal" colors, regardless of whether the language had terms available to refer to those colors (Heider, 1971, 1972; Heider & Olivier, 1972; Rosch, 1975).

In twenty years there has been a change from apparent acceptance of the "traditional relativistic hypothesis concerning the nature of human color categorization" (Berlin & Kay, 1969, p. 12) to the assertion that "color categorization is not random and the foci of basic color terms are similar in all languages" (Berlin & Kay, 1969, p. 10) and that these are universal aspects of colors. This change in viewpoint is associated with seemingly small changes in procedure used to study color terms and judgments about colors. In fact, of course, the findings from the two lines of inquiry are not contradictory, and seemingly incompatible inferences about cultural relativity or universality may be premature, at best.

That premature inferences can interfere with careful study is illustrated by a recent report of observations made about cognitive development in Guatemala (Kagan, 1972; Kagan & Klein, 1973). The observations led to an assertion that it is necessary

> ... to reorder the hierarchy of complementary influence that biology and environmental forces exert on the development of intellectual functions that are natural to man. Separate maturational factors seem to set the time of emergence of those basic abilities. Experience can slow down or speed up that emergence by several months or several years, but nature will win in the end. (Kagan & Klein, 1973, p. 949)

This assertion was based on observations that were interpreted as showing retardation in cognitive development in Guatemalan infants compared to American infants, but comparable levels of cognitive functioning in older

Guatemalan and American children (p. 957). However, there are some matters of procedure, both in testing the infants and in testing the older children that render that interpretation dubious at best.

Infants in one locale, an isolated Indian village, were described as being passive, fearful, and quiet (Kagan & Klein, 1973, pp. 949–50). Infants in other Spanish-speaking villages were shown sequences of events and the infants' fixation times, vocalizations, etc. to the events were recorded. American infants, tested previously, were said to have looked longer at the events than did the Guatemalan infants, and the latter were interpreted as being retarded in their cognitive development (Kagan & Klein, 1973, p. 951). Since the Spanish-speaking infants tested seemed more mature than those in the Indian village who were not tested, the retardation of the latter was regarded as being more severe (Kagan & Klein, 1973, p. 951). But in order for these findings to be evidence of retarded development, the conditions of testing would have to be similar for the Americans and for the Guatemalans. Also, before extending downward the interpretation of retardation to infants other than those tested, it seems desirable to give those infants an opportunity to perform the task. In addition, the cognitive skills required by the tasks need specification. When other tests were used with infants in the same or similar villages, the performance of Guatemalans was said to be similar to that of Americans (Sellers, Klein, Kagan, & Minton, 1972).

As part of the same investigation, tasks requiring identification, recognition, or recall of objects or drawings were given to groups of children between the ages of five and twelve in a variety of Guatemalan locations. One recognition memory task was also given to a group of American children (Kagan et al., 1973). Generally, the children's performance on the tasks improved with age. Performance differences among groups were much greater at younger ages than at older ages for some tasks and these findings were interpreted as reflecting the partial reversibility of the early retardation of cognitive development (Kagan & Klein, 1973, p. 957). However, ceiling effects are apparent in the scores of some groups of older children from some tasks (e.g., Kagan & Klein, 1973, p. 957). Furthermore, even scores on standardized tests of intellectual functioning in infancy are not related reliably to performance several years later (Bayley, 1970, pp. 1173–74). In the case of this investigation, infants were tested with one set of tasks and concurrently, groups of older children were tested with another set of tasks. The scores were interpreted as reflecting developmental changes, over time, when there was no information about whether performance on the two sets of tasks was related.

If the conclusion made from Bayley's findings is tenuous, it is nonetheless clear from the publicity surrounding her report that the issue of cultural relativity or universality of cognitive functioning is of much public interest (e.g., *New York Times*, December 1972; *Los Angeles Times*, February 1973; *Saturday Review of Education,* April 1973, *New York Times Magazine,* June 6, 1976). Perhaps this discussion is appropriately concluded with the comment that cross-cultural researchers must take some responsibility for communicating their findings accurately and with appropriate caution when the topic under investigation is a socially or politically sensitive one. If they do not, then whatever knowledge is obtained about relations between culture and cognition, and whatever conclusions can be reached about cultural influences on how people think and learn may well be ignored, distorted, or misapplied.

Note

1. This chapter is based partly on a review conducted while the author was a Fellow at the Center for Advanced Study in the Behavioral Sciences, Stanford, California, and held Special Fellowship no. 1F03HD54324 from the National Institute of Child Health and Human Development. The facilities of the Center and the skills of its staff are extraordinary; support from the Center in many forms is acknowledged with gratitude. In addition, Judith Allen and Marsha Unze contributed greatly to the preparation of this chapter which was supported also by Program Project Grant no. P01HD0502706 from the National Institute of Child Health and Human Development to the University of Minnesota.

References

ABIOLA, E. T. The nature of intellectual development in Nigerian children. *Teacher Education,* 1965, *6,* 37–58.

BARNES, R. H., MOORE, A. U., REID, I. M., & POND, W. G. Effect of food deprivation on behavioral patterns. In N. S. Scrimshaw & J. E. Gordon (Eds.), *Malnutrition, learning, and behavior.* Cambridge: MIT Press, 1968.

BAYLEY, N. Development of mental abilities. In P. Mussen (Ed.), *Carmichael's manual of child psychology,* Vol. 1. New York: Wiley, 1970.

BERLIN, B., & KAY, P. *Basic color terms: their universality and evolution.* Berkeley: University of California Press, 1969.

BERRY, J. W. Temne and Eskimo perceptual skills. *International Journal of Psychology,* 1966, *1,* 207–29.

———. Radical cultural relativism and the concept of intelligence. In J. Berry & P. Dasen (Eds.), *Culture and cognition: readings in cross-cultural psychology.* London: Methuen, 1974.

BIESHEUVEL, S. Psychological tests and their application to non-European peoples. In G. B. Jeffery (Ed.), *The yearbook of education.* London: Evans, 1949.

————. The study of African ability, Part I: The intellectual potentialities of Africans. *African Studies*, 1952, *11*, 45–57.

————. Objectives and methods of African psychological research. *Journal of Social Psychology*, 1958, *47*, 161–68.

————. Adaptability: its measurement and determinants. In L. J. Cronbach & P. J. D. Drenth (Eds.), *Mental tests and cultural adaptation*. The Hague: Mouton, 1972.

BIESHEUVEL, S., & LIDDICOAT, R. The effects of cultural factors on intelligence-test performance. *Journal of the National Institute of Personnel Research*, 1959, *8*, 3–14.

————. Reply to Dr. Langenhoven's comments on "The effects of cultural factors on intelligence test performance." *Journal of the National Institute of Personnel Research*, 1960, *8*, 153–55.

BRAZELTON, T. B. Implications of infant development among the Mayan Indians of Mexico. *Human Development*, 1972, *15*, 90–111.

BRAZELTON, T. B., ROBEY, J. S., & COLLIER, G. A. Infant development in the Zinacanteco Indians of southern Mexico. *Pediatrics*, 1969, *44*, 274–90.

BRISLIN, R. W., LONNER, W. J., & THORNDIKE, R. M. *Cross-cultural research methods.* New York: Wiley, 1973.

BROWN, R. W., & LENNEBERG, E. H. A study in language and cognition. *Journal of Abnormal and Social Psychology*, 1954, *49*, 454–62.

CAMPBELL, D. T. Distinguishing differences in perception from failures of communication in cross-cultural studies. In F. Northrop & H. Livingston (Eds.), *Cross-cultural understanding: epistemology in anthropology*. New York: Harper & Row, 1964.

CHAMPAKAN, S., SRIKANTIA, S. G., & GOPALAN, C. Kwashiorkor and mental development. *American Journal of Clinical Nutrition*, 1968, *21*, 844–52.

CIBOROWSKI, T., & COLE, M. Cultural differences in learning conceptual rules. *International Journal of Psychology*, 1971, *6*, 25–37.

————. A cross-cultural study of conjunctive and disjunctive concept learning. *Child Development*, 1972, *43*, 774–89.

————. A developmental and cross-cultural study of the influences of role structure and problem composition on the learning of conceptual classifications. *Journal of Experimental Child Psychology*, 1973, *15*, 193–215.

COLE, M. *Toward an experimental anthropology of thinking.* Paper presented at the joint meeting of the American Ethnological Society Council on Anthropology and Education, Montreal, April 1972.

COLE, M., & BRUNER, J. Cultural differences and inferences about psychological processes. *American Psychologist*, 1971, *26*, 867–76.

COLE, M., GAY, J., & GLICK, J. Some experimental studies of Kpelle quantitative behavior. *Psychonomic Monograph Supplements*, 1968, *2* (Whole No. 26), 173–90.

COLE, M., & SHARP, D. Linguistic structure and transposition. *Science*, 1969, *164*, 90–91.

————. *The cultural context of learning and thinking.* New York: Basic Books, 1971.

COLE, M., & SCRIBNER, S. *Culture and thought: a psychological introduction.* New York: Wiley, 1974.

COLLISON, G. O. Concept formation in a second language: a study of Ghanaian schoolchildren. *Harvard Educational Review*, 1974, *44*(3), 441–57.

COWLEY, J. J. Time, place, and nutrition: some observations from animal studies. In N. S. Scrimshaw & J. E. Gordon (Eds.), *Malnutrition, learning, and behavior.* Cambridge, Mass: MIT Press, 1968.

CRAVIOTO, J., & DELICARDIE, E. R. Mental performance in school age children. *American Journal of Diseases of Childhood,* 1970, *120,* 404–10.

CRAVIOTO, J., & BIRCH, H. G. Nutrition, growth and neurointegrative development: an experimental and ecologic study. *Pediatrics,* 1966, *38,* 319–72.

CRAVIOTO, J., & ROBLES, B. Evolution of adaptive and motor behavior during rehabilitation from Kwashiorkor. *American Journal of Orthopsychiatry,* 1965, *35,* 49–64.

CRYNS, A. G. J. African intelligence: a critical survey of cross-cultural intelligence research in Africa south of the Sahara. *Journal of Social Psychology,* 1962, *57,* 283–301.

DASEN, P. R. Cross-cultural Piagetian research: a summary. *Journal of Cross-Cultural Psychology,* 1972a, *3,* 23–39.

———. The development of conservation in Aboriginal children. A replication study. *International Journal of Psychology,* 1972b, *7*(2), 75–85.

———. The influence of ecology, culture and European contact on cognitive development in Australian Aborigines. In J. Berry & P. Dasen (Eds.), *Culture and cognition: readings in cross-cultural psychology.* London: Methuen, 1974.

———. Concrete operational development in three cultures. *Journal of Cross-Cultural Psychology,* 1975, *6*(2), 156–72.

DAVID, K. H. Cross-cultural uses of the Porteus Maze. *Journal of Social Psychology,* 1974, *92,* 11–18.

DAWSON, J. L. M. Cultural and physiological influences upon spatial-perceptual processes in West Africa. *International Journal of Psychology,* 1967, *2,* 115–28 (Part I); 171–85 (Part II).

DELACEY, P. R. A relationship between classificatory ability and verbal intelligence. *International Journal of Psychology,* 1972, *7*(4), 243–46.

DE LEMOS, M. M. The development of conservation in Aboriginal children. *International Journal of Psychology,* 1969, *4,* 255–69.

———. The development of spatial concepts in Zulu children. In J. Berry & P. Dasen (Eds.), *Culture and cognition: readings in cross-cultural psychology.* London: Methuen, 1974.

DERĘGOWSKI, J. B. Difficulties in pictorial depth perception in Africa. *British Journal of Psychology,* 1968, *59,* 195–204.

———. Effect of cultural value of time upon recall. *British Journal of Social and Clinical Psychology,* 1970, *9,* 37–41.

———. Orientation and perception of pictorial depth. *International Journal of Psychology,* 1971, *6,* 111–14.

———. Pictorial perception and culture. *Scientific American,* 1972a (November), *227,* 82–88.

———. The role of symmetry in pattern reproduction by Zambian children. *Journal of Cross-Cultural Psychology,* 1972b, *3,* 303–07.

———, & SERPELL, R. Performance on a sorting task. A cross-cultural experiment. *International Journal of Psychology,* 1971, *6,* 273–81

EVANS, J. L., & SEGALL, M. H. Learning to classify by color and by function: a study of concept discovery by Ganda children. *Journal of Social Psychology*, 1969, *77*, 35-53.

FAHRMEIER, E. D. The effect of school attendance on intellectual development in northern Nigeria. *Child Development*, 1975, *46*, 281-85.

FAVERGE, J. M., & FALMAGNE, J. C. On the interpretation of data in intercultural psychology. A paper written in recognition of the work done in this field by Dr. S. Biesheuvel. *Psychologia Africana*, 1962, *9*, 22-36.

FELDMAN, C. F. *The development of adaptive intelligence.* San Francisco: Jossey-Bass, 1974.

FELDMAN, C. F., & HASS, W. A. Controls, conceptualization, and the interrelation between experimental and correlational research. *American Psychologist*, 1970, *25*, 633-35.

FURBY, L. A theoretical analysis of cross-cultural research in cognitive development: Piaget's conservation task. *Journal of Cross-Cultural Psychology*, 1971, *2*, 241-55.

GLADWIN, T. *East is a big bird.* Cambridge, Mass.: Harvard University Press, 1970.

GOLDBERG, S. Infant care and growth in urban Zambia. *Human Development*, 1972, *15*, 77-89.

GOLDSCHMID, M. L., BENTLER, P. M., DEBUS, R. L., RAWLINSON, R., KOHNSTAMM, D., MODGIL, S., NICHOLLS, J. G., REYKOWSKI, J., STRUPCZEWSKA, B., & WARREN, N. A cross-cultural investigation of conservation. *Journal of Cross-Cultural Psychology*, 1973, *4*, 75-88.

GOODNOW, J. A test of milieu effects with some of Piaget's tasks. *Psychological Monographs: General and Applied*, 1962, *76* (36, Whole No. 555).

————. Problems in research on culture and thought. In D. Elkind & J. Flavell (Eds.), *Studies in cognitive development: essays in honor of Jean Piaget.* New York: Oxford University Press, 1969.

————. Cultural variations in cognitive skills. In J. Hellmuth (Ed.), *Cognitive studies.* New York: Brunner/Mazel, 1970.

GOODNOW, J., & BETHON, G. Piaget's tasks: the effects of schooling and intelligence. *Child Development*, 1966, *37*, 573-82.

GREENFIELD, P. M. On culture and conservation. In J. Bruner, R. Olver, & P. Greenfield (Eds.), *Studies in cognitive growth.* New York: Wiley, 1966.

————. Comparing dimensional categorization in natural and artificial contexts: a developmental study among the Zinacantecos of Mexico. *Journal of Social Psychology*, 1974, *93*, 157-71.

GREENFIELD, P. M., REICH, L. C., & OLVER, R. R. On culture and equivalence: II. In J. Bruner, R. Olver, & P. Greenfield (Eds.), *Studies in cognitive growth.* New York: Wiley, 1966.

GUTHRIE, G. M. Unexpected correlations and the cross-cultural method. *Journal of Cross-Cultural Psychology*, 1971, *2*, 315-23.

HAWARD, L. C. R., & ROLAND, W. A. Some inter-cultural differences on the Draw-a-Man test: Goodenough scores. *Man*, 1954, *54*, 86-88.

————. Some inter-cultural differences on the Draw-a-Man test: Part II, Machover scores. *Man*, 1955a, *55*, 27-29.

————. Some inter-cultural differences on the Draw-a-Man test: Part III, Conclusions. *Man*, 1955b, *55*, 40-42.

HEIDER, E. R. "Focal" color areas and the development of color names. *Developmental Psychology*, 1971, 4, 447–55.

———. Universals in naming and memory. *Journal of Experimental Psychology*, 1972, 93, 10–20.

HEIDER, E. R., & OLIVIER, D. C. The structure of the color space in naming and memory for two languages. *Cognitive Psychology*, 1972, 3, 337–54.

HERON, A., & DOWEL, W. Weight conservation and matrix-solving ability in Paupuan children. *Journal of Cross-Cultural Psychology*, 1973, 4, 207–19.

HERON, A., & SIMONSSON, M. Weight conservation in Zambian children. A nonverbal approach. *International Journal of Psychology*, 1969, 4, 281–92.

HUDSON, W., ROBERTS, A. O. H., VAN HEERDEN, C. D., & MBAU, G. G. The usefulness of performance tests for the selection and classification of Bantu industrial workers. *Psychologia Africana*, 1962, 9, 189–203.

IRWIN, M. H., & MCLAUGHLIN, D. H. Ability and preference in category sorting by Mano school children and adults. *Journal of Social Psychology*, 1970, 82, 15–24.

IRWIN, M. H., SCHAFER, G. N., & FEIDEN, C. P. Emic and unfamiliar category sorting of Mano farmers and U. S. undergraduates. *Journal of Cross-Cultural Psychology*, 1974, 5(4), 407–23.

JAHODA, G. Assessment of abstract behavior in a non-Western culture. *Journal of Abnormal and Social Psychology*, 1956, 53, 237–43.

———. A cross-cultural perspective in psychology. *The Advancement of Science*, 1970, 27, 57–70.

KAGAN, J. Cross-cultural perspectives on early development. Paper presented at the Meeting of the American Association for the Advancement of Science, Washington, D. C., 1972.

———. A conversation with Jerome Kagan. *Saturday Review of Education*, 1973, 1(3), 41–43.

KAGAN, J., & KLEIN, R. E. Cross-cultural perspectives on early development. *American Psychologist*, 1973, 28, 947–61.

KAGAN, J., HAITH, M. M., & MORRISON, F. J. Memory and meaning in two cultures. *Child Development*, 1973, 44, 221–23.

KELLAGHAN, T. Abstraction and categorization in African children. *International Journal of Psychology*, 1968, 3, 115–20.

KLEIN, R. E., FREEMAN, H. E., KAGAN, J., YARBROUGH, C., & HABICHT, J. P. Is big smart? The relation of growth to cognition. *Journal of Health and Social Behavior*, 1972, 13, 219–25.

KLEIN, R. E., HABICHT, J. P., & YARBROUGH, C. Effects of protein-calorie malnutrition on mental development. *Advances in Pediatrics*, 1971, 18, 75–91.

LANDAUER, T. K., & WHITING, J. W. M. Infantile stimulation and adult stature of human males. *American Anthropologist*, 1964, 66, 1007–28.

LANGENHOVEN, H. P. A note on "The effects of cultural factors on intelligence test performance" by S. Biesheuvel and R. Liddicoat. *Journal of the National Institute of Personnel Research*, 1960, 8, 151–52.

LANTZ, D., & STEFFLRE, V. Language and cognition revisited. *Journal of Abnormal and Social Psychology*, 1964, 69, 472–81.

LAOSA, L. M., SWARTZ, J. D., & DIAZ-GUERRERO, R. Perceptual-cognitive and personality development of Mexican and Anglo-American children as measured by human figure drawings. *Developmental Psychology*, 1974, 10(1), 131–39.

LENNEBERG, E. H., & ROBERTS, J. The language of experience: a study in methodology, Memoir 13. *International Journal of American Linguistics*, 1956, 22 (Whole No.).

LESTER, B. M., & KLEIN, R. E. The effect of stimulus familiarity on the conservation performance of rural Guatemalan children. *Journal of Social Psychology*, 1973, 90, 197–205.

LeVINE, R. A. Cross-cultural study in child psychology. In P. Mussen (Ed.), *Carmichael's manual of child psychology*, Vol. II. New York: Wiley, 1970.

LEVITAS, G. Second start. *New York Times Magazine*, June 6, 1976, 42–48.

LITTLEJOHN, J. Temne space. *Anthropological Quarterly*, 1963, 36, 1–17.

LLOYD, B. B. The intellectual development of Yoruba children: A reexamination. *Journal of Cross-Cultural Psychology*, 1971, 2, 29–38.

————. *Perception and cognition: a cross-cultural perspective*. Middlesex, England: Penguin, 1972.

MacARTHUR, R. S. Sex differences in field-dependence for the Eskimo. Replication of Berry's findings. *International Journal of Psychology*, 1967, 2, 139–40.

MACCOBY, M., & MODIANO, N. On culture and equivalence: I. In J. Bruner, R. Olver, & P. Greenfield (Eds.), *Studies in cognitive growth*. New York: Wiley, 1966.

McFIE, J. The effect of education on African performance on a group of intellectual tests. *British Journal of Educational Psychology*, 1961, 31, 232–40.

MEACHAM, J. A. Patterns of memory abilities in two cultures. *Developmental Psychology*, 1975, 11(1), 50–53.

MERCADO, S. J., GUERRERO, R. D., & GARDNER, R. W. Cognitive control in children of Mexico and the United States. *Journal of Social Psychology*, 1963, 59, 199–208.

MUNDY-CASTLE, A. C. An experimental study of prediction among Ghanaian children. *Journal of Social Psychology*, 1967, 73, 161–68.

MUNROE, R. L., & MUNROE, R. H. Effect of environmental experience on spatial ability in an East African society. *Journal of Social Psychology*, 1971, 83, 15–22.

NAROLL, R. Cross-cultural sampling. In R. Naroll & R. Cohen (Eds.), *A handbook of method in cultural anthropology*. New York: Columbia University Press, 1973.

NERLOVE, S. B., MUNROE, R. H., & MUNROE, R. L. Effect of environmental experience on spatial ability: a replication. *Journal of Social Psychology*, 1971, 84, 3–10.

NISSEN, H. W., MACHOVER, S., & KINDER, F. F. A study of performance tests given to a group of native African Negro children. *British Journal of Psychology*, 1935, 25, 308–55.

OHUCHE, R. O. Piaget and the Mende of Sierra Leone. *The Journal of Experimental Education*, 1971, 39, 75–77.

OKONJI, M. O. The differential effects of rural and urban upbringing on the development of cognitive styles. *International Journal of Psychology*, 1969, 4, 293–305.

————. A cross-cultural study of the effects of familiarity on classificatory behaviour. *Journal of Cross-Cultural Psychology*, 1971, 2, 39–49.

————. The development of logical thinking in preschool Zambian children: classification. *The Journal of Genetic Psychology*, 1974, 125, 247–55.

OWOC, P. J. On culture and conservation once again. *International Journal of Psychology*, 1973, 8, 249–54.

PELUFFO, N. Culture and cognitive problems. *International Journal of Psychology*, 1967, 2, 187–98.

PICK, A. D., & PICK, H. L., Jr. Culture and perception. In E. C. Carterette & M. P. Friedman (Eds.), *Handbook of perception*. New York: Academic Press, in press.

PICK, H. L., Jr., & PICK, A. D. Sensory and perceptual development. In P. Mussen (Ed.), *Carmichael's manual of child psychology*. New York: Wiley, 1970.

PORTEUS, S. D., & GREGOR, A. J. Studies in intercultural testing. *Perceptual and Motor Skills*, 1963, 16, 705–24.

PRICE-WILLIAMS, D. R. A study concerning concepts of conservation of quantities among primitive children. *Acta Psychologica*, 1961, 18, 297–305.

———. Abstract and concrete modes of classification in a primitive society. *British Journal of Educational Psychology*, 1962, 32, 50–61.

PRICE-WILLIAMS, D. R., GORDON, W., & RAMIREZ, M. Skill and conservation: a study of pottery-making children. *Developmental Psychology*, 1969, 1, 769.

RAY, V. F. Techniques and problems in the study of human color perception. *Southwestern Journal of Anthropology*, 1952, 8, 251–59.

———. Human color perception and behavioral responses. *Transactions of the New York Academy of Sciences*, 1953, 15 (Serial II), 98–104.

RICHARDSON, S. A. The influence of social-environmental and nutritional factors on mental ability. In N. S. Scrimshaw & J. E. Gordon (Eds.), *Malnutrition, learning, and behavior*. Cambridge, Mass.: MIT Press, 1968.

ROSCH, E. Universals and cultural specifics in human categorization. In R. W. Brislin, S. Bochner, & W. J. Lonner (Eds.), *Cross-cultural perspectives on learning*. Beverly Hills: Sage/Halsted, 1975.

SCHMIDT, W. H. O., & NZIMANDE, A. Cultural differences in color/form preference and in classificatory behavior. *Human Development*, 1970, 13, 140–48.

SCHWITZGEBEL, R. The performance of Dutch and Zulu adults on selected perceptual tasks. *Journal of Social Psychology*, 1962, 57, 73–77.

SCRIBNER, S. Developmental aspects of categorized recall in a West African society. *Cognitive Psychology*, 1974, 6, 475–94.

SCRIBNER, S., & COLE, M. Cognitive consequences of formal and informal education. *Science*, 1973, 182, 553–59.

SECHREST, L., FAY, T. L., & ZAIDI, H. S. M. Problems of translation in cross-cultural research. *Journal of Cross-Cultural Psychology*, 1972, 3, 41–56.

SEGALL, M. H., CAMPBELL, D. T., & HERSKOVITS, M. J. *The influence of culture on visual perception*. Indianapolis, Ind.: Bobbs-Merrill, 1966.

SELLERS, M. J., KLEIN, R. E., KAGAN, J., & MINTON, C. Developmental determinants of attention: a cross-cultural replication. *Developmental Psychology*, 1972, 6, 185.

SERPELL, R. Cultural differences in attentional preference for colour over form. *International Journal of Psychology*, 1969a, 4, 1–8.

———. The influence of language, education, and culture on attentional preference between colour and form. *International Journal of Psychology*, 1969b, 4, 183–94.

———. Discrimination of orientation by Zambian children. *Journal of Comparative and Physiological Psychology*, 1971a, 75, 312–16.

———. Preference for specific orientation of abstract shapes among Zambian children. *Journal of Cross-Cultural Psychology*, 1971b, 2, 225–39.

SHAPIRO, M. B. The rotation of drawings by illiterate Africans. *Journal of Social Psychology*, 1960, *52*, 17–30.

SIANN, G. Measuring field dependence in Zambia: a cross-cultural study. *International Journal of Psychology*, 1972, *7*, 87–96.

SMITH, M. W. Alfred Binet's remarkable questions: a cross-national and cross-temporal analysis of the cultural biases built into the Stanford-Binet intelligence scale and other Binet tests. *Genetic Psychology Monographs*, 1974, *89*, 307–34.

STEFFLRE, V., VALES, V. C., & MORLEY, L. Language and cognition in Yucatan: a cross-cultural replication. *Journal of Personality and Social Psychology*, 1966, *4*, 112–15.

SUCHMAN, R. G. Cultural differences in children's color and form preferences. *Journal of Social Psychology*, 1966, *70*, 3–10.

SUCHMAN, R. G., & TRABASSO, T. Color and form preference in young children. *Journal of Experimental Child Psychology*, 1966, *3*, 177–87.

TEKANE, I. Symmetrical pattern completions by illiterate and literate Bantu. *Psychologia Africana*, 1963, *10*, 63–68.

TRIANDIS, H. C., MALPASS, R. S., & DAVIDSON, A. R. Psychology and culture. *Annual Review of Psychology*, 1973, *24*, 355–78.

TRONICK, E., KOSLOWSKI, B., & BRAZELTON, T. B. Neonatal behavior among urban Zambians and Americans. Paper presented at the Biennial meeting of the Society for Research in Child Development, Minneapolis, 1971.

VERNON, P. E. Administration of group intelligence tests to East African pupils. *British Journal of Educational Psychology*, 1967, *37*(Part 3), 282–91.

VETTA, A. Conservation in Aboriginal children and "genetic hypothesis." *International Journal of Psychology*, 1972, *7*(4), 247–56.

WAGNER, D. A. The development of short-term and incidental memory: a cross-cultural study. *Child Development*, 1974, *45*, 389–96.

WHITING, J. W. M. Socialization process and personality. In F. L. K. Hsu (Ed.), *Psychological anthropology*. Homewood, Ill.: Dorsey, 1961.

WHITING, J. W. M., & CHILD, I. L. *Child training and personality: a cross-cultural study*. New Haven: Yale University Press, 1953.

WIEMAN, R. J., & GUTHRIE, G. M. The effects of age and cultural familiarity on children's categorization responses. *Journal of Social Psychology*, 1972, *86*, 299–308.

WITKIN, H. A. A cognitive-style approach to cross-cultural research. *International Journal of Psychology*, 1967, *2*, 233–50.

WITKIN, H. A., & BERRY, J. W. Psychological differentiation in cross-cultural perspective. *Journal of Cross-Cultural Psychology*, 1975, *6*, 4–87.

WITKIN, H. A., DYK, R. B., FATERSON, H. F., GOODENOUGH, D. R., & KARP, S. A. *Psychological differentiation*. New York: Wiley, 1962.

WITKIN, H. A., LEWIS, H. B., HERTZMAN, M., MACHOVER, K., MEISSNER, P. B., & WAPNER, S. *Personality through perception*. New York: Harper & Row, 1954.

WITKOP, C. J., BALDIZON, G. C., CASTRO, O. R. P., & UMANA, R. Auditory memory span and oral stereognosis in children recovered from Kwashiorkor. In J. F. Bosma (Ed.), *Second symposium on oral sensation and perception*. Springfield, Ill.: C. C. Thomas, 1970.

WOBER, M. Adapting Witkin's field independence theory to accommodate new information from Africa. *British Journal of Psychology*, 1967, *58*, 29–38.

————. Culture and the concept of intelligence: a case in Uganda. *Journal of Cross-Cultural Psychology*, 1972, *3*, 327–28.

ZA'ROUR, G. I. The conservation of number and liquid by Lebanese school children in Beirut. *Journal of Cross-Cultural Psychology*, 1971, *2*, 165–72.

4

Anthropological Approaches to Cognition and Their Relevance to Psychology[1]

Douglass R. Price-Williams

Contents

Abstract

The chapter opens with a discussion of the differing attitudes towards cognition held by the disciplines of anthropology and psychology. There is a tendency in anthropology to treat cognition more as a matter of product than process, and to be more group and institutionally oriented than individually oriented. A substantial segment of what is called cognitive anthropology is concerned with indigenous forms of classification. The techniques and approaches of ethnoscience are reviewed. Debates within anthropology concerning the implications of ethnoscience are discussed. Examples of the approach are given from diverse cultures.

The next section deals with modes of thought, a name given to that spectrum of anthropological studies that is involved with belief systems and the kind of thinking associated with them. A brief history is provided, outlining early ideas about the primitive mind through contemporary examples that have focussed on ideas in religion and magic. Levi-Strauss's ideas that focus on the emphasis on concrete thought that traditional peoples entertain are provided.

The following section is concerned with anthropological perspectives on intelligence and their relation to psychological notions of intelligence. In particular dichotomies such as analytic versus relational thinking and propositional versus appositional thinking, are commented upon.

The final section discusses the question of theory within anthropology, inasmuch as it touches on cognition. The questions of context and institutionalization of thought are raised and discussed. Two anthropological notions are selected for analysis: Bateson's concept of *eidos* and Wallace's idea of mazeway. The psychological implications of these concepts are discussed.

Introduction

A preliminary difficulty in discussing anthropological perspectives on cognition is that the very term is interpreted differently by anthropologists and psychologists. A convenient starting point is a consideration of the problem undertaken by Colby and Cole (1973). After remarking that "scholars in the two fields are scarcely concerned with the same topics, even though both groups profess to study cultural differences in modes of thinking" (p. 63), Colby and Cole go on to make the distinction between what people think and how they think, between the content of cognitive activity and processes. Another way of phrasing this distinction is to distinguish cognitive *product* from cognitive *process*. Thus, anthropologists have been more concerned with various cultural differences in cognitive products: belief systems, values, classifications. They have been less concerned with questions of how classifications are formed, what kind of strategies are utilized in forming concepts, what rules are followed for the solution of problems, and similar topics that are discussed in Pick's chapter in this volume. As a rule anthropologists have accepted the doctrine of psychic unity to settle for the view that cognitive processes are the same all over the world; it is only the product or content that is different. As Colby and Cole report (1973, p. 63) an anthropologist responded to a cross-cultural psychological study on thinking by stating that: "The reasoning and thinking processes of different people in different cultures don't differ . . . just their values, beliefs, and ways of classifying things differ." The distinction between cognitive product and process is reflected in the methods adopted to determine each. Cognitive process is generally determined by experiment. Cognitive products are discovered through observation, question and answer techniques, and more sophisticated linguistic methods.

In addition to the matter of interpretation, there is another decided difference between the perspectives of psychology and anthropology. Cognitive psychologists tend to work on the basis of a theory, and their findings have reference to a general theory of cognition. Cognitive anthropologists have no theory of mind, no general theory of cognition. Their concern (Tyler, 1969) is the discovery of how different peoples organize their cultures. Their emphasis, unlike other types of anthropologists, is not on the material phenomena or social organization units in themselves, but how they are organized in the minds of men. It is the search for these principles of mental organization that provides the rationalization for the use of the word *cognitive*. The entire enterprise is nevertheless one of translation: how to interpret in a systematic manner the organizational behavior of the informant.

While the main thrust of cognitive anthropology is of this nature, it can also be said that there are occasional side attempts at what might be called a search for cognitive styles. For psychologists this latter term is restricted to the borderland of research between personality and cognition, as evidenced by the works of people like Witkin, Lewis, Hertzman, Machover, Meissner, and Wapner (1954) and Gardner, Holzman, Klein, Linton, & Spence (1959). In an anthropological journal Cohen (1969) introduced the term *conceptual style* that carries much the same meaning as the psychological *cognitive style*; it might be wiser for expositional purposes to adhere to this terminology when discussing anthropological forays into the subject. The further term *Modes of Thought*, an actual title of a book concerned with basic differences in thinking between Western and non-Western societies (Horton and Finnegan 1973), is aimed at the same target. A conceptual style, as interpreted by anthropologists, is not identical with what was previously labelled as cognitive product; on the other hand it is not what a psychologist would understand as cognitive process. It reflects more a manner of organizing things, of putting things in a certain way, of looking at the world in a distinct fashion. This chapter will describe various attempts by anthropologists to delineate conceptual styles.

A further preliminary clarification must be made before entering into substantive material. There has always been a tendency in anthropology to adopt a perspective on cognition from a group position and not an individual position. Early incursions into thinking were interested in the Durkheimian notion of "collective representations." What was at stake were ideas common to all members of a social group. Later considerations about cognition in the era of ethnoscience still maintain this attitude.

It would be a mistake, though, to characterize anthropology's interest in cognition as a uniform phenomenon. There have always been a number of independent thinkers in the discipline that have struck out lines of their own. A description of anthropological perspectives on cognition has of necessity, then, to be fragmented. There is no theory of cognition; there is no common standpoint concerning cognition; it is difficult even to find a definition of the term. The subject will have to be followed in a fractionated manner from the psychologists' vantage point, looking at how a sister discipline deals with a common interest, and attempting to assess what implications this treatment has for psychologists.

Classification and Ethnoscience

Since the publication of Durkheim and Mauss's study on indigenous classification (1903), how various people categorize the world about them has been a target of anthropological inquiry. During the middle 1950s, a systematic approach was used by a group of anthropologists who had the adjective *cognitive* as a prefix. Basically their approach focussed on some particular domain, such as botany, to find out how a specific group of people with a common language catalog the world of plants and flowers. The native terminology is the starting point. A notation is invented to translate the native terminology into terms that reveal the basic structure. One technique for doing this is that of componential analysis.

Componential analysis is a method through which a system of rules underlying a taxonomy is discovered. The starting point is a collection of terms concerning a single domain—kinship, plants, color, or illness. Then the procedure is to determine how all of the terms in the domain are related to one another or contrasted with one another. The resulting schema is a model for understanding how a particular group employs classification procedures for any given area of discourse. Triandis has given a concise description of the flow of operations, with kinship as the domain:

> Briefly, the following steps are required. First it is necessary to collect a large sample of expressions that belong to a particular universe of meaning, e.g. kinship terms. Second, it is necessary to translate the kinship terms into a basic notation which consists of simple elements such as Fa (Father), Mo (Mother), Br (Brother). Now a particular relative may be described in terms of these basic components, e.g. he is the Fa Mo Br (a great uncle). Third it is possible to examine the way in which the lexical field is structured. For instance, a kinship term field may employ as basic structural elements (a) the seniority of the generation of the relative, (b) the sex of the relative, (c) the sex of the relative in relation to ego's sex, and (d) the degree of affinal removal. (Triandis, 1964, p. 8)

In following through this method with particular examples, a controversy that has dogged the passage of ethnoscience since its start must be raised;

namely, whether the analysis of a native language in a particular domain is simply a matter of detecting a terminological usage, or whether the analysis has some kind of psychological validity, discovering how peoples' "minds" work. The distinction has been labelled *formal linguistic analysis versus psychological reality*. Some anthropologists have adopted the former position, others the latter.

Tyler (1969) has covered the main schools in introductions to sections three and four of his book. The two approaches will be examined using kinship as an example, as this domain has become the *locus classicus* of the debate. The first is the position of formal analysis, by a person who has explicitly eschewed the psychological reality thesis (Burling, 1964). The second is by a person who has adopted to some extent the psychological reality position. The target of enquiry is the American kinship system in both cases. The analyses are identical to that which would be afforded to any other kinship system outside our own culture. The first example is that of Burling (1970). He adopts as his starting point a complaint that previous work on the subject has been too rigid, not allowing for alternative or variable usages. Moreover, he focusses on children as exemplars of terminological usage that has not been wholly mastered, pointing out the obvious inference that adult terminological usage is the end product of an ontogenetic process, which might be more readily understood if seen as that. For the psychological student, who is more accustomed to studies of this nature involving a sample of specific children, upon whom experiments or questions are imposed by an experimenter, it has to be made clear that a typical anthropological study is styled in the abstract and generalized. With Burling's study for example, the method is simply that of the participant observer, who is generalizing his inferences from observations of children at large—in this case presumably those in his own community. The target of Burling's study is the principles underlying American kinship terminology. He sees it developmentally, as a sequence of principles that really constitute a learning paradigm. The core principles, first in the sequence, are the principles of sex and age. These principles are reflected in the use of the four terms: mother, father, brother, and sister. The author then points out a principle that Piaget has made so much of in his exposition of the child's grasp of family relationship (Piaget, 1928), namely that of relational perspective. A kinship term is used with reference to some understood ego. A child has to understand that different terms can be used to refer to the same person according to the relationship with that person. To put it simply, a child's father's wife. Burling does not attach chronological ages to the grasp of this distinction: we know from the work of Piaget and others that it is about the age of seven that this principle of relativity is attained, as far as Euroamerican culture is concerned. Continuing his sequence, Burling distinguishes the principles of consanguinity (i.e., kinship through a physical relationship) and generation as the next to be attained. Then follow more elaborate principles that the child has to attain on his or her way to adult terminology. One of these is what Burling calls *cover terms*. These are terms like parent, child, spouse, and sibling that override the distinctions of sex, and are more "abstract" inasmuch as they apply to more than one type of individual. The last two principles apply to more complicated cases: secondary kinsmen, and relationships like in-laws or half-brothers and half-sisters, or again step and foster relationships. The details are not important here.

The point is that the sequence is put forward as a terminological series in which the immediate nuclear family terms act as the core relationships upon which the rest is built. It needs to be repeated that Burling's presentation is concerned with formal analysis. He does not adduce psychological principles, at least explicitly or overtly. Burling considers this particular article an advance on more traditional attempts at finding components of language and/or thought in anthropological approaches, in which only the finished adult paradigm is considered.

Next, an example of *psychological reality* is considered. A necessary preface to this example is provided by one of Tyler's Introductions in his *Cognitive Anthropology* (Introduction to Part 4, 1969, p. 343):

> Once the anthropologist has completed a formal analysis and judged it complete, consistent and parsimonious, what evidence does he have that his result corresponds to the way a native speaker would isolate and arrange the features of this same semantic domain? Is this a relevant question? Anthropologists are sharply divided on these points. Some assert a direct correspondence between the anthropologists' and native speakers' models. Others argue that there may be a correspondence between the two, but that it must be demonstrated by operations external to the methods of formal analysis. Still others maintain that the question is simply irrelevant.

It is to the point that "it must be demonstrated by methods external to the methods of formal analysis" that there emerges an approximation to psychological experimentation. Wallace (1965; reprinted in Tyler 1969, p. 397) makes the crucial point that: "The claim that a componential analysis represents a native speaker's cognitive world is now often avoided . . . One reason for this shyness has been, I think, the traditional lack of interest in testing the validity of hypotheses by experimental research methods."

An example of psychological reality is found in an article on American-English kin terms by Sanday (1971). In a previous article Sanday had distinguished between two methods—that of componential analysis and that of concepts deriving from the information-processing approach to human thinking. Sanday thinks that the advantage of each method is related to distinct goals, which can be labelled cross-cultural versus intracultural. Where there is to be comparison *between* cultures the formal analytic approach is seen as desirable, inasmuch as it can abstract relatively culture-free dimensions. However, when the goal is that of variation *within* culture, where individual differences would be emphasized, then the information-processing approach has more advantages. It is the latter method that Sanday considers to be appropriate in establishing the psychological reality of terminology. Now, in formal componential analysis, the essence of the technique is to extract from some given lexical domain, specific semantic dimensions that then are posited as a paradigm or model (Sanday, 1971, p. 556). The formal analysis school simply leaves the matter at that. For those "psychological realists" like Wallace and Sanday herself, there is felt a need to go beyond this level. In Sanday's case, the need expresses itself in hypothesizing psychological terms that are affiliated to the linguistic terms—indeed are recognized as equivalent, and then testing out the model through experiment. As she phrases it:

> . . . the equivalent of semantic dimension is cognitive process and the equivalent of the componential model is cognitive structure. Cognitive process refers to the processes by which kinship terms are interrelated and generated from memory; cognitive structure refers to the format by which terms are stored in memory. The question to be investigated is the empirical equivalence of the componential paradigm and cognitive structure on the one hand, and of semantic dimension and cognitive process on the other (Sanday 1971, p. 556).

It might be noted that this distinction of cognitive process versus structure is similar to the cognitive process versus product that was adopted earlier in this chapter. Sanday's approach requires closer inspection to see how an anthropologist arrives at much the same conclusion.

The empirical part of Sanday's analysis consists first of asking a respondent to free recall "all the words for kinds of relatives and family members you can think of, just list the words as if you were giving them to yourself, not to somebody else" (p. 557). In addition respondents were asked to name all the relatives living in their household and in their neighborhood. The resulting list is then analyzed for *cognitive process* and for *cognitive structure*, as defined above by Sanday. Both terms are identified by a set of *decision rules*, outlined in full by Sanday in an appendix to the article (Sanday, 1971, p. 568–69). While it would be too lengthy here to itemize all these rules, it nevertheless is necessary to indicate the general nature of each group. The decision rules that identify cognitive process (which is defined as being the way in which kinship rules are interrelated and generated from memory) are characterized by principles of relation. Thus one decision rule is labelled a lineal path, in which terms or pairs of terms from two generations are contiguous, and where the terms are not isolated family clusters: for example the pairs of terms: mother/father, son/daughter. Another decision rule, the sex rule, is identified by that situation where contiguous terms are identical except for differences in sex. Whereas the main principle underlying cognitive process is that of *relations between* terms, the principle underlying the classification of cognitive structure is that of *frequency* of terms. The latter decision rule is related to the decision rules of cognitive process, by virtue of the fact that the cognitive structure decision rules are computed from a ratio derived from the number of terms taken from the lineal path to the number of terms taken from the collateral path. In essence, this particular approach to the inference of psychological reality consists of an attempt to coordinate semantic dimensions (that is, the purely terminological) with inferred connections taken from informants' memory banks. Sanday concluded from the results of this experiment that there is an overlap between the concepts of semantic dimension and cognitive process (p. 558), and pointed out that contiguous terms or pairs of terms were found to be connected by semanticlike dimensions. She pointed out that this agrees with the statement by Romney and D'Andrade (1964, p. 168) that people do respond to kinship terms as if each term contained a bundle of semantic dimensions (sememes).

These two studies by Burling and by Sanday have been quoted in detail in order to give a contrasting picture, both in terms of substance and of method, of the way in which anthropologists tackle the problem of cognition. In this case it is the same domain: kinship. The orientation of this chapter is to present the differing concepts of cognition as they are treated by anthropology and psychology. Thus certain salient points that are habitually treated by the anthropologist but that may be novel or even overlooked by the psychologist must be identified. The first point is anthropologists' heavy reliance on linguistic foundations. Cognition has come to anthropology through the medium of linguistic theory and linguistic terminology. This gives rise to a set of problems that psychologists, on the whole, are not concerned with, except for that group dealing with psycholinguistics. The second point is that anthropologists are at variance over the subject matter of cognition. For those anthropologists like Sanday, who feel the need to promote psychological meaning to their studies, there arises the necessity to experiment, to gather information from a sample of individuals, to make inferences about psychological functions. In such a case, the only difference from that of the psychologist proper is that while a psychologist would refer his observations to theoretical frameworks, such as Piaget or Bruner or Vygotsky, the framework of the anthropologist is that of linguistic theories. This still presents a challenge for anthropology. In a recent historical account of the subject, the necessity to conjoin language and thought can be picked up in a statement of Colby that "the ultimate goal is the understanding of the evaluations, emotions, and beliefs that lie behind word usage" (Colby 1966, p. 3). On the other hand, some anthropologists have criticized the entire venture.

For example Harris in his historical account *The Rise of Anthropological Theory* (1968, pp. 582–83) has this trenchant criticism:

> The fundamental error of the new ethnography is that it is based upon a patently false analogy between vernacular code on the levels of phonemes, morpheme and syntax on the one hand, and on the other, the higher-order codes which are in some way related to the semantics of everyday speech behavior and the historical unfolding of nonverbal behavior-stream events.

It is not the purpose of this chapter to cast judgment on the purposes and on the validity of cognitive anthropology within its own framework; rather it is to indicate its nature and approach, and especially to point out the differing schools within anthropology itself.

The concern with terminological usage, either recognized as a matter of formal analysis or interpreted psychologically, has intruded into other domains. There has been attention given to the classification of colors, to plants, and to illness, to name three domains (Conklin, 1955; Frake, 1961). The domain of colors, their recognition and labelling, has much in common with explicitly psychological studies (Rosch, 1973) and has generated substantial research (see Berlin & Kay, 1969). Exploration of illness and disease has given rise to more sophisticated methods than the ones outlined so far. For example, D'Andrade and his colleagues (D'Andrade, Quinn, Nerlove, & Romney 1972) employed the techniques of multidimensional scaling with reference to categories of disease in two language systems. Micklin and his collaborators (Micklin, Durbin, & Leon, 1974, pp. 143–56) explored the lexicon for madness in a town in Colombia, using the method of tree analysis. While even further sophistication in this matter may be anticipated, there is still the basic datum of how people express themselves.

The application of ethnoscientific techniques to domains such as kinship involve classificatory schemes that tax only slightly an individual's reasoning abilities. Domains that involve more dynamic situations can be illustrated with the following three studies about: (1) the adaptive strategies of urban nomads, (2) travelling on ice, and (3) planting practices. The first example from Spradley (1972), of a subculture within the United States has as its starting point two problems that continually crop up in the methodology of cross-cultural psychological work. The first, the emic-etic debate (see Volume 2 of this *Handbook*), is the problem of defining the cognitive world. The emic point of view states that this is done from the perspective of the inhabitants of that world, and not on premises imposed from without. In Spradley's study, the target is the population on skid row. Eschewing both the medical problem of alcoholism and the way in which the ordinary person, and indeed the urban specialist, tends to carve up the city, Spradley approached the ideal of providing a folk taxonomy from the point of view of the skid row inhabitants themselves. The

questions that are relevant are: What areas of the city are culturally significant to these people? What language terms do they use in describing
these areas? These questions lead naturally onto the second problem of
providing the units of description that are relevant. The particular en-
deavor goes beyond the mere listing of categories into strategies of adaptation that these urban nomads utilize. Following the prescription of
category systems as identifying aspects of the environment that provide
direction for instrumental activity and anticipating future events, Spradley
(1972, p. 241) evaluates that "an important avenue to understanding both
the *strategies of adaptation* and the *environment* to which urban groups are
adjusting is the study of category systems through ethnoscientific techniques." In order to contrast what would be an etic description of the
world in which these people live, against how they themselves categorize
it, Spradley will be followed precisely in identifying the relevant features.

The salient point here is the way in which Spradley's informants
identify themselves. They do this with a category system that an outsider
would not think of. Specifically they label their fellow members as: working stiffs, mission stiffs, bindle stiffs, airedales, rubber tramps, home guard
tramps, box car tramps, and dings. Some of this nomenclature is meaningful to the outsider and can be inferred from the labels: other terms are
not so obvious. Thus while home guard and box car tramps would be
fairly easily understood as representing those nomads who travel little
versus those that travel by freight car; "rubber tramps" are not easily understood, and are applicable to those that travel in their own car. As
Spradley pointed out, it is the superordinate concept of "homelessness"
that ties all these terms together. The airedale and bindle stiff tramps carry
their home with them in the form of a pack and bedroll. While rubber
tramps live in their cars, mission stiffs live at the mission; dings are professional beggars who have no home base. Using this method, a number of
further key terms are detected from the working language that provide
material that can be analyzed. For example, the term "flop" emerges as a
salient usage: making a flop, flopping out, kinds of flop. A folk taxonomy
of flop thus can be made, which is represented in full in Table 4–1, taken
from Spradley (Spradley, 1972, p. 250, Table 13–2). What is significant
in the area of cognition lies in the products of labelling and discrimination. Information is not gained directly about the process of discrimination, but at least the functional basis on which discriminations are made is
learned.

The second example comes from data collected among Slave Indians
living in northern Canada concerning their travel across frozen lakes and
rivers. The author notes (Basso, 1972) that the Slave have a highly involved taxonomy for ice. Ice is divided into three main subcategories:
solid ice, melting ice, and cracking ice, which are directly related to the
function of travelling over it; but there are further terms within each sub-

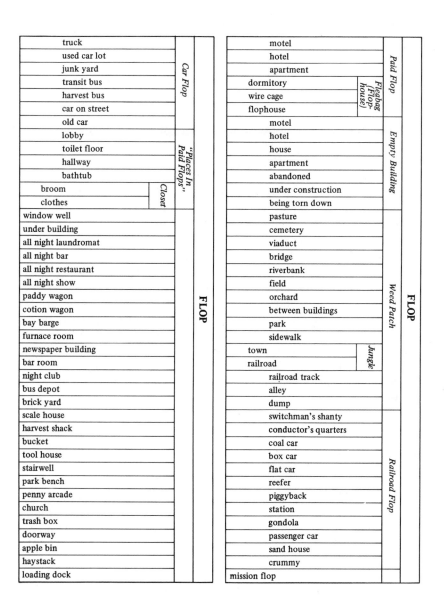

truck		*Car Flop*	
used car lot			
junk yard			
transit bus			
harvest bus			
car on street			
old car			
lobby		*"Places In Paid Flops"*	
toilet floor			
hallway			
bathtub			
broom	*Closet*		
clothes			
window well			
under building			
all night laundromat			
all night bar			
all night restaurant			
all night show			
paddy wagon			
cotion wagon			
bay barge		*FLOP*	
furnace room			
newspaper building			
bar room			
night club			
bus depot			
brick yard			
scale house			
harvest shack			
bucket			
tool house			
stairwell			
park bench			
penny arcade			
church			
trash box			
doorway			
apple bin			
haystack			
loading dock			

motel		*Fleabag (Flop-house)*	*Paid Flop*
hotel			
apartment			
dormitory			
wire cage			
flophouse			
motel			*Empty Building*
hotel			
house			
apartment			
abandoned			
under construction			
being torn down			
pasture			*Weed Patch*
cemetery			
viaduct			
bridge			
riverbank			
field			
orchard			
between buildings			
park			
sidewalk			
town	*Jungle*		*FLOP*
railroad			
railroad track			
alley			
dump			
switchman's shanty			*Railroad Flop*
conductor's quarters			
coal car			
box car			
flat car			
reefer			
piggyback			
station			
gondola			
passenger car			
sand house			
crummy			
mission flop			

Table 4-1   Taxonomic Description of "Flops" (Taken from Spradley, 1972)

category. Thus solid ice has eight further discriminations: "thin ice," "brittle ice," "hollow ice," and so on. This is akin to the well-known nomenclature among Eskimos of categorizing different shades of snow, and can be elicited directly from the language. However Basso goes one step further into the structure underlying the criteria for ice by using a modified version of the paired-comparison tests used by Berlin, Breedlove, and Raven (1968). It turns out that there are a whole group of morphological attributes of ice that contain the following criteria: state, subsurface water, surface water, texture, thickness, clarity, color, and states of the cracking process.

Morphological properties of ice constituted only one side of the coin. The other side constituted the situations wherein ice is encountered: that amounts to kinds of travel. There is a general term for travel; more specifically it is put in a participating sense, "travelling from place to place," pertinent to winter hunting and trapping. This generic term is subdivided into three kinds of "travelling from place to place": namely, "travelling on foot," "travelling by snowshoe," and "travelling by dogsled." The properties of ice are now correlated to the specific kind of travelling, as it apparently made no sense for the Slave to be asked "what kinds of ice are suitable for travel?" Such a question had to be asked only with reference to the specific kind of travel—by foot or by dog-sled, for instance. The resulting matrix of questions, formed by the conjunction of the various types of ice with the various types of travel, could then be made for Slave informants, asking them to respond in appropriate terms. These appropriate terms, found out also by empirical study, were put in terms of function for the informant. There were three such appropriate responses. The ice was judged suitable for that kind of travel and could therefore be traversed. The ice was judged unsuitable and a detour was considered necessary. Or the ice was considered dangerous and could only be traversed with caution. In the conclusion of this study Basso makes a point which relates cognition to action:

> It has become a commonplace in writings on contemporary methodology to observe that the discovery and statement of cultural rules is facilitated by the analysis of native classification systems. In this paper, I have tried to show that although such analyses are indeed fundamental, they are by no means sufficient. In order to arrive at productive rules for behavior, we must also know how the referents of native categories are appraised and acted upon. And this, I have argued, requires that explicit attention be given to the analysis of situations (Basso 1972, p. 46).

Basso's emphasis on the analysis of situations, and how the various referents discussed are actually acted upon by informants, leads to the third study. This is a study of planting practices in a slash-and-burn agricultural system in northeast Brazil. Johnson (1974) wanted to find out "the extent to which cognitive models generated by ethnoecological techniques may be used to predict actual practices in specific contexts" (p. 88). Agricultural categories, of this sharecropper group living in northeast Brazil, were teased out through eliciting questions. The first question: "what are the kinds of land that one has?" elicited two levels of contrast, that referring to the use of materials for house construction, and the other referring to different types of agricultural land. This latter set reduced to eight stable concepts: first, second, and third (old) swidden, sandy hillside, river margin, river bottom in dry season, low/moist, and saline lands.

This classification constituted the first step only. The second step was taken to find the interrelationships between these terms, elicited by the question: "What is the difference between ——— and ——— ?" (Johnson, 1974, p. 89). The answers resulted in two major dimensions of contrast, signified by the pair of polar opposites of strong versus weak on the one hand, and hot versus cold on the other. Thus all eight types of land could be plotted on a coordinate system assigned to these two dimensions. All this represented the cognitive model. The intention was to see whether the actual *practices* of planting as such corresponded with what was *said* about land and crops. Johnson considered that indeed there was a statistically significant correspondence (one would not expect a complete one-to-one correspondence); there was relatively close agreement.

The foregoing examples of the application of ethnoscientific techniques do not exhaust the repertoire of the subject. It is trusted that giving illustrative examples does not mislead in assuming that there is firm agreement within the field of cognitive anthropology as to the efficacy or even meaning of such techniques. There is extreme variability. Apart from the terminology versus psychological argument, there are other basic differences. Some users of the method have established rigorous mathematical techniques (e.g., Romney & D'Andrade, 1964). They chose American kinship terms for their target of analysis. It has been argued that by contrast many domains in the "real" world do not provide a finite set of rules, which can be given so orderly an analysis. Thus Harris (1970) has shown by reference to the Brazilian terminology of racial identity that there is an inherent noise and ambiguity in the system itself. He argues that in modern Brazil there may be a sociopolitical reason for keeping racial identity ambiguous. Class confrontations might develop if there were a perceived correspondence between class and race. Even if Harris's example is extreme, it seems clear that ethnoscientific techniques work best with relatively "closed" categories, such as color and plants. However, there have been other domains, which seem far less "closed." For example, Abrahams and Bauman (1971) broke down the domain of "talking nonsense" among peasants of St. Vincent in the British West Indies, a style of speech behavior that is heavily laden with value connotations among these people. While there have been ingenious examples carried out by anthropologists such as this one, there are signs that terminology as an index of cognitive behavior is more complicated than the supporters of ethnoscience had earlier anticipated. Sankoff (1972) indicated in an examination of New Guinea social organization that the tribe's (the Buang Dgwa) concept of kin affiliation not only differed from person to person, but also differed from occasion to occasion. Sometimes this feature can be fully explicated as was the case with Frake's earlier study of skin disease concepts in the Philippines. Nevertheless as Colby and Cole have commented (1973, p. 69):

> Anthropologists are beginning to realize that it is quite possible not only for different individuals in the same culture-using group to have different semantic structures in their heads, but that the *same* individual can have different semantic structures for the same terminology set and that the usage of these different structures depends upon the context of situation.

The first wave of ethnoscience might be considered to have lost its energy. Keesing's witty article (1972) entitled "Paradigms Lost" probably best summarizes the present position. The question is where does cognitive anthropology go from here? It might be that Wallace's suggestion (1971) that the logic of relations be pursued rather than the logic of classes would be a fruitful line to follow. It certainly would plummet cognitive anthropology into the arena of cognitive process more directly than it has previously been involved. If it has proved difficult for anthropologists to hitch terminological systems onto psychological systems, there is still left the ambiguity whether category systems formulated by psychologists reflect the "real" external world or the attributes of language. In a paper analyzing personality trait theory through the techniques of componential analysis, D'Andrade (1965) raised the strong possibility that classifications used by psychologists can be derived from similarities in the meanings of words solely. Since the time D'Andrade wrote this paper the rise of attribution theory in psychology (e.g., Jones & Davis, 1965; Kelley, 1967) may help to accept this suggestion better. Nevertheless the entire issue of language, communication, and cognitive relationships continues to beset its inquirers.

Modes of Thought

This section title is taken from the book edited by Horton and Finnegan (1973), which is a seminal publication for a different anthropological perspective on thought than the one discussed in the previous section. Despite the decline and fall of the primitive mentality thesis, an awareness (or suspicion) that there is a basic difference in thought between Western and non-Western societies has continued to develop. This viewpoint differs from the earlier formulations of Levy-Bruhl (1923, 1926, 1928) on a number of points. First, it is far more cautious. Second, there is no longer any question on primitiveness in the sense of inferiority or deficiency; rather it is the sense of a different mode of thinking. Further, this mode of thought can be found here and there within Western systems, though not dominant. Moreover, if there is a difference between Western and non-Western thought, the difference lies with criteria through which the chain of thought is led, and not necessarily with the machinery of thinking.

It is to be kept in mind that the idea of "modes of thought" is associated with belief systems and ideologies. From the vantage point of general psychology, this is more of a social psychological conception such as the one used by Rokeach (1960) in "The Open and Closed Mind." Belief systems have concepts, codes, and consensus strategies that bring them into the cognitive realm. For anthropologists there has always been the urge to "get into" belief systems other than their own. Black (1973) has comprehensively covered the main anthropological schools on this topic. Historically, Levy-Bruhl provided the first formulations of how to consider the cognitive components of belief systems that appeared so very different from those of the educated world of his time. Towards the end of his career (1949), Levy-Bruhl revised his earlier notions (see Cazeneuve 1972, pp. 85–87), inasmuch as he abandoned the key term "prelogical." Two passages from his notebooks of 1949 indicate his final position:

> ... I still want to account for participation, if not from the logical point of view, at least from the viewpoint of the knowledge of objects, and of their understanding—while recognizing that this understanding, when it concerns participations, entails an important part of affective, not cognitive elements.

> There is a mystical mentality which is more marked and more easily observable among "primitive people" than in our own societies, but it is present in every human mind. From the moment that it is no longer set up as something which is opposed to a different mentality, all the above problems disappear.

A category difficulty now occurs when cognition is conjoined with affective elements. From the time of Kant and Tetens at any rate, and possibly earlier, the history of psychology has been marked by clear division between cognition and affect. It was indeed the lack of this division in so-called primitive societies that had made people like Levy-Bruhl (1923, 1926, 1928) and Werner (1957) suspect that there was a different type of mentality operating. Curiously, with all of the Freudian input into anthropology at that time and since, the notion of positing the problem into terms of primary process versus secondary process thinking never emerged dominantly. The problem is even more confounded when another language system is dealt with. As Evans-Pritchard put it in a foreword to a posthumous edition of one of Levy-Bruhl's books (1966):

. . . but what the words in their own languages mean to those who speak them may not correspond exactly, or even at all, with what the words by which we translate them means to us. In the process of translation, or mistranslation, we may easily put into the thought of primitive people ideas quite foreign to them, and that is what Levy-Bruhl holds has only too often happened.

To tap the cognitive components of something other than what is usually labelled cognitive is not an easy matter. It requires the investigator to be aware of what precise system is operating. Lienhardt has given a classic example with the belief system of the Dinka of the southern Sudan:

> The Dinka have no conception which at all closely corresponds to our popular modern conception of the "mind," as mediating and, as it were, storing up the experiences of the self. There is for them no such interior entity to appear, on reflection, to stand between the experiencing self at any given moment and what is or has been an exterior influence upon the self. So it seems that what we should call in some cases the "memories" of experiences, and regard therefore as in some way intrinsic and interior to the remembering person and modified in their effect upon him by that interiority, appear to the Dinka as exteriorly acting upon him, as were the sources from which they derived. Hence it would be impossible to suggest to Dinka that a powerful dream was "only" a dream, and might for that reason be dismissed as relatively unimportant in the light of day, or that a state of possession was grounded "merely" in the psychology of the person possessed. They do not make the kind of distinction between the psyche and the world which would make such interpretations significant for them. (Lienhardt, 1961, p. 149)

The basic question is: what are modes of thought? It is perhaps significant that the Horton and Finnegan book of that name has run into difficulties of primary definition. In their introduction to the book (Horton & Finnegan, 1973, p. 17) they have specified the differentiating characteristics that are thought to distinguish one mode of thought from another. They specify rationality versus nonrationality; the findings of science versus non-science/mistaken notions/false ideas; openness versus closure; secularism versus religiousness and/or magic; high versus low division of labor (a criterion which they consider to be more relevant to modes of thought than at first appears); and tradition versus creativity and individual expression. It can be seen that all these polarities have social elements, indeed may be thought of as being exclusively social. Again, for psychology, the references lies in that realm that might be called the social psychology of cognition.

Of all these dichotomies, the open versus closed variety has probably been given most attention. Horton, for example, in a couple of articles (1967) characterized African traditional thought as being, on the whole, much the same as is customary in Western science, but distinguished on one crucial point. Namely, that while Western thought in the name of science is continuously open to empirical checks, is on the look out for falsification and is competitive with alternative theories, the so-called traditional thought has no alternatives. The belief system and the thought processes that go along with it have nothing outside of the system that might assist the thinker in a reconsideration of the data. Gellner (1973) has criticized Horton's viewpoint on two grounds: first, it is not true that the thought of Western science is invariably so open. Western scientists are frequently quite obstinate in considering world views that deviate from their own paradigm. And second, it is also not true that traditional people have this tunnel vision about their own beliefs. Gellner quotes the observation of Leach with the tribesmen of highland Burma (Leach, 1954), who tend to oscillate between two competitive views of their own society. Nevertheless, other people have focussed on the key point of verification. Tambiah (1973), for instance, brought this criterion into line with cognitive processes, when the role of analogy in magical acts was considered. Tambiah found that analogy is certainly used both in science and in magic, but the criteria used for judging its applicability differs between the two:

> . . . whereas in science the use of an analogy is closely linked to prediction and verification, and its adequacy judged in terms of inductive support, or of meeting standards of probability criteria, or standing up to tests of falsifiability and the like, the semantics of a magical rite are not necessarily to be judged in terms of such "true/false" criteria of science but on different standards and objectives. The corresponding objectives in (magical) ritual are "persuasion," "conceptualization," "expansion of meaning" and the like, and the criterion of adequacy are better conveyed by notions such as "validity," "correctness," "legitimacy," and "felicity" of the ceremony performed. (Tambiah, 1973, p. 219)

One inference to be taken from Tambiah's analysis is that one cannot ignore the subject of epistemology when paying attention to non-Western thought processes. The two are intertwined. This is perhaps not so surprising when their close connection with Western thought processes as specified by Piaget (1970b) is noted. This is the reason why the consideration of a different epistemology when paying attention to the data coming from the altered-states-of-consciousness field (Price-Williams, 1975) is offered here. On the anthropological material, epistemology cannot be avoided, as it is aligned with the inferences drawn from an alien belief system. Hahn (1973) has put it very well when he writes:

> The interaction between the belief of anthropologist and native . . . might be labelled "epistemic;" it is a logical consequence of the process by which the anthropologist comes to know and formulate the native's beliefs.

A different approach to modes of thought is found in the writings of Levi-Strauss. His theories have often proved difficult for even his fellow anthropologists to follow; it may be somewhat intrepid for cross-cultural psychology to make a foray into his line of thought. In *The Savage Mind* (1966)—particularly in the very first chapter entitled "The Science of the Concrete"—Levi-Strauss upsets the customary abstract-concrete dichotomy by pointing out that the so-called primitive's version of the concrete is far more sophisticated than the Western mind usually suspects. Levi-Strauss introduces the French word *bricoleur* to specify a more precise meaning to the usual term of *concrete*. In the American translation of the book, the translator provides a note (Levi-Strauss 1966, p. 17) that clarifies the term: "The '*bricoleur*' has no precise equivalent in English. He is a man who understands odd jobs and is a Jack-of-all-trades or a kind of professional do-it-yourself man . . ." Levi-Strauss himself talks of mythical thought as being a kind of intellectual *bricolage*, and contrasts the engineer or scientist with the *bricoleur*. In a passage later on in the same chapter, Levi-Strauss says that while the engineer works by means of concepts, the *bricoleur* works by means of signs. In yet another passage he indicates that the elements of mythical thought lie halfway between percepts and concepts. However concrete the references in mythical thought may be, such as references to food, animals, and things, Levi-Strauss's proposition about the underlying logic they pertain to in mythical stories is thoroughly abstract. By pointing to a number of myths all over the world (though his immediate referencing mostly pertains to his South American material), Levi-Strauss claims that a kind of algebra of signs is operating. The algebra is made up of relations between people, or animals, or material things, and their statuses, which are given in the stories. He sees a consistency in the underlying structure behind the manifest account. The consistency is that of binary oppositions. Although this no doubt oversimplifies the issue, what Levi-Strauss finds in these stories is the kind of relationship that is often found in intelligence tests; e.g., sky is to under the earth as birds are to worms. This kind of opposition has expression as metaphor. However, Levi-Strauss introduced a further element in his theory that adds a note of complexity. Basic to the theory is the notion that myths have forms or structures, which are largely, if not exclusively, unconscious to those that hold them. The elements of myths combine in a certain way to communicate their meaning. Basically the idea is that myth is constructed such that content and setting form a combined matrix. As Levi-Strauss himself has put it (1968, p. 17):

> The sequences form the apparent content of the myth; the chronological order in which certain things happen. . . . But these sequences are organized, in planes of different levels (of abstraction) in accordance with schemata, which exist simultaneously, superimposed one upon another.

There followed a reference to the analogy with musical composition that suggested that the construction of myths is not wholly lineal, and thus that a wholly lineal analysis would not do justice to the understanding of myths. Previously, Lee's (1950) analysis of Trobriander thought claimed that whereas Western thought is imbued through and through with the underlying notion of the uninterrupted line, the Trobrianders' thought is not:

> I believe that, where valued activity is concerned, the Trobrianders do not act on an assumption of lineality at any level. There is organization or rather coherence in their acts because Trobriand activity is patterned activity. One act within this pattern brings into existence a preordained cluster of acts (Lee 1959, p. 113).

Levi-Strauss indicated that something of this kind is prevalent in myths in addition to the undoubted lineal aspect of a chronological sequence. Leach (1970) indicated that there is a parallel tendency to the distinction in grammar between parts of speech and the sentence, and points out that the two factors are close, if not identical, to the psychological processes of similarity and contiguity, the two principles that Frazer picked as underlying the thought of magic. Levi-Strauss, of course, goes much further than the early anthropologists, and stipulates that myth is a kind of magical mediation for resolving paradoxes represented by irreconcilable opposites.

The Levi-Strauss movement has been mentioned here as it has become a leading example of what some anthropologists have represented as cognition. But it is hard to find what place psychology per se has in all this. Very few modern psychologists have indeed accepted mythical thought as an arena of investigation; of these it has been the depth psychologists—Freud, Fromm, Jung, and their successors. When such psychological processes such as similarity and contiguity have been examined, it has not been in the context of mythical thought but in the psychological analysis of retention or intelligence. The question arises for psychology as to whether investigation of such factors as these might not reveal something different if they are studied in such contexts as mythical tales. There is the further query as to the similarity, if any, between the theory of structuralism as it is conceived in anthropology and the theory of structuralism as put forward by some schools of psychology (e.g., Piaget 1970a).

Intelligence

Whereas intelligence testing has always been left to psychologists by anthropologists—often disdainfully—the *concept* of intelligence and its entanglement with the concept of race have been met head-on by anthropology as a discipline. It will not be a concern of this present section to enter into the debate over the Jensen controversy (for positions taken by anthropologists see, inter alia, Brace, Gamble & Bond, 1971; Montagu, 1975). The concern here will be to choose here and there representatives who have entered into the region of styles of intelligence. Of these Cohen is a good example (1969, 1971), particularly as some of her formulations criss-cross ideas expressed by psychologists. Cohen's starting point is the school culture in the United States versus the cultures of minorities. Her claim is that there are two distinct cognitive organizations operating. In the school culture there is operating what she calls the *analytic style*; in the culture of minorities there is operating the *relational style*. She borrows much from cognitive style notions germane to Witkin et al. (1954), Witkin, Dyk, Faterson, Goodenough and Karp (1962/1974) and to Kagan (Kagan, Moss, & Siegel, 1963), but she ploughs new ground when she links distinct cognitive and conceptual styles to modes of social organization. Specifically she connects the relational conceptual style with group organizations based on shared-function styles of relationship, and the analytic conceptual style with groups based on formally organized relationships. A later article (Cohen, 1971) spelled out precisely what is meant by these key terms of analytic versus relational. These are interpreted as polar categories, the first being associated with that pattern of thought inculcated or required by the school, the latter appearing in those children that did poorly in schools. The term analytic includes the following properties: being stimulus centered, sensitive to the specific parts of the stimulus, looking for nonobvious attributes, and seeking for properties with formal meaning. The relational style is predominantly self-centered, seeks for descriptive properties, is global, and is inclined to embed rather than to extract properties. A later addition to these two categories included two further styles that are conceived as two alternative ways of dealing with the mutual incompatibility of the analytic-relational dyad. The first is called simply the *flexible style* that shares certain properties with the analytic style, such as being stimulus centered, is parts-specific, and looks for formal attributes. However, it shares with the relational style the property of selectively embedding and identifying the unique as being meaningful. The other alternate style that Cohen calls *conflict-concrete* is stimulus centered and looks for formal attributes as with the fully analytic style; but it is global and descriptive as is the fully relational style. As with the initial two modes of intelligence, the alternative styles are thought to be associated with specific kinds of social organization. Cohen's (1971) paper fits the schema into occupational roles. Thus analytic styles are considered to be prominent among businessmen, executives, and certain kinds of academic fields. The alternate flexible style is characteristic of social workers, nurses, and elementary school teachers. The conflict-concrete alternate style goes with engineers, craftsmen, and small businessmen; the relational style, with artists, creative writers, and sensitivity group leaders and counselors.

What is characteristic of Cohen's scheme is the anthropological/sociological approach to psychological concepts. It has affinities with Bernstein's early distinctions of private versus public codes of communication that were thought to characterize different social classes, and which were linked to perception (Bernstein, 1961). The approach to intelligence by these disciplines is somewhat similar to the personality-and-perception class of psychologists. They look for representative types of perceptual inferences from classes of individuals. There is no implication of one class perceiving "better" than another class of individual; it is merely considered "different." Another way of regarding the sociological input is to see it as an extension of cognitive style procedures to the domain of intelligence. A consequence of this approach would be to think of *intelligences*—in the plural—rather than an overall homogenous factor that is taken as a universal standard.

Another example originates from the neurological sciences (Bogen, DeZure, Tenhouten, & Marsh, 1972) but has been extended to the cultural area by sociologists (Tenhouten & Kaplan, 1973). The basic hypothesis is that the right and left hemispheres of the brain are associated with two distinct modes of thought, called appositional and propositional, respectively. Appositional thought is predominantly spatially oriented, is holistic rather than analytical, is inductive rather than deductive, and deals with simultaneous analysis as distinct from linear analysis. Propositional thought is more language oriented, or more precisely, is more concerned with the use of words in propositions. It excels in linear and sequential tasks, is highly analytic, and is digital distinct from analogue. The two modes are to be considered as a ratio, with one dominating over the other for certain types of actions, for individuals and perhaps for cultural groups. The material has been largely collected by Bogen (1969a, 1969b). The question here is: brain lateralization aside, are some cultures more appositionally inclined, and are some cultures more propositionally inclined? It can be seen that the appositional-propositional distinction has conceptual links with other dichotomies, such as global-analytic, Cohen's relational-analytic, and the differentiation ratio of Witkin. Inasmuch as cultural differences have been found with the application of these factors (e.g. Witkin & Berry, 1975; Berry, 1976) it would not be surprising to find cultural differences with the appositional-propositional model. At present the experimental evidence is limited. Using such a test as the Street Test to represent appositional thought, and such subtests as the Wechsler similarities and language to represent propositional thought, Tenhouten (1971) found that minority groups within the United States (blacks and Hopi Indians) scored higher on the Street Test than comparable urban whites, and scored lower than the whites on the Wechsler subtests.

The upshot of anthropological or sociological perspectives on intelligence is to question the monolithic concept of intelligence, and even of the broader concept of *knowing*. It also ties in the different types of intelligence and cognition with variant modes of social organization. In doing so, anthropological perspectives are continually hampered by the current state of knowledge and terminology in the psychological sciences. It seems clear, for instance, that the idea of conceptual style goes beyond what most psychologists would identify as cognitive style, in that the former notion veers more to what one would usually think of as *process* than merely as mode. Nevertheless there are indications that within psychology the dividing line between process and style is becoming less clear (see e.g. Shouksmith, 1970).

A not insignificant contribution of the nonpsychological disciplines to the study of intelligence lies with the labelling problem. This is proving to be another region where old dividing lines are becoming muddied. It has been apparent for sometime now that such a concept as intelligence does not operate in a social vacuum. Mercer (1973) in particular and Edgerton (1970) have shown how the notion of mental retardation is reactive to labelling procedures by society. Psychologists are more prone to encapsulate in society the concept of intelligence than they used to be. Olson, for example (1970), is ready to define intelligence as a factor operating in a particular medium, and others (e.g., Wober, 1974) are on the look-out for alternate concepts in non-Western societies.

Theoretical Concerns and Psychological Implications

As has been said previously, there are no anthropological theories about cognition. What theoretical concerns there are have been imported from psychology. LeVine (1963), Jones (1971) and Wallace (1970) have all described the relationships of various psychological theories of learning and cognition to anthropological matter. These theories include behavioristic concepts such as drive, reinforcement, stimulus-generalization and primacy effects. They include the direct paradigm of operant conditioning, and they include the information theory model. The dependence on purely psychological theories would seem to indicate that anthropology feels the need for probing beneath the surface material that it deals with. There is a recognition of the process versus product distinction. The Rylean (Ryle, 1949) separation of *knowing how* from *knowing that* is essential to understanding this distinction. Yet there is an important element, which anthropology has always recognized and placed in front, that negates a simple polarity on this basis. This element is context. The distinction of process from product is useful and indeed necessary for the problem of sorting out the "machinery" of thought from the materials with which the machinery is operating. But this does not mean that the so-called products of thought are unreactive factors that have no effect on the process itself. It is clear, for example, that improved—that is, more advanced—techniques of mathematics have a positive feedback effect on the mentality operating them. The social disciplines have always recognized this interdependence. As Geertz has put it:

> ... the prevailing view that the mental dispositions of man are genetically prior to culture and that his actual capabilities represent the amplification or extension of these pre-existent dispositions by cultural means is incorrect.

> ... cultural resources are ingredient, not accessory, to human thought.

> ... human thinking is primarily an overt act conducted in terms of the objective materials of the common culture, and only secondarily a private matter. (Geertz, 1962, pp. 736–37)

The reactive element of cultural products of thought is reflected in the psychologists' stress on context and situation. As Cole and his associates have said: ". . . cultural differences in cognition may more nearly reflect changes in the situations to which various cognitive skills are applied, than they do general processes" (Cole, Gay, Glick, & Sharp, 1971, p. 226). The term situation implies more than just technology. The mathematical ability of an educated Westerner entails more than just the employment of a mechanical calculator as distinct from an abacus. It entails learning new sets of rules, being immersed in a culture that has preceded the contemporary Westerner for hundreds of years. In turn the mechanical calculator facilitates further conceptual rules that would have been impossible to formulate without it. This viewpoint need not go to the extreme of regarding culture as an all-determining envelope—to the conclusion, as White (1956) puts it, that if Newton had been a Hottentot he would have calculated like a Hottentot. It does mean that in the history of human thought the prevailing *eidos* of the times cannot be ignored. It is in fact this term—*eidos*—coined by Bateson (1958) that points to the direction to which anthropologists have always been pointing, and to which many cross-cultural psychologists are now going. Bateson amplified this important concept:

> ... It is probable that cultures may vary in the species of steps which link their premises together and that the word 'logic' must therefore be interpreted differently in every culture (p. 25).

> We defined social structure in terms of ideas and assumptions and "logic," and since these are, in some sense, a product of cognitive process, we may surmise that the characteristics of Iatmul culture which we are now studying are due to *a standardization of the cognitive aspects of the personality of the individu-*

als. Such a standardization and its expression in cultural behavior I shall refer to as the *eidos* of a culture (Original italics. Bateson, 1958, p. 220).

It is doubtful whether there has ever been a programmatic research into the *eidos* of a culture since Bateson's first incursion into the area, a point recognized also by Gladwin (1964), who perhaps gave subsequent amplification to the idea in his book concerning navigation and logic in a Pacific atoll (Gladwin, 1970). Such a research certainly means going beyond the products of cognition, but it needs to use these products as a starting point. The concept of *eidos* entails a particular cultural context. *Eidos* cannot be studied by methods that originate from outside of that culture. For cross-cultural psychology the search for cognitive process lies in ferreting out the "species of steps which link (a particular culture's) premises together," and following the processual track from there. As Bateson has again put it (p. 32): "From the examination of the premises in the structure of a particular culture we can fit them together into a coherent scheme and finally arrive at some general picture of the cognitive processes involved." This kind of approach to cognition, as Bateson and Benedict recognized (see Bateson, 1958, p. 33) is configurational and has little affinity to approaches that are based on more atomistic principles. Bateson's notions are mentioned as they represent an important contribution to cognition from the standpoint of anthropology. At present these notions present a challenge to the cross-cultural cognitive psychologist.

It also seems that the concept of "mazeway" introduced to the anthropological world by Wallace (1956, 1957, 1961) has a number of parallels with Bateson's ethos. In the same way as *eidos* is opposed to *ethos* in Bateson's scheme, Wallace wishes to find a concept that distinguishes the cognitive from the affective and motivational aspects of personality; indeed a concept that gets away somewhat from the notion of personality altogether. Therefore, he defines mazeway as "the meaningfully organized totality of learned cognitive representations of people, things, processes, and values held at a given time by an individual" (Wallace, 1961, p. 139). Wallace would recognize the "know-how" to make a mask or the "know-how" to smoke a cigarette as an element of mazeway. The relationship to culture is given in the following passage:

> The elements of mazeway are the totality of what has been learned and is now known. But it is a totality which possesses an organization, a structure, that is not wholly inherent in the separate learnings themselves, but has been formed by such process as generalization, logical analysis, and imagination reconstructing learned materials in memory. Whatever the relationship between the individual learnings and mazeway *Gestalt,* however, by virtue of the learning process the individual members of a society will learn to predict one another's behavior. They will maintain a set of mutually equivalent (not necessarily identical) learned meanings for stimuli which are continuously available, during all their transactions, as statements of the boundaries and

conditions of their mutual behavior. Thus the statement that given learning capacity, the members of a society will produce a culture, has as its corollary the statement that the members of that society will individually possess mazeways whose contents, including mutually predictive cognitions, are equivalent. In other words, the culture concept implies a Principle of Mazeway Equivalence for members of a culturally organized social group (Wallace, 1961, p. 141).

The cognitive search of Bateson and Wallace refers to some quality that the psychologist is not aiming at directly. Such concepts as *eidos* and mazeway, presume an organization that is linked with noncognitive elements of a culture. The search or inquiry is for how cognition is tied in with these other noncognitive elements. That it *is* tied in is assumed from a Durkheimian thesis of interlocking unity of a culture. A speculation might be hazarded that the independent variables of the cross-cultural cognitive psychologist are just those elements inherent in *eidos* and mazeway. But this would overlook the fact that just the mere setting up of independent and dependent variables enacts a state of abstraction from the culture that the anthropologist is loath to do. Cole (1975, p. 163) summarized the difference between the two disciplines on this:

> . . . there is a very wide gulf between ethnographic and psychological approaches to the study of cognition. The two disciplines do not share the same data base: ethnographers rely for the most part on naturally occurring, mundane events, while psychologists rely on experiments. Ethnographers reject experiments as artificial, while psychologists avoid natural behavior sequences as ambiguous.

To leave the issue at this point, however, would be inadequate. There are points of rapprochement between the two disciplines that are making for convergence. One is the matter of context. In the same way as the study of linguistics has recently witnessed a moving away from the word to the sentence, so are there signs of cross-cultural psychology exhibiting a parallel tendency. Certainly an inclination towards context has been seen. Some cross-cultural psychologists are paying attention to the emic perspective. The notion of varying stimulus preferences has been entertained. The entire relationship of communication to cognition—a vital link for study by psychology—is a further element of study that needs amplification from psychology, although it is one that some have touched on (see Cole, 1975). If there is a lesson that anthropology has to teach psychology on the subject of cognition, it is that the cognitive realm of individuals is substantially greater than that explored by the odd experiment. The tapping of this wider world presents difficult challenges for the methodological ingenuity of the psychologist. A failure to explore, however, will always have the consequence of a continual divergence between the two disciplines.

Note

1. The writing of this chapter was in part supported by PHS grant ʋ04612, NICHD, Mental Retardation Center, University of California at Los Angeles. The author wishes to thank the following for their helpful advice in the preparation of the manuscript: Harry Triandis, Walter Lonner, Robert Edgerton, Ronald Gallimore, Cecile Edgerton; and those members of the East-West Culture Learning Institute, Honolulu, who worked on a first draft.

References

ABRAHAMS, R. D., & BAUMAN, R. Sense and nonsense in St. Vincent: speech behavior and decorum in a Caribbean community. *American Anthropologist,* 1971, *73,* 762–72.

BASSO, K. Ice and travel among the Fort Norman Slave: folk taxonomies and cultural rules. *Language in Society,* 1972, *1,* 31–49.

BATESON, G. *Naven: a study of the problems suggested by a composite picture of the culture of a New Guinea tribe drawn from three points of view,* 2nd ed. Stanford: Stanford University Press, 1958.

BERLIN, B., BREEDLOVE, D. E., & RAVEN, P. H. "Covert" categories of folk taxonomies. *American Anthropologist,* 1968, *70,* 290–99.

BERLIN, B., & KAY, P. *Basic color terms: their universality and evolution.* Berkeley: University of California Press, 1969.

BERNSTEIN, B. Aspects of language and learning in the genesis of the social process. *Journal of Child Psychology and Psychiatry,* 1961, *1,* 313–24.

BERRY, J. W. *Human ecology and cognitive style: comparative studies in cultural and psychological adaptation.* Beverly Hills, Calif.: Sage/Halsted, 1976.

BLACK, M. B. Belief Systems. In J. J. Honigmann (Ed.), *Handbook of social and cultural anthropology,* Chicago: Rand McNally, 1973.

BOGEN, J. E. The other side of the brain. I: dysgraphia and dyscopia following cerebral commissurotomy. *Bulletin Los Angeles Neurological Society,* 1969a, *34,* 73–105.

BOGEN, J. E. The other side of the brain. II: an appositional mind. *Bulletin Los Angeles Neurological Society,* 1969b, *34,* 135–62.

BOGEN, J. E., DeZURE, R., TENHOUTEN, W. F., & MARSH, J. F. The other side of the brain. IV: the A/P ratio. *Bulletin Los Angeles Neurological Society,* 1972, *37,* 49–61.

BRACE, C. L., GAMBLE, G. R., & BOND, J. T. (Eds.), *Race and intelligence.* Washington, D. C.: American Anthropological Association, 1971.

BURLING, R. Cognition and componential analysis: God's truth or hocus-pocus? *American Anthropologist,* 1964, *66,* 20–28.

———. American kinship terms once more. *Southwestern Journal of Anthropology,* 1970, *26,* 15–24.

CAZENEUVE, J. *Lucien Levy-Bruhl.* New York: Harper & Row, 1972.

COHEN, R. Conceptual styles, culture conflict, and non-verbal tests of intelligence. *American Anthropologist,* 1969, *71,* 828–56.

————. The influence of conceptual rule-sets on measures of learning ability. In C. L. Brace, G. R. Gamble & J. T. Bond (Eds.), *Race and intelligence.* Washington, D.C.: American Anthropological Association, 1971.

COLBY, B. Ethnographic semantics: a preliminary survey. *Current Anthropology,* 1966, *7,* 3–32.

COLBY, B., & COLE, M. Culture, memory and narrative. In R. Horton and R. Finnegan (Eds.), *Modes of thought: essays on thinking in Western and non-Western societies.* London: Faber and Faber, 1973.

COLE, M. An ethnographic psychology of cognition. In R. Brislin, S. Bochner, & W. J. Lonner (Eds.), *Cross-cultural perspectives on learning.* New York: Sage/Halsted, 1975.

COLE, M., GAY, J., GLICK, J. A., & SHARP, D. W. *The cultural context of learning and thinking.* New York: Basic Books, 1971.

CONKLIN, H. Analysis of Hanunoo color categories. *Southwestern Journal of Anthropology,* 1955, *11,* 339–44.

D'ANDRADE, R. G. Trait psychology and componential analysis. *American Anthropologist,* 1965, *67,* 215–28.

D'ANDRADE, R. G., QUINN, N. R., NERLOVE, S. B., & ROMNEY, A. K. Categories of disease in American-English and Mexican-Spanish. In A. K. Romney, R. N. Shepard, & S. Nerlove (Eds.), *Multi-dimensional scaling: theory and application in the behavioral sciences.* Vol. 2, Applications. New York: Seminar Press, 1972.

DURKHEIM, E., & MAUSS, M. De quelques formes primitives de classification. *Année Sociologique,* 1903, *6,* 1–17. Reprinted in R. Needham (Ed. and Tr.), *Primitive classification.* Chicago: Chicago University Press, 1963.

EDGERTON, R. Mental retardation in non-Western societies: towards a cross-cultural perspective on incompetence. In H. C. Haywood (Ed.), *Socio-cultural aspects of mental retardation.* New York: Appleton-Century-Crofts, 1970.

EVANS-PRITCHARD, E. E. Foreword to L. Levy-Bruhl, *The 'soul' of the primitive,* Gateway Edition, Chicago: Henry Regeny Co., 1966.

FRAKE, C. O. The diagnosis of disease among the Subanum of Mindanao. *American Anthropologist,* 1961, *63,* 113–32.

GARDNER, R. W., HOLZMAN, P. S., KLEIN, G. S., LINTON, H. B., & SPENCE, D. P. Cognitive control: a study of individual consistencies in cognitive behavior. In G. S. Klein (Ed.), *Psychological issues.* New York: International Universities Press, 1959.

GEERTZ, C. The growth of culture and the evolution of mind. In J. M. Scher (Ed.), *Theories of the mind.* New York: Free Press, 1962.

GELLNER, E. The savage and the modern mind. In R. Horton and R. Finnegan, *Modes of thought: essays on thinking in Western and non-Western societies.* London: Faber and Faber, 1973.

GLADWIN, T. Culture and logical process. In W. H. Goodenough (Ed.), *Explorations in cultural anthropology: essays in honor of George Peter Murdock.* New York: McGraw-Hill, 1964. Reprinted in J. W. Berry & P. R. Dasen (Eds.), *Culture and cognition: readings in cross-cultural psychology.* London: Methuen, 1974.

———. *East is a big bird: navigation and logic on Puluwat Atoll.* Cambridge, Mass.: Harvard University Press, 1970.

HAHN, R. A. Understanding beliefs: an essay on the methodology of the statement and analysis of belief systems. *Current Anthropology,* 1973, *14,* 207–29.

HARRIS, M. *The rise of anthropological theory.* New York: Thomas Y. Crowell, 1968.

———. Referential ambiguity in the calculus of Brazilian racial identity. *Southwestern Journal of Anthropology,* 1970, *26,* 1–4.

HORTON, R. African traditional thought and Western science. Part I: from tradition to science. Part II: the "closed" and "open" predicaments. *Africa,* 1967, *37,* 50–71; 155–87.

HORTON, R., & FINNEGAN, R. (Eds.), *Modes of thought: essays on thinking in Western and non-Western societies.* London: Faber and Faber, 1973.

JOHNSON, A. Ethnoecology and planting practices in a swidden agricultural system. *American Ethnologist,* 1974, *1,* 87–101.

JONES, E. E., & DAVIS, K. C. From acts to dispositions: the attribution process in person perception. In L. Berkowitz, (Ed.), *Advances in experimental social psychology,* Vol. 2. New York: Academic Press, 1965.

JONES, J. A. Operant psychology and the study of culture. *Current Anthropology,* 1971, *12,* 171.

KAGAN, J., MOSS, H. A., & SIEGEL, I. E. Psychological significance of styles of conceptualization. In *Basic cognitive process in children.* Society for Research in Child Development Monograph 86. Chicago: University of Chicago Press, 1963.

KEESING, R. Paradigms lost. *Southwestern Journal of Anthropology,* 1972, *28,* 299–332.

KELLEY, A. H. Attribution theory in social psychology. In D. LeVine (Ed.), *Nebraska Symposium in Motivation.* Lincoln, Nebraska: University of Nebraska Press, 1967.

LEACH, E. *Political systems of highland Burma.* London: London School of Economics and Political Science, 1954.

———. *Claude Levi-Strauss.* New York: Viking Press, 1970.

LEE, D. Codifications of reality: lineal and non-lineal. *Psychosomatic Medicine,* 1950, No. 12. Reprinted in D. Lee, *Freedom and Culture.* New York: Prentice-Hall. Spectrum Book, 1959.

LEVI-STRAUSS, C. *The savage mind.* London: Weidenfeld and Nicolson, 1966.

———. The story of Asdiwal. In E. Leach (Ed.), *The structural study of myth and totemism.* London: Tavistock Publications. Social Science Paperback Edition, 1968.

LEVINE, R. A. Behaviorism in psychological anthropology. In J. M. Wepman & R. W. Heine (Eds.), *Concepts of personality.* Chicago: Aldine Publishing Co., 1963.

LEVY-BRUHL, L. *Primitive mentality.* New York: Macmillan, 1923.

———. *How natives think.* London: G. Allen and Unwin, 1926.

———. *The "soul of the primitive."* New York: Macmillan, 1928.

LIENHARDT, G. *Divinity and experience: the religion of the Dinka.* Oxford: Clarendon Press, 1961.

MERCER, J. R. *Labelling the mentally retarded.* Berkeley, Calif.: University of California Press, 1973.

MICKLIN, M., DURBIN, M., & LEON, C. A. The lexicon for madness in a Colombian city: an exploration in semantic space. *American Ethnologist,* 1974, *1,* 143–56.

MONTAGU, A. (Ed.). *Race and I.Q.* Oxford: Oxford University Press, 1975.

OLSON, D. R. *Cognitive development: the child's acquisition of diagonality.* New York: Academic Press, 1970.

PIAGET, J. *Judgment and reasoning in the child.* London: Routledge and Kegan Paul, 1928.

———. *[Structuralism]* (C. Maschler, Ed. and trans.). New York: Basic Books, 1970a.

———. *[Genetic epistemology]* (E. Buckworth, trans.) New York and London: Columbia University Press, 1970b.

PRICE-WILLIAMS, D. R. Primitive mentality: civilized style. In R. Brislin, S. Bochner, & W. Lonner (Eds.), *Cross-cultural perspective on learning.* New York: Wiley, 1975.

ROKEACH, M. *The open and closed mind.* New York: Basic Books, 1960.

ROMNEY, A. K., & D'ANDRADE, R. G. Cognitive aspects of English kin terms. *American anthropologist,* 1964, *66,* 146–70.

ROSCH, E. Natural categories. *Cognitive Psychology,* 1973, *4,* 328–50.

RYLE, G. *The concept of mind.* London: Hutchinson's University Library, 1949.

SANDAY, P. R. Analysis of the psychological reality of American-English kin terms in an urban poverty environment. *American Anthropologist,* 1971, *73,* 555–70.

SANKOFF, G. Cognitive variability and New Guinea social organization: the Buang Dgwa. *American Anthropologist,* 1972, *74,* 555–66.

SHOUKSMITH, G. *Intelligence, creativity and cognitive style.* New York: Wiley-Interscience, 1970.

SPRADLEY, J. P. Adaptive strategies of urban nomads. In J. P. Spradley (Ed.), *Culture and cognition: rules, maps and plans.* San Francisco: Chandler Publishing Company, 1972.

TAMBIAH, S. J. Form and meaning of magical acts: a point of view. In R. Horton & R. Finnegan (Eds.), Modes of thought: essays on thinking in Western and non-Western societies. London: Faber and Faber, 1973.

TENHOUTEN, W. D. Cognitive styles and the social order. Final Report, Part II, Office of Equal Opportunity Study B00-5135: *Thought, race and opportunity.* Los Angeles, California, 1971.

TENHOUTEN, W. D., & KAPLAN, C. D. *Science and its mirror image: a theory of inquiry.* New York: Harper & Row, 1973.

TRIANDIS, H. Cultural influences upon cognitive processes. In L. Berkowitz (Ed.), *Advances in experimental social psychology,* Vol. I. New York: Academic Press, 1964.

TYLER, S. A. (Ed.), *Cognitive anthropology.* New York: Holt, Rinehart and Winston, 1969.

WALLACE, A. F. C. Mazeway resynthesis: A biocultural theory of religious inspiration. *Transactions of the New York Academy of Sciences,* 1956, *18,* 626–38.

————. Mazeway disintegration: the individual's perception of socio-cultural disorganization. *Human Organization,* 1957, *16,* 23–27.

————. The psychic unity of human groups. In B. Kaplan (Ed.), *Studying personality cross-culturally.* Evanston, Ill.: Row, Peterson and Co., 1961.

————. The problem of the psychological validity of componential analysis. *American Anthropologist,* 1965, *67,* 299–48.

————. Culture and cognition. In A. F. C. Wallace (Ed.), *Culture and personality,* 2nd ed. New York: Random House, 1970.

————. A relational analysis of American kinship terminology: an example of relations between process and structure in cognition. In P. L. Garvin (Ed.), *Cognition: a multiple view.* New York: Spartan Books, 1971.

WERNER, H. *Comparative psychology of mental development,* revised edition. New York: International Universities Press, Inc., 1957.

WHITE, L. A. The locus of mathematical reality: an anthropological footnote. In J. R. Newman (Ed.), *The world of mathematics,* Vol. 4. New York: Simon and Schuster, 1956.

WITKIN, H. A., LEWIS, H. B., HERTZMAN, M., MACHOVER, K., MEISSNER, P. B. & WAPNER, S. *Personality through perception.* New York: Harper & Row, 1954.

WITKIN, H. A., DYK, R. B., FATERSON, H. F., GOODENOUGH, D. R., & KARP, S. A. *Psychological differentiation: studies of development,* New York: Wiley, 1962. (Republished, Potomac, Md.: L. Erlbaum Associates, 1974).

WITKIN, H., & BERRY, J. Psychological differentiation in cross-cultural perspective. *Journal of Cross-Cultural Psychology,* 1975, *6,* 4–87.

WOBER, M. Towards an understanding of the Kiganda concept of intelligence. In J. W. Berry & P. R. Dasen (Eds.), *Culture and cognition: readings in cross-cultural cognition.* London: Methuen, 1974.

5

Cross-Cultural Perspectives on Emotion and Emotion Communication

Carroll E. Izard

Contents

Abstract

This chapter focuses primarily on the facial expression of emotions, since it is the expressive component of emotion that is particularly well suited to cross-cultural research. A review of various theories of the origin of facial expressions suggests that the evolutionary-genetic theory, originated by Darwin and clarified and extended by contemporary ethologists and psychologists, appears most consistent with existing data.

Cross-cultural studies have developed robust evidence for the universality of certain emotion expressions. Since all human beings recognize these expressions and attribute to them the same experiential significance, it is reasonable to infer that they are genetically based or preprogrammed.

Other cross-cultural studies show, however, that cultures may have different rules for displaying various emotions under different conditions. Such display rules may effect some modifications in facial expressions. Complex facial expressions involving components of more than one emotion are not recognized and described as well across cultures as are the expressions of fundamental emotions.

Research has also shown that different cultures vary significantly in their attitudes toward various emotions. This, in turn, affects socialization practices and subsequent adult personality traits. In addition, the level of emotion experience and expression can affect values, beliefs, social organization, and other aspects of the social system. The final section of the chapter discusses what might be called the inherently adaptive, conspecific functions of the fundamental emotions.

Introduction

This chapter will be concerned primarily with the discrete emotions that characterize human experience and human relations. Theories of emotion will be reviewed only selectively and briefly since several reviews are readily available (Cofer, 1972; Strongman, 1973; Izard, 1971, 1972, 1977; Arnold, 1960, 1970). More extensive treatment of the psychophysiology and neurophysiology of emotion is available (Jacobsen, 1967; Pribram, 1971; Delgado, 1971; Glass, 1967; Black, 1970; Malmo, 1975). The principal focus in this chapter will be on the expressive or communicative function of emotion and on its role as a motivational/experiential variable. While this work will not be confined to any one theoretical approach, as is inevitably the case, certain conceptions about what is important in the field of emotion for cross-cultural psychology influenced the selection and presentation of material. The choice to emphasize emotion expression and emotion communication will seem perfectly obvious to some, but it will not seem central to others.

Several factors support the emphasis on emotion expression. The most important reason is a pragmatic one—most of the cross-cultural studies of emotion have been concerned with the expressions of the emotions. A second reason is that expression is recognized by a number of major theories as a significant aspect of emotion. Some define it as an integral component; others see it as an immediate and telltale effect. Virtually all remaining theories at least acknowledge that it is an accompaniment of emotion. Finally, emotion expression constitutes the central component of nonverbal communication, and since it is nonverbal it can be studied with minimal language translation problems.

The external expression of emotion (as distinguished from the internal activity of the glandular-visceral system) may well include most of the striate muscles of the body, as when we "freeze" in "terror" or explode with anger, but the focus here will be on the facial expressions of fundamental emotions. The elaboration of the concept of fundamental emotion is linked to a theoretical framework (Izard, 1971, 1972) that will not be presented here. For present purposes fundamental emotion can be defined as an affect that has a characteristic neuromuscular-expressive pattern, an expression that can be consensually validated. If the expressive pattern of an emotion proves to be a transcultural phenomenon, then it will be possible to make certain important inferences regarding the nature of that emotion and its role in the biological and cultural evolution of human beings. A central aim of this chapter, then, will be to examine the evidence relating to Darwin's century-old thesis that the expressions of the emotions in human beings are innate and universal. Before considering the relevant evidence, however, it seems appropriate to place it in the context of a brief survey of the major theories of facial expression.

Theories of Emotion Expression and Emotion Communication

Despite the fact that facial expressions have been the subject of scientific controversy for well over a hundred years, there are only three major theories of their origin and significance. Two of these theories were presented in the nineteenth century, and the newest is more than a half-century old. One of these theories holds that expressions can be explained in terms of the electro-mechanical laws of neuromuscular function. A second theory suggests that facial expressions derive from sensory reactions, and the third maintains that facial expressions result from reactions that originally served other purposes of the organism in the course of evolution.

The Electro-Mechanical Explanation of Facial Expressions

This theory dates back to Spencer's (1855) notion that the emotion-specific character of facial expression is purely physiological or mechanical in nature. He maintained that whenever a weak neural impulse passes through the nervous system it acts with greatest strength where muscles have to overcome the least resistance. The facial muscles are small, highly mobile, and attached to easily movable parts. Consequently, it is this group of muscles on which the excitation associated with emotion becomes most clear and distinct.

Spencer believed that any sentiment or emotion is accompanied by a diffuse motor discharge proportional to its intensity and independent of its pleasant or unpleasant nature. He considered the neural impulses to be distributed in the organism in strict conformity with mechanical laws, the muscles being affected directly in proportion to the resistance they generate and inversely with their importance for work and locomotion. Large muscles that can manifest their excitation only in actuating the legs or other heavy masses will remain immobile after a weak or moderate neural discharge. But the small muscles, which can actuate themselves by over-coming very little resistance, will respond visibly even to weak impulses. It is for this reason, aside from all psychological and social considerations, Spencer argued, that the facial muscles are such marvelous instruments of expression.

Spencer's principle fails to explain why the diffuse discharge from a mild stimulation causes the precise pattern known as a smile rather than movements of, for example, only half of the fifteen or so muscles involved in this relatively simple emotion expression. Since the laws of simple electro-mechanical functioning do not explain the different facial patterns associated with each of the discrete emotions, Spencer supplemented his strictly quantitative theory with an evolutionary principle relating to qual-ity of emotion. He thought that in order to explain the association of spe-cific expressions with particular discrete emotions it was necessary to assume in addition to the diffuse discharge, a pattern of restrained neural discharge that depends not only on the intensity of the emotion but on its quality. In the course of evolution the neural discharge that was depen-dent upon the quality of a specific emotion became associated with the particular muscles necessary to execute the expression of that emotion.

Dumas (1948) accepted Spencer's first principle but rejected his no-tion of a "restrained" discharge determined by the quality of the emotion. Dumas maintained that the sets of muscles involved in the expressions of the various emotions can be arranged hierarchically in terms of the quan-tity of neural energy required to fire them. In this way he was able to stick with a strictly electro-mechanical explanation of expressions. Dumas maintained that while the expression of joy could be explained as a truly electro-mechanical function of the emotion of joy, the process by which the smile comes to represent or symbolize emotion depends upon the law of association working in a social context where other people need to in-terpret the physiological pattern. Dumas recognized that the use of the smile as a symbol of joy may or may not be associated with genuine joy experience. Thus, in summary, "the smile is originally a simple mechani-cal reaction: then it appears to us by virtue of a physiological association as the natural expression of joy, and finally we make it the voluntary symbol of this sentiment" (Dumas, 1948, p. 77). A particular emotion has a specific expression by virtue of the fact that the different combination of muscles required for each expression offers a different degree of resistance and requires a different degree of excitation or depression of neural activ-ity. Thus Dumas explained differentiated expressions, but he did not ex-plain how each expression became associated with one particular emotion. Apparently he assumed that each emotion generated a different amount of energy, each generating the amount required for its specific expressive movements.

The Dimensional Approach: Arousal, Activation,
and Dimensions of Emotion and Behavior

Spencer (1860) was one of the early scientists to conceptualize the experiential component of emotions or feelings as dimensions or states of consciousness, and hence as dimensions of personality and behavior. Wundt (1896) extended the Spencerian tradition and proposed that the sphere of consciousness described by emotion or feeling could be accounted for by three dimensions: pleasantness-unpleasantness, relaxation-tension, and calm-excitement. As will be described, Wundt's dimensions were revived by Woodworth (1938) and Schlosberg (1941) and their colleagues in a long line of successful research on the dimensions of emotion expression.

Emotion as organismic arousal.   Building on the conceptions of Spencer and Wundt, Duffy (1934, 1941, 1951, 1962) proposed that all behavior can be explained in terms of a single phenomenon, organismic arousal, a concept having apparent similarity to Wundt's dimension of relaxation-tension. Duffy (1962) maintained that behavior varies in only two dimensions, direction and intensity. She defined direction in terms of selectivity of response, a selectivity based on the expectancies and goal-orientation of the organism and the relationships among the preceived stimuli. An individual goes toward or away from a situation depending on its incentive value or threat value.

Intensity was defined as general organismic arousal or energy mobilization, and level of arousal "as the extent of release of potential energy, stored in the tissues of the organism, as this is shown in activity or response" (Duffy, 1962, p. 17). According to Duffy, emotion is simply a point or range of points toward the high end of the arousal dimension. Hence emotion as such can vary only in intensity, there being no allowance for discrete types of emotion experience.

Neural activation, emotion, and behavior.   Following Moruzzi and Magoun's discovery of certain functions of the brain stem reticular formation, Lindsley (1951, 1957) developed his activation theory of emotion and behavior. His theoretical formulation attempted to replace Duffy's (1962) broad and difficult-to-measure concept of organismic arousal with a concept of activation, defined as neural excitation of the brain stem reticular formation and concomitant changes in electroencephalographic patterns in the cortex. His explanation of emotion presupposes antecedent emotion stimuli, either external and conditioned or internal and unconditioned. Such stimuli initiate impulses activating the brain stem which, in turn, sends impulses to the thalamus and cortex. A hypothetical activating mechanism transforms these impulses into behavior characterized by "emotional excitement" and into cortical EEG patterns, characterized by low amplitude, high frequency, and asynchrony.

When impulses initiated by a reduction of emotional stimuli influence the thalamus directly, synchronized, high-amplitude, low-frequency EEG patterns may be established. Under these conditions, Lindsley predicted observable behavior opposite to that seen in "emotional excitement": namely, "emotional apathy." Lindsley acknowledged that his theory could not elucidate the nature of discrete emotions. His primary concern was with the relationship beween certain antecedent conditions, changes in electrical activity of the brain (as measured by the EEG), and observed behavior.

Dimensions of emotion expression.   Since Darwin published his famous work on *The Expression of the Emotions in Man and Animals* in 1872, the complex field of facial expression of emotion has received a great deal of attention. However, many of the contributions to the analysis and understanding of facial expression have not focused on the relationship between expressive behavior and other personality and social variables.

The approach to the study of facial expressions of concern here was initiated when Woodworth (1938) proposed the first really successful system for classifying the facial expressions of discrete emotions. He showed that many different facial expressions could be reliably categorized by use of the following six-step linear scale: (1) love, happiness, mirth; (2) surprise; (3) fear, suffering; (4) anger, determination; (5) disgust; and (6) contempt.

After applying the Woodworth classification scheme to various series of photographs of facial expressions, Schlosberg (1941) proposed that facial expressions could be more adequately described by considering the Woodworth scale as a circular surface with two axes or dimensions: pleasantness-unpleasantness (P-U) and attention-rejection (A-R). Later Schlosberg added a third dimension, sleep-tension (S-T) and thus came very close to adopting and verifying empirically the usefulness of the three dimensions of feeling originally proposed by Wundt in 1896.

Schlosberg's approach was similar to that in a psychophysical experiment where judgments are based on physical dimensions. His instructions required subjects to make their ratings on the basis of observable physical characteristics of the photographed expressions. In his earlier experiments Schlosberg had his subjects rate each photograph of a facial expression on two nine-point scales: pleasantness-unpleasantness and acceptance-rejection.

For each picture, the average rating was computed for each dimension. With P-U and A-R scales represented by perpendicular lines intersecting at scale point 5, the circular suface can be represented by a circle connecting the ends of the P-U and A-R axes. Any given picture (expression) can be represented as a point on the space within a quadrant of the circle. By drawing a line from the origin (intersection of P-N and A-R) through the plotted point to the rim of the circle, the circular scale value and the emotion category of the particular expression can be determined. The correlation between the circular scale values obtained via the category sorting technique and those determined or predicted by the dimensional ratings was .76. Thus facial expressions as represented in still photographs can be relatively accurately classified into discrete emotion categories on the basis of the P-U and A-R dimensional ratings.

Schlosberg and his colleagues (Engen, Levy, & Schlosberg, 1958) added the dimension of sleep-tension because they became impressed by the work of Duffy and Lindsley and the evidence that a dimension of "activation" was important in emotion. With a specially developed series of facial expressions (the Lightfoot series) they demonstrated test-retest reliabilities of .94, .87, and .92 (N=225) for the P-U, A-R, and S-T dimensions respectively. Triandis and Lambert (1958) applied Schlosberg's three dimensions in a cross-cultural study and showed that they were as valid for Greek subjects as for Americans. Later investigators (e.g., Abelson & Sermat, 1962; Ekman, 1964) showed that the acceptance-rejection and sleep-tension dimensions were highly correlated (thus not independent dimensions) and raised the question of their meaningfulness as separate dimensions of emotion expression. Several other investigators have made contributions to the dimensional approach to the study of facial expressions and emotion (Hofstatter, 1955, 1956; Izard & Nunnally, 1965; Plutchik, 1962). Some of their research led to the development of new dimensions, such as control or deliberative-impulsive (Osgood, 1966), attention-inattention (Frijda & Phillipszoon, 1963), and self-assured–insecure (Frijda, 1970).

Osgood's extensive analysis of live expressions yielded three dimensions that he interpreted in terms of his semantic dimensions of linguistic signs. He concluded that his expression dimensions of pleasantness, activation, and control correspond to the semantic dimensions of evaluation, activity, and potency. Osgood's interpretation may be an important one for students of emotion-cognition interactions.

Sensory Reactions as the Origin of Facial Expressions

Based on his work with blind people, Piderit (1925) maintained that Darwin overemphasized the role of heredity in facial expressions. He supported this conclusion with the observation that expressiveness around the eyes in blind people was positively correlated with the relative amount of time that the individual had enjoyed sight. That is, expressive movements around the eyes tend to deteriorate in people who lose their sight early in life, while no such loss in expressive movements occurs around the mouth and lower face. Thus, according to Piderit, while heredity may play some role in the expressive movements, expressions are primarily dependent upon the interaction of mental and sensory functions. Modern students will recognize the weakness of Piderit's argument against the role of heredity, since more recent research has shown that any behavioral mechanisms, no matter how thoroughly preprogrammed genetically, require some practice or exercise in order to achieve normal function.

Nevertheless, Piderit pointed out an important relationship between the sensory organs of the face and expressive movements. He maintained that there were different expressive movements associated with pleasant and unpleasant sensory impressions. For example, certain specific mouth movements occur in response to a bitter taste in the mouth. By the process of association an unpleasant idea can become the stimulus for the same mouth movement as an unpleasant object in the mouth. All ideas have pleasant or unpleasant qualities and can become stimuli for positive or negative expressive movement. According to Piderit, the frequency of occurrence of expressive movement is a function of the relative activity and excitability of the various sensory organs. "Thus most frequent are movements of muscles of visual organs, less frequent of the gustatory organ, even less frequent of the olfactory organ, and most rare of the auditory organ" (Piderit, 1925, p. 39).

Wundt (1877, cited in Peiper, 1963) proposed the theory of expression which like Piderit's leaned heavily on the basic principle that the expressions are associated with sensory process. According to Wundt an inner psychological state, such as fear or sadness, becomes linked with movements and sensations of movement corresponding to the natural reactions of sensory organs to external perceptions. Facial expressions that originally indicate simply the reactions of the perceiving organ to a sensory stimulus gradually become a form of expression of sensations and emotions. When a person feels "bitter anger" his mouth takes on the expression seen when one is tasting a bitter substance. More recently Lersch (1957) has extended and developed the principles laid down by Piderit and Wundt. Lersch noted that the sensory theory of facial expression could not explain the positive expressions of smiling and laughing. He introduced the "law of contrasting accentuation" to explain these expressions: smiling and laughing are expressions contrasting with those that follow from the quality of bitterness.

The most extensive contemporary statement of the sensory theory of facial expressions is that of Peiper (1963). Peiper pointed out that the muscles or expressions are primarily the muscles that form the radiating and circular frames of the mouth, nose, and eyes, "the seat of the three senses whose original mission is increasing the perceptive ability for welcome stimuli and decreasing it for unwelcome ones" (p. 112). Peiper pointed out that in addition to the primary or immediate sensory reaction to a stimulus there is often a secondary or spreading reaction to a non-stimulated sensory organ. The movements brought about by the primary and spreading reactions of the sensory organs can account for many facial expressions, according to Peiper. Peiper also pointed out that the sensory reactions to unpleasant stimuli may be considered defensive movements; and he noted that changes in the respiratory rhythm caused by sensory stimuli influence facial expression. Thus the position of the mouth in the crying infant is the combined result of respiratory changes and sensory re-actions. Peiper's theory is well summarized in the following statement:

> The development of each child teaches us again and again that crying and screaming are originally elicited only by unpleasant sensory perceptions, the only effective cause at all ages. From this fact we can postulate that the facial expression of a bad mood had its origin in the defensive sensory reactions which diminish the undesired sensory stimuli as much as possible and thus make them innocuous. This can still be seen today as the expressive movement of a bad mood in the infant and in the adult (Peiper, 1963, pp. 121–22).

Peiper, like the earlier sensory theorists, recognized that his theory was more applicable to negative expressions than to positive ones. Peiper did not accept the notion of some of the earlier theorists (Wundt, 1877) that smiling derived from the sensory movements made in response to a sweet taste. Peiper noted that infants do not smile in response to a sweet substance; they suck and swallow. Peiper had no clear and firm statement as to the origin of the positive expressions, but he leaned toward a notion similar to that of Lersch's Law of Contrast. He also seemed willing to accept the evolutionary significance of the smile, noting that at a phylogenetically lower stage this expression could have been "the key to the vital distinction between the other man's friendly or hostile intentions" (p. 131). In concluding his analysis of the origin of facial expressions, Peiper indicated that only negative emotion expressions could be well explained by the sensory theory and that positive expressions are better explained by a combination of inborn tendencies and social learning.

The Evolutionary-Genetic Theory of Facial Expression

Darwin (1872) placed facial expressions in evolutionary perspective with the statement of three principles. At least part of the substance of each of the three principles still finds some support in the contemporary theorizing of ethologists, but in the elaboration and explanation of these principles Darwin made some errors characteristic of the biological thought of his day.

Expressive movements derived from adaptive acts.   Darwin called this idea the principle of serviceable associated habits, but the term *habit* tends to conceal the power and continued plausibility of Darwin's notion. The part of this principle that is still supported by contemporary theory and evidence is the idea that an expressive movement is originally part of an adaptive act that helped the organism cope in the stimulus situation. As Darwin put it, expressive movements derived from serviceable acts that satisfied a certain state of mind—sensation, desire, or intention. The part of the principle that has fallen into disrepute was Darwin's belief that the expressive movement eventually became habitual and that the habit was transmitted to the next generation and inherited as an emotion expression. Thus Darwin was mistakenly adopting a Lamarckian position on the inheritance of acquired traits.

The principle of antithesis.   Darwin maintained that once there was a connection between a state of mind and an expression, the arousal of the opposite state of mind would tend to evoke the opposite expression even if such a movement had not been of service to the organism. The weakness of this principle is that Darwin again used the concept of habit to explain the connection between the state of mind and the expression, and in this sense the principle is dependent upon the inheritance of acquired characteristics. This is probably the least plausible and least supported of Darwin's original ideas on the origin of expression.

The principle of direct action of the nervous system.   This principle is similar to the one enunciated by Spencer (1855); it suggests that a neural discharge may affect directly the expressive musculature associated with a particular emotion. To some extent Darwin leaned on the concept of habit formation and acquired traits in elaborating on this principle, but importantly he also considered that the direction of the neural discharge was determined, in part, by the innate structure of the nervous system. This point was confirmed by his statement that the principle of direct action is independent of the will and to a large extent of habit. With this idea Darwin anticipated Tomkin's (1962) and Izard's (1971) theories that postulate innate subcortical programs for the expressions of each of the fundamental emotions. For other critiques of Darwin's theory, the reader is referred to Arnold (1960) and Honkavaara (1961).

Tinbergen's (1952, 1973) extensive study of bird displays led to the development of two concepts that support Darwinian thought. His first idea about the evolutionary development of expressive or display behavior is summarized by the term "displaced activity." An example of such displaced activity (a seemingly irrelevant act) is grass pulling in the herring gull during social encounters. Grass pulling is part of the normal activity in nest building. In the course of evolution, the grass-pulling movement came to communicate threat and to release retreat behavior in the opponent. The releasor function started a new evolutionary development termed "ritualization" (after Huxley, 1923, cited in Tinbergen, 1952) in which the displacement activities became increasingly adapted to their releasor function. The ritualization gradually brings about changes in morphological structures and these in turn result in an exaggeration and simplification of the displacement activity. Gradually the ritualized act is subserved by an independent neural mechanism and the display loses its displacement character and becomes more strictly an element of social communication.

Tinbergen's second idea about the origin of display behavior is summarized in his concept of "intention movements," incomplete movements caused by a drive of low intensity. Such movements signal to an observer what an animal intends to do.

The recent work of Andrew (1963, 1965) supported the basic ideas contained in Darwin's principle as well as the ideas of Tinbergen. According to Andrew, movements that conveyed information to the animal's fellows about the future behavior of the animal served adaptive purposes. Because of this adaptive-communicative function, the movement was passed along genetically through natural selection. Andrew supported the notion that expressive movements are transmitted to subsequent generations by virtue of their communicative function, pointing out the apparent correlation between animal sociability (communicativeness) and expressiveness. The relatively social wolf displays a far greater range of facial expressions than the solitary bear. Andrew supported the Darwinian notion that the facial expressions were originally associated with other adaptive acts and were not originally expressions of emotion. He suggested that the movements involved in facial expression were originally responses designed to protect vulnerable areas, especially sense organs, and responses associated with vigorous respiration and grooming. While Piderit and Peiper saw the responses associated with the protection of sensory organs as a vehicle for the ontological development of expression, the position represented by Darwin, Tinbergen, and Andrew suggests that sensory reactions were the movements from which expressive behavior derived through evolutionary-genetic processes.

Cross-Cultural Evidence for the Universality of the Fundamental Emotions

The physiological-mechanical theory and the sensory theory allow for relatively more influence from sociocultural factors on the development of expressive movements. The evolutionary-genetic theory states unequivocally that when a particular pattern of facial movements took on a standard intraspecific communicative function that served adaptive purposes, it was passed on to subsequent generations through natural selection. The evolutionary-genetic theory can subsume the sensory theory by allowing for the fact that sensory reactions provide many of the phylogenetically early movements from which facial expressions derived.

Most of the cross-cultural research on emotions has been designed to evaluate Darwin's hypothesis of innateness and universality of the expressions of emotions. Darwin's (1872) early work was truly cross-cultural, but he had to depend on verbal descriptions and anecdotal reports of observers (friends and acquaintances) residing in other parts of the world. Extensive cross-cultural research on emotions has been reported by Ekman, Friesen, and Ellsworth (1972); Izard (1971); and Sorenson (1975). The original research of these investigators was done against a background of within-culture research in the United States and various countries of Western Europe; both Ekman and his colleagues and Izard were guided by some common theoretical conceptions regarding the emotions.

Since the within-culture research on facial expressions has been reviewed and critically analyzed in the references cited in the foregoing paragraph, only a brief summary will be given here. After Darwin's impressive and highly stimulating research on the expressions of emotions in animals and man in 1872, there was a gap of nearly fifty years when there was virtually no scientific activity in this realm. Biologists abandoned the field of emotion expression until the discipline of ethology began to gain impetus in the second quarter of this century. Ethologically trained biologists focused on the study of behavior of animals in their natural habitat, and most of their contributions came from studies of the display and communicative systems of lower animals— bees, birds, fish and others (e.g., Tinbergen, 1952; Lorenz, 1966). In the late fifties and early sixties some of the ethologists turned their attention to higher primates and their work tended to substantiate Darwin's notion of the continuity of expressions in animals and man (Hinde & Rowell, 1962; Van Hoof, 1963; Bolwig, 1964; Altman, 1967).

In the late sixties and seventies ethologists began the study of behavior patterns in human beings (e.g., Blurton-Jones, 1972; McGrew, 1972). Most of this work has been within-culture research with children. Their approach to the study of expressions or displays began with defining small, easily observable, and readily defined units of behavior. As a rule they make no assumptions regarding the possible underlying internal states or motivational processes. One of the aims of these investigators, as stated by some of them, is to construct a complete ethogram (repertory of expressive movements), and to fit these into a more complete ethogram of behavior that describes all the interactions of the organism with the environment. Only then, they maintain, will it be possible to analyze the antecedent and consequent responses associated with expressions or displays.

Although a few studies in the first quarter of this century showed that it was possible to obtain a fairly high degree of concensus in the classification-of-facial-expressions-by-emotion category, when psychologists finally became serious about the study of facial expression American psychology was beginning to fall under the domination of behaviorism. Actually, Watson (1919) spoke of the innateness of three primary emotions (love, rage, and fear), but subsequent behavioristic investigators (Irwin, 1932) discredited the studies on which Watson based his inferences about primary emotions.

Behaviorism's denial of inner experience as a proper subject for scientific psychology was not the only problem besetting those who would study emotion and emotion expression. More importantly there was no theoretical framework to help the investigator define an emotion or to draw the limits on the range of states that would be considered as emotion. As a consequence investigators tried to find facial expressions to represent such widely different inner states as anger and admiration on the one hand, and fear and doubt on the other. Although some advances have been made in theory and empirical research, the basic question raised by James nearly a century ago is still with us: "What is an emotion?"

The way James worded the answer to his own question seemed to put the neck of emotion research in a noose from which it has never completely escaped. He said emotion was the *perception* of certain *bodily changes.* For many psychologists even today it is an easy step from James's "perception" to cognition and from "bodily changes" to glandular-visceral activity, and herein lies the chief source of controversy in defining emotion and in determining the relationship between emotion and expression.

Considerable confusion has resulted from the failure of many investigators to consider both somatic and glandular-visceral bodily changes in emotion research. Because of the influence of Lange, the merging of James's and Lange's theory, and the current of belief in James's day, the "bodily changes" that James spoke of came to be synonymous with changes in the glandular-visceral organs innervated by the autonomic nervous system. As a consequence, investigators in the field of emotion saw changes in heart rate, respiration, and skin conductance as far more important (objective and "scientific") indexes of emotion than changes in the facial muscles that shape expressions.

A critical factor in defining emotion is the decision as to whether emotion has a cognitive component. Psychologists are divided on this issue, with the majority explicitly or implicitly accepting a definition in which emotion involves cognition (e.g., Arnold, 1960; Lazarus and Averill, 1972; Frijda, 1970; Mandler, 1975; Schachter, 1971; Simonov, 1975). In discussing emotions they included such concepts as admiration, awe, bewilderment, and doubt. They tended to classify anything that has an affective component as an emotion. In this framework it would be possible to generate a virtually endless number of emotions, and it would be difficult if not impossible to say which of these were more primary or fundamental than the others. It was in part this kind of definitional problem that led to so many controversial findings in the early research on facial expressions. Some investigators seemed to have assumed that it was as appropriate to search for a unique expression of admiration as it was to search for one of anger.

Another resolution to the definitional problem is that found in Tomkins's (1962, 1963) and Izard's (1971, 1972) theories of emotion. They assume that just as there is a cognitive system and cognitive processes, there is a relatively independent emotion system, consisting of the fundamental emotions, their interactions, and interrelationships. Thus emotion can exist in consciousness independent of cognition. While they recognize that normally emotion and cognition interact and mutually influence each other, their recognition of separate cognition and emotion processes is crucial to the question of how to define emotion and, hence, how to study its expression. Izard and Tomkins see the sensory data (proprioceptive and cutaneous impulses) of facial expression as the source of sensory data that is processed as emotion. While the internal emotion process that generates subjective experience from facial feedback may follow from perceptual or cognitive processes, this need not necessarily be the case. An emotion may be generated by a drive state or by another emotion, apart from any cognitive process. Tomkins and Izard classify a concept like admiration or bewilderment as an interaction of emotions and cognition (affect-cognition interaction), and since the cognitive component would be subject to learning and idiosyncratic experience, they would not necessarily expect such a complex concept to be represented by a universal expression. Izard defines an emotion as fundamental when it has a universal facial expression fired by an innate neural program that leads to a specific experiential-motivational state. Thus one way to define the fundamental emotions is through a cross-cultural search for expressions that are transcultural and universal for human beings. This was the approach followed by Izard (1971) and Ekman et al. (1972) in their cross-cultural studies of facial expressions.

The first extensive and systematic cross-cultural studies of facial expression were reported nearly a hundred years after the publication of Darwin's famous treatise (Izard, 1968). The data from these studies and those from several other investigators are reported in Table 5-1. The data in this table were obtained by using photographs of facial expressions and by having subjects classify them into emotion categories. These data demonstrate rather convincingly that eight different emotion

Table 5-1 Percentage of Subjects Who Agreed on the Emotion Category of Photographs Selected to Represent Fundamental Emotions Cultural (National) Group

	American	English	German	Swedish	French	Swiss	Greek	Japanese (Tokyo)	Mexican[a]	Brazil[b]	Chile[b]	Argentina[b]
N=	89	62	158	41	67	36	50	60	616	82	90	168
Interest-Excitement	84.5	79.2	82.0	83.0	77.5	77.2	66.0	71.2				
Enjoyment-Joy	96.8	96.2	98.2	96.5	94.5	97.0	93.5	93.8	97	97	90	94
Surprise-Startle	90.5	81.0	85.5	81.0	84.2	85.5	80.2	79.2	54	82	88	93
Distress-Anguish	74.0	74.5	67.2	71.5	70.5	70.0	54.5	66.8	61	83	90	85
Disgust-Contempt	83.2	84.5	73.0	88.0	78.5	78.2	87.5	55.8	61	86	85	79
Anger-Rage	89.2	81.5	83.2	82.2	91.5	91.8	80.0	56.8	86	82	76	72
Shame-Humiliation	73.2	59.5	71.8	76.2	77.2	70.0	71.0	41.2				
Fear-Terror	76.0	67.0	84.0	88.8	83.5	67.5	67.8	58.2	71	77	78	68
Average	83.4	77.9	80.6	83.4	82.2	79.6	75.1	65.4				

a. The Mexican data were obtained by Dickey & Knower (1941).
b. The data from Brazil, Chile, and Argentina were obtained by Ekman & Friesen (1972). Ekman and Friesen also obtained data from a Japanese sample on the same six emotions they studied in South America, and they obtained somewhat higher percentages of agreement than those obtained in Izard's sample.

expressions are interpreted in the same fashion in a wide sample of literate cultures. In a subsequent study (summarized in Izard, 1971) it was shown that disgust and contempt can be represented by distinctly different expressions that are correctly identified in different cultures (American, Turkish, Indian, and Japanese).

Extension of Emotion Expression and Emotion Recognition
Studies to Preliterate Children

Ekman and his colleagues extended the study of the expression and recognition of the emotions to preliterate cultures in Borneo and New Guinea. In extending the work to preliterate cultures, Ekman chose to work only with six emotion categories that had been most consistently validated by other investigators. They are the same as six of the categories used by Tomkins and McCarter (1964) and Izard: happiness (joy), sadness (distress), disgust, surprise, anger, and fear.

In the first study (Ekman, Sorenson, & Friesen, 1969) the investigators used a categorization procedure similar to that of Izard, except that the subject was required to select from among only six categories instead of eight or nine. For the subjects in Borneo and New Guinea the emotion category words were translated into locally understood languages (Pidgin, Fore, and Bidayuh). The agreement or accuracy of emotion recognition in the preliterate cultures was less than that which Ekman et al. and Izard found in literate cultures, but it was significantly better than chance in three different preliterate samples. No emotion category was misidentified by the majority of observers in more than one of the preliterate samples.

In a follow-up study Ekman et al. (1969) sought even more completely isolated preliterate cultural samples. They returned to New Guinea and located subjects (189 adults and 130 children) who had never seen movies or magazines, spoken or understood English or Pidgin, lived in any Western settlement or government town, or worked for a Caucasian. Deciding that with this sample they would need to follow a more simplified procedure, the investigators adopted a format similar to the one Izard used in studies with children (Izard, 1971). They showed the subjects a triad of three pictures (emotion expressions), then told them a brief story that depicted one of the emotion expressions and required the subject to identify the emotion the experimenter was describing. The triad always included at least one emotion which in past studies with literate cultures had not been most frequently mistaken for the correct emotion.

The binomial test was applied to the responses for each picture, assuming chance performance to be one in three. It was found that all pictures were identified correctly at a significant level, with the exception of those sets where subjects had to distinguish between fear and surprise. (Fear and surprise were identified correctly when compared with other emotions. Poor discrimination occurred only when both appeared on the same triad.) A more stringent binomial test, assuming chance to be one in two, still showed that all pictures were identified in significantly correct proportions except when it was necessary to discriminate fear and surprise. By omitting the difficult discrimination between fear and surprise, Ekman et al. (1969) obtained essentially the same results with a sample of 130 children between the ages of six and fifteen as they did with their adult subjects.

In another experiment on the second trip to New Guinea, the same authors got nine male New Guinea subjects to express facially the emotion which would be felt by the person in each of the emotion stories used in the first experiment. All the subjects met the experimenters' criteria for visual isolation from Western civilization. The subjects' efforts were recorded on video tapes and later shown in random order to thirty-four American university students who were asked to judge the emotion intended by the New Guineans. The American observers judged the New Guinean poses of happiness, sadness, anger, and disgust with a significant degree of accuracy, though they, like the New Guineans, confused fear with surprise.

The data of Ekman and his associates (see also Ekman, 1973) constitute impressive evidence for the innateness and universality of six of the fundamental emotions: enjoyment (happiness), distress (sadness), anger, disgust, surprise, and fear. Izard's work together with that of Ekman and his colleagues seems to put to rest the question of the innateness and universality of emotion expressions. As regards the other fundamental emotions, the evidence already presented is quite robust, though the case would be strengthened by confirming data from preliterate cultures.

In addition to the systematic data on recognition of expressions of fundamental emotions presented in the foregoing summary, a number of ethologists have supported the Darwinian position. Haas (1970) argued that the innate recognition observed in relation to innate releasor mechanisms in animals extends to human beings. He speculated that disgust was an innate reaction to rotting substances or excrement or other matter detrimental to health, and that fear was innately released by darkness, steep drops, and large approaching bodies. A study of candid films made in several different primitive cultures led Haas to conclude that the expression of interest is transcultural. His description of the facial and head movements observed in interested people in the different cultures is quite similar to those described in the psychological investigations cited above. Haas suggested that the widening of the eyes and orienting of the head in the direction of the object of interest may have been of crucial importance among primitive peoples when they were in potentially dangerous situations.

Haas maintained that in Southern Europe innate (hence strong, clear) facial expressions are employed deliberately to suit the purposes of the communicator. That is, the expression of the emotion of distress may be simulated simply for reasons of politeness. This speculation is consistent with considerable folklore about the expressiveness of Southern Europeans, but he presented no systematic supporting data.

Eibl-Eibesfeldt (1971) described a transcultural greeting response and illustrated it with photographs of French, Waika Indian, Balinese, and Papuan people. The common elements in the photographs are raised eyebrows and transverse wrinkles across the length of the brow. Eibl-Eibesfeldt maintained that in the greeting response the eyebrows are jerked upward for about a sixth of a second. The expression on most of the eight faces presented by Eibl-Eibesfeldt has some of the components of interest, surprise, and joy; these photographs were taken with cameras using mirror lenses and prisms that permitted filming to the side without the subjects' knowledge. Eibl-Eibesfeldt also presented photographs demonstrating the marked similarity in the rage expression of a mandril, a Kabuki actor portraying the emotion, and a candid shot of a small girl experiencing rage. A rather detailed presentation of similarities between nonhuman primate and human facial expressions has been presented by Chevalier-Skolnikoff (1973).

Eibl-Eibesfeldt (1972) noted that there are some basic movements other than facial expressions that are essentially instinctive and transcultural. He discussed the example of head nodding to signal "yes" and head shaking to signal "no." He pointed out that the signals are the same across many cultures, but noted some differences. For example, Ceylonese have two ways of signaling yes. They nod the head in the usual fashion when answering yes to a simple factual question, but to indicate agreement to do something (for example, to join one in a cup of tea) they sway the head in a slow sideways movement. Eibl-Eibesfeldt thought that such examples illustrate slight cultural variations in the use of what are probably inborn behavior patterns. Darwin speculated that head shaking originated from food refusal, as when the satiated baby refuses the breast by turning its head away. Similarly Eibl-Eibesfeldt suggested that the head shaking may have its roots in a shaking-off movement, which is part of the behavioral repertory of birds and fur-bearing mammals. He observed that deaf- and blind-born children express refusal by head shaking.

Universality of Expression and Recognition
Limited to Fundamental Emotion

In another series of studies Izard assessed emotion recognition in another way, and the results have some bearing on the underlying hypothesis relating to the generalizability of emotion recognition across cultures. The stimuli were photographs containing cues for two or more emotions in the same face; that is, they presented a Complex Emotion Recognition Task (CERT). Since complex expressions presumably derive from interactions and combinations of primary emotions, and since the linkage between one emotion and another often involves other personality subsystems (e.g., cognitive) and social interactions (e.g., socialization), it was expected that there would not be as much cross-cultural similarity in responses to complex expressions (CERT stimuli) as to expressions of fundamental emotions. The results confirmed this expectation.

First it was determined that the categorization of the complex expressions of CERT was not random; then CERT was administered to forty-one American and thirty-seven French university students. In contrast to the expressions of fundamental emotions, seventeen of the thirty-four complex expressions yielded significantly different response distributions for the French and American samples. This finding suggests some important problems for future research, since expressive cues that convey emotion in everyday life are frequently embedded in complex expressions.

However, the amount of agreement that was actually obtained was remarkable, considering the fact that for each photograph subjects had to agree on the emotion that was most prominent, the one that was next most prominent, and so forth. There was no significant difference in the distribution of responses in the emotion categories for 50 percent (seventeen in thirty-four) of the pictures. Further research with emotion that blends using photographs carefully standardized within a given culture could yield information on idiosyncratic, culture-specific, and transcultural components of facial expressions.

Cross-Cultural Similarities and Differences in the Labelling of Facial Expressions

Since there now exists a number of cross-culturally standardized sets of facial expression photographs, it seems that there would be numerous studies of cultural similarities and variations in the labeling of universal expressions. Such data might be a quite fruitful source of information on cultural similarities and differences in the realm of expression interpretation and emotion communication. They might also furnish leads relating to a number of other emotion characteristics or emotion-related phenomena of personality and social interactions. Only a few studies have touched these problems.

Izard (1971), using the same photographs he used in cross-cultural studies of emotion recognition, conducted emotion labeling studies in four cultures—American, English, French, and Greek. He projected the photos (slides) onto a screen and asked the subjects to make a free-response description of the emotions or feelings portrayed by the person in the photo. Considering the responses with frequencies of two or more, the 268 subjects from the four cultures used 224 different words or labels in responding to the thirty-two photographs. Twenty-seven of the words were unique to female subjects and nineteen were unique to males. Thirteen judges were asked to categorize the 224 words into one of the eight fundamental emotion categories. In placing the free-response descriptions into emotion categories, the judges could place each in one of the emotion categories, indicate that the response connoted two or more emotions, or indicate that the label had no emotion connotation. Twenty-seven of the words were categorized by the judges as having no emotion connotation and forty-six were judged as connoting two or more emotions. The remaining 151 free response descriptions were assigned to one of the eight emotion categories by a majority of the thirteen judges. The judges' placement of the 151 terms in the emotion categories is shown in Table 5–2.

Interestingly, in terms of vocabulary there were few unique descriptions for any culture, although frequency of usage for different labels var-

Table 5–2   **"Correct" Free-Response Labels for the Series 1 Photos of Fundamental Emotions**
N = 268—89 Americans, 62 British, 67 French, 50 Greeks (A Priori Emotion Categories Are Centered, Followed by Correct Transcultural Free-Response Labels)

INTEREST-EXCITEMENT

attentive	fervor[b]	questioning
concentration	inquisitive	reflection[a]
concern[a]	interest	religious fervor[b]
contemplation[a]	observation[b]	seriousness
curiosity	pensive	somber reflection
deliberating	pondering	thoughtfulness
excitement[b]	puzzlement	wonder
expectation[a]		

ENJOYMENT-JOY

amusement	gratitude[b]	playful
bliss[a]	happiness	pleasantness
clowning	humor[a]	pleasure
contentment	jovial	rapture
delight[a]	joy	satisfaction
ecstasy	laugh	sees something pleasant
elation	merry	self-satisfaction[a]
enjoyment[b]	mystical ecstasy	serenity[a]
gaiety	optimism	smile
glee[a]		

Table 5-2   (continued)

SURPRISE-STARTLE

amazed	pleasant astonishment	surprise
amused surprise[b]	pleasant surprise[b]	surprise, fear
astonishment	shock	surprise, joy
fearful astonishment	startle[a]	surprise with fear
joyful surprise		

DISTRESS-ANGUISH

about to cry[a]	grief	sad
anguish	hurt	sorrow
bad news	loneliness	suffering[a]
crying	melancholy[b]	troubled[a]
dejected	misery[a]	uneasiness
dejection	not going well	unhappy
depression	pain[a]	unloved[a]
despair	pathetic	upset[a]
disappointment	pity[b]	worry
distress		

DISGUST-CONTEMPT

aversion[b]	dislike	scorn
contempt	distaste	skepticism
cynical	insolence[b]	smirk[a]
derision	mockery[a]	smug[b]
disapproval	repugnance[a]	sneer
disdain	repulsion	superiority
disgust	sarcasm	

ANGER-RAGE

aggressive	furious	revenge[a]
anger	fury	spite
bitterness[b]	mad	vengeful[a]
enmity[a]	rage	vexation[b]
ferocity[a]		

SHAME-HUMILIATION

ashamed	guilt	shame
bashful[b]	penitent	shyness
embarrassment	repentance[b]	timidity

FEAR-TERROR

anxious	fright	scared
apprehension	horror	terror
fear	panic[a]	

a. Words unique to females
b. Words unique to males

ied considerably. The percentages of appropriate labeling responses for each emotion category and for each culture are presented in Table 5–3. For female subjects the average number of correct responses considering all emotion categories and all cultures was 56 percent while the corresponding figure for male subjects was 50 percent. Although this is substantial agreement for the unstructured task of free-response descriptions of stimuli, it is considerably lower than the 70–80 percent obtained in the emotion recognition studies where subjects were provided with a list of labels to choose from. The data were transformed to angles and submitted to an analysis of variance. Neither the variance due to culture nor to sex was significant. There was a significant difference in the accuracy with which the various emotions were appropriately labeled. As can be seen from inspection of Table 5–3, the emotion of joy is labeled correctly by 71–90 percent of the subjects, while the emotion of shame was labeled correctly by as few as 7 percent of some groups. The emotion of interest was the next lowest in terms of frequency of correct responses. If the emotions of interest and shame are removed from consideration, the average percent of correct responses is 61 percent for males and 65.4 percent for females.

The difference between accuracy in the emotion labeling task and the emotion recognition task may be accounted for by a number of factors. In the first place the structure of the two tasks would account for some of the difference. The emotion recognition task is structured and the number of correct responses expected by chance is approximately one in ten while the number expected by chance in the emotion labeling task is one in an infinitely large number. Another factor might be that the relative infrequency with which people practice the labeling of emotion expressions may mean that subjects in judging the photos simply did not think through the various alternatives well enough to make the best possible choice. There is also the possibility that something was lost in translations and in the problems presented by idiosyncratic responses.

Emotion-Related Attitudes and the Socialization of Emotions in Different Cultures

The research reviewed in the foregoing section suggested that the emotions may be among the most fundamental and universal phenomena in personality and culture. This raises the question about the importance of emotions in determining social systems, cultural processes, and individual personality. Not much research has been directed specifically toward answering these questions, but some that will be reviewed in this section has a bearing directly or indirectly.

Table 5-3 Percentage of Subjects Giving "Correct" Response on Emotion Labeling Task

| | American | | English | | French | | Greek | |
	Male (N=50)	Female (N=39)	Male (N=23)	Female (N=39)	Male (N=14)	Female (N=53)	Male (N=25)	Female (N=25)
EMOTION								
Interest-Excitement	31.7	43.5	27.9	36.0	25.1	34.1	36.5	35.2
Enjoyment-Joy	90.2	89.3	71.3	84.7	93.9	82.1	80.0	80.4
Surprise-Startle	87.9	89.7	73.1	83.4	60.7	65.8	52.7	60.0
Distress-Anguish	57.6	63.4	54.4	68.9	82.2	53.2	43.9	55.3
Disgust-Contempt	45.4	53.6	44.5	47.5	39.4	48.8	42.1	55.3
Anger-Rage	63.2	70.4	56.0	57.0	37.5	58.0	39.6	54.6
Shame-Humiliation	9.1	14.7	9.5	6.9	7.2	18.2	33.9	18.4
Fear-Terror	62.4	56.1	54.4	61.5	58.9	63.2	74.0	67.7

% Using Label

(Taken from *The Face of Emotion* by C. E. Izard, Appleton-Century-Crofts, 1971)

In addition to the facial expression research, the work of Benedict (1934), Mead (1937), and Whiting and Child (1953) attests to the fact that the emotions and emotion concepts are transcultural phenomena. Concepts of joy, anger, disgust, contempt, sadness, fear, shame, and guilt are common in cross-cultural research reports. Although the emotions are not treated systematically in cultural anthropology, the literature of that field gives the impression that emotions and emotion expressions play a role in social interactions and in the development of social norms and other aspects of social organization.

Spiro's (1961) analysis of the relationship between personality and social systems gives a special place to what he terms emotional needs. He makes the assumption that human social systems are a functional requirement of human life. Thus human existence requires socially shared behavior patterns that satisfy "(a) biological needs, (b) those needs that are an invariant concomitant of social life, and (c) those emotional needs that develop in the interaction between biology and society" (p. 96).

A number of psychological and anthropological investigators have given a substantial place to the emotions in explaining social and cultural phenomena. Fear or anxiety, love, hostility, disgust, and contempt have often been considered as important motivators in the socialization process (Dollard & Miller, 1950, chapter 20). Piers and Singer (1953) and Mead (1956) used shame or guilt concepts to explain individual conscience and social sanction. Whole cultures have been stereotyped as friendly, hostile, contemptuous, or fearful (Leeper & Madison, 1959, pp. 98–133), or as "shame" cultures or "guilt" cultures (Benedict, 1946).

Using data on seventy-five primitive societies from the cross-cultural file of the Institute of Human Relations, Whiting and Child (1953) showed some relationships between types of socialization and later susceptibility to various emotion reactions such as anxiety. For example, they showed that the greater the severity of socialization in a particular system of behavior (e.g., oral or genital), the greater the anxiety associated with that system and the more that system would be the focus of concern and worry in adult life.

Knapen (1958) used observational and interview techniques to study the effects of the Batongo society's practice of allowing the child almost complete indulgence up to the age of weaning. Until this age the child is subjected to moral sanctions only after the performance of such a highly undesirable behavior that it would cause great embarrassment to the clan. Even then punishment is light or negligible when the behavior occurs in the relative privacy of the family. The same offense may provoke intense reprobation if it is more public. Thus internalized values tend to be purely social values operating only in a social context. He maintained that this type of socialization caused "fear of others" to be stronger and more frequent than "guilt reactions." This is opposite to the order of the frequency of these emotions in Western cultures (Izard, 1971).

Siegel (1955) studies the role of anxiety in cultural integration and societal cohesion. Cultural integration was defined as the interrelatedness among elements of a social system. "A tightly integrated system is characterized by the strong centralization of values; that is, the tendency for broad sections of the culture to be related to a few key values supported by a strong *emotional* reluctance to change" (p. 42). He defined anxiety in such a way as to make it equivalent to the concept of fear; i.e., as the anticipation of danger, and he pointed out that whole groups or societies may develop the habit of responding to certain cues with anticipation of danger and fear. Siegel analyzed three cultures—the Hopi, the East European Jewish Shtetl, and the Hutterites. In each of these societies he found a high level of anxiety and a high degree of cultural or social integration. He argued:

> Assuming that anxiety states are painful, especially when experienced intensely, it is expected that some opportunities are necessary to relieve tensions and to dispel them temporarily. The only universally approved mode of behavior which has this function is participation in communal life itself. Many of the real and supposed dangers of individuals are removed, at least in part, by common participation in group-centered activities (Siegel, 1955, p. 43).

From Siegel's argument one can infer that the cultural pattern of responding to fear generated by cues perceived by many members of a society leads to a decrease in individualism, an increase in group cohesion, and a strengthening of the values, beliefs, and practices that maintain it. Siegel's cross-cultural work anticipated Schachter's (1959) finding that experimentally induced anxiety or fear increased the affiliative motive in American college students. More specifically, Schachter showed that a threatened individual preferred the company of similarly threatened people to people in other conditions.

Grinder and McMichaels (1963) and McMichaels and Grinder (1964, 1966) have shown that personal behaviors in relation to shame and guilt vary with cultural concepts and practices. In the first experiment they studied the relative effect of "a shame and a guilt culture" on resistance to temptation. Following Mead's (1956) observation that Samoans are guilt-free since their behavior control depends entirely on external sanctions, Grinder and McMichael hypothesized that in a temptation situation where subjects could envision no social sanction for transgression Samoan children (from a shame culture with behavior control by social sanction) would show less resistance to temptation than would American children (from a guilt culture with behavior control by own sanction). They measured resistance to temptation by a game in which children had to cheat to win the offered prize or reward. The children did not know that the experimenter had a sure way of detecting those who falsified their scores in the target-shooting game. Two weeks after the target-shooting session subjects were administered a multiple-choice story completion measure of guilt. The stories described a transgression wherein the transgressor could not be detected, and the children were required to check the response that best described what they would feel and do if they were the character in the story. They did find, as predicted, that significantly more of the Samoan children (100 percent) yielded to temptation and falsified their scores on the target-shooting game. Further, the Samoans had significantly lower means on all three dimensions of the story completion guilt measure—remorse, confession, restitution. However, the magnitude of the Samoans' scores on the story completion test showed they were far from free of guilt or the effects of conscience as Mead implied.

In a later study, using the same tests, McMichael and Grinder (1964) found no differences between Japanese-Americans and white Americans in Hawaii. Although it was the study of the Japanese that led Benedict (1946) to the shame-culture concept, it might be argued that there has been much cultural change since her study and that Hawaii may not provide an adequate testing ground for the hypothesis. In a third study McMichael and Grinder (1966) found some evidence that guilt development as measured by their procedures was weaker in Japanese-American children in Hawaii who had little exposure to American culture than in those with greater exposure.

Munroe and Munroe (1975) summarized the evidence from cultural anthropology bearing on the question of the relationship between affective experiences in infancy and early childhood, on the one hand, and adult personality and social relations, on the other. While they could find no evidence that any society deprived infants of positive emotions and emotional attachments as severely as some orphanages and foundling homes in the West, they did find data on a few societies around the world where the socialization of infants minimized positive emotions and positive affective relationships. They found a correlation between neglect of the infant's emotional needs and adult personality traits of fearfulness and suspicion. More generally, neglectful treatment of the infant appeared to be associated with maldevelopment of the emotion system and emotion related behavior: "Societies that were scored as typically rejecting of children produced a familiar syndrome of adult personality characteristics—low emotional responsiveness, emotional instability, low self-evaluation, low generosity, and dependence" (Munroe & Munroe, 1975, p. 40). They also reviewed some evidence that supported Mead's (1928) idea that the practice of using a large number of caretakers for an infant produces adults who form only shallow emotional ties. They cited a number of studies that supported the notion that intensity of emotional attachments to individuals varied inversely with the number of caretakers in infancy. They cited a study by Rabin (1965) showing that children reared in Israeli kibbutzim formed stronger ties to peers than to parents. Interestingly, the effects of single versus multiple caretakers can be observed in a comparison of two species of monkeys—rhesus macaques who form strong mother-infant (one on one) relationships, and bonnett macaques whose infants receive social support from all the adults in the troupe. Rosenblum and Kaufman (1968) showed that pigtail macaque infants suffer lasting separation distress and depression in mother-infant separation studies, while bonnett macaque infants show only a mild and temporary reaction. When bonnett infants are separated from their mothers and left with other bonnett macaques, the social support received from their conspecifics apparently prevents separation distress and depression. However, if a bonnett infant living in a mixed group of bonnetts and pigtails is separated from its mother and left with only the pigtail macaques (who do not provide social support in the same way as bonnetts), the separated bonnett infant shows all the classic signs of separation distress, depression, and withdrawal (Kaufman & Rosenblum, 1969; Kaufman & Stynes, 1978).

Blurton-Jones and Konner (1973) found some sex and cultural differences in the play behavior of London and Bushman children. Of particular interest were their observations of the facial behavior that accompanies rough and tumble play—closed-mouth smile, open-mouthed smile, smile with squared lower lip, and laugh. Boys in both cultures displayed these facial expressions (and engaged in rough and tumble play) more frequently than girls, but Bushman girls displayed them much more frequently than London girls. The latter finding was accounted for by the fact that Bushman girls play more with boys than with other girls. Bushman girls showed more play faces and the reverse was true for London girls. It seems reasonable to assume a correlation between the Bushman sex-role training implied by these findings and the fact that men and women in the Bushman hunter-gatherer culture share the work of providing food about equally. In general, Blurton-Jones and Konner found that the relationship between specific facial expressions and bodily actions was the same in both cultures.

Izard obtained evidence that some apparent intercultural differences in emotion-related behavior may stem from differences in attitudes toward the emotions rather than simply from the emotions themselves. Subjects from ten different cultures were instructed to answer certain questions about one of the emotions on the list of fundamental emotions that had been previously used by the subjects in an emotion classification experiment. These data have been reported in detail (Izard, 1971) and only highlights of the answers to a few of the questions will be presented here. An overall analysis of the data for each question was accomplished by analysis of variance. When there was a significant culture x emotion inter-action, as was almost always the case, differences between cultures were measured in terms of standard deviations from the grand mean for all cultures taken together.

One of the questions was "What emotion do you understand the best?" As expected, from the percent agreement scores obtained in previ-ous research, the highest average percentage of responses fell in the cate-gory of joy. However, a significant culture x emotion interaction showed that the cultural samples differed significantly in their choice of which emotion they understood best. The English selected interest-excitement more frequently than joy; the Swedes and Japanese had very large per-centages in joy with correspondingly small percentages in other cate-gories. The French and the Greeks distributed their responses somewhat more evenly between the three categories of interest, enjoyment, and dis-tress. Not a single subject in the Swedish and Japanese samples indicated that distress was the best understood emotion.

Another question was "Which emotion do you understand least?" In answering this question the Japanese males put 68 percent of their re-sponses in the shame category, placing them two standard deviations above the overall mean. The data did not furnish concrete evidence about why the Japanese should deviate so strongly on this emotion, but it was not simply an East-West difference. A relatively large percentage of the Swiss (58 percent) also selected shame as the least understood emotion. The explanation as to why a large majority of the Japanese gave this re-sponse is not helped by Benedict's (1946) classification of the Japanese as an example of a "shame culture," unless it is assumed that the prevalence of shame contributes more to repression of its significance than to the un-derstanding of it.

A third question that may help illuminate the data from the foregoing one was "Which emotion do you dread the most?" In answering this question the modal category for all cultural groups except the Japanese, was either fear, shame, or anger. By far the most deviant response to this question came from the Japanese, who placed a little more than 70 percent of their responses in the category of disgust-contempt. The percentage of responses the Japanese placed in the shame category was below the mean. Putting the findings for this and the preceding questions in juxtaposition suggests that the negative emotions of shame and disgust-contempt are of considerable importance in the personality and culture dynamics of the Japanese. It is interesting to note that Tomkins (1963) speculated that shame and contempt are sometimes confused with each other, and Izard (1971) observed that contempt from another may be the most important single instigator of the emotion of shame.

In commenting on the Japanese responses to the foregoing questions, Professor Yoshihisa Tanaka of the University of Tokyo suggested that part of the explanation may lie deep in Japanese history. When the Samurai were the elite ruling class of Japan, a very strict and rigid ritual was followed in the event that a Samurai was looked upon with contempt. When this occurred, the only alternative open to the Samurai was either to kill the person who held him in contempt or to kill himself. If it is correct to assume that contempt tends to elicit shame, then we might consider that contempt from another person evoked shame in the Samurai, and his violent reaction to the contempt of another was, at least secondarily, a response to his own shame. This reasoning is made more plausible by the fact that the Samurai was considered to have regained his honor if he killed the offender or committed suicide. The look of contempt led to loss of honor, and it is reasonable to infer that loss of honor activated the emotion of shame.

The Functions of the Emotions in Biological and Cultural Evolution

The thoughts expressed in this section are necessarily speculative. There is no evidence and indeed no known method of obtaining direct evidence in support of some of the ideas expressed. They are based on the assumption that the emotions have served adaptive functions throughout human history. Other behavioral scientists have argued in favor of such an assumption (Averill, 1968; Hamburg, 1963; Jolly, 1966; Mead, 1950). In a paper on the role of emotions in primate cultures and the evolution of human beings, Hamburg wrote:

> The principal points I want to make are as follows: primates are group-living forms; the primate group is a powerful adaptive mechanism; emotional processes that facilitate interindividual bonds (participation in group living) have selective advantage; the formation of such bonds is pleasurable for primates; they are easy to learn and hard to forget; their disruption is unpleasant and precipitates profound psychophysiological changes that tend to restore close relations with others of the same species (p. 305).

The emotion of interest plays a vital role in the development of skills and competencies, and the threshold and viability of one's interest is crucial to adaptation and effective functioning. This emotion also guarantees response to complexity, novelty, and change; and since human beings are complex and everchanging, interest facilitates the formation and maintenance of social relationships.

Joy complements interest in guaranteeing that human beings will be social creatures. A smile of joy on the human face is the most general and effective social stimulus that exists. The reciprocal smiling of mother and infant fosters attachment and the development of a strong interpersonal tie that facilitates the infant's survival and healthy development. Laughter games show that when a potentially distressing or frightening, ambiguous situation is resolved favorably and the infant laughs, the mother or caretaker tends to repeat the situation and the infant increases his or her participation (Sroufe and Wunsch, 1972). Thus joy and laughter preclude the strain of negative emotion and enhance infant-environment interaction.

Surprise clears the neural pathways of other messages and prepares the individual to deal effectively with a new or sudden event and the consequences of such events. From an evolutionary standpoint surprise can be seen as the emotion that functions to change the organism's motivational set. Failure to make such a change in the face of sudden danger could prove fatal.

As Tomkins (1963) pointed out, the emotion of distress tells the individual that all is not well, and it provides the motivation to address the problem and alleviate the distress. Distress also serves as the basis for empathy and altruism—it enables people to feel with the other individual who suffers, and empathic distress motivates the individual to work toward alleviation of the suffering of others.

Averill (1968) made a strong case for the biological origin and adaptive value of grief, of which the central affective component is distress. He argued that grief insured group cohesiveness in all species where a social form of existence was necessary for survival. Grief and anticipation of grief can serve as powerful forces motivating mutual care and protection.

Anger was classified by Cannon (1929) as one of the emergency emotions. Anger mobilizes energy and renders the individual capable of defending self with great vigor and strength, very useful attributes in the early history of the human species. While this function of anger became rarely needed with the rise of civilization, appropriately expressed anger may still be justifiable and adaptive when it is the necessary motive force that enables an individual to "speak up for self" and to defend against an attack on personal integrity, needless restraints, and oppression (Holt, 1970). Anger-related communications are effective in ongoing relationships when the anger is expressed in such a way as to avoid cutting off communication with the other individual.

During the course of evolution disgust probably helped prevent organisms from eating spoiled food and drinking polluted water and motivated them to maintain an environment sufficiently sanitary for their health. Disgust probably also played a role in the maintenance of body hygiene and the establishment of social standards for cleanliness.

In evolutionary perspective, contempt may have emerged as a vehicle for preparing a group to face an adversary. In contemporary life, occasions that elicit contempt are those in which the individual needs to feel stronger, more intelligent, more civilized, or in some way better than the opponent. It is difficult to see an adaptive role for contempt in contemporary life. Perhaps contempt for forces that pollute the environment and deface nature can be condoned, and maybe any contempt that falls on the human beings most responsible for such problems will help keep them in check and make them undesirable models for aspiring leaders.

The principal function of fear in evolution was to motivate the individual to escape from danger and to mobilize the necessary energy to accomplish this. Fear also serves as a force for social cohesion and collective action when the group or community is threatened (Eibl-Eibesfeldt, 1971). Fear anticipation or fear avoidance serves the same functions today. From their own experience (and the cumulative experience of the group) parents know that the most reliable way to keep their children safe from harm is to teach them to be afraid of dangerous situations.

In evolutionary terms, shame probably developed from a need for social norms, common patterns of socialization, and group cohesiveness. If a child's speech, manners, or other social behavior does not conform reasonably well with that of other persons of the group, he may be "shamed" or subjected to contempt that leads to shame. Using contempt and other techniques of eliciting shame are still frequently used to keep people in line. But shame heightens self-awareness, motivates self-improvement, and facilitates the development of self-identity (Lynd, 1961; Lewis, 1971).

Guilt and the motive to avoid guilt heighten one's sense of personal responsibility and guilt complements shame in fostering social responsibility. Without guilt and shame people would lose their grip on morality and ethics. Guilt becomes a built-in monitor of the rules of fair play and provides the structure for social order (see Mead, 1950).

Summary

This chapter focused on the discrete emotions of human experience, their expressions, and their roles as motivational/experiential variables in individual and social behavior. It gives considerable attention to the facial expression of emotion, since such expression is generally considered either a component or concomitant of emotion and since most cross-cultural studies of emotions have been concerned with their expressions. A substantial part of contemporary emotion theory and research places relatively more emphasis on the role of the somatic nervous system and the striate musculature (including that of the face) than on the glandular-visceral system.

One theory of facial expression holds that specific muscle patterning occurs simply as a result of electro-mechanical laws that govern neurophysiological responses. This theory has difficulty explaining how a particular expression became associated with a specific subjective experience.

Another tradition holds that facial expression can be described in terms of certain dimensions such as pleasantness-unpleasantness and relaxation-tension. While certain forms of this theory tend to discount the existence or significance of discrete emotions, Schlosberg and his associates feel that such dimensions could be used to predict or identify consensually validated emotion or expression categories. Two other theories are rooted mainly in the evolutionary-biological tradition. The first of these maintains that facial expressions derive mainly from defensive movements of the muscles surrounding the sensory organs of the face. While this principle explains the origin of certain of the negative emotion expressions rather well, it has no explanation of the development of expressions of positive emotions. Finally, Darwin supported the notion that expressions were derived from movements that were originally adaptive acts. He also proposed a principle of direct action of the nervous system that can be interpreted as favoring the existence of innate subcortical programs for specific facial expressions. Contemporary ethologists generally support the Darwinian position and some make explicit their belief that expressive movements were transmitted genetically by virtue of their communicative function, a function that is related to animal sociability.

Robust cross-cultural data and evidence from studies of the born-blind now lend strong support to Darwin's thesis that the expressions of the emotions are innate and universal. Some studies suggest that universality is limited to certain primary or fundamental emotions. However, even some blends (expressions representing components of two or more fundamental emotions) are correctly identified across certain cultures, though blends do not yield as high agreement as unitary expressions when naive judges are used.

Although the expressions and inner experiences that characterize the fundamental emotions are innate and universal, there are numerous cultural differences in attitudes toward the emotions and their expressions. Each culture tends to have its own set of display rules, and these norms tend to restrict the expression of emotions in terms of time and circumstance. For example some studies have shown that under certain conditions, subjects from some ethnic groups yield to temptation more frequently and express güilt less intensely than subjects from other ethnic groups. Other studies have shown that certain child-rearing practices or the socialization process changes the threshold for positive and negative emotions and significantly affects adult personality and social behavior.

Theoretical arguments and some empirical data support the notion that each of the fundamental emotions has an inherently adaptive function. Negative emotions play a role in defensive and corrective behavior and also play a role in the development of self-identity and social organization. The positive emotions facilitate the development of skills and competencies and the formation of interindividual bonds.

References

ABELSON, R. P., & SERMAT, V. Multidimensional scaling of facial expressions. *Journal of Experimental Psychology*, 1962, *63*(6), 546–54.

ALTMAN, S. A. *Social communication among primates.* Chicago: University of Chicago Press, 1967.

ANDREW, R. J. Evolution of facial expression. *Science*, 1963, *142*, 1034–41.

———. The origins of facial expressions. *Scientific American*, 1965, *213*, 88–94.

ARNOLD, M. B. *Emotion and personality*, Vol. I: *psychological aspects.* New York: Columbia University Press, 1960.

———. *Feelings and emotions.* New York: Academic Press, 1970.

AVERILL, J. R. Grief: its nature and significance. *Psychological Bulletin*, 1968, *70*, 721–48.

BENEDICT, R. *Patterns of culture.* Boston: Houghton-Mifflin, 1934.

———. *The crysanthemum and the sword.* Boston: Houghton-Mifflin, 1946.

BLACK, P. *Psychological correlates of emotion.* New York: Academic Press, 1970.

BLURTON-JONES, N. *Ethological studies of child behavior.* Cambridge, England: Cambridge University Press, 1972.

BLURTON-JONES, N., & KONNER, M. J. Sex differences in behavior of London and Bushmen children. In R. P. Michael and J. Crook (Eds.), *Comparative ecology and behavior of primates.* London: Academic Press, 1973.

BOLWIG, N. Facial expression in primates with remarks on a parallel development in certain carnivores (a preliminary report on work in progress). *Behavior*, 1964, *22*, 167–92.

CANNON, W. B. *Bodily changes in pain, hunger, fear, and rage*, 2nd ed. New York: Appleton, 1929.

CHEVALIER-SKOLNIKOFF, S. Facial expression of emotion in nonhuman primates. In Paul Ekman (Ed.), *Darwin and facial expression: a century of research in review.* New York: Academic Press, 1973.

COFER, C. N. *Motivation and emotion.* Illinois: Scott Foresman, 1972.

DARWIN, C. *The expression of the emotions in man and animals.* London: John Murray, 1872.

DELGADO, J. M. R. *Physical control of the mind.* New York: Harper & Row, 1971.

DICKEY, E. C., & KNOWER, F. H. A note on some ethnological differences in recognition of simulated expressions of the emotions. *American Journal of Sociology*, 1941, *47*, 190–93.

DOLLARD, J., & MILLER, N. E. *Personality and psychotherapy.* New York: McGraw-Hill, 1950.

DUFFY, E. Emotion: an example of the need for reorientation in psychology. *Psychological Review*, 1934, *41*, 184–98.

———. An explanation of "emotional" phenomena without the use of the concept "emotion." *Journal of General Psychology*, 1941, *25*, 283–93.

———. The concept of energy mobilization. *Psychological Review*, 1951, *58*, 30–40.

———. *Activation and behavior.* New York: Wiley, 1962.

DUMAS, G. *La vie affective*. Paris: Presses Universitaires de France, 1948.

EIBL-EIBESFELDT, I. *Love and hate*. New York: Holt, Rinehart and Winston, 1971.

——. Similarities and differences between cultures in expressive movements. In R. A. Hinde (Ed.), *Nonverbal communication*. Cambridge, England: Cambridge University Press, 1972, pp. 20–33.

EKMAN, P. Body position, facial expression, and verbal behavior during interviews. *Journal of Abnormal and Social Psychology*, 1964, *68*(3), 295–301.

EKMAN, P., (Ed.), *Darwin and facial expression*. New York: Academic Press, 1973.

EKMAN, P., FRIESEN, W. V., & ELLSWORTH, P. *Emotion in the human face*. New York: Pergamon, 1972.

EKMAN, P., SORENSON, E. R., & FRIESEN, W. V. Pan-cultural elements in facial displays of emotion. *Science*, 1969, *164*, 86–88.

ENGEN, R., LEVY, N., & SCHLOSBERG, H. The dimensional analysis of a new series of facial expressions. *Journal of Experimental Psychology*, 1958, *55*(5), 454–58.

FRIJDA, N. H. Emotion and recognition of emotion. In M. Arnold (Ed.), *Feelings and emotions*. New York: Academic Press, 1970.

——, & PHILLIPSZOON, E. Dimensions of recognition of expression. *Journal of Abnormal and Social Psychology*, 1963, *66*, 45–51.

GLASS, D. C. *Neurophysiology and emotion*. New York: Rockefeller University Press, 1967.

GRINDER, R. E., & MCMICHAELS, R. E. Cultural influence on conscience development: resistance to temptation and guilt among Samoans and American Caucasians. *Journal of Abnormal and Social Psychology*, 1963, *66*(5), 503–07.

HAAS, H. *The human animal*. New York: G. P. Putnam's Sons, 1970.

HAMBURG, D. A. Emotions in the perspective of human evolution. In P. H. Knapp (Ed.), *Expressions of emotion in man*. New York: International Universities Press, 1963, pp. 300–17.

HINDE, R. A., & ROWELL, T. E. Communication by postures and facial expressions in the rhesus monkey (*Macaca mulatta*). *Proceedings of the Zoological Society of London*, 1962, *138*, 1–21.

HOFSTATTER, P. R. Dimensionen des mimischen ausdrucks. *Zeitschrift für Angewandte und Experimentelle Psychologie*, 1955–56, *3*, 503–09.

HOLT, R. R. On the interpersonal and intrapersonal consequences of expressing or not expressing anger. *Journal of Consulting and Clinical Psychology*, 1970, *35*(1), 8–12.

HONKAVAARA, S. The psychology of expression. *British Journal of Psychology*, 1961, Monograph Supplement 32.

HUXLEY, J. S. Courtship activities in the red-throated diver (*Colymbus stellatus Pontopp.*), together with a discussion on the evolution of courtship in birds. *Journal of the Linnean Society of London*, 1923, *25*, 253–92.

IRWIN, O. C. Infant responses to vertical movements. *Child Development*, 1932, *3*, 167–69.

IZARD, C. E. The emotions as a culture-common framework of motivational experiences and communicative cues. Technical Report No. 30, 1968, Vanderbilt University, Contract No. 2149(03)–NR 171–6090, Office of Naval Research. In E. G. Beier, *The silent language: an annual of nonverbal communication*. New York: Psychological Dimensions, in press.

————. *The face of emotion.* New York: Appleton-Century-Crofts, 1971.

————. *Patterns of emotions: a new analysis of anxiety and depression.* New York: Academic Press, 1972.

————. *Human emotions.* New York: Plenum Press, 1977.

IZARD, C. E., & NUNNALLY, J. C. Evaluative responses to affectively positive and negative facial photographs: factor structure and construct validity. *Educational and Psychological Measurement,* 1965, *25,* 1061–71.

JACOBSEN, E. *Biology of emotions.* Springfield, Ill.: Thomas, 1967.

JOLLY, A. Lemur social behavior and primate intelligence. *Science,* 1966, *153,* 501–06.

KAUFMAN, C., & ROSENBLUM, L. A. The waning of the mother-infant bond in two species of macaque. In B. M. Foss (Ed.), *Determinants of infant behavior,* Vol. IV. London: Methuen, 1969.

KAUFMAN, C., & STYNES, A. J. Depression can be induced in the bonnett macaque infant. *Psychosomatic Medicine,* 1978, *40*(1), 71–75.

KNAPEN, M. L. Some results of an inquiry into the influence of child training practices on the development of personality in a Bacongo society (Belgian Congo). *Journal of Social Psychology,* 1958, *47,* 223–29.

LAZARUS, R. S., & AVERILL, J. R. Emotion and cognition: with special reference to anxiety. In C. D. Speilberger (Ed.), *Anxiety: contemporary theory and research.* New York: Academic Press, 1972.

LEEPER, R., & MADISON, P. *Toward understanding human personalities.* New York: Appleton-Century-Crofts, 1959, pp. 98–133.

LERSCH, P. Zur theorie des mimischen ausdrucks. *Zeitschrift für Angewandte und Experimentelle Psychologie,* 1957, *4,* 405–19.

LEWIS, H. *Shame and guilt in neurosis.* New York: International Universities Press, 1971.

LINDSLEY, D. B. Emotion. In S. S. Stevens (Ed.), *Handbook of experimental psychology.* New York: Wiley, 1951, pp. 473–516.

————. Psychophysiology and motivation. In M. R. Jones (Ed.), *Nebraska symposium on motivation.* Lincoln: University of Nebraska Press, 1957, pp. 44–105.

LORENZ, K. *On aggression.* New York: Harcourt, Brace, and World, 1966. (Original printing, 1963.)

LYND, H. M. *On shame and the search for identity.* New York: Science Editors, 1961.

MCGREW, W. C. *An ethological study of children's behavior.* New York: Academic Press, 1972.

MCMICHAELS, R. E., & GRINDER, R. E. Guilt and resistance to temptation in Japanese and white Americans. *Journal of Social Psychology,* 1964, *64,* 217–23.

————. Children's guilt after transgression: combined effect of exposure to American culture and ethnic background. *Child Development,* 1966, *37*(2), 425–31.

MALMO, R. B. *On emotions, needs, and our archaic brain.* New York: Holt, Rinehart and Winston, 1975.

MANDLER, G. *Mind and emotion.* New York: Wiley, 1975.

MEAD, M. *Coming of age in Samoa.* New York: William Morrow, 1928.

————. *Cooperation and competition among primitive peoples.* New York: McGraw-Hill, 1937.

————. Some anthropological consideration concerning guilt. In M. L. Reymert (Ed.), *Feelings and emotions.* New York: McGraw-Hill, 1950.

————. Social change and cultural surrogatic. In C. Kluckhohn and H. A. Murray (Eds.), *Personality in nature, society, and culture,* 2nd ed. New York: Alfred A. Knopf, 1956.

MUNROE, R., & MUNROE, R. *Cross-cultural human development.* Monterey, Calif.: Brooks/Cole, 1975.

OSGOOD, C. E. The semantic differential technique in the comparative study of culture. *American Anthropologist,* 1966, *66,* 171–200.

PEIPER, A. *Cerebral function in infancy and childhood.* New York: Consultants Bureau, 1963.

PIDERIT, T. *Mimik und Physiognomik.* Detmold, 1925. (Originally published in 1867.)

PIERS, G., & SINGER, M. *Shame and guilt: a psychoanalytic and a cultural study.* Springfield, Ill.: Thomas, 1953.

PLUTCHIK, R. *The emotions: facts, theories, and a new model.* New York: Random House, 1962.

PRIBRAM, K. H. *Mood states and mind.* Harmondsworth: Penguin Books, 1971.

RABIN, A. I. *Growing up in the kibbutz.* New York: Springer, 1965.

ROSENBLUM, L. A., & KAUFMAN, I. C. Variations in infant development and response to maternal loss in monkeys. *American Journal of Orthopsychiatry,* 1968, *38,* 418–26.

SCHACHTER, S. *The psychology of affiliation.* Stanford, Calif.: Stanford University Press, 1959.

————. *Emotion, obesity, and crime.* New York: Academic Press, 1971.

SCHLOSBERG, H. A scale for the judgement of facial expressions. *Journal of Experimental Psychology,* 1941, *29,* 497–510.

SIEGEL, B. J. High anxiety levels and cultural integration: notes on a psycho-cultural hypothesis. *Social Forces,* 1955, *39,* 42–48.

SIMONOV, P. V. *Vishaya nervnaya, deyatelnost cheloveka: Motivatsionnoemotsionalnie aspekts.* Moskva: Izdatelstvo, 1975.

SORENSON, E. R. Culture and the expression of emotion. In T. R. Williams (Ed.), *Psychological anthropology.* The Hague: Mouton, 1975.

SPENCER, H. Psychology of laughter. MacMillian Magazine, 1860, *1,* 395. (Reprinted: *Essays: scientific, political, and speculative,* Vol. 2. New York: Appleton, 1910)

————. *The principles of psychology,* Vol. I. New York: Appleton, 1855.

SPIRO, M. Social systems, personality, and functional analysis. In B. Kaplan (Ed.), *Studying personality cross-culturally.* New York: Harper & Row, 1961.

SROUFE, L. A., & WUNSCH, J. P. The development of laughter in the first year of life. *Child Development,* 1972, *43,* 1326–44.

STRONGMAN, K. T. *The psychology of emotion.* London: Wiley, 1973.

TINBERGEN, N. "Derived" activities: their causation, biological significance, origin, and emancipation during evolution. *Quarterly Review of Biology,* 1952, *27*(1), 1–26.

————. *The animal in its world: explorations of an ethologist.* London: Allen and Unwin, 1973.

TOMKINS, S. S. *Affect, imagery, consciousness,* Vol. I: *the positive affects.* New York: Springer, 1962.

————. *Affect, imagery, consciousness,* Vol. II: *the negative affect.* New York: Springer, 1963.

TOMKINS, S. S., & McCARTER, R. What and where are the primary affects? some evidence for a theory. *Perceptual and Motor Skills,* 1964, *18,* 119–58.

TRIANDIS, H. C., & LAMBERT, W. W. A restatement and test of Schlosberg's theory of emotions with two kinds of subjects from Greece. *Journal of Abnormal and Social Psychology,* 1958, *56,* 321–28.

VAN HOOF, J. A. R. A. M. Facial expression in higher primates. *Symposia of the Zoological Society of London,* 1963, *10,* 103–04.

WATSON, J. B. *Psychology: from the standpoint of a behaviorist.* Philadelphia: Lippincott, 1919.

WHITING, J. W. M., & CHILD, I. L. *Child training and personality: a cross-cultural study.* New Haven, Conn.: Yale University Press, 1953.

WOODWORTH, R. S. *Experimental psychology.* New York: Holt, 1938.

WUNDT, W. *Deutsche Rundschau,* 1877, *3*(7), 120. (Cited in A. Peiper, *Cerebral function in infancy and childhood.* New York: Consultants Bureau, 1963.)

————. *Grundriss der psychologie.* Germany: W. Englemann, 1896. [*Outlines of psychology*] (C. H. Judd, Tr.). New York: G. E. Stechert, 1897.

6

Cross-Cultural Research on Motivation and Its Contribution to a General Theory of Motivation*

H.-J. Kornadt, L. H. Eckensberger,
and W. B. Emminghaus

Contents

Abstract

This chapter explores the relationship between cross-cultural psychology and motivational psychology. The focus is on the contribution of cross-cultural psychology to the development of a general *theory* of motivation. In the first section, general approaches to motivation theory are examined. Three motive systems (attachment/dependency, aggression, and achievement) were chosen to illustrate these approaches in order to show how

* The authors gratefully acknowledge the assistance of H. C. Triandis and W. J. Lonner, who patiently read earlier versions of the chapter, thereby improving our English and the style of the final version and making critical comments and valuable suggestions.

cross-cultural psychology has contributed to the development of motivation theory.

A review of selected literature suggests how cross-cultural psychology has led to a differentiation of theoretical concepts. Also discussed is the extent to which these motive concepts are culture-bound (i.e., in most cases confined to Western cultures). Finally, those elements that can serve as the basis for a universal theory of motivation are examined.

The authors assume the transcultural validity of (a) a hedonistic principle, (b) the influence of certain biological factors, and (c) opportunities to experience the environment. These constancies provide a framework that also allows for an account of the development of culture-specific motives. The framework enables comparison of different cultures via common features. Thus, culture-specific facts can be understood on the basis of a general, transcultural theory of motivation, and motive development.

Introduction

In this chapter, the phenomena dealt with are rather inexactly referred to as "motives" that include wishes, desires, needs, drives, instincts, wants and so forth, whether they are understood as innate or learned; in short, the chapter will be concerned with all those factors that have an activating, energizing, and goal-directing effect on behavior, generally maintaining it until the goal has been attained.

Goals and Possibilities of Cross-Cultural Research

In cross-cultural research the concept of "motive" has attained its significance on two epistemological levels. On the one hand, motives and needs are dealt with, in some culture theories, as reductionist principles in explaining culture. Culture is interpreted as a result of the mutual influences of basic human needs and social and material environmental factors (Malinowski, 1944; Spiro, 1961). On the other hand, "cultural conditions" are considered to be antecedent conditions for the variation of human motives. The latter viewpoint examines a purely psychological set of questions. Efforts to discuss the combination of these two levels were pioneered in "Personality and Culture Studies" (cf., e.g., Kluckhohn & Murray, 1948; Kluckhohn, Murray, & Schneider, 1953; Kardiner, 1945; Aronoff, 1967; McClelland, 1961; and Whiting, 1968). Instead of discussing the considerable methodical difficulties that are connected with this attempt (cf., Dogan & Rokkan, 1969; Eckensberger & Kornadt, 1977), this chapter will be limited primarily to investigations on the individual level.

On this individual level the motive concept has the function of a *hypo-*

thetical construct interpreting certain ("dynamic") aspects of human behavior and individual differences. It encompasses postulations about (a) the structure, function, and development of motives as enduring dispositions, (b) the conditions for their instigation and deactivation, and (c) their combined functions (e.g., as in a conflict).

Cross-cultural research is understood to mean "the explicit systematic comparison of psychological measures obtained under different cultural conditions" (Eckensberger 1973, p. 45; cf. also Boesch & Eckensberger, 1969; Eckensberger 1970). Unsystematic investigations that are not based on motive-theoretical questions are considered only marginally.

The systematic description of the expression of motives (kind and strength) provides a kind of "psychogeographical map." So far, however, most of this work has been theoretically unproductive because "culture" was usually dealt with as a global descriptive characteristic. To be useful, studies must consider intracultural differences (Lesser & Kandel, 1968) and make precise statements about the cultural conditions that are effective. Without such statements and a theoretical framework within which relationships and differences may be interpreted, such investigations can produce only trivial and perhaps even misleading, results (Eckensberger, 1973; Boesch & Eckensberger, 1969).

Therefore, the focus will be on research that supplies explanations about universals of individual motivation or about the conditions that lead to culture-bound motives affecting an individual's behavior.

The advantages of cross-cultural comparisons for motivation are similar to the advantages in general psychology and are summarized in the following points (see also Triandis, Introduction to this *Handbook*): general goals are (a) the generation and (b) the worldwide testing of hypotheses.

1. Most psychology was developed in European-derived cultures. Data from non-European–derived cultures can stimulate hypotheses from outside the realm of European-derived experiences. Many of these could never emerge from European-derived experiences. Such hypotheses can refer to (a) the manner of functioning of motives (attachment), (b) specific forms of expression of the motives under the influence of particular social or ecological conditions (achievement), and (c) the existence of unknown motive systems. Kagan & Klein (1973, p. 948) pointed out, for example, that "seeking serenity" can be a goal of life. Also, are terms like *philotimo* in Greek culture (Triandis, 1972; Vassiliou & Vassiliou, 1973) linked to culture-specific motives unknown in the hitherto existing literature?

2. Cross-cultural research offers the following opportunities for the examination of hypotheses and/or of their generalizability:
   a. *Maximizing the Systematic Variance*
      Generally speaking cultures are sought that have large differences in (a) motivated behavior or (b) antecedence conditions. Margaret

Mead's assertion that the frustration-aggression hypothesis is not true for the Balinese is an example (Mead, 1954, p. 378). It requires cross-cultural research, as do other promising hypotheses.

b. *Control of Extraneous Variance*
Cultures could be found in which motivational variables that are usually confounded are disentangled. Then a "clearer" test of the hypothesis is possible. The classical example is the cross-cultural test of the universality of the Oedipus Complex and the importance of sexual rivalry between father and son (Freud, 1912). In the matrilineal society of the Trobriand Islands the boy's hostility was addressed to his uncle, who is the disciplinarian in that society, and not to his father, who is his mother's lover (Malinowski, 1927).

c. *Utilizing "Natural Experiments" to Avoid Ethical Problems of Experimentation*
If, for example, the question of interest is whether extreme restriction of movement in infancy has an influence on the development of dependency and/or aggressiveness, then this cannot be investigated in Western cultures. However, since swaddling is practiced in some cultures anyway (Gorer, 1949; Gorer & Rickman, 1949), its effects can be studied.

Among the methodological problems in cross-cultural research an especially interesting one for motivation research is the functional equivalence of indicators (e.g., Sears, 1961). The question of which indicators for a specific hypothetical motive construct are functionally equivalent in various cultures can be treated only within the framework of a theory that should include assumptions about the culture-bound modification of a motive. Such a theory is the object of cross-cultural research.

Problems of Structuring This Chapter

A treatment of single motives "one after the other" was rejected, because this would require a taxonomy of motives. Existing classifications (e.g., Murray, 1938; Maslow, 1954), are speculative and may be ethnocentric. Adequate classification systems will emerge only from empirical research done in many cultures.

For this reason, a hypothesis-oriented developmental approach will be used here. Such hypotheses should account for processes and explicate the conditions for motivated actions and of the developmental courses that influence these processes. Single motives do not develop completely independently of other motives. They may be under the influence of common developmental conditions or be dependent upon one another.

This approach was also adopted because longterm effects can be comprehended by cross-cultural research that, as a rule, are not accessible to experimental research. Motives are conceived as enduring behavioral dispositions that form and stabilize gradually. The developmental approach allows examination of the earliest and least complicated motive structures first and the more complicated later.

Motivation: theoretical problems.   Cross-cultural research should deal with the questions of (1) universals in human motivation, and (2) the culture-bound, possibly culture-specific, peculiarities in the formation of motives and/or the effects of motives on behavior.

1. *Hypotheses about universals* can be based on the following (Sears, 1961):
   a. genetically determined physiological mechanisms on which may be based universal innate motives or needs directed at specific goals;
   b. an inborn activating and energizing capability that is, however, undirected and totally unspecific;
   c. a physiological mechanism, including innate capacities for emotional reactions that have certain (psychophysical) qualities, seen as an essential basis for the otherwise learning-dependent development;
   d. an innate mechanism capable of arousing certain processes of learning and thinking, dependent on experience;
   e. the biological nature of humans, their capacity to learn, leads to common experiences that are processed similarly. For example, all human beings are initially dependent on others for care and affection; all are little and inexperienced among taller, and more experienced humans; and, for everyone the stream of impressions is initially without order and gradually susceptible to external influences. Universal learning conditions can, moreover, be seen in a basically similar ecology all over the world.
2. *Culture specific influences.*
   a. Some experiences are available in some ecologies but not in others; some forms of sanctioning, or cognitive regularities, or values and convictions are found in only some cultures.
   b. Many factors may regulate the processing of experiential influences. Some may inhibit innate motives; others may change the development of motives through conditioning or the formation of cognitive schemata (Bartlett, 1932; McClelland, 1951). Furthermore, complex interactions of such influences may shape motive development (Heckhausen, 1968).
   c. Cultures may influence specific aspects of the development of motives, as well as specific features of behavior patterns. Quantitative (e.g., low versus high need achievement) as well as qualitative differences (e.g., in Culture A more "hope of success"; in Culture B more "fear of failure") can arise between cultures. One can even formulate hypotheses about completely culture-specific motives. Furthermore, hypotheses must be formulated about the categorization of motives, and their distinction from one another, based on the processes of their development. Cross-cultural research is particularly suited for the testing of such hypotheses, but must be embedded in a broad theory of motives and their development.

The treatment of three motivational systems will be concentrated on: dependency/attachment, aggression, and achievement. A complete discussion of all motives would have included many others, such as hunger, thirst, sexuality, fear, affiliation, approval, power, and perhaps attitudes toward pain and death. Limitations of space make such broad coverage impossible; only a superficial treatment would have been possible.

The three motive systems chosen correspond approximately to those that Sears (1961) identified as probably being transcultural. The discussion of these three motive systems allows for a review of (a) the contributions that cross-cultural comparisons have made to the general formation of theories, and (b) progress during the last fifteen years.

Motivation—Theoretical Approaches and Their Role in Cross-Cultural Research

Psychoanalytic Theories

The psychoanalytic theory of motive development has two essential aspects: (a) *a biological-genetic orientation*, with the emphasis on biologically determined basic drives, phases of development, and mechanisms; and (b) *a social learning aspect* with the assumption that motives are formed only through the socially determined vicissitudes of drives, which exist in changing relations to objects and changing satisfactions or frustrations.

Hence, it is incorrect to classify psychoanalysis as an "instinct theory" as has been done in the American literature (Hall & Lindzey, 1968; Newcomb, 1950; Singer, 1961, p. 32). All that is taken into account here is that the *libido* is assumed to be a biologically determined innate energizing drive that originates spontaneously and "pushes" the organism toward satisfaction. This basic drive finds its gratification through certain organic areas, and is directed at objects, both changing in the course of infant and child development. With the later inclusion of *thanatos*, as a sort of counterpoint to *eros*, Freud postulated two basic antagonistic drives.

What is not taken into account is the fact that the specific sociocultural environmental conditions influence this developmental process through the opportunities for satisfaction and the sources of frustration that lead to the development of defense mechanisms as, for example, sublimation or displacement.

This incorrect classification may be the consequence of a "transcultural error" emanating from a mistake in the translation of Freud's concept of *Trieb* (drive) as "instinct" (Hartmann, 1948, Mitscherlich & Muck 1969, p. 112). Freud did assume the genetic determination of the origin of drive energy and the urge toward satisfaction. But he did *not* assume genetically determined kinds of object-related behavior. That psychoanalysis could become so fruitful for cross-cultural research is based on the fact that although it is differentiated, it is not a rigidly systematic theoretical system. This allowed a utilization of single concepts without compelling the acceptance of the validity of the whole system. Creative researchers could develop quite ingenious hypotheses, under license from Freudian theory.

Numerous researchers analyzed the universality of certain psychoanalytic assumptions (e.g., repression, Oedipus Complex, Roheim, 1932; Seligman, 1924, 1932; Kardiner, 1939, 1945; Malinowski, 1927; Eggan, 1943). Others were stimulated by the psychoanalytic concept of the development of culture (Freud, 1912; Karinder, 1939, 1945; Parsons, 1950, 1961) and examined the "basic personality structure" and the "modal personality" (cf. Singer, 1961, p. 14; Kardiner, 1939; Linton, 1945; Gorer & Rickman, 1949), or they examined the general social learning aspect of culture (Mead, 1939) that emphasizes the extraordinary adaptability of human nature, an approach that was also influenced by John Dewey (1922).

The assumed consequences that child rearing has for the "vicissitudes of drives" by satisfying or frustrating needs led to the investigation of weaning, breast feeding, the age and severity of toilet and sex training, and the Oedipus Complex (e.g., Blackwood, 1935; Eggan 1943; Whiting & Child, 1953). Dependency was seen as a secondary drive based on the universal need for nourishment (Freud, 1940; Spitz, 1957; cf. also Bowlby, 1969, p. 364). Aggression was conceived of as a reaction to the inevitable universal frustration of drive satisfaction. A more stringent behavioristic formulation of the frustration-aggression hypothesis later followed a more precise examination of the relationship between this hypothesis and displacement as a "vicissitude" of this need. The assumption of a universal drive, *thanatos*, aimed at destruction, death, and Nirvana, became less important for empirical research.

The *methods* of research were also influenced by psychoanalysis. Dream analyses (Seligman, 1924; Roheim, 1949), symbol analyses (DeVos, 1961; Fisher, 1950), and psychiatric interviews (e.g., Leighton and Leighton, 1944; Carstairs, 1957, 1961), as well as the later use of projective tests, can be attributed to the influence of psychoanalysis.

The Learning Theory Interpretation of Motives

The core concept of this research tradition is the postulate that behaviors or habits are learned by "reinforcement" of responses. The original Law of Effect (Thorndike, 1911; 1932) has been essentially retained: if a certain behavior is followed by a *satisfying state of affairs* it will tend to be repeated. Such positive consequences (*rewards*) are often viewed by learning theorists as a *reduction of drive*.

The essential motivational concept of this mechanistic stimulus-response theory is drive. Its significance has changed from the early work of Woodworth (1918) to the explicitly behavioristic theory of Hull (1943), in which drive was only understood as a general (unspecific) state or as an energizer. The behavior-directing, guiding aspect of goal-directed behavior is clearly separated in this theory, and is conceived of as the result of reinforcement.

Although a motivational principle has a central role in behavior theory, a precise motive theory has not grown from it. Correspondingly, drive theory has not become fruitful in cross-cultural research, particularly if occasional applications are disregarded, which really were *post hoc* interpretations. An exception may be Whiting & Whiting (1975, pp. 7-8). Atkinson (1964) provided a comprehensive review of theory development.

However, the attempt, coming from the experimental tradition, to make the concepts of learning theory as precise and operational as possible, became especially successful in one branch of motivational theory. Psychoanalytic concepts were phrased in terms of general behavior theory and were made experimentally testable. Good examples are the formulation of the frustration-aggression hypothesis (Dollard, Doob, Miller, Mowrer, & Sears, 1939), the theory of *acquired drives* by Mowrer (1950) and their experimental support by Miller (1941, 1948), and Miller's (1944) conflict theory and its experimental confirmation (Brown, 1948; Miller, 1959).

Then, certain concepts were formulated and tested cross-culturally (Whiting & Child, 1953). Also, stressing those elements of motivated behavior that depend on experience, and the attempt to reveal the role of these elements experimentally, learning theory drew attention to the relationship between physiological or homeostatic needs (hunger, thirst, sex) and learned motivated behavior, and also contributed to the differentiation between *biogenic* (or primary) and *sociogenic* (learned or secondary) motives. Kardiner's (1939, p. 418) cross-cultural research originally departed from psychoanalysis, but later included a distinction between hunger, sex, and the need for protection as innate "basic needs," and other motivated behavior as dependent on experience and culture.

A favored area of application is the study of child rearing that can be investigated, from a psychoanalytic point of view, as a frustrating condition, but also as a special reinforcement pattern. In both cases there is a link between psychoanalytic and more precise behavioristic concepts. This research orientation has benefited especially from the development by Murdock, Ford, Hudson, Kennedy, Simmons and Whiting (1950) of the Human Relations Area Files. HRAF allowed the systematic evaluation of many hypotheses by using already collected ethnographic materials. (See chapters by Barry and Naroll, Michik, & Naroll in Volume 2 of this *Handbook*.)

Cognitive Theories of Motivation

McClelland (1951) established a new, theoretically and empirically fruitful direction of research, which gained special importance in the study of need achievement (e.g., McClelland, Atkinson, Clark, & Lowell, 1953). At the beginning motives were considered homogeneous, complicated systems forming functional units that determine behavior. Explicit hypotheses were formulated about their function in determining motivated action, as well as concerning their structure and development.

It is useful to differentiate between *motive* as a "relatively general and stable personality disposition which is assumed to be one of the determinants of motivation" (Atkinson, 1964, p. 263) and *motivation* as a term that "refers to the strength of the (aroused) tendency to act in a certain way in order to get on to the goal."

In what follows a *motive* will be conceived as the goal state striven by an individual within a certain person-environment relationship, and as a relatively enduring disposition of evaluation (Heckhausen, 1972). A motivated action will be determined by (a) the strength of the instigated enduring motive (or motives), (b) the expectation to attain the motive goal by definite instrumental actions, and (c) the incentive or value of goal attainment. Therefore, situational conditions, as well as individually enduring dispositions, play a role in the motivation of an action. The class of person-environment relationships which constitutes a motive depends upon experience. The goal state striven for, and the estimation of the probability of success of a particular action in a given situation are based on innumerable experiences.

McClelland, Clark, Roby, and Atkinson (1949) emphasized the anticipatory, future-oriented aspect of motivation in contrast to the "looking backwards" oriented conception of association-mechanistic S-R theory, according to which an action occurs because it had previously been reinforced (Atkinson, 1964, p. 115). Subsequently, the cognitive character of the motive system, especially the setting of a goal and the expectancy, became an essential aspect of this viewpoint (Heckhausen & Weiner, 1972; Fuchs, 1963; Heckhausen, 1963b, 1973).

Another branch of research led to many studies of imitation learning. Bandura was able to show that observing the behavior of a model alone can lead to the establishment of a behavior disposition. This can be understood also as a (motivated) process, of cognitive structuring of one's own possibilities of behavior. Imitation learning has been especially studied in the case of aggressive behavior (Bandura, 1962, 1973).

In the late 1960s attribution theory (Weiner, 1972; Heckhausen & Weiner, 1972) clarified a further component of motive systems. Motivated actions depend on both the motive-relevant interpretation of the situation and the causal attributions made by the observer concerning the effects of actions. Enduring individual characteristics can exist in these cognitive components.

This group of theories, although it is the most recent, has had the most significant influence in the history of cross-cultural research. Numerous investigations were stimulated by this clearly formulated theory, from which were derived precise hypotheses about cultural influences on motivation and cultural consequences of motive structures. McClelland (1961) used not only cross-cultural but also historical data. Historical and cross-cultural data serve similar purposes in testing hypotheses, and hence it is appropriate to discuss historical data in this *Handbook* (see Berry's chapter in Volume 5 of this *Handbook*).

The general principles of cognitive motivation theory were applied also to a series of other motives (hunger, affiliation, power, aggression, fear, sex; Atkinson, 1958). So far, however, cross-cultural research in this potentially fruitful domain has been limited almost exclusively to the study of need achievement.

The questions examined from this theoretical perspective concern (a) the comparison of the expression of a motive in different cultures, (b) the connections of the motive with definite cultural developmental and child rearing conditions, and (c) the cultural (especially economic) effects of the motive.

Some of the results of cross-cultural research on the achievement motive brought into focus certain central problems of motive theory. This fruitful application of the theory will be discussed in detail in the section on the achievement motive and in the final section.

The *methods* used by McClelland and his associates in their research have enriched cross-cultural psychology. McClelland's "thought sampling method" was especially successful. It used a specific system of scoring and evaluating responses to the Thematic Apperception Test (TAT). The still popular TAT was adapted for many cultures (e.g., blacks: Nuttall, 1964; Mingione, 1965; Chagga: Ostheimer, 1969; in Kenya: Kornadt & Voigt, 1970; in India: McClelland & Winter, 1969; Singh, 1969, 1970a; in Hawaii: Sloggett, Gallimore, & Kubany, 1970; in Jamaica: Tidrick, 1973). Moreover, questionnaires, and other instruments, directly related to the theory were developed and subsequently translated into many languages. Furthermore, content analyses of folk tales were employed to measure the intensity of the achievement motive in a culture, and economic indicators were used to measure the effect of the achievement motive in a society (see note 20).

Ethological Instinct Theory

Instinct theory or ethology has surprisingly gained new importance since the 1950s. Interest in the older instinct theory, emanating from Darwin and continued by James (1890) and McDougall (1908), among others, had waned in the twenties (under the influence of behaviorism). By an *instinct* McDougall meant an "inherited or innate psychophysical disposition which determines . . . to perceive . . . objects of the certain class . . . and to act in regard to it in a particular manner . . ." (McDougall, 1908, p. 30). He put together a list of such instincts.

The concept of instinct has been revived by ethologists (Eibl-Eibesfeldt, 1974; Lorenz, 1963; Tinbergen, 1951). These researchers and their numerous followers have produced more precise descriptions, by means of careful observations of animal behavior, and have also created a more differentiated instinct concept.

The central assumption of this theoretical approach assumes that with human beings, too, a large part of motivated behavior is based upon inherited biological mechanisms. This view contrasts sharply with behavioristic learning theory. On the basis of animal behavior research at least four possibilities for such mechanisms can be differentiated.

1. *Instinctive Reaction Patterns*
   As biologically determined forms of behavior, these are the most complicated and most complete. Individuals react with definite behavior in a species-specific way to certain releasing stimulus configurations. Complicated patterns of behavior, like mating or the defense of territory, which were assumed by the early instinct theoreticians to be a single "instinct," were proven, after careful observation, to be a complicated chain of enmeshed instinctive reactions.
2. *Species-specific Releasing Effects of Specific Key Releasers*
   Through "innate release patterns" a nonrigid behavior, but also impulses to certain classes of behavior, can be released. For human beings this was assumed in the case of the configuration of the infant's face (babyishness) or early smiling response (Gray, 1958).
3. *Endogenous Emergence of Specific Drive Energy Linked to Certain Endocrine or Homoeostatic Conditions*
   This form of behavior is empirically well-documented in the case of animals. Lorenz (1963) claimed that such a mechanism accounts for aspects of human aggression. He assumed that if the inborn aggression drive is not satisfied, its energy is accumulated and dangerous eruptions can occur, when the threshold for releasing stimuli is lowered.
4. *Imprinting*
   A kind of learning process, imprinting must be understood as a special interaction of biogenic conditions and experience. During a "critical period" of the organism's life, latent behaviors (e.g., approaching, following) can be linked almost irreversibly with the specific characteristics of

perceived objects. This led to the hypothesis that, in humans, infant dependency contains features of imprinting and is partly encoded in the genotype (Wiggins, Renner, Clore, & Rose, 1971, p. 169).

The extension of theoretical concepts, gained from the observation of animal behavior, to human beings, takes place most often in the form of imprecise analogies. Nonetheless, corresponding hypotheses cannot be dismissed without investigation. Ethologists point to the regulation of such behaviors by neurophysiological mechanisms. There is no doubt that similarities exist between people and animals in such mechanisms. Furthermore, they join with Darwin, in arguing that such hereditarily determined behaviors would have to have been formed in the genotype. Lorenz also postulates, for human aggressiveness, a phylogenetic selection advantage.

Relatively few cross-cultural investigations have been stimulated by these theories. The *questions* raised by these concepts relate to the proof of biologically firmly established specific systems of needs and releasers for certain patterns of behavior or motivational tendencies (e.g., infant dependency and aggressive behavior). Mead's widely known view, which explains differences between male and female behavior by means of sex roles shaped by culture, may have to be reexamined because there is now considerable evidence that sex-linked behaviors depend also on hormones. The research methods used by ethologists require behavioral observations. They were developed for studies of animal behavior and contain careful records of behavior and releasing conditions.

Personality Theory

Though personality theory has not provided a special motive theory, it is relevant to motive research, as well as to cross-cultural research. Early representatives of this direction are J. McK. Cattell (1890), William Stern (1911, 1912), and H. Rorschach (1921), who wished to describe human personality. They developed their own procedures, namely personality tests. Murray (1938) attempted to provide a complete description of personality. Murray's personality theory emphasized motives and was influential in the development of McClelland's theory of achievement motivation. Murray's thema concept furnished an important starting point for modern cognitive motivation theories. It already contained the idea of a special motivational person-environment relationship.

In cultural anthropology, personality theory has contributed to the intensification of "culture and personality" studies, which have also indirectly yielded information about motivational phenomena, and to the especially strong tendency to carry out cross-cultural studies with the aid of projective techniques. Besides Murray's TAT, the Rorschach and the sentence completion technique are used in cross-cultural comparisons. Rosenzweig (1944) introduced the Picture Frustration Study. The TAT appeared virtually predestined for cross-cultural studies. It seemed to be culture-free, since the pictures presented are nonverbal stimuli. According to the basic projection theory of Frank (1939) which can be roughly traced back to Freud, it was assumed that people, from whatever culture they might come, would express in these tests their inner motivational dynamics. Thus the central functions of their personality could be comprehended. Within the Euroamerican cultural realm and in cross-cultural comparisons, it has become clear now that projective methods have essential limitations (Hörmann, 1964; Kornadt, 1964; Lindzey, 1961; Murstein, 1963).

Comment. The grouping of motivation theories undertaken here is problematic and selective, but includes an appropriate sampling of theories for cross-cultural research and outlines their historical development. All of the theories summarized continue to evolve, and most still thrive. Thus, none of these theories is definitely out of date; however, each researcher emphasizes a different theory.

A motivation theory developed within the framework of cognitive theories will prove most fruitful. Such a theory integrates most completely the available knowledge from experimental psychology, developmental psychology, social psychology, clinical personality, and cross-cultural research, and can most quickly absorb new results. It might assimilate appropriately other areas, such as, perhaps, neurophysiological or ethological research.

Dependency/Attachment

Sears (1961) defined dependency as the "instigation to be oriented toward and cared for by another person" (p. 452). He perceived in this aspect of the human "motivational system" a "secondary drive," also called a "sociogenic motive" (cf. McDavid & Harari, 1968). According to Sears this secondary drive is transcultural because its origins can be derived (1) from a species-specific and hence a universal learning situation, and (2) from—presumably likewise universal—appropriate environmental events. Sears expanded on this by saying that man

> has such a long period of *physical dependency*, [that] he [therefore] has a tremendous number of reinforcements of maternal orientations toward him, *accompanied by primary drive gratification*. As a consequence it *may* be assumed that this *orientation, and other signs of care-taking behavior*, become the appropriate Environmental Events for the gratification of a secondary drive of dependency (p. 452, author's italics).

More recently the concept of "dependency" and its theoretical explanation have been attacked, partially modified, and replaced (cf. Hartup, 1963; Ainsworth, 1969; Walters & Parke, 1964; and Maccoby & Masters, 1970). Only the most important general aspects of this motive system will be discussed here.

The Significance of Dependency-Attachment for the
Development of the Whole Personality

Prescientific reports have long pointed to the vital importance of attachment. For instance, in an attempt to learn which language children would speak spontaneously, Friedrich II forbade newborn children any kind of verbal or physical contact with their caretakers. As a result, many of the children died. Another historical example is the essentially futile efforts of Doctor Itard to "socialize" a boy who had grown up in isolation (known as "Kaspar Hauser"). Both examples demonstrate the role of the "dependency motive" in infancy.

In investigations in foster homes, conducted by Ribble (1941, 1944), Spitz (1946, 1949, 1965), Goldfarb (1943a, 1943b, 1944a, 1944b, 1945a, 1945b, 1947), and Bowlby (1951), the significance of infant interactions for the development of personality was emphasized.

This work demonstrated that, first, this sociogenic motive is significant for normal development of different aspects of personality, because the importance of the mother or any constant caregiver is emphasized for positive development. The "deprivation" of the motive on the other hand, leads to abnormal development (anaclitic depression, Marasmus), a typical syndrome that was marked initially by weepy behavior, then by withdrawal from the environment and the people in the surroundings, insomnia and loss of weight, and finally by a frozen rigidity (cf. Spitz & Wolf, 1946, p. 313).

In addition, the importance of infancy for later personality development, postulated by Freud's analysis of adults, was confirmed empirically. Finally, the irreversibility of the deficit was stressed.

However, additional conditions in the hospital and selection mechanisms as genetic and class specific conditions (cf. Pinneau, 1950, 1955; Casler, 1961) make a unicausal interpretation of the symptoms difficult. And there Bakwin (1942) considered a more general "sensory deprivation" and not "maternal deprivation" to be the determinant of an abnormal development.

Child-rearing investigations in the fifties (cf. e.g., Sears, Maccoby, & Levin, 1957) were likewise affected by confounding countless situational and child-rearing variables. Therefore, animal experiments became important in examining the meaning of *single* antecedent conditions for the development of "cognitive," affective, social, and physical variables.

These studies were, however, naturally burdened by the *problem of their va-lidity for humans.*

Since, for ethical reasons, a replication of animal experiments for the purpose of examining their generalizability to humans is forbidden, *the cross-cultural method assumes central significance in this connection.* By employing it one can at least try to look for unconfounded conditions in real-life set-tings, which correspond to the animal experiments used in artificial con-ditions of the laboratory.

In fact, Mead (1953) as well as Bakwin (1942) doubted that the symp-toms described by Spitz were essentially caused by a *social* understimula-tion, the lack of a constant caregiver or even by the separation from the mother, because in many primitive communities the care of infants is not always delegated to a single person alone;[1] yet negative consequences are not observed. In fact, although the mother is most frequently the caretaker of the child (Mead 1953), this function can also be performed effectively by *other people:* by nurses (cf. Stevens, 1971); by older siblings (cf. Ains-worth, 1963), and by the father (cf. Marvin, Van Derender, Iwanaga, LeVine, & LeVine, 1977). It can also be performed by a variable *number* of them (cf. Stevens, 1971; Leiderman & Leiderman, 1974; Marvin et al., 1977).

*Specification of the "Dependency/Attachment" Concept and
Examination of its Transcultural Validity*

Ainsworth (1969) emphasized that within different theoretical positions entirely different *concepts* have been developed to explain the infant-mother interaction: *object relation* within *depth psychology,* the *dependency con-cept* within *learning theory,* and the *attachment concept* within *ethologically oriented theories.* Attachment appears to be relatively neutral and does not, for example, provoke negative connotations (non-self–reliance, etc.), as does the concept of "dependency." Henceforth, the term *dependency* will be used, but does not imply blanket acceptance of the ethologically oriented theoretical position. Rather, its critical examination is one of the topics in a subsequent section. Coates, Anderson, and Hartup (1972a) following Maccoby & Masters (1970), combined three behavioral aspects under this concept: *"seeking proximity* with some specific person, and *seeking attentive,* and *nurturant behaviors* from that same individual" (Coates et al., 1972a, p. 231).

Following Campbell and Fiske (1959) and Fiske (1973) and their logic of *convergent* and *discriminant* validity, the three aspects of "attachment be-havior" (motive) named by Coates et al. (1972a) must be related to (a) *one another* and (b) to *other* likewise *socially oriented* behavior.

From this theoretical position it follows methodologically that, al-though a goal orientation (hence, a motive) within a single individual is the basis of attachment behavior, it cannot be clearly deduced from the behavior of *the individual alone*. Strictly speaking, the *individual* cannot be taken as the "bearer of data," but only the *dyad* as a whole. The *intercorrelation of different* socially oriented behaviors, therefore,. is a highly insufficient operationalization of the convergent and discriminant validity of so-called dyadic variables.

Structural cluster formation of attachment indicators and their transcultural generalizability.   Concurring with the definition of Coates, Anderson, and Hartup (1972b) and Maccoby & Masters (1970, p. 74), the following "rough indicators" can be differentiated from one another for the construct of "attachment": (1) seeking physical contact (intensity, frequency of clinging, touching), (2) proximity-seeking (seeking to be near), (3) attention-seeking, (4) seeking praise and approval, (5) resistance to separate, and (6) seeking help and support. As will be shown later—especially from ethological points of view and in the period of infancy—there are much more differentiated indicators of attachment. Nonetheless, the above six indicators suffice as a preliminary description of the concept.

The detailed analysis of available data by Maccoby & Masters (1970) produces the following trend, although it largely excludes "nurturance" and "help-seeking" (see Fig. 6-1):

1. Rating scales for different indicators for the "dependency/attachment" system correlate substantially with one another (about .60), but observation scores do not. Since this points to a possible error of judgment in rating scales, it appears reasonable to rely primarily on observational data.
2. In observation scores *three* clusters can be differentiated from one another with certainty:
   a. *proximity-seeking* (touching, being near)
   b. *attention-seeking* (approval-seeking) and
   c. *securing aid for self* (nurturance- and help-seeking)
3. The embedding of these three aspects of the dependency-attachment system in the entire context of socially oriented behavior, as demonstrated by an integration of the work of Baumrind and Black (1967), Becker and Krug (1964), and Schaefer (1961), allows an association with very different areas of behavior:
   a. *proximity-seeking* with the area "friendliness/affiliation";
   b. *attention-seeking* with the area of assertive, active social behavior; and
   c. *help-seeking* is represented by the passive-dependent pole (cf. also the indicators touching or holding; "positive attention-seeking" and "securing aid for self" in Emmerich's investigation, 1964).

Attention-seeking and *nurturance-seeking* thus have a negative relation to one another, while proximity-seeking relates orthogonally to both.

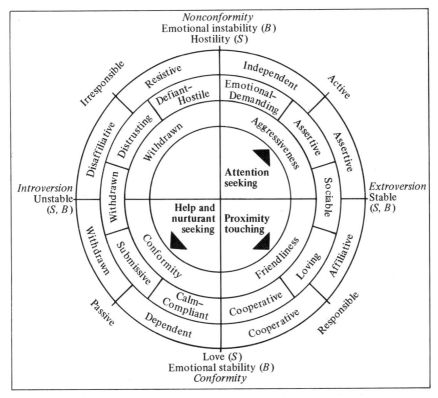

Figure 6-1   Relation of Different Indicators of Attachment/Dependency (Prox-imity-Seeking, Seeking Attention, Seeking Help) to One Another and Their Classification in a General Interactional System (Convergent and Discriminant Validity of the Attachment/Dependency Construct) after an Overall View by Maccoby & Masters (1970). The figure was slightly modified for the present purpose. From D. Baumrind & A. E. Black, Socialization practices associated with dimensions of competence in preschool boys and girls. *Child Development* 1967, *38*, 291-327. By permission from The Society for Research in Child Development.

The separation of attention-seeking from both other aspects of the at-tachment concept (*seeking help* and *seeking proximity*), however, appears to be more valid and reliable (see also Maccoby & Feldman, 1972) than a sepa-ration of these two aspects from one another. That is, behaviors (sociabil-ity, conformity) related to *proximity-seeking* rest partly on the stable extraversion pole, and partly on the passive area of the circumplex. Thus, seeking proximity surely can have an assertive-aggressive function *as well as* a help-seeking one. This fact mathematically leads to orthogonality.

First, these findings explain the partly contradictory results in regard to the relation between "dependency" and other socially oriented behav-iors, inasmuch as they refer to different aspects of this complex system.

Second, it does not seem reasonable, at least at preschool and school age, to speak of "the" dependency or "the" attachment and lastly, it is obvious that attachment in a narrower sense—the positive evaluation of persons qua persons (cf. Hartup, 1963)—is most closely represented in *proximity-seeking*.

An explicit cross-cultural study that was carried out to investigate the attachment concept on an individual level stems from Maccoby & Feldman (1972). They compared a part of an American longitudinal section sample of children (ages two, two and one-half, and three years) with a kibbutz sample (mean age of two years and seven months). In their structural analysis (correlation between attachment indicators) the authors employed (a) a proximity summary score, (b) the frequency of looking at the mother, (c) frequency of other distance bids (SSS-score: smiling at the mother, speaking to her, showing objects to her), (d) incidence of crying when mother leaves the child with a stranger, and (e) crying when the mother leaves the child alone. It is evident that "proximity-seeking" is represented most nearly by variable (a) and "attention-seeking" by variable (b).

The findings of the intercorrelation analysis of these behaviors of American children (see Maccoby & Feldman, 1972, p. 41) at all age levels and in different situations confirm the trends described earlier: "proximity-seeking is not related to either looking at the mother or directing other distance bids toward her" (p. 40). It is interesting that the significance of *"visual regards"* apparently changes with the situation: depending on the presence or absence of a stranger, this behavior can be subsumed under proximity-seeking *or* attention-seeking, respectively.

These authors unfortunately do not report the correlations of the same variables from the kibbutz sample. Since, however, most significance tests for single variables between the cultures were negative, it can be cautiously concluded that the relations between the variables, that is, the structural distinction of proximity- and attention-seeking, are transculturally stable, even if this finding is not a necessary and not a sufficient condition for this argument.

For a further discussion of this question, some findings from the famous Six Cultures Study of the Harvard-Cornell-Yale group, (Whiting, 1973; Whiting & Whiting 1975) will be presented and the observational data gathered in the six cultures (Longabaugh, 1966) will be referred to.

In this investigation behavioral observations were carried out in six local communities on three- to eleven-year-old children. The cultures have been described by Whiting (1963), Minturn & Lambert (1964), and Whiting and Whiting, (1975). They included (1) the community of *Taira* on the northeast coast of Okinawa, (2) families of hamlets in *Tarong*, in the Philippines; (3) families from the Rajput caste in the town of *Khalapur*, located in northern India; (4) *Nyansongo*, in Kenya, a sublocation of the

Gusii; (5) the community of *Juxtlahuaca* in the western highlands of the Mexican state of Oaxaca, and (6) United States families from *Orchard Town* in New England. From these, sixty-seven boys and sixty-seven girls (twenty-four from Taira; twenty-four from Tarong; twenty-four from Khalapur; twenty-two from Juxtlahuaca; twenty-four from Orchard Town; sixteen from Nyansongo) were chosen and observed. The twelve observation categories were differentiated. It was observed that the child (1) offers help, (2) suggests responsibility, (3) reprimands, (4) seeks dominance, (5) acts sociably, (6) seeks attention, (7) offers support, (8) touches, and (9) seeks help. Further categories were (10) assaults sociably, (11) assaults, and (12) symbolic aggression (cf. Whiting & Whiting, 1975, Appendix 17, pp. 187–96).

The observational data were collected in five-minute behavior samples. From these, two sets of *relative* data were derived: (a) Rate scores: the frequency of a certain behavior relative to the *time* during which the child was observed *in toto*. The values that thus ensued were called *rate scores;* (b) Proportion scores: the frequency of a behavior per child relative to the *entire number* of interpersonal activities of the individual child.

Methodological Excursus
1. The findings of the analyses by Longabaugh (1966) and Whiting & Whiting (1975) differ from one another in the relationships of just those items that represent attachment aspects (touches; seeks attention; seeks help). This difference is not to be attributed to the application of different statistical methods (Eckensberger, 1978)—Longabaugh (1966) did a factor analysis; the Whitings employed a multidimensional scaling method—but to the *kind of aggregation of the data*. Whiting & Whiting (1975) aggregated at an early stage, by computing the *median scores* of the proportion scores of the behavior categories per culture, and correlated them on the cultural level. By contrast, Longabaugh (1966) took this step later, since he computed an intercorrelation matrix between *individual* proportion scores *per* culture. Longabaugh (1966) calculated *the mean of the relations between two categories computed on the individual level;* whereas the Whitings formed *relations of averaged (median) scores of the categories on the aggregate level*. Longabaugh's analysis appears, therefore, more comparable with the data gathered on the individual level.
2. This discussion will be limited to a description of the proportion scores, since "there was considerable variation in the overall rate of interaction from culture to culture . . . (that) . . . could either be a true difference or attributable to the different techniques and skills of observers" (Whiting & Whiting, 1975, pp. 64f).
3. It is known that results from empirical investigations of the attachment system are systematically different depending on (a) age; (b) sex, and (c) target person. These differences concern the single behavior categories of the system (seeking attention, touching) differentially. Later this chapter will pursue these results more exactly from functional points of

view. The question of whether the conditions mentioned produce *different* interactions in different cultures cannot be answered, as no appropriate analysis is available from the Harvard group because of the few subjects in each culture used in this research.

Longabaugh's principal component analysis of the average intercorrelation matrix between the twelve observation categories of the six cultures produced two interpretable factors. Longabaugh's results are illustrated graphically in Figure 6–2. The names of the observation categories are geared to the nomenclature of Whiting & Whiting (1975).

The result of this analysis is interesting for three reasons:

1. The total pattern of the observation categories corresponds to the data from Baumrind & Black (1967), Becker & Krug (1964) and Schaefer (1961). The behaviors typed as dependent-passive are opposed to the assertive-active ones. Orthogonal to that factor is the affiliation cluster. This result speaks for the generalizability, therefore, of some basic factors of human (child) interactions (see also Lonner's chapter in Volume 1 of this *Handbook*).
2. A closer inspection of the behaviors included in the dependency/attachment concept (seeks attention, touches, seeks help) shows that they break down into *two clusters:* "seeks attention" is clearly distinguished from both other aspects. However, since it is close to the center of this

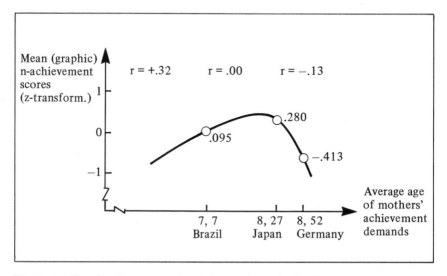

Figure 6–2 Graphic Representation Adapted from the Findings of Longabaugh's Factor Analysis (1966). Principal component analysis of average intercorrelations of the twelve categories of behaviors in six cultures after varimax rotation.

system, it is not reflected positively in it. Interestingly enough, this kind of behavior constitutes, along with *reprimands*, the third factor in Longabaugh's (1966, p. 451) analysis (although not interpreted there): the loading for *reprimands* is −.63 and for *seeks attention* is −.58. Since both load on the negative side (positive loadings are for *offers help:* +.36 and *offers support:* +.38) and since *reprimands* has clearly assertive, active components, the structural differentiation of the *attention-seeking* from the *attachment/dependency* dimension is transculturally supported.

3. With respect to the question of how far proximity-seeking can be separated for help-seeking, the data give a rather negative answer: *touches, seeks help,* and *acts sociably* (here rather an adaptable way of social behavior in contrast to *offers support*), lie closely together in the same quadrants. These results, nonetheless, call for further research because *culture-specific interactions* between situations, target, and age are not available. They are just the *smallest common denominator* for analyses of attachment behaviors. The question as to whether the two factors of attachment can be differentiated just up to preschool age (Maccoby & Masters, 1970), or, whether one is dealing with two distinct stages or phases in the development of attachment (Maccoby & Feldman, 1972) is open. According to the current state of research in Western cultures, the answer seems to read: in *proximity-seeking* (touching, clinging, following, etc.) and the *more distal forms of attachment behavior* (above all, "vocalizing," cf. Coates et al., 1972b; Lewis & Ban, 1971; Maccoby & Feldman, 1972; but also "looking," cf. Lewis & Ban, 1971; Maccoby & Feldman, 1972; "speaking," "smiling," and "showing," cf. Maccoby & Feldman, 1972), separate aspects of the attachment system emerge at an early age; i.e., before the completion of the *first year of life.* Unfortunately, however, there are no equivalent statements of the social behavior of infancy, in the investigation of Maccoby & Feldman nor in all other works within this area. A transcultural test of the "attachment-differentiation hypothesis" is not yet available.

Functional cluster formation of attachment-indicators and their transcultural generalizability. The change in the meaning of "visual regards" that was reported by Maccoby & Feldman (1972), gives a hint that next to the possibility of a *structural* differentiation of at least two forms of attachment their *functional* separability is indicated.

Data obtained in western cultures do not permit observations of single isolated conditions. More differentiated reanalyses of the data of Sears, Rau, and Alpert (1965) and Rosenthal (1965), by Maccoby and Masters (1970), show complex interactions between age, target, and form of attachment behavior (proximity- versus attachment-seeking). Moreover, there are interactions between target, anxiety arousal, and both forms of attachment. Unfortunately the data stem from children of preschool age and relate to relatively short age ranges (ca. two years).

Considering different results, Maccoby & Masters (1970, p. 146) come to the following conclusion: "(1) proximity-seeking declines with age, attention-seeking does not; (2) proximity-seeking is increased by fear arousal, attention-seeking is not; (3) attention-seeking generalizes from adult to child targets, proximity-seeking does not."

These global tendencies, can be checked with cross-cultural data from the Six Cultures Study (Whiting & Whiting, 1975). The following must be considered: (a) the above-mentioned interactions are not explained, and (b) *age trends* can be interpreted only with uncertainty, since the study is a cross-sectional one and an explanation by a cohort effect is probable, (Schaie, 1965; Baltes, 1968), especially in the case of cultures that are in a state of rapid social change.

Additionally when the Whitings attempted to form *functional* clusters of their observation categories they applied two criteria for the formation of clusters, (a) the same developmental course, and (b) sex differences in the same direction. In order to determine the clusters, the frequency values of the behavior categories were standardized for each culture, and mean differences between the cultures were removed from the data. The combination of these two characteristics (developmental course x differences in sex) leads to six clusters: (1) intimate dependency (touches, seeking help); (2) dominant dependency (seeks attention, seeks dominance); (3) nurturance (offers help, offers support); (4) aggressive behavior (assaults, insults, assaults sociably); (5) prosocial behavior (suggests responsibility, reprimands); and (6) sociability (acts sociably).

Both structural aspects of *attachment behavior* can also be classified functionally into two different clusters: *touches* (proximity-seeking) together with *seeking help* form the intimate-dependency cluster; *seeks attention* joins with *seeks dominance* to form the dominance-dependency cluster. Both cluster formations fit into the differential active-passive dimension.

Differential age trends of proximity- and attention-seeking in cross-cultural comparison of the pooled developmental trends over the behavior categories (cf. Whiting and Whiting, 1975, pp. 138–43) and single behaviors—touches, seeks help, seeks attention and seeks dominance—were clustered into the dimensions "intimate-dependent" and "dominant-dependent" (see p. 138).

The product-moment correlations of these dimensions with chronological age (three to eleven years) were computed separately for boys and girls. Values were given for the entire sample ("all cultures") as well as for the individual cultures. Although these analyses did not consider different target people, these data at least show the same trend that exists in Western cultures: the cluster that contains "proximity-seeking" *decreases* with age (especially in girls); the cluster that contains "attention-seeking" on the whole shows no significant age trends.

Differential generalizability of "proximity-" and "attention-seeking" to different target people in cross-cultural comparison. The Whitings' data (1975) allow a first transcultural examination of Western findings, viz., that proximity-seeking varies from target to target person (age of targets ranged from children to adults), much more than attention-seeking. A far greater percentage of *intimate-dependent* behavior is shown (pooled over all cultures) toward adults than toward peers and infants (see Whiting & Whiting, 1975, Fig. 18, p. 156). They do not, however, find the same gross difference in the *dominant-dependent* behavior cluster. Secondly, the rank-order of the frequency value of all six behavior clusters toward infants, peers, and adults across and within all cultures changes (Whiting & Whiting, 1975, p. 157f). Both clusters are at the end of the rank-order toward infants (rank 5 and 6), for peers *dominant-dependent* is in fourth place, and *intimate-dependent* is in third place. In the same direction, however, the "differentiation" of reactions develops (that is, the relation of these ranks *between* the cultures), with the greatest concurrence of the rank orders between the cultures being toward infants (median rho = +.83), somewhat less toward peers (median rho = +.66), and least of all toward adults (median rho = +.54).

The correlations between the intimate-dependent and dominant-dependent scores were computed by taking into account the different targets. Accordingly (Whiting & Whiting, 1975, p. 163), the dominant-dependence (the scores include attention-seeking) shown toward peers and parents (Pearson r) correlated +.35 ($p < .001$), while the intimate-dependent scores (which contain touching and seeking help) correlated only +.11 (n.s.). According to these data, then, attention-seeking also appears to be generalizable to different target people, but not proximity-seeking.

The differential effect of fear arousal on proximity- and attention-seeking. Although "stranger anxiety" as a fundamental phenomenon has been investigated in cross-cultural research, the differential effects of a stranger as a fear-arousing stimulus or of other fear-arousing stimuli in relation to the aspects of attachment, as have been outlined, have seldom been taken into account. And it is unfortunately not guaranteed that a differential effect of fear arousal is always reported. Leiderman & Leiderman (1974), for instance, studied in polymatric infants of the East African Highlands the effect of a stranger on such behavior as: lifts arms to be picked up; smiles, joyous movements; indifferent staring; frowns, restless; turns away or buries face. The authors, however, sum these reactions algebraically (that is, they treated them as a *single* dimension), although a separate evaluation of "smiles," and "lifts arms to be picked up," as separate indicators of attention and proximity-seeking, was an obvious possibility.

Some indications that fear-arousal can also result in functional differentiation of the two aspects of attachment, already discussed, were gleaned from the investigation of Maccoby & Feldman (1972), though this separation is not explicitly identified by them. They reported (p. 27) that in the American sample proximity-seeking toward the mother *rises* in the *presence of the stranger* for all age groups (two, two and one-half, and three years). For all age groups, the cluster *"speaks, smiles, shows (SSS),"* however, *decreases* relative to reactions to the mother in the *presence of the stranger* (p. 29). On the other hand, the comparison of American children with kibbutz children shows that neither the SSS cluster nor "crying" produced a statistically significant difference between the two cultures. Probably attention-seeking toward the mother also took place in the kibbutz in the presence of the stranger. Proximity-seeking apparently increases toward the mother in kibbutz children, too, in the presence of a stranger, even if a direct comparison between these values was not technically possible. As a whole all the data of cross-cultural research from the structural as well as functional point of view show that the "attachment system" really does concern a "transcultural variable," and that at least proximity- and attention-seeking are the two critical aspects to be considered.

Development of Dependency/Attachment

Conditions for the emergence of attachment in infants.   The human infant under normal conditions displays a tendency around the seventh month to prefer a *specific person*, that is he or she greets him or her in a specific way and is irritated by his or her absence, i.e., the infant develops by this age a "specific attachment." This occurs before the infant can distinguish people from one another and is used to express his or her dislike of being left alone. The protest against separation is not, however, confined to a specific person. About one month after the emergence of this "specific attachment" a child develops a distinct fear of strange people. Simultaneously, however, the number of people toward whom the child develops a specific attachment increases (see Schaffer & Emerson, 1964).

There is little doubt that Freud's analysis of the developmental conditions for the choice of the first "drive object," *mother's breast* or *mother*, emphasized the central significance of orality, the reduction of the nourishment drive. In addition he stressed the significance of *general socially oriented interaction patterns* like kissing, stroking, rocking of the baby (Freud, 1905), *fear of separation* (Freud, 1926), and the *phylogenetic function* of the child/mother tie (Freud, 1938). The significance of orality, however, was certainly strengthened by the work of his daughter Anna Freud (1946, 1954), who conceived the emergence of the child/mother tie from orality in three phases. The first is when libidinous energy is associated with the experience of *tension reduction* in the *feeding process;* in the second, the child "loves" the *nourishment itself,* and in the third, love is finally transferred to the *provider of food. Social smiling* is regarded by Spitz (1965) as an important element that is a species-specific reaction to the human face, but can also be evaluated as an "affective sign" of *expected* gratification (therefore a cognitive condition). Likewise *crying* when the mother leaves is an affective indicator of the child/mother relation. The emerging *fear of strangers* (the so-called eighth-month anxiety) is interpreted as *separation fear*, which the child shows if it sees a stranger instead of the expected mother. Hence, the object relationship (attachment/dependency) is already determined by behaviors like proximity-seeking and resistance to separation, as well as by distant bids (crying).

The interpretation of stranger anxiety as a sign for fear of separation from the mother has been questioned since a child can also show signs of fear toward an approaching stranger if it is *simultaneously* in the mother's arms (Szekely, 1954). But the significance of orality for the emergence of the child/mother tie was initially also fully accepted within the framework of learning theory attempts to explain this phenomenon (Dollard & Miller, 1950; Sears, Whiting, Nowlis, & Sears, 1953; Sears, Maccoby, & Levin, 1957; Sears, Rau, & Alpert, 1965; Beller, 1957, 1959).

In cross-cultural research Whiting (1944) concluded, from investigations of the Kwoma, that dependency reactions were not strengthened just by consistent, positive reinforcements, but appeared predominantly after frustrations as well.

Harlow and his colleagues, by experimentally manipulating nourishment and skin contact with rhesus monkeys, demonstrated that skin contact and not nourishment appeared to be the key antecedent in the formation of attachment (cf. Harlow, 1958). However, these studies did not question the possibility that dependency is a secondary drive that could be built upon the reduction of another primary drive, for example, on Harlow's concept of "contact comfort" (see McDavid & Harari, 1968).

The biophysiologically given deficient maturity of the human being at birth leads to a close association of these conditions in all cultures. Whiting & Child (1953), for example, showed that transculturally, oral training and dependency training are strongly correlated with one another. Konner (1972), too, who is strongly influenced by ethological theory, feels unable to distinguish between the comforting and nourishing function of breast feeding in the Zhun/Twasi Bushmen.

Actually the process of breast feeding has or can have several functions, a fact that usually does not become clear in studies done in Western cultures. Brazelton (1972), for example, reported that the breast is given to infants by the Zinacanteco Indians also to soothe them, and not just when they are hungry. The positive relationship between breast feeding (when done, duration, etc.) and attachment, therefore cannot be employed unequivocally as a criterion for the hypothesis that the reduction of the hunger drive is the key antecedent to attachment.

The most significant empirical counterarguments against this hypothesis, however, come from the "Glasgow Study," in which Schaffer & Emerson (1964) investigated sixty Scottish mother/child pairs. The intensity of specific attachment had no connection to the schedule of feeding or the age and duration of weaning. Instead, the authors discovered a positive connection between specific attachment and the amount of *general interaction* between mother and child, as well as "maternal responsiveness," and a *negative* trend between the number of caregivers and the amount of attachment to a person.

These findings are essentially supported by work in other cultures. Marvin et al. (1977), for example, investigated a sample of eighteen Hausa children, who had been raised in a polymatric society. They had an average of almost four caregivers where feeding and the reduction of other physical needs were looked after by caregivers different from those who were responsible for the general care of the children. For attachment formation the *general interaction* with the baby was more important than feeding. The children were, moreover, also attached to more than one person.

On the basis of a great number of indicators, Ainsworth (1963, 1967) was able to classify twenty-three of twenty-eight children in Uganda as "secure attached" and five as "not attached" . . . perhaps expressed better as "not yet attached." She did not find a connection between security of the child's attachment and general "warmth" of the mother (amount of affection she expressed) or a "schedule of feeding" (1963). But in considering sucking more closely she ascertained that children, who had been fed thoroughly on demand, and had also been given the breast for comfort, were more disturbed at the time of weaning (ca. twelve months) than those children who had either been fed "on schedule" or those who had been given the breast exclusively when they were hungry (1967). The reduction of the hunger drive itself, though not necessarily an antecedent condition for attachment, can become an integrated part of it. In weaning, the withdrawal of the mother then is experienced *as rejection*, and the termination of attachment (by rejecting the child) is then interpreted as the beginning of independence of the child from the caretaker (Albino & Thompson, 1956). In accordance with that interpretation, Goldberg (1972) reports that the Zambians train independence along with weaning. Also Stevens (1971) asserted, from data collected in a Greek hospital, that unproblematic feeding is less a prerequisite than the result of successful attachment.

Though work in other cultures confirms that the reduction of an infant's hunger drive is not the most important antecedent for the development of attachment, the significance of "contact comfort" is also weakened with this work, since in humans general stimulation (not just contact) appears to be the key variable. Parenthetically this assumption agrees with Rheingold (1961), who stressed the importance of visual and kinesthetic stimulation. However, these findings alone do not irrevocably damage the application of secondary drive theory to the emergence of attachment, since its occurrence could theoretically also be attributed to another primary drive—for example, a general primary need for stimulation.

Perhaps the most important implication of this position would be that one would have to be able to "deprive" such a "drive." This appears, however, to be doubtful (cf. the works of Walters & Parke, 1964; and Walters & Ray, 1960 which was apparently conducted outside the realm of cross-cultural comparison). It follows for instance from the concepts of Beller (1955) that the "general dependency drive" is formed from the components of attention, help, recognition, and physical contact, and it follows according to Sears et al. (1953) that the same drive would have to manifest itself in relation to different targets. This chapter's interpretation of the structural and functional cluster formation of the dependency/attachment concept in Western culture, *as in cross-cultural comparison*, contradicts both assumptions.

In the course of the general shift from the Hullian model to the Skinnerian "operant conditioning model" (Ainsworth, 1969, p. 992), "secondary drive theory" was discarded even in learning theory. Dependency was simply viewed "as behavior" that is learned through reinforcements in a learning process, in which the mother also receives positive reinforcement and thus lays the foundation for the further social development of the child (cf. Bijou & Baer, 1965; Gewirtz, 1961, 1969). In these interpretations "primary reinforcers" though still required, are relatively arbitrary. But behavior itself does not require a "need" or "drive."[2] Nevertheless, objections were raised against the application of associative learning by ethologically oriented researchers, especially by Hess (1970) and by Bowlby (1969).

The most comprehensive and most differentiated ethologically oriented theories (cf. Ainsworth 1969, 1973 and Bowlby, 1969) assume that human attachment behavior has biological roots and must be understood in the context of Darwinian evolutionary principles, that is, by its "survival value" for the species. Second, the child/mother relationship is viewed neither alone from the point of the child nor from the mother, but both partners in this dyad form *one system*. Schaffer (1963), therefore, prefers the term "attachment couple." Third, mother and child mutually regulate one another to achieve an optimal spatial distance or to maintain it, which guarantees the protection of the child from enemies. Fourth, before the child is capable of locomotion the scheme "babyishness" (Lorenz, 1943) is used by the child; the mother herself is induced by the child's *crying* and *smiling* to move toward him. Fifth, as soon as the child can locomote on his or her own the maintenance of the optimal distance on the part of the mother is further ensured by the emotional conduct of "care need," on the part of the child by "attachment" (in animals by imprinting). The mother serves thereby as a "secure base for exploration," as a secure platform from which the protected child can explore the environment. And sixth, with regard to evolution theory it follows that this "goal-corrected system" is "genetically biased;" that is, the principal elements lead, in the case of infants, to fixed action patterns, which then may subsequently "lose their fixed-action qualities and become modified through experience or coordinated into goal-corrected systems: regardless of this loss, neither Bowlby nor the ethologists lose sight of their species-characteristic features" (Ainsworth, 1973, p. 6).

This ethologically conceived model has the great advantage of representing attachment in a *functional relationship* to other action and interaction patterns of infancy. It includes the previously appearing discrimination capacities, the simultaneously increasing locomotive skills, and the later fear reactions. The developmental model of Bowlby (1969), has four phases. It systematizes observations of the primary orientation reactions of the child (visual fixation, visual tracking, listening, phase 1), the ensuing social responsiveness (crying, smiling, vocalizing, phase 2), active initiative in seeking proximity and contact (phase 3), and the significance of the early cognitive processes of the child (phase 4). Attachment, in the strict sense of the word, belongs to phase 3. The integrating function of this model accounts for its enormous influence.

This theory also revolutionized research methods, since (a) mother/child dyads have been increasingly investigated in "natural settings" and (b) the catalogue of behaviors in infancy has been vastly broadened. In such methods the following three classes of indicators have been differentiated: (1) signaling behavior (crying, smiling, vocalizing), (2) orienting behavior (looking, following, approaching), and (3) active physical contact behavior (clambering up, embracing, clinging). In addition, systematic variations of situations are undertaken, which relate chiefly to *exploration behavior*, to *separation situations* and to reactions toward *strange people* as well as their interactions (e.g., exploration in the presence and absence of the mother or in the presence of a stranger, e.g., Ainsworth & Wittig, 1969).

The chief distinction between learning theory (e.g., Gewirtz, 1969) and ethology centers on the assumption that these single elements of the control system are supposed to have a biophysiological basis. They are supposed to function "similarly to instinct," and thus it is assumed that (a) single stimuli (babyishness, smiling, crying) have a "release function" and (b) the reactions of these stimuli are, to a certain extent, "genetically biased."[3]

Fortunately, aspects of the question of the plasticity of the assumed regulatory mechanism and the species-specificity of "action patterns," can be tested in cross-cultural psychology. When looking at the results of cross-cultural research, it is first worthwhile to note that some indicators for an attachment pattern, derived from experiences in Western cultures (e.g., kissing, hugging), are of no importance at all in some cultures (in Uganda, for example). This pattern seems to be influenced by a *specific learning* process (cf. Ainsworth, 1967, pp. 344f). Further, it is known from Ainsworth (1963) that specific attachment emerged *earlier* on the average in babies in Uganda than in the sample of infants from Glasgow (Schaffer & Emerson, 1964).[4] This difference can, of course, be attributed to the differences in methods employed by the authors (operationalization of attachment, see Stevens, 1971). But a more intensive stimulation of the African children can also play a role here. Géber & Dean (1957) and Ainsworth (1963, 1967) have reported that the general amount of stimulation by the caregivers to Ugandan children is greater than that given in Western cultures (see also Goldberg, 1972). It is also greater in traditional African families when compared with acculturated families in Africa (cf. Géber, 1958a, 1958b). From the investigations of Géber (1958a, 1958b), that related partly to the Ainsworth sample, it is known that the Ugandan babies got higher scores on Gesell tests than European children.[5] It is also known that the amount of general stimulation, in an optimal range, has a positive correlation with *general development*, as has been shown by animal experimental investigations on *physiological* (Guttmann, 1972), *morphological* (Reugamer, Bersntein, & Benjamin, 1954; Weininger, 1956) and *behavioral development* (Thompson, 1968), as well as by the cross-cultural work by Gunders & Whiting (1968), done with data from sixty-nine societies on the aggregate level. Since it is also known that the amount of general stimulation is an important antecedent condition for attachment, there could be a theoretically important functional connection between general stimulation, the general developmental state of the organism, and attachment, which suggests less of an "instinct analogous" process of attachment than a mutual interaction between the state of maturation of the organism and external stimulation by which the organism would be capable of earlier differentiation and categorizations of stimuli. Therefore, within the first year of life, in the traditional environment, development may be improved by the kind of stimulations that are available; further development (in the second year of life) then may require stimulation of a different kind, which is often missing. This results in compensation, relative to the precocity of African children, during the first two years of life, as reported by Géber (1958a, 1958b). Additionally, nourishment as well as genetic factors cannot be definitely excluded as contributing factors (Goldberg, 1969; Lusk & Lewis, 1972).

Also, the "releasers" relevant to the core behavior of the mother—*crying, smiling, eye contact* and so-called *"babyishness"*—as well as the reactions of caregivers to these stimulative conditions, show considerable plasticity. This makes an "instinct-analogous" interpretation of human behavior at least questionable.

Third, Ainsworth's study (1967), shows that in the African sample differential crying, and in the American sample differential smiling, was the first sign of attachment. Culture-specific behavior patterns of the caregivers could be responsible for this. For example, Marvin et al. (1977) reported that the Hausa responded much more quickly to crying than is usual in the United States (see Bell & Ainsworth, 1972). Konner (1972) reported the same for the Zhun/Twasi Bushmen. This difference can perhaps be attributed to the fact that United States babies do not disturb their mothers as quickly because of the buffering effect afforded by bedroom walls, and on the other hand, to the greater likelihood that crying has a more serious basis in less developed and dangerous environments. It appears, however, to be transculturally possible to differentiate the crying of children in danger from "normal" crying (see Wolff, 1969; Konner, 1972).

On the contrary, Ainsworth (1973) reported that Americans more often try to gain contact with infants by "smile evoking" than the caregivers in the Ugandan sample. Also the Zhun/Twasi (!Kung) provoke smiling of children at an early stage, and show a prompt reaction to smiling (Konner, 1972). By contrast, Zinacanteco Indian children are seldom encouraged to smile, and there is seldom a reaction to smiling at all (Brazelton, 1972). Kilbride & Kilbride (1975), in their survey of differences between cultures, concluded that the frequency and duration of social smiles of infants are closely connected with social stimulation, but that the first emergence of a smile is in part determined by biological factors.

These studies show that children's crying and smiling, as well as reactions to them, are subject to considerable cultural variation. It therefore may be unwise to link them with the instinct-analogous model, by making them the functional equivalent of "releasing stimuli."

Eye contact, too, which is considered to be an important prerequisite for developing attachment in Western cultures (Robson, 1967), is likewise not present to the same degree in all cultures. This is partly because in many cultures children are carried on the back most of the time (cf. Brazelton, 1972; Goldberg, 1972) and partly because children are held on the lap, so that caregiver and child look in the same direction. Yet the development of attachment does not appear to be hindered under these conditions.

Finally, the interpretation of "babyishness" as a releasing stimulus is questioned by the fact that in some cultures mothers kill their newborn if their rearing is endangered (cf. Konner, 1972), an action not undertaken "light-heartedly," but experienced as a conflict situation (see Eibl-Eibesfeldt, 1972). Characterizing it as "conflict," though, should not alone suffice as an argument, for conflicts can be formulated and corroborated without referring to instincts or "genetically biased principles."

The universality of a central aspect of ethologically oriented attachment theory, namely the *dynamic balance* between exploration behavior of the child and the function of the caregiver as a firm exploration basis, is also challenged by cross-cultural data (Marvin et al., 1977). They showed that the caregiver was not used as a basis for locomotive, but for manipulatory exploration,[6] and that the otherwise customary reactions to separation from the caregiver (emotional upset, following, etc.) did not appear. Also, the assumption that attachment is initially limited to one person is placed in question by Marvin and his colleagues as well as Leiderman & Leiderman (1974).

One aspect in the work of Marvin et al. that is claimed for *support* of the validity of ethological theory is more likely to *question* it. Ethological theory postulates that "the 'biological function' of a behavioral system is that which gave the species (or the individual) survival advantage in the 'environment of evolutionary adaptedness'—the original environment in which the species first emerged" (Ainsworth, 1973, p. 5). Marvin and associates conducted their study in a natural setting that corresponds closely to Ainsworth's "original environment." It is manifest there, though, that the locomotory exploratory behavior of the child is *not limited by its attachment to the safe base for exploration,* but by the *intended restriction of the caregivers who allow exploration only to a very limited degree.* This finding leads to the dilemma that attachment behavior is supposed to have a function that is no longer important in Western society, but that it is also unimportant in a dangerous environment because it is the *caregiver* who reacts to the *perceived* dangers.

The search for species-specific universals and the underlying assumption of a biologically rooted model of man is the main reason why ethologically oriented researchers especially use the cross-cultural method as a touchstone (cf. Blurton-Jones, 1972). However, it appears that results from cross-cultural research will more strikingly show the *limitations* of the ethological interpretation of the emergence of attachment rather than support its validity. It is clearly one of the merits of this approach to interpret the emergence of attachment of a child as an outcome of the *mother-child dyad.* Unfortunately, however, the mutual regulating interrelationship between both partners within the dyad is sometimes neglected when compared with the equilibrium between the proximity-seeking and exploratory activities of the child. It would be highly beneficial, for theory and research on attachment, if two conditions (and their interactions) would be recognized more than has been done in the past: (a) the changing organismic state of the child, especially its growing *cognitive* capacities; and (b) the nurturant and retrieval *intentions* of the mother as well as the correlated *cognitions* she has (concerning the developmental state of the child, its capacities and limitations, as well as to possible "dangers" within the environment). It is highly questionable, however, whether such cognitive variables could still be handled by the theory as epiphenomena or whether they necessarily would lead to a radical change in the underlying paradigm.

Conditions for the further development of attachment/dependency.   The few investigations on the further development of dependent behavior after infancy shows that this behavior (especially proximity-seeking) decreases with age, and that—if one accepts separation upset as an indicator—this decline takes place at four to four and one-half years (see Shirley & Poyntz, 1941). The *stability* of dependent behavior (defined by intercorrelations of dependent behavior at different ages; i.e., in the *relative* position of individual children in a sample) is, on the whole, moderate and usually significant for most indicators and age intercorrelations. Stability is, though, greater for adjacent ages, with ages three to ten years being most distinct, and greater for girls than for boys (Kagan & Moss, 1962). (For a summary of this work, see Maccoby & Masters, 1970.)

Within the Six Cultures study, the decrease of the functional cluster formation of dependent behavior was also demonstrated. A transcultural check of the stability measures is impossible for the age groups investigated by Kagan & Moss (1962), since corresponding longitudinal data are lacking. Maccoby and Feldman (1972) only give values (for very differentiated indicators) for ages two to three for their American samples, but no corresponding values for the kibbutz sample.

The literature review by Maccoby & Masters (1970) on the preconditions for further development of dependent behavior shows that the "warmth" pole of the "warmth versus hostility" factor of parental behavior unexpectedly has no noteworthy relation to dependent behavior (cf. Becker, 1964), while the "hostility" or "rejection" pole definitely has. This finding is supported by Rohner (1975), whose data came from an ethnographic analysis of 101 societies from around the world. He reports a correlation of $-.30$ for children and $-.39$ for adults between dependence and "parental acceptance-rejection," a relationship he attributes to a frustration of a "generalized need" for positive evaluation, which additionally leads to socially and psychologically rather "negative" behaviors (hostility, aggression, feelings of low self-esteem, low self-adequacy, negative view of the world). Unfortunately, however, Rohner's data are calculated on the aggregate level and are difficult to interpret on the individual level. Maccoby & Masters (1970) offered an alternative interpretation for such a relationship: the parents can be rejecting *because* the children are dependent. It is unclear which *mechanism* operates in such circumstances or how it is put into motion. For example, rejection by the parents can lead to *fear arousal* that leads to increased proximity-seeking. It is also possible that to some extent more general conditions of an unspecific development of competence are concealed behind this correlation. Since dependency is "immature behavior" it may be presumed that human beings develop other, more adaptive techniques in the course of their development, and that "the rejecting parent probably does a poor job of helping the child to acquire more mature behavior" (Maccoby & Masters, 1970, p. 141). The important role of such conditions is supported by the relationship that generally exists in Western research between the second important child-rearing factor of "permissiveness versus restrictiveness" (Becker, 1964) and dependent behavior. Parental restrictiveness correlates positively with dependent behavior toward the parents. The development of *independence and self-reliance* appear to develop along with child-centered responsibility (Baumrind & Black, 1967; Sears et al., 1965). This is supported transculturally by the Six Cultures Study (Whiting & Whiting, 1975), even if their data are statistically questionable (cf. Eckensberger, 1978). In trying to cluster these behavior categories the Whitings suggest two dimenions: dimension A that can be characterized by "dependent-dominant versus nurturant-responsible" behaviors, and dimension B that combines the behaviors that are described as "authoritarian-aggressive versus sociable-intimate." *Cultures* that are classified in the "nurturant-responsible" pole of dimension A (Tarong, Juxtlahuaca, Nuansongo) are characterized by less cultural complexity (defined by the scale of Murdock & Provost, 1973). The *cultures* that display a high degree of complexity (Khalapur, Orchard Town, Taira) can be classified in the "dependent-dominant" pole. From the psychological viewpoint, however, it is important that *leeway for behaviors and for proving oneself* differs in amount for the children according to the complexity of cultures. These different margins correspond well with the development of responsibility in children. Children in less complex cultures do not only take over generally more household tasks at an earlier age than children in more complex cultures, but also qualitatively different ones. Thus, the children in less complex cultures are entrusted with chores that have, for the child, a sensible meaning for the household system such as fetching wood and water, cooking, helping with the harvest, taking care of livestock, and looking after younger brothers and sisters. *Negligence* of such chores has *immediate consequences* for the child. Their *fulfillment* on the other hand leads (via causal attribution) to a "strengthening of the ego" and responsibility for oneself, too. Children in more complex cultures help with household chores whose significance for the household and for themselves is less clear.

These last examples demonstrate that dependency is not only a prerequisite for the functioning of learning principles (praise, social reinforcement, imitation, modeling, etc.) in a later stage of life, but it is a precursor for other motive systems, and is especially significant for the development of need achievement (see pp. 273f). A close attachment to members of the cultural group is furthermore one precondition for the

child to learn values and actions of his reference group. This is one function of attachment that ethologists also consider important (Bowlby, 1969,
pp. 225f, and Konner, 1972).

The Aggression Motive

Definition of the Concept

Research on aggression involves the study of behavior that has the potential to produce physical injury or an injury of interests (e.g., of self-esteem, social status, property) of another person (Berkowitz, 1962, 1965;
Feshbach, 1964, 1970; Bandura & Walters, 1963; Bandura, 1973; Hartup &
DeWit, 1974). In a somewhat broadened sense, the breaking of taboos and
laws or disdaining the group consensus can be included in this definition.
"One obvious distinction that needs to be made is between acts that accidentally lead to an injury and acts that are 'intentional' or 'motivated' "
(Feshbach, 1970, p. 161). Thus actions that accidentally lead to injuries are
excluded from the definition of aggression used in this chapter.

Behaviorism rejects the inclusion of "intention" in defining aggression
as being too subjective (Buss, 1961). Bandura (1973) stresses that aggressive behaviors can be elicited by the expectation of *every kind* of positive
benefit. Recent summaries about aggression research do not regard intention as a necessary element in defining aggression (Hartup & DeWit, 1974;
Stonner, 1976). Concentration will be on an aggression construct, theoretically understood as a motive, and goal directedness or intention itself is
an indispensable component for a motive construct (Kornadt, 1974). Otherwise this chapter concurs with the positions of Feshbach (1970), Berkowitz (1974) and Werbik (1974).

Further, "hostile," intended aggression can be differentiated from an
"instrumental" one (Feshbach, 1970), where injuries occur as side effects
in the pursuit of nonaggressive goals. Special avoidance motives could
oppose an aggressive action, representing specific inhibition of aggression
(as in fear of punishment or guilt—Olweus, 1969, 1973; Whiting & Child,
1953; Kornadt, 1974). Then, certain kinds of conflict behavior are assumed
to occur, for example, displacement or projection.

Indicators of aggressiveness. Aggressiveness is implicated in the following
behaviors:

1. physical aggression, such as beating, kicking, temper tantrums;
2. verbal aggression, such as screaming, scolding, insulting;

3. indirect or symbolic aggression like threatening, disobeying, not greet-ing, sorcery, and so forth.

These actions are evaluated differently in different cultures; verbal and symbolic aggression are especially variable. An action intended to of-fend may be understood in one culture, but be entirely meaningless in another culture. In evaluating aggressive indicators it must be considered that aggression is a dyadic variable (Sears, 1951) and like attachment it can only be expressed and interpreted interpersonally. Aggressive behavior requires that the other person involved attribute it to an aggressive motive, otherwise it will have another meaning.

Investigations of aggression only partly refer to direct observations. Indirect sources of information such as questionnaires or tests are often employed, whose results are usually interpreted in a global sense. Experi-mental investigations have hardly played a role in cross-cultural compari-sons. Finally, on an aggregate level, the topic of criminality has received considerable attention (Clinard & Abbott, 1973; DeVos & Mizushima, 1973; Gurr & Duvall, 1973).

Interpreting indicators of aggressiveness involves the following problems:

1. With regard to the inhibition of aggression a low aggression "score" can be interpreted as:
   a. a low strength of the aggression motive,
   b. a higher strength with concomitant high aggression inhibition, and
   c. a limited expression of "aggressiveness" under specific situational conditions.
2. The generalizability of any indicator to all aspects of aggressiveness is problematic. This is closely linked to the question of whether different behavior and indicator areas can be attributed to a single motive con-struct. This is a problem of construct validity and must be especially taken into account when "fantasies" (from projective methods) are em-ployed as the only indicators of aggressiveness.
3. Since specific indicators are subjected to different evaluations and sanc-tions in different cultures, it is incautious to interpret them intercul-turally in the same way.

Finally, in aggression the behavior of adults plays a much greater role than in attachment. Furthermore, the form and function of aggressive be-havior changes during the life span.

Problems of the theoretical approach.   Theoretical assumptions about the structure and function of aggressiveness, aggression inhibition, and about their genesis are numerous (see especially Freud, 1920, 1932; Dollard et al., 1939; Buss, 1961; Sears et al., 1957; Berkowitz, 1962; Bandura, 1973;

and Lorenz, 1963). In recent years the role of learning and cognitive structuring processes are no longer disputed (e.g., cf. Bandura, 1973; Feshbach, 1974; Eibl-Eibesfeldt, 1974), and a certain biological basis is being taken more seriously (Hartup & DeWit, 1974; Stonner, 1976).

Newer developments dealing with a systematic motivation theory of aggression within cognitive theories have hardly begun (e.g., Feshbach, 1974). Tedeschi, Smith, and Brown (1974) attempted a reformulation in terms of attribution and social equity. Kornadt (1974; 1979) expanding Feshbach's (1964) theory applied the general motivation theory of McClelland et al. (1953), Atkinson & Feather (1966) and Heckhausen (1968) to aggression.

This theoretical heterogeneity is also reflected in the use of inconsistent terminology. In the following the term *aggressiveness* will be used as a synonym for "enduring aggression motive." The term *aggression* stands for aggressive action actually performed. Furthermore, there are assorted differentiations in the literature with regard to different directions, e.g., extrapunitive versus intropunitive or directed versus indirected aggression, or to different forms of aggression, e.g., impulsive versus nonimpulsive, overt versus covert, and instigated versus self-instigated or spontaneous. In the following the different researchers' terminology will be retained in an effort not to add to the list of varying forms.

Validity of the concept.   There is no systematic summary of research examining the convergent and discriminant validity of the aggression construct. The observations made within the framework of the Six Cultures Study could, however, partially fill this gap (Whiting & Whiting, 1975). Aggressive behaviors were originally differentiated according to "opportunity aggression" (carried out purely for the sake of hurting someone) and "instrumental aggression" (to achieve some end).

Further evaluation rests upon the behaviors classified as "instrumental aggression" that were differentiated in physical and symbolic acts. As the former category was further differentiated, three categories emerged: *"assaults* (seriously); *assaults sociably* or horseplay, and *insults"* (Whiting & Whiting, 1975, p. 61).

The median proportion scores of the behaviors can be classified in two dimensions. Dimension B evinces a sociable-intimate cluster score (acts sociably + assaults sociably + touches) and an authoritarian-aggressive polar cluster score (reprimands + assaults). *Insults* (symbolic aggression) does not display a high value on any of the dimensions (see Whiting & Whiting, 1975, p. 69). So aggression proved to be a transcultural variable, since the behaviors investigated in different cultures could be arranged on one dimension. Thus the assumption regarding the universality of aggressiveness (Whiting & Child, 1953) was confirmed.

Expression and Functional Forms of Aggressiveness

A motivational theory of aggressiveness should first consider cultural variations in aggression. Such an inexact and theoretically neutral interest was the basis of many older impressive descriptions of aggressive behaviors on an aggregate level. If raids, violent crime, warlike conflicts, theft of livestock, and similar indicators are used, differentiation can be made between "peaceful cultures" e.g., Hopi (Thompson & Joseph, 1944); !Ko-Bushmen (Eibl-Eibesfeldt, 1972); Semai (Dentan, 1968); Abron (Alland, 1972); Hutterites (Eaton & Weil, 1955); Polynesians (Levy, 1969) and "warlike-aggressive cultures," Kwoma and Papuans of New Guinea (Whiting, 1944; Berndt, 1964); Apaches (Goodwin, 1942); Comanches (Linton, 1945); Rajput (Triandis & Lambert, 1961); Dagum Dani (Gardner & Heider, 1969); and the Yanamani and Eipo (Eibl-Eibesfeldt, 1976). In addition, culture-specific preferences of certain aggressive forms have been described, e.g., frequency of violent criminal acts, wars against neighboring tribes, combats between peers, deceits, sorcery, gossip, and calumny.

These differences can be attributed to the *targets* (ingroup versus outgroup; authorities versus peers), and/or the *forms* of expression (e.g., war and fighting as physical versus sorcery as symbolic aggression). But it may be assumed that differences of "strength" are included, that is, the fundamental underlying *energizing variable* (approximately measured in the frequency and intensity of the responsiveness or the relative "severity" of the aggression) may be reflected in cultural differences. However, the instigating conditions and the intended goals of aggression, and the regularities linking both must be known before asking more precisely about the way aggression functions.

Expressive forms of aggressiveness.   Triandis & Lambert (1961) computed, in a secondary analysis of sixty primitive cultures, which "sources of frustration" were considered to be the cause of a (more or less) comparable event, namely, damage to the food supply, and against whom aggressions were directed. Considerable intercultural differences were found for both. Objects of aggression include spirits, peers, or neighboring tribes. Further, the authors distinguished between two kinds of societies: one in which people express their aggression spontaneously in unstructured situations; in the other they devise more structured means for aggressive outlets (p. 646).[7]

In comparing cultures with differences in aggression, the complexity of the cultures should also be taken into account. Complexity probably determines which patterns seem adequate to interpret frustrations and reactions to them. Different levels of knowledge and kinds of social relationships (illiterate versus industrial society) apparently lead to different forms of aggressive reaction and expression, an assumption supported by Whiting & Whiting (1975). Differences in preferred *aggression targets* were uncovered by Whiting (1963) and Minturn & Lambert (1964).

Differences in forms of *expression of aggressiveness* or *directions* of aggression have been frequently investigated on the individual level using samples from different cutlures (with no claims to representativeness). In addition to direct observations, questionnaires and projective methods were employed, chiefly the Picture-Frustration Test (PFT) by Rosenzweig (1945), Rosenzweig, Fleming, and Rosenzweig (1948). For example, Takala & Takala (1957) examined 632 Finnish children between four and eleven years of age and found them to have higher extrapunitive scores on the PFT than American children. Similarly, McCary (1950) earlier showed, in an intracultural comparison, that more overt aggression and less passive reactions to frustration emerge in the Northern than in the Southern United States. Related investigations were also carried out in Japan by Sumida & Hayashi (1956, 1957) and in India by Pareek (1964). According to Pareek, who compared these data with those of Rosenzweig from the United States, the Japanese have an especially strong tendency toward intrapunitive reactions and usually ascribe the responsibility for a frustration to themselves.

Findings by others (cf. DeVos, 1973a; Frost, Iwawaki, & Fogliatto, 1972; Triandis, 1972; Trommsdorff, 1978; Nakane, 1970; Hoshino, 1970) support the assumption that there are unusual kinds of aggressiveness. The data point to a slighter or to a more strongly inhibited aggressiveness, or to an aggressiveness differently structured among adult Japanese. However, the aggression data collected in Okinawa during the Six Cultures Study (Whiting & Whiting, 1975) do not suggest less aggressiveness among Japanese children. (But the Okinawan village of Taira should not be taken as representative of Japan.[8])

Differences between subcultures in forms of expression of aggressiveness may be valid transculturally. Madsen (1966) compared differences in "overt" versus "covert" aggression between urban and rural children in the United States of America and Mexico. She assumed, from the frustration-aggression hypothesis, that rural children would be more likely to show displaced and covert aggression. In both nations the rural had higher Rorschach "covert aggression" scores than the urban groups. "Overt aggression" indicators (teacher ratings) were, however, more frequent in the urban than in the rural Mexican, but not in the United States samples.

Differences in aggression as a function of sex and socioeconomic status in Guatemala and the United States were investigated by Adinolfi, Watson, and Klein (1973) by using the Picture-Frustration Study and peer ratings, but the differences could not be clearly ascertained. Such differences are frequently employed as arguments for the learning-theoretical or the frustration-aggression interpretations of aggressiveness (e.g., Madsen, 1966). They could also be explained from a psychoanalytic or ethological point of view. A final choice of only one of these theories would be possible only after a more exact investigation that included the study of inhibition, displacement processes, and developmental conditions.

Similarly, global comparisons of whole cultures are insufficient, because they do not include all indicators relevant to aggression and cannot determine the relative significance of the indicators. Whether the aggression motive in its "energetic core" is variably strong in different cultures thus cannot be answered.

The evidence based on test comparisons is full of methodological deficiencies (e.g., unrepresentative samples, the unchecked equivalence of the indicators, etc.). For example, it is often overlooked that the evaluation categories of the PFT are a priori classifications, which are only loosely derived from psychoanalytic theory and the frustration-aggression hypothesis, and are not anchored in the network of a comprehensive motivational system.

Functional forms of aggressiveness.   Whiting & Child (1953) in their cross-cultural testing of aggressive functioning were guided by the psychoanalytic projection hypothesis and certain displacement assumptions of frustration-aggression theory, designed to explain processes at the individual level. The transference of these assumptions to the cultural level is problematic.

Whiting & Child, departing from Miller's conflict model (Miller, 1948), which they modified by assuming a curvilinearity of the inhibition gradient (1953, p. 288, Fig. 1), postulated a connection between aggression anxiety and displacement. "Aggressive habits" directed toward parents or close relatives as the original frustrators, cannot really be expressed toward them, but towards other objects; the dissimilarity of the objects increases with increasing aggression anxiety. Such objects are, among others, spirits: "Spirits of the dead, or ghosts, should be much more similar to a person's relatives than should animal spirits" (Whiting & Child, 1953, p. 286). In the case of stronger aggression anxiety a "custom potential[9] fear of agent," regarded as a projection of aggression, related more to dissimilar animal spirits than to ghosts (cf. 1953, p. 296, Fig. 3).

A secondary analysis of HRAF data from thirty-two cultures confirms these hypotheses (see Figure 6–3). These findings and the interpretations suggested by Whiting & Child provide data that attest to a universality of certain functions of aggressiveness and aggression inhibition. For example, the emergence of definite kinds of projection and displacement (as in fear of sorcerers), is more exactly predictable within a precise conflict theory.

A similar investigation of projection and displacement was done by

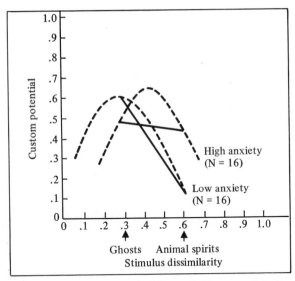

Figure 6–3   "Mean Custom Potential of Fear of Ghosts and Animal Spirits, for Societies with High and with Low Anxiety about Aggression" (Whiting & Child, 1953, p. 297). The hypothetical curves drawn in are solely to show the principal compatibility with the hypothesis of Whiting & Child. Adapted with permission from Whiting and Child, *Child Training and Personality*, Yale University Press.

Wright (1954). In both these studies, however, some ex-post facto interpretations are employed, many quantifications are arbitrary, and only two points of measurement are available for each group. Nevertheless, the assumption of a certain universal validity of psychoanalytic displacement theory appears to be plausible, especially in regard to a number of further investigations and observations. In cultures in which overt aggressive behaviors are more suppressed, one finds less direct aggression (cf. Hopi: Thompson & Joseph, 1944; Abron: Alland, 1972; Navaho: Kluckhohn, 1944; Honigman, 1972; Worchel, 1974).

Modifications according to age and sex.   To date the Six Cultures Study represents the most systematic available cross-cultural study of aggression.

At ages three to eleven years, the frequency of all observed forms of aggression combined remains constant within each of the six cultures (see Lambert, 1974; Whiting & Whiting, 1975, p. 143, Fig. 16). Nevertheless, the proportion of different forms of aggression changes with age. It appears that the rougher, less inhibited, forms of aggression (assaults) are replaced by more socially acceptable forms (cf. Whiting & Whiting, 1975, p. 138, Fig. 15). In all cultures a "self-instigated" form of aggression, as well as one of retaliation, can be observed. The frequency of both forms is relatively similar across cultures. Generally, all forms of aggression are to be found more frequently in boys than in girls.[10] Finally, there are differences in the targets of aggression (infants, peers, and parents) (Whiting & Whiting, 1975, p. 156, Fig. 18).

The rank scores that the aggression cluster received in comparison to the other behavior clusters (Whiting & Whiting, 1975, p. 158) were very similar in the six cultures studied. It must be considered whether these proportions concur with the frequency of instigated aggression experienced by children. Lambert denies this and from immediate observations suggests that the "passing-down" of aggression (that is the older child directing its retaliation against the younger ones) is a form of displacement that occurs in all cultures. In defining the "real" frequencies this has to be taken into account. This may support the displacement hypothesis investigated by Whiting & Child (1953).

Antecedent Conditions for the Development of Aggressiveness

The focus here is no longer simply the instigating circumstances for the individual aggressive act; there are as well enormous individual differences in frequency, multiplicity, and gravity of "frustrative" events as well as in reacting to them. The problem is, then, how enduring individual differences of this kind can result in an aggression motive with its specific motivational dynamics.

All theories assume critical conditions for the development of aggressiveness in child rearing practices. Starting from the frustration-aggression hypothesis, in all cultures the control of the child's needs can be understood as being frustrating. In estimating the *degree* of frustration, correlations can be examined between the extent of demands to control the child's needs and aggressiveness.

Within the framework of *reinforcement learning,* punishment or reward of aggressive behaviors in child-training are investigated. In *imitation learning,* parental behaviors are regarded as models for the strength (intensity) and forms of the child's aggressive behavior. In *psychoanalysis* the parental influence is moulded into the *ego-ideal* and *superego* of the child by identification, resulting especially from the dynamics of the solution of the Oedipus complex. The child both strives toward ideals and is anxious to avoid guilt feelings associated with not reaching one or the other ideal.

A series of investigations made relatively simple assumptions within "unifactorial" theories. According to the newer, pluralistic theories on the genesis and development of aggressiveness (Kornadt, 1966; Feshbach, 1970, 1974; Bandura, 1973; cf. as well Heckhausen, 1966), such principles do not cancel out one another (even if they can become effective in different directions). The entire range of child rearing variables might be effective. It is increasingly realized that a more complicated reciprocal relationship exists between parents and children.

Frustration.   According to Miller's (1941) revision of the Dollard et al. (1939) frustration-aggression hypothesis, aggression is always a consequence of a frustration, and frustration produces generally, but not exclusively, an instigation to aggression. Frustration is understood as "an interference with the occurrence of an instigated goal response at its proper time in the behavior sequence" (Dollard et al., 1939, p. 7). Later frustration was employed less precisely, as if it were synonymous to an aversive stimulation.[11]

The transcultural validity of the frustration-aggression hypothesis was examined by Bateson (1941). The aggressive behavior of the Iatmul (New Guinea) apparently corresponded to the frustration-aggression hypothesis. In contrast, in Bali the blocking of a goal-directed action did not lead to aggression in adults.

Bateson explains that Bali children learn "to see life as composed of smooth series of enjoyable acts rather than as separate sequences of acts where each sequence leads up to some satisfying climax" (p. 353). They apparently live "in the immediate present not in some distant goal" (p. 355). Nonetheless, this does not contradict the frustration-aggression hypothesis, since a theoretically necessary stipulation is lacking. Obviously, the *time perspective* is significant for the aggression motive, but even on Bali the children display *temper tantrums.* Equally, the nearly unfrustratable adults, who are, in general, "indefinitely willing to suffer interruption" (p. 353) suddenly show outbursts of rage (e.g., lynching of a cattle rustler caught red-handed.) No goal-directed aggression motive seems to develop from early anger effects. Instead, also in adults, unstructured anger is an aggressive response form, that is—in Western society—usually confined to exceptional (pathological) cases.

Child rearing.   Whether frustration engendered in child rearing, and its differing ranges of severity, also has a distinct effect on aggression, cannot be definitely answered as yet. While some investigations seem to support this hypothesis (Ainsworth & Ainsworth, 1962), there are cultures and subcultures in which, in spite of much frustration in child rearing, only limited aggression appears (e.g., among the Hopis, studied by Thompson & Joseph, 1944; the Hutterites, studied by Eaton & Weil, 1955). Here again, the problem of interpreting the indicators of aggressiveness, especially of lower scores, is important.

Russell's (1972) HRAF-based finding of the relationship between warfare and developmental conditions is a further, though very global, linking of "frustration" with different forms of aggression. Mainly on the basis of factor analysis, Russell concluded that "non-indulgent child rearing practices, punitive emphasis on achievement, social anxiety and punishment of premarital and extramarital sexual relations" can be viewed as causes for high warfare and crime (Russell, 1972, p. 304). Those frustrations in child rearing are surely confounded with a number of other variables in an unknown manner and preclude a causal interpretation. Such variables may, for example, result in a suppression or displacement of aggression previously built up. Additional variables could also, independently of possible frustrations, account for a strong aggression motive. In the case of the Abrons, aggression is severely punished (Alland, 1972). An aggression-inhibition conflict can be hypothesized to be operating in such cases, the confirmation of which may be the emergence of less overt aggression with concomitantly increased indirect aggression (torturing animals, mischievousness, and a high frequency of sorcery).

A specific form of a frustration-aggression hypothesis was set forth by Prescott (1975). Starting from observations of the effects of maternal-social deprivation producing aggression in monkeys (Harlow & Harlow, 1962) and from neurological processes underlying somato-sensory deprivation, Prescott (1970) examined the hypothesis that "punishment of premarital sexual behavior would lead to high aggression in adults." He arrived at a "two-stage developmental theory . . . in short, violence may stem from deprivation of somato-sensory pleasure, either in infancy or in adolescence" (Prescott, 1975, p. 67). The connection made by Prescott does not correspond to the general frustration-aggression hypothesis, but rather to psychoanalytic and ethological hypotheses about the (innate) importance of a need for "somato-sensory" pleasure. Surely, the multiplicity of possible effective relationships makes inadmissable the explanation of the data by a single causal factor. The hypothesis, however, is interesting and politically relevant.

In order to recognize real causal relationships, the interactions of factors relevant to aggression in a more detailed and systematic way would have to be assessed. Included should be longitudinal studies that permit an analysis of processes in motive development. Since the interrelation of indirect aggression and suppressed direct aggression is not yet clear, it is open to question whether an evaluation of aggression in toto could prove effective.

As the child rearing methods that are said to be relevant for the development of aggressiveness are culturally variable, cross-cultural comparison would permit an assessment of functional relationships. The infants of the (aggressive) Kwoma do not develop a frustration-aggression sequence. Instead, as a result of excessive mothering they develop a frustration-dependency sequence (Whiting, 1944). This is thoroughly consistent with the modified frustration-aggression hypothesis (Miller, 1941). Yet later, when older children can successfully act aggressively toward their juniors, a link between frustration and aggression is observed, which is, moreover, rewarded by social approval from the parents. According to Levy (1969; 1973, p. 580) the Tahitians, who are not considered to be aggressive, usually allow children to have short "cathartic" outbursts of anger, but a longer serious angry behavior is hindered. Similarly, Semai children who beat each other are separated but not punished (Dentan, 1968). In both cases, lower rather than inhibited aggressiveness seems to develop.

Parental (and cultural) responses to child aggression vary widely (Minturn & Lambert, 1964)[12] and influence the development of aggressiveness in different ways that are, however, still largely unknown. But it has been shown that child-rearing methods lead, in different ways, to the development of *aggression anxiety* followed by aggression conflict and displacement (Whiting & Child, 1953).

These early investigations may be interpreted in terms of mutual relatedness between child-rearing practices and socialization anxiety of children, and between certain characteristics of aggressiveness and guilt feelings. But this is a post hoc interpretation that is only possible by assuming additional prerogatives and variables.

In the Six Cultures Study (Whiting & Whiting, 1975; Lambert, 1974), the relationship between child-rearing conditions and the development of aggressiveness was not investigated systematically. But the cultures could be classified on one dimension in regard to the children's aggressive behavior (sociable-intimate versus authoritarian-aggressive).

A dichotomy appeared according to differences in family structure. In those cultures where children show social intimate forms of aggression (Orchard Town, Juxtlahuaca, Tarong) the nuclear family is the dominant domestic unit. In the other cultures (Taira[13], Khalapur, Nyansongo) the patrilineal stem of the extended family dominates (cf. Whiting & Whiting, 1975, p. 114).

The extended family appears to supply antecedent conditions for the acquisition of aggressive behavior, since it offers models for identification and role imitation. The relationships between father and mother are more hostile, mother and grandmother live in conflict with one another, and the grandfather assumes an authoritarian role (Whiting & Whiting, 1975, p. 181). The prescriptively patrilocal residence rules resulted in additional frustrating conditions (Whiting & Whiting, 1975, pp. 176f).

Lambert (1974), concerned with the social context of aggressive behavior, was able to judge the observed aggressive acts according to whether they occurred spontaneously or by virtue of an instigation, and could relate this differentiation to the proportional frequency of aggres-

Table 6-1   Medians for Children of Each Culture on Dimension B (Based on Proportion Scores for Each Child Standardized Over the Whole Sample)

Nyansongo	Khalapur	Taira	Juxtlahuaca	Orchard Town	Tarong
−1.37	−0.46	−0.10	+0.20	+0.41	+0.70
Authoritarian-aggressive				Sociable-intimate	

sion targets. Lambert assumed that in all cultures there emerges a "massive displacement of aggression toward young children" (1974, p. 451).

This transcultural phenomenon, however, presumably also shows that peers provide a high degree of the feedback for aggressive acts. In formulating hypotheses about the development of aggressiveness, such painstaking cross-cultural observations permit recognition of the significance of peer interaction.

An interesting finding is the importance of a further differentiation: "retaliation on the spot" as compared with "hurting at some more opportune time." Lambert reports that "the higher the tit-for-tat score in a culture, the lower is the proportion of aggressive instigations received on the average by a child" ($r = -.59$ n.s., Lambert, 1974, p. 456f). Moreover, on the individual as well as on the cultural level, "the relationship between retaliation and being picked on ... becomes strongly and reliably negative," (p. 457) if, by the use of partial correlations, "the overall aggressive output proportion" is considered.

Lambert (p. 457) presumes that "a strategy of retaliation on the spot when attacked tends to inhibit attack over time." This hypothesis can be helpful in identifying the characteristics of low-aggression cultures. Lambert (p. 458) named three such indices: (1) the rates or proportions of hurts received as instigations to the child; (2) the rates and proportions of hurting effect acts received by the child; and (3) the "sneaky" hurts that others visit on the child as effect acts that follow nonhurting behavior on the child's part. These aspects are not yet sufficiently recognized, but they are important in the scope of a motivation theory of aggression.

One of them is the possibility of experiencing frustrations because of an anticipated threat to attaining distant goals, which is surely in part dependent on the kind and number of long-term goals. This is also important for the choice of aggressive reactions and retaliation strategy. A delayed retaliation requires a longer time perspective and a greater delay of gratification.

In addition, and this is another aspect, the distinction is not made here between hostile and instrumental aggression. In principle, this differentiation should be defended for theoretical reasons, though it is difficult to do so.

Certainly goals of other motives are frequently mixed with aggression goals, and their rewarding attainment is also important for the development of aggressiveness (e.g. taking away a toy from a peer, thereby angering him and simultaneously displaying superiority). Instrumental aggression, however, can also be understood as displaced aggression that is less tabooed and can be more easily justified and equally satisfy the "genuine" goals of aggression. Two conditions may have to be met: (1) the capability of delaying gratification is high, and (2) the structure of the aggression goal becomes correspondingly more differentiated.

The value of such detailed cross-cultural analyses becomes obvious: aside from frustration and learning by success, other factors play an important role in the development of aggressiveness. For instance, multiple cognitive processes of "weighing up" and "structuring," exist in aspects of retaliation. Furthermore, the role of social equity and the attribution of the causes of frustration are presumably important for developing nonaggressive, constructive goals and dispositions of action as forms of coping with frustrations (Pitkänen, 1974; Pitkänen-Pulkkinen, 1976; Rosenzweig, 1974). Factors that have been investigated in cross-cultural comparisons under the influence of cognitively oriented motive theories include: (1) The availability of aggressive models and the possibility of observing the effects of their behavior, (2) cognitive modes of structuring present in and transmitted by society, and (3) the evaluations of different aggressive behaviors.

Imitation learning. A post hoc interpretation (Bandura, 1973) points out that in some societies, especially the "warlike" ones, children are systematically offered the opportunity to observe aggressive models. In other cultures, whose members are considered as nonaggressive, child-rearing techniques apparently preclude representing models for aggressive behavior.

With data from forty-eight cultures Bacon, Child, and Barry (1963) found that, in boys, lack of *male identification figures* is conducive to aggressiveness. There are apparently mutual interactions of such factors as an ideal view of "manliness" in a society, opportunities for learning from models, previous identification with the mother and later "masculine" overcompensation, and the frustration of the dependency and approval motives. Whether sex-role identity is built up through identification with the father, or whether it is, conversely, a precondition for father identification has not been established.

Peer influence might be of special importance if clear discrepancies in behavior and/or values exist between the "subculture of the peers" and the adults. In an experiment concerning resistance to temptation in a play situation, Fry (1975) documented that Indian children are less influenced than United States children by a deviant model. This finding points out that culture-bound differences may exist in the development of self-control.

Evaluation and cognitive structuring. The Kwoma, the Naven, and the Yanamani associate aggressive behavior with the "ideal" character of a man (Whiting, 1944; Bateson, 1936; Chagnon, 1968). The Nunivak Eskimo do not esteem aggressive behavior (Lantis, 1959; cf. Honigman, 1972); likewise, aggressiveness is not respected by the Hopis, and may in fact lead to rejection.[14] Single aggressive behaviors are also subject to evaluation:

whether "revenge" leads to the building up of self-esteem or social acceptance. Furthermore, there are cognitive structures, concepts, and judgments in regard to "frustration" that are dependent on culture. Frustrations can be perceived as natural and unchangeable or as arbitrary, avoidable, nasty, and contemptful. Correspondingly, a frustration may or may not be interpreted as an injury of social equity or of one's own worth. Furthermore, whether or not one must aggressively fight in order to become respected as a man, or whether one can get along with frustrations depends on culture (Feshbach, 1974).

Such judgments, formerly studied under the viewpoint of the "arbitrariness of frustration," gain a new meaning within the context of attribution theory. East Asian, Central and East African cultures, and certain religious subgroups seem to have "frustration tolerance" that is clearly different from Euroamerican modes. It would be fruitful to study this cross-culturally within the framework of a cognitive motive theory of aggression.

Inhibition. It is open to question whether human beings can be said to have an innate, instinctive inhibition of aggression, (Lorenz 1963, Eibl-Eibesfeldt, 1974, and Merz, 1965.) Aggression anxiety is certainly conditioned through the punishment of aggressive acts (see e.g., Dollard et al., 1939). But numerous cognitive processes are involved, as in developing guilt oriented along internalized standards, or in evaluating the degree of retaliation that is adequate (and not excessive) to the injury experienced. An inhibition construct in aggression may be suggested, analogous to the two-component theory in achievement motivation to have the functional characteristics of a motive component (Kornadt, 1974; Olweus, 1969). The exact kind and function of cognitive aspects and affective elements (for instance, anticipation of negative affects) are, in any case, not yet known. Whether the widely accepted mechanistic conflict model by Miller (1944, see also Epstein, 1962) is valid for the interaction of aggressiveness and aggression inhibition or whether it would not have to be replaced by a cognitive model of conflict-solution may be answered in part by cross-cultural investigations.

Summary. Obviously a whole complex of factors leads to different degrees or forms of aggression inhibition, or even to low aggressiveness. On the basis of the available data it is impossible to provide an unequivocal evaluation of the various operative factors. The pluralistic model mentioned earlier is suitable as a framework for the developmental processes leading to aggressiveness and aggression inhibition. It needs to be complemented by considering cognitive processes, as derived from attribution theory, and social values.

This model and the difference in the evaluation of frustrations, in preferred targets, and forms of aggression, mean that a concept of a homogeneous and generalized disposition toward aggressive behavior (one global, undifferentiated aggression motive) that might predict all possible kinds of aggressive behavior is not tenable. However, the question remains whether, in spite of all differentiations of the special forms of the aggression *motive*, Sears's (1961) assumption that there is a universal "genotypic quality of aggression" can be endorsed.

On the Universality of Aggressiveness

The existing cross-cultural literature shows culture-bound differences between individuals in the form, direction, and strength of aggressive behavior. It suggests that some forms of aggressiveness occur in all cultures (see e.g., the summary interpretations of Bacon et al., 1963; Russell, 1972; Whiting & Whiting, 1975). This statement includes inferences from aggregate as well as individual levels, and stipulates an acceptance of the assumption that different phenomena (like fighting and murdering, mockery and sorcery) could be understood as different forms of expressing the motive of aggression.

The "face-slapping rituals" and song duels of the Eskimos (Eibl-Eibesfeldt, 1974) and the property destroying potlatch rituals of the Kwakiutl (Benedict, 1934) may be viewed as substitutes for destructive forms of physical aggression. The justification of such an assumption must, however, be examined within a theory of the structure of the aggression motive, its function, and its development. Such a theory is still in its infancy.

An approach in this direction could be derived from ethological theories. Ethologists assume an inherited tendency toward aggressive behavior, which is supposed to be universally rooted in the biological outfitting of the human being.

Biological components.   Biology would generally support the assumption that humans have certain brainstem regions that when stimulated cause aggressive behavior, and that a connection between testosterone and aggressiveness is evident (Hamburg, 1971; Moyer, 1971). Ethologists assume both certain motoric patterns characteristic for aggression and the susceptibility to typical releasing situations to be genetically determined. They can point to impressive similarities in the behavior between children and young primates, especially chimpanzees. Kicking, hitting, spitting, stamping of the feet, waving branches or sticks with a raised hand, and throwing objects are mentioned as examples of motoric patterns. Typical facial expressions for anger and threat are added. Hamburg and Van Lawick-Goodall (1974, p. 81–82) mentioned typical eliciting situations: survival threat, frustration of self-esteem, frustration of crucial interpersonal relationships (especially in the early mother-child relationship), and threat to the sense of belonging. A cross-cultural study was carried out by Eibl-Eibesfeldt (1972) with the children of the !Ko-Bushmen, a society described as nonviolent. He reported that all forms of aggression mentioned above appear in appropriate situations, and that they gradually disappear under the influence of socialization.

In the Six Cultures Study (Whiting & Whiting, 1975; Lambert, 1974), an aggression cluster proved to be transcultural. The observed behaviors correspond to those postulated by the ethologists; the younger the children, the greater the correspondence. With increasing age culture-bound socializing influences become more and more effective.

Also the other investigations support the impression that, at least in early infancy, similar forms of aggression appear universally. They exist in the form of temper tantrums (Hamburg & Van Lawick-Goodall, 1974), as reactions to (a) frustrations of attachment, (b) threats to social security (Alland, 1972; Albino & Thompson, 1956; Whiting, 1964), or (c) sibling and peer rivalry (Alland, 1972). Furthermore, there is a form of rough-and-tumble play of boys that can be regarded as universal, too (Hamburg & Van Lawick-Goodall, 1974). Even in the play of the peaceful !Ko-Bushmen, Sbrzesny (1976) discerned various aggressive acts. Likewise, the peaceful Zhun/Twasi show aggression in children's play (Konner, 1972). There is also the frequently described (e.g., Lambert, 1974; Hamburg and van Lawick-Goodall, 1974; Feshbach, 1970, 1974; Hoving, Laforme, & Wallace, 1974; Whiting & Whiting, 1975) greater tendency of boys to display aggressive behavior. It is, of course, in many cultures the male sex role that determines the methods and ideals of child rearing. However, that need not be a contradiction to a simultaneously possible biological explanation. The development of social sex roles may be influenced by experiences of biologically based, therefore universal, behavior differences.

Whether biological determinants exist in the form of a spontaneous drive, as ethological theory postulates, is not clear. Facts may support more closely the assumption of a disposition responsible for certain complex cues activating affect. This activation of affect consists of a definite psychophysical total reaction, including vegetative, motoric (facial expression, gestures, and body motorics), and emotional constituents such as anger.

Such a presumably universal disposition toward the emergence of aggression in infancy does not predispose the universality of aggressiveness in adults.

Supporting social conditions.   A series of universal conditions that foster the development of aggressiveness must also be assumed. That is, all humans certainly have frustrating experiences and everybody receives some positive rewards for aggressive acts (Hamburg & Van Lawick-Goodall, 1974, assume this especially for temper tantrums). A child usually grows up with others who behave aggressively. The conditions for modeling, for positive feedback (Lambert, 1974) and for the successful development of displaced aggression in the form of "passing down" aggression are therefore evident. The further development of such a "primary aggression motive" is certainly dependent upon numerous conditions in the sociocultural learning environment. They are responsible for differences in conceptual classifications and evaluations, goals, expectations and affective links, stored-up possibilities of instrumental action, anxieties, and avoidance reactions.

It is reasonable, however, to assume a universal aggression motive, with an essential root in the innate anger-affect reactions to certain instigating situations. Its cognitive structure can be defined as a goal to eliminate the source of frustration "at all costs"—even violently. Insofar as aggression is a dyadic (Sears, 1951), socially directed motive, its further development will depend especially upon (1) how far frustrations are experienced as having been caused by others; (2) how much they are seen as accountable causative agents (so that retaliation is appropriate); (3) the success experiences obtained after aggressive acts (through direct reward, modeling, social approval), and (4) which values develop in relation to this class of behavior. Child-rearing methods and the totality of sociocultural learning and developmental conditions represent a number of further causal factors that, in a supposedly lawful though complicated manner, contribute to the development of such a motive.

Each of these assumptions could be made precise and be detailed within a motivation theory of aggression. An adequate form of such a theory seems to be a cognitive motivation theory, which includes certain ethological assumptions (Feshbach, 1974; Kaufmann, 1970; Kornadt, 1974, 1979). Clear hypotheses according to differences in sociocultural developmental conditions can be formulated and can be tested cross-culturally. Such a motivation theory of aggression, in spite of the assumed genetically inherited component of aggression, would permit the assumption that there can be certain developmental conditions that lead to minimal (even uninhibited) aggression. A host of favorable conditions would then be necessary, e.g., little opportunity for successful aggressive behavior, the observation of nonsuccessful aggressive models, and the absence of positive social evaluation of aggression. Furthermore, fully nondestructive forms of behavior could be developed and employed, thereby eliminating frustration and anxiety when coping with problems; this nonaggressive behavior must also be convincingly anchored to positive social evaluations.

The Achievement Motive[15]

The area of achievement motivation is the classical example of fruitful cross-cultural research in motivation. Max Weber's thesis, linking Protestantism and capitalism, is closely connected with the development of research on need achievement.

The "achievement motive" construct developed by McClelland includes learning processes, and thus culture-bound antecedent conditions. Interests in both antecedent and consequent variables in the social area have stimulated many systematic cross-cultural studies.

Achievement motivation has been discussed in other chapters of this *Handbook* especially by Berry (Volume 5) and by Jahoda (Volume 1) therefore only the motive's theoretical aspects and its possible universality of the achievement motive will be discussed here.

The Concept of the Achievement Motive

McClelland assumed that "a motive is a learned result of pairing cues with affect or the conditions which produce affect" (1953, p. 38) and "motives should be distinguishable primarily in terms of the *types of expectations* involved, and secondarily in terms of the types of action" (McClelland et al., 1953, p. 76). The precise defining condition for the achievement motive is "a competition with some standard of excellence" (1953, p. 110). This motive provides the decisive psychological link between social and religious values (the Protestant ethic) and economic development (McClelland, 1961, p. 58).

Serpell elucidated (1976, p. 29) the complicated structure of interrelations described by McClelland by using a modified model originally suggested by B. B. Whiting (1963).

This model depicted in Figure 6-4 contains antecedent conditions, and numerous characteristic indicators of need achievement, which have been investigated in cross-cultural research. This research typically relies upon the assessment of covert rather than overt behavior, test data (TAT, questionnaires, and the like), content analyses of folk tales, and the analysis of economic indicators, such as economic development and consumption of energy. Child-rearing data were mostly obtained from interviews or questionnaires, and only in a few cases from direct observations.

Differentiation of the concept.   Many cross-cultural investigations departed from McClelland's achievement motive: *One* highly generalized motive

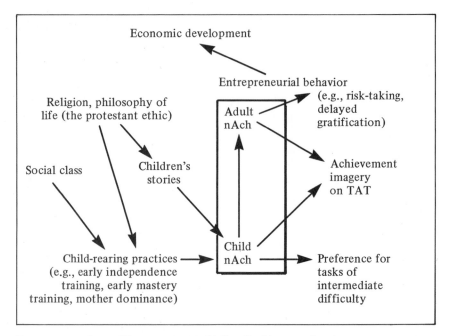

Figure 6–4   Some Elements in McClelland's Theory of Achievement Motivation and Economic Development (from Serpell, 1976, p. 29)

was assumed. However, four developments made possible the formulation of more differentiated hypotheses.

1. *Cognitive processes* related to the goal area have received considerable attention. The concept of a "standard of excellence," and competition with such a standard, which implies an evaluation of one's own performance and expectations of the effects of this performance are included in this domain of inquiry. Cognitive structures associated with person-environment relationships, related to achievement themes, and their generalizability, the *kind* of standards of excellence and the subjectively experienced causes of the effects of actions were also considered.

   Although McClelland's definition is general, virtually only individual academic and professional achievements, especially competitive and economic-entrepreneurial activities (as these relate to Weber's thesis), were examined. Cross-cultural research raised the question of whether different goal areas and standards of excellence need to be differentiated. Gradually the generalized status and the universality of the achievement motive began to be doubted.

2. The attainment, or surpassing, of the standards of excellence has *positive* affective consequences; falling short of these standards results in *negative* affect. This can lead to a generalized, affectively tuned expectancy, in

the form of *hope of success* or *fear of failure* (McClelland, 1951). A two-component model of need achievement was developed later (Atkinson & Litwin, 1960; Heckhausen, 1963a; and Birney, Burdick, & Teevan, 1969). "The theory asserts that a person's motive to achieve (need achievement), his motive to avoid failure and his expectation of success in some venture, strongly influence the character of his motivation . . ." (Atkinson and Feather, 1966, preface). Later further differentiations of the affective orientation were added.

3. A motive system develops gradually, in the course of ontogenesis, by manifold learning processes. The first hypotheses about socialization conditions (McClelland et al., 1953), became more precise and differentiated. Doubts were expressed about the supposed important role of "the philosophy of life; and religious values." LeVine (1966) suggested that it is rather the presence of status differences, and the possibility of status mobility which are the essential antecedent conditions for need achievement at the individual level.

4. A motive system is *activated only in certain situations* because of relevant cues that these situations contain (remember the differentiation between "motive" and "motivation" discussed at the beginning of this chapter). Obviously, the cue value of situations activating need achievement may vary from culture to culture. McClelland et al. (1953) aspired to develop a theory that would apply to "all cultures" (p. 289).

These four areas have thus became the foci for the generation and testing of hypotheses within cross-cultural research. As a result of the enormous volume of research spawned by these four areas the initially rather homogeneous conception of the achievement motive became so fractionated that it is now questionable whether it is possible to speak of *the* achievement motive at all.

Antecedent Conditions for the Development
of the Achievement Motive

McClelland assumed that motives "develop out of repeated affective experiences connected with certain types of situations and types of behavior" (McClelland et al., 1953, p. 275). In the development of need achievement these are conditions favorable to competition with standards of excellence that should (a) produce positive affect and (b) occur often. As originally stated, "Cultures of families which stress 'competition with standards of excellence' or which insist *that the child be able to perform certain tasks well by himself* . . . should produce children with high achievement motivation" (McClelland et al., 1953, p. 275).

Practices of socialization.   McClelland & Friedman (1952) investigated the relation of independence training and the achievement motive in eight North American Indian tribes. They relied on data concerning three variables of independence training (initial indulgence, age of training, severity of training), which had already been developed using the HRAF (see Whiting & Child, 1953). They estimated the achievement scores from folk tales, which were analyzed the same way as TAT stories. Independence training and the strength of need achievement were connected positively despite the small number of cultures. For the variables of age and severity of independence training combined, the significance was especially high ($p < .0005$, Kendall's (1948) Tau, a correlation coefficient of $+.91$).[16]

On the individual level Winterbottom (1953, 1958) was likewise able to show, with a sample of thirty American white middle class mothers, that those who expected early self-reliance and imposed fewer restrictions had sons (eight to ten years old) with high need achievement. This sample of mothers also valued more highly the accomplishments of their sons, and were more rewarding than the mothers of sons with low need achievement.

Other findings in different social and cultural conditions were reviewed by McClelland (1961). These studies explored particularly the importance of *age* and of *kind of training* for the development of the achievement motive. Both *age* of the beginning of independence training and *severity* were initially regarded as one indicator of the extent to which the child is forced to master things on its own (McClelland et al., 1953).

In the tradition of developmental psychology, however, it is useful to consider age as a separate factor, which could be significant. For example, psychoanalytic considerations could justify that early experiences are more strongly and more persistently effective (see also McClelland et al., 1953, p. 295), (e.g., early demands cause children to accept values more readily because of anxiety, Rosen, 1964; slighter discriminating capacity leads to greater generalization of experiences, Veroff, 1965).

Therefore, an optimal age for independence training whose impact on need achievement exists universally must be found. McClelland's hypothesis contains two different *kinds of training*, namely *achievement training* and *self-reliance training* (see Rosen, 1959, p. 51 footnote), which should be studied separately, since their relation to the achievement motive could stem from different regularities in psychological development.

In child rearing that explicitly demands *achievement* the essential mechanisms could be the direct reinforcement of achievement behavior, the mediation of achievement values and high achieving models. By contrast, *independence training* could be effective just in meeting the child's desire for doing things by himself, "wanting-to-do-it-alone" and selecting his optimal level of difficulty himself. In this respect, Heckhausen (1966) conceived of self-reliance as being a precursory motive of need achievement. Thus, an optimum of positive experiences leads to the formation of success expectations and possibly to a generalized self-confidence. This view does not require a narrow culture-bound conceptualization of achievement.

Age of independence/achievement training.   Investigations of the correlation between early self-reliance training and the strength of the achievement motive have produced contradictory findings. Heckhausen & Kemmler (1957) were able to corroborate the Winterbottom findings with school beginners in Germany; Chance (1961), Bartlett & Smith (1966), and Smith (1969) were not able to do so in the United States. In Japan, Hayashi & Yamauchi (1964) could also find no relation. A cross-cultural investigation on an aggregate level by Child, Storm, and Veroff (1958), which used the McClelland & Friedman (1952) methodology in thirty-three cultures, also failed to produce any relation between the onset of self-reliance training and scores reflecting the achievement motive. Rosen (1959), employing the Winterbottom method in different ethnic subgroups of varied religious affiliations in the United States and Canada, found a partial confirmation. The overall tendency of the relation between independence training and the achievement motive was, however, not very encouraging (F value 1.92, $p. < .10$). The absence of such a relation in the lower class failed to support McClelland's (1961) assumption of its universality. However, the data supported McClelland's hypothesis positing the importance of religious affiliation for the achievement motive.

In a Winterbottom-type study of mother-son couples in Brazil, Japan, and Germany, McClelland initially ascertained that in Brazil there existed a positive correlation between early independence training and need achievement scores, in Germany, a negative one, and in Japan none at all (see Table 6-2). He was able to explain these contradictions from a developmental viewpoint (1961).

A comparison of the pretraining mean ages showed that the different correlations refer to different age levels (Figure 6-5).

McClelland assumed a curvilinear relationship between age of onset of training for self-reliance and need achievement, with an optimum

Table 6-2   Age of Mothers' Achievement Demands and Sons' n Achievement (Graphic) in Brazil, Japan, and Germany (from McClelland, 1961, p. 346)

Age and correlations		*Brazil* *N = 118*	*Japan* *N = 115*	*Germany* *N = 300*
Average age of mothers'	M	7.70	8.27	8.52
achievement demands	SD	1.46	1.39	1.37
		diff.=.57	diff.=.25	
		t=3.04,p<.01	t=1.64, p ~.10	
Correlations				
Achievement demands x sons'				
n Achievement (graphic)		+.32,p<.01	.00	−.13,p<.02

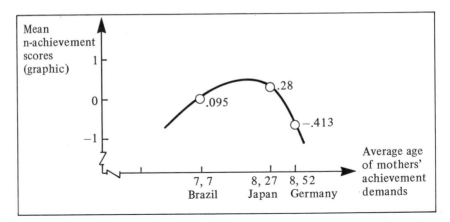

Figure 6–5 Graphic Representation of the Relation between the Average Age of Mother's Achievement Demands and Mean nAch Scores of the Sons—According to the Different Correlations Given in Table 6–2 (Data taken from McClelland 1961, p. 77 and p. 346)

starting age being at about the eighth year. The opposite direction of correlations within two groups showed that in one group the mean age of achievement demands was before and in the other it was after the optimum point.

This conception was supported by a longitudinal study by Moss & Kagan (1961) in the United States, which related maternal "acceleration pressure" to the achievement of the son. They found the highest correlation in the age six to ten range with an optimal at eight years (see Table 6–3).

High need achievement is not fostered, therefore, by self-reliance training provided as early as possible, but by training at the optimal age, which may be at age eight (Heckhausen, 1966, 1972; Veroff, 1969). Accordingly, there may also be such a thing as "premature" self-reliance training (which contradicts Rosen's hypothesis, see p. 70). Premature demands for self-reliance can evoke failure (see also McGhee & Teevan, 1965). Specifically, early self-reliance demands of the mothers (scored

Table 6–3 Correlations between Maternal Acceleration and Achievement in Different Age Groups (from Vontobel 1970, p. 85; According to the Data of Moss & Kagan, 1961)

Age Period	Maternal Acceleration and Achievement Motivation
0–3 years	.11
3–6 years	.37
6–10 years	.51

after Winterbottom) were correlated with fear of failure (TAT). Similar conclusions are suggested by Meyer, Wacker, Heckhausen, & Oswald (1969) and Meyer and Wacker (1970) in Germany. Furthermore, Heckhausen (1966) stressed that early self-reliance training fosters need achievement development only if it is *suited to development*.

Consequently, a universal statement on *the optimal* age of *the* independence training can hardly be made. Most methods employed fail to tap the developmental suitability variable. Questions concerning the age at which a child may, for example, play alone when outside the house, surely mean very different things from culture to culture, or even from subgroup to subgroup.

Severity of independence/achievement training. The different *kinds of socialization* will now be discussed. McClelland's hypothesis confounds self-reliance and achievement training (e.g., in the Winterbottom index). However, the separation demanded by Rosen is justified, as was shown by the Child et al. (1958) investigation, which showed the achievement training to be connected with the achievement contents of folktales; McClelland wrote: "apparently it is the achievement rather than the self-reliance aspect of Winterbottom's child-training variable which is more universally associated with achievement fantasies" (1961, p. 343). Rosen and D'Andrade (1959) reached the same conclusion in a study of the interaction of sons and their parents: the mediation of achievement norms and positive sanctioning are more important for need achievement development than is self-reliance training. Further confirmation is suggested by the findings of Hayashi, Okamoto, & Habu (1962) in Japan. They found no relation at all between self-reliance training and the achievement motive, in the case of sons, but the parents of highly motivated sons care more about a good education.

Another differentiation of kinds of socialization was suggested. In contrast to a developmentally suited self-reliance training, a premature cue can result in the neglect of the capabilities and interests of the child. This is especially true for *parent-centered* in contrast to *child-centered* self-reliance training. If, in addition, as a consequence of premature demands, failures are frequently punished, one approaches an "authoritarian" or cold, rejecting atmosphere of child training.

Lower class families are more restrictive and more prone to strict control, immediate intervention, negative sanctions, and parent-centered self-reliance training (Rosen, 1959). This study showed no correlation between independence training and need achievement, in lower class families. However, boys had a higher need achievement score (t = 4.22, $p < .001$) when achievement training was stressed earlier than caretaking was.

A series of other experiments supported the assumption that a warm atmosphere, positive reinforcement of achievement, and child-centered self-reliance are favorable for the development of need achievement. In contrast, restrictive, parent-centered, and demanding and punishing child training practices are likely to have a paralyzing effect (Morrow & Wilson, 1961; Nuttall, 1964, in the case of blacks; Strodtbeck, 1958). Similarly, Child et al. (1958) found that the more restrictive and stricter a culture's methods of child rearing the *less* developed is the achievement motive.

Influence of child rearing agents: role the father in the development of need achievement.   Rosen and D'Andrade (1959) stressed the importance of the setting of a high level of aspiration by both parents and the parental emphasis on recognition and warmth in socialization. In addition they suggested the need for a differentiation between the behavior of the parents of highly motivated sons. Whereas the mother of highly achievement motivated sons displays dominance, reacts angrily and with reproach to failures, urges achievement, offers direct hints, and thus demonstrates quite clearly her standards of excellence, the father maintains benevolent reserve. In the case of low achievement motivated sons the distribution of roles between mother and father was the reverse. This observation drew the attention of researchers to the *role of (a) the father, (b) father dominance, and (c) father absence for the development of need achievement.*

In Brazil, where the husband-father dominated family prevails, Rosen (1962) found that children receive little independence and achievement training. In all the social classes investigated, the need achievement scores were lower than those of a comparable American sample. Rosen attributes this finding to father dominance. Strodtbeck (1958) attributed the relatively low need achievement of sons in United States upper classes to the dominance of the father. The first systematic investigation of this hypothesis was done by Bradburn (1960, 1963). Because of the traditional Islamic stress on male dominance he chose Turkey. Bradburn stated that Turkish students actually did have lower need achievement scores than those of a comparable American sample, and that those who had the highest achievement motive scores had been separated from their fathers (the separation must have occurred by the age of fourteen, and not later).

Mischel (1961a) related the influence of *father absence* to another indicator which (as he showed earlier—1961b) correlated positively with the achievement motive: the preference for delayed reinforcement or immediate reinforcement. With samples from Trinidad he showed that father absence in the case of eight- to nine-year-olds was significantly related to the preference for immediate reinforcement, but not in the case of eleven- to fourteen-year-olds. Such findings suggest that the father does not always have an inhibitory influence on the development of the son's achievement motive. It is plausible that when the father's superiority of power and ability is strongly felt, in a critical period for the development of need achievement, the need achievement of his son is inhibited. This is likely to be the case, if the father intercedes very actively in the socialization process.

The father's inhibitive function is apparently only relevant in societies in which the father occupies a particularly dominant position. Nuttall (1964) showed that early father absence also leads to lower need achievement. In his investigation (interviews of black adults from 200 household units) people who had grown up without their fathers attained moderate achievement motive scores. Only those persons whose fathers were present during their childhood had high achievement motive scores.

For now, it must remain unsettled whether the father has a positive model role which is lost when he is absent, or a negative role when he is excessively dominant and/or if this function depends on the age of the sons.

Kornadt and Voigt (1970) studied boys in Kenya separated not only from their fathers but also from their whole families. They examined whether a rise of need achievement appears with secondary school students attending a boarding school, when compared to day school boys. They confirmed the hypothesis for those boys who attended secondary school for more than three years.

Excursus: influence of the mother in the development of need achievement.   The allusion must suffice here that the dominant behaviors of mothers, too, in the form of direct intervention, restrictions of the child's self-reliance, and predominantly negative sanctioning leads to lower need achievement. This was noted by Rosen and D'Andrade (1959) in observations of parent-child interaction in the United States and in a similar investigation by Heckhausen and Oswald (1969), in Germany. According to Kagan and Moss (1962, p. 221f), Crandall, Dewey, Katkovsky & Preston (1964), and Shaw and Dutton (1962), there are characteristic differences in child-rearing techniques, and the functioning of each parent as a model, of the same or the opposite sex, for the development of the achievement motive in boys and girls. In a study of Chinese children of an agricultural village in Northern Taiwan, Olsen (1971) found a positive correlation between self-reliance training and need achievement, but only for boys thus corroborating the results of Lowell (see McClelland et al., 1953).

Madsen & Kagan (1973) showed, in separate experiments, that a sample of American mothers encouraged motivation for high achievement to a greater extent than did a sample of Mexican mothers. The American mothers expected higher achievement before they rewarded their six- to nine-year-old children and gave significantly less reward after failure than did their Mexican counterparts. After a failure the majority of the American mothers admonished their children to attempt the same task again, whereas the Mexican mothers usually lowered the difficulty of the task.

Summary.   The following universal conditions foster the development of the achievement motive:

First, children are given the opportunity to pursue their own goals. Children can then "optimally," (that is, suited to their abilities and interests) try out their skills and prove themselves thus establishing a sense of competence. Second, the parents make developmentally suited demands in a warm, understanding climate, are generally encouraging, provide positive sanctions, and facilitate by identification the adoption of parental values. Third, the parents do not narrow the range of the child's development and do not burden the child with anxiety by an excess of parental superiority and dominance. Lastly, there is a sociocultural context in which achievement is socially and positively evaluated, and opportunities are provided for successful achievement behaviors.

Sociocultural determinants.   The investigations already summarized here were all derived from McClelland's basic theoretical position. LeVine (1966, p. 81), in contrast, departed from the assumption that every social system has clearly marked status ranks. Insofar as people have the opportunity to change their status, those who do engage in behaviors that allow an upward movement get positive rewards. Thus a concept of the "ideal successful man" is developed, which is highly valued by the parents and influences their child-rearing practices.

Accordingly, differences in the status system would be connected with differences in need achievement: "If status mobility systems determine frequencies of achievement motivation in populations, a change in the nature of status mobility will cause a change in the relative frequency of achievement motivation" (LeVine, 1966, p. 21).

LeVine tested his hypothesis in Nigeria among the Ibo who constitute the group that excels in remarkable entrepreneurial activities. The Ibo, who had a status system strongly oriented *along professional lines,* actually showed a higher percentage of people with achievement dreams than did the Hausa, whose *status mobility* was traditionally far lower. This percentage was intermediate in the case of the Yoruba who had more restrictions of status mobility by birth, but greater professional mobility than the Hausa.[17] However, LeVine's status mobility hypothesis does not contradict the central theoretical assumptions of McClelland and his school.

Social and Economic Consequences of the Achievement Motive

The studies discussed here are interesting only insofar as they can supply explanations about the structure of the achievement motive and the way in which it functions. McClelland (1961) employed the achievement thematic content of folk tales, primer stories, or certain graphical expressions (using the method of Aronson, 1958) as indicators of the strength of achievement motive. He related this dimension to different indicators of economic development and even made statements about ancient societies. He thus noted positive relations between high need achievement and the extension of the trade areas of ancient Greece between 900 and 100 B.C. Similar relations were obtained for Spain in the late Middle Ages, England before the Industrial Revolution, and the United States from 1800-1950. By examining ornaments, similar results were found about the ancient Peruvian culture from 800 B.C. to 700 A.D.

McClelland's general finding is that a period of elevated achievement motive always preceded an economic rise; decrease in achievement motive always preceded a decline. This finding suggested that need achievement is a cause of economic growth and not the other way around.

At the individual level Hayashi, Rim, and Lynn (1970) compared students from nations with different levels of economic growth. They found that the occupation of the independent entrepeneur was more readily preferred in the countries with low economic growth (Ireland, Great Britain) than in those with a high rate of growth (Japan, Israel).

McClelland (1961) reports a quasi-experimental observation, on the aggregate level, which demonstrates the influence of the Protestant ethic. A Mexican mountain village that has recently been converted to Protestantism was compared to an equivalent village that had remained Catholic. About ten years after the conversion, the boys in the Protestant village actually did display clearly higher scores on a series of achivement motive indicators.[18]

At the individual level, long-term changes of the achievement motive were also possible and resulted in increased achievement (e.g. Kolb, 1965). In Germany, a change of the causal attribution for failure (Heckhausen, 1974), resulted in greater achievement behavior.

McClelland and Winter (1969) developed a similar individual training program, in India, within a foreign aid program. It was at least partially successful, for half of the businessmen trained actually increased their entrepreneurial activities and their economic achievements. Surprisingly, though expected from the theoretical viewpoint, there was no proportionate change in their achievement motive scores.[19]

Differentiation of the Achievement Motive Concept.

Affective orientations.   Doubts were occasionally aroused, when lower than expected achievement motive scores, or unclear results, appeared in comparing cultures or subgroups.[20] A cause for doubt was presented very early, for instance, in a comparison of men and women (cf. McClelland et al., 1953; McClelland, 1958).

One approach to solving this problem explored the possibility that the cue value of the TAT pictures is not independent of sex or more generally of culture (Lesser, Krawitz, & Packard, 1963; French & Lesser, 1964). Only those women who conceived of their own female sex role as being compatible with "male" (intellectual) forms of efficiency expressed higher need achievement to TAT male figures. Another achievement area was relevant for more traditionally minded women.[21] Furthermore, McClelland's idea of a differentiation of *hope of success* and *fear of failure* was considered. These orientations may be operating when a person strives to achieve a standard of excellence, for both expectation of success and anticipations of failure may occur. As a result they may develop into enduring dispositions. Achievement approach and avoidance behaviors correspond to these emotions.

Atkinson, Birney, and their coworkers, in the United States, and Heckhausen and his coworkers, in Germany, have developed a systematic two-component model of the achievement motive. Many experimental, empirical investigations have demonstrated that achievement behavior, the level of aspiration, risk-taking behavior, and other kinds of achievement motivated behaviors can be comprehended more precisely within the framework of this model.

This differentiation of affective orientation is a striking alteration of McClelland's conceptualization of need achievement as a highly generalized and homogeneous, unidimensional variable. The high scores of McClelland's method express preponderantly hope of success, while the lower scores express either fear of failure or low motivation. To date the two component model and scoring methods (Moulton, 1958; Alpert & Haber, 1960; Birney, Burdick, & Teevan, 1961; Heckhausen, 1963b) have been employed very little in cross-cultural research. However, Singh (1970a) found that unsuccessful Indian farmers are higher on fear of failure than their successful counterparts (see also Singh, 1970b, Verma, 1973).

Worth mentioning is a cross-cultural comparison of the Heckhausen and Birney fear-of-failure measures. Heckhausen developed a key for fear of failure, found in the achievement oriented content of TAT stories, and Birney developed a key for *hostile press* "which is thought to be an equivalent of fear of failure. However, this takes into account not only achievement oriented content but every threat theme involving the main protagonists in the TAT stories" (Heckhausen, 1967, p. 17).

Anxious subjects, identified by means of the hostile press measure, avoid work situations implying failure or including a threat of social evaluation more than subjects identified with Heckhausen's fear of failure measure. They were also less able to improve their performance in a competitive situation. Heckhausen (1968, p. 125) concluded from these and other findings that the two measures activate *different aspects of the fear-of-failure orientation.*

Perhaps culture-bound differences in the conception of fear of failure

are suggested by these findings. Birney and Heckhausen used both measures with German and American students and found a cultural difference. Specifically, Americans appear to have learned to deny failure
experiences and reinterpret them as vague hostile press feelings (covert reaction), whereas Germans appear to have learned to admit their failures
(overt reaction).

McClelland and Winter (1969) tried to increase need achievement of
Indian businessmen (p. 79). Successfully influenced subjects did not, surprisingly enough, change their achievement scores. Pareek and Kumar
(1969), after a factor analytic study, tentatively suggested that Indian entrepreneurs could be more marked by status needs than by achievement
needs. Heckhausen (1971) postulated that the paradox is due to a lack of
differentiation between the two affective orientations (fear of failure, hope
of success).

A reanalysis showed, in fact, that those subjects who after the course
became more active entrepreneurs, initially had higher fear-of-failure
scores. The successful participants increased their net hope (NH = hope of
success minus fear of failure) more during the program than did the
others; this was confirmed three years later. These findings indicate that
need achievement can be changed in adults and that the concept of different affective orientations clarifies many inconsistencies. Both the Ameri-
can-rooted concept and the German-made method can be successfully
applied transculturally.

In the United States Horner (1968, 1972) discovered *fear of success* as a
further affective orientation in talented female students. She assumed that
women developed fear of success because they fear negative consequences, in the form of social rejection or the loss of femininity from too
much success—especially in high academic achievement.[22]

Six years after Horner's first investigation a rise in fear of success
among male students could be shown (Hoffman 1974). Whereas 8 percent
of the males in Horner's sample expressed fear of success, 77 percent did
so in Hoffman's study. A content analysis of TAT stories showed that the
content area of fear postulated by Horner for girls was different from that
found in boys. The latter appear to be more cynical than the former and to
emphasize a doubt that achievement per se is worthwhile. Cross-cultural
studies are needed to determine whether the reasons for the development
of fear of success in women, postulated by Horner, are transculturally
valid. Since the assignment of sex roles is dependent on culture, such
work should prove most informative.

Weston and Mednick (1970) actually found less fear of success in
black female students in the United States, than in their white counterparts. They argue that black women have a more dominant and more aggressive sex-role identity pattern, and that the aggressive overtones of
intellectual achievement are, therefore, more acceptable to them. As a

bonus, for a black man a successful woman is more attractive than she is threatening, because she is an economic asset.

Goal areas. DeVos (1968) alluded to the fact that Indians and Chinese achieve economically outside their native cultures, although their cultures appear to have a low need for achievement. This finding points to the significance of the socioeconomic context in activating or fostering the achievement motive. McClelland's conception was criticized because of its biases toward individual success or success connected with economic achievement in social competition (Berrien, 1964).

In fact, in spite of the *abstract* definition of the achievement motive, both in the measuring instruments and in construct validation, the focus was on *personal individual* achievements. In addition, the criteria of achievement required people to concentrate on the task at hand, which is to be done as well as possible. The tasks stress problems of predominantly intellectual efficiency, of motor skills, or activities related to professional work. Helping in problem solving is rejected (Winterbottom, 1958); pressures to conform proved less effective (McClelland et al., 1953). High achievers preferred a competent to a socially attractive work partner (French, 1956). Rewards not relating to achievement (social reward, money and the like) did not activate need achievement. If Mexican children are—as they are often portrayed—(see Madsen & Shapira, 1970; Kagan & Madsen, 1971, 1972a, 1972b) less competitive and more cooperative than American children, can it really be concluded that the Americans have higher need for achievement?

Similarly, DeVos (1968) questioned the transferability of McClelland's model to the Japanese. The Japanese show, despite many preoccupations with achievement and accomplishment, a high need for affiliation (cf. Caudill, 1952; Caudill & DeVos, 1956; DeVos, 1960; DeVos & Wagatsuma, 1961; DeVos, 1965), which contradicts Western experiences and theories about the independence of need achievement and need affiliation. A major part of Japanese need achievement can be understood "in terms of a continuing need to belong and to participate cooperatively with others" (DeVos, 1968, p. 363).[23] For the Japanese it is not the individual who represents the traditional standard, but the greater social unit of the "family": "success only for oneself has been considered a sign of excessive, immoral egoism" (DeVos, 1973b, p. 181).

Thus peculiarities of the goal structure of need achievement contradict the unity and generalizability of the original conception of need achievement. According to Gallimore (1969) high and low achieving male Hawaiian students (grades ten to twelve) do not differ in the intensity of their achievement motive. Success depends on need affiliation, which is correlated with behavior relating to achievement in a risky task. Kubany, Gallimore, and Buell (1970) showed, in the case of fourteen- to sixteen-year-old Hawaiian boys, that the preference for a middle range of risks was higher when the boys were observed than when they were alone. According to Western findings (McClelland, 1958; Atkinson & Feather, 1966) this preference is characteristic of people high in need achievement and hope of success if there is no additional activation of social aspects of the situation.

Further Specific Differentiations

Because of the variety of findings reviewed, the achievement motive is no longer treated as a global, unidimensional concept. The differentiation derived from conceptualizing different causes, which a person can attribute to success or failure (Weiner, 1970, 1972; Weiner & Kukla, 1970; Heckhausen & Weiner, 1972; and others), belongs here. Veroff's (1973) factor analytic studies suggest that people notice different aspects of a goal state. Veroff's differentiation included *three dimensions* of achievement orientations: *affective orientation, future orientation,* and the *definition of success.* In regard to future orientation he distinguished between a realistic, instrumental (as he found, for example, among white males in the United States) and an unrealistic, defensive orientation (which appeared in black females in the United States, for example).

Veroff further differentiates the cognitive structure of the goal system (see 1973, p. 106) into aspects of what is experienced as success and what goals are considered an achievement. *Success* can be defined rather according to the *action* itself or to the evaluation of the *success of the action. Criteria of success* can likewise be derived from different systems of reference: from one's own self, from the social environment (e.g., competition), or from nonsocial conditions (e.g., the orientation toward the solution of a task). He was able to show, in a nationwide investigation, the usefulness of this differentiation.

Regarding the development of need achievement it can be suggested now that the disparity among experiences, models, rewards, and punishments can lead to the development of different concerns for achievement, different success criteria, and different domains of action.

Achievement *behavior* is influenced by the socially determined evaluations of achievements. In each culture different areas of achievement are thematized, and achievements are evaluated differently. For example, a culture may emphasize achievements in academic or economic fields (as in Western cultures), in religious activity, obedience, modesty, in hobbies or in criminality. Rosen (1956, 1959) was able to show this in a study with subjects of different socioeconomic backgrounds. Veroff (1973) reported that women with high need achievement make child rearing an achievement goal.

The achievement attitude of Japanese and Hawaiians could correspond to the type of achievement orientation in an area of action that Veroff described as a socially oriented feeling of effectance. In this the feeling of success does not grow out of the knowledge "I did it *myself*" (as in the case of autonomy orientation), but "*We* did it," or perhaps "I did it for others." That kind of motive is likely to correspond to the *setting of group-related goals* among Russian pupils (Bronfenbrenner, 1962), a goal that appears also to be fostered in China. Competitiveness appears to be a kind of success orientation favored in the United States.

Family achievement among Mexican-Americans and black Americans can be considered a social orientation for evaluating achievement. Mexican-American children were found to have a stronger tendency to attain something for others (cf. Ramirez & Price-Williams, 1976, p. 51). Israeli kibbutz children, whose child training is focused upon cooperation instead of competition, showed more cooperative achievement behavior than children from urban families (Shapira & Madsen, 1969).

Finally, the necessity of considering value orientations specific to each culture may be viewed with respect to the notion of *delay of reinforcement.* Gallimore, Weiss, and Finney (1974) found, in a comparison of Hawaiian- and Japanese-American students, that the Hawaiians preferred more immediate reinforcement. What is usually interpreted as a lack of planning, and thereby as an indicator of low achievement motive (Raynor, 1969; Veroff, 1973), can mean an emphasis on social aspects of the achievement motive. The subjects were asked what they would do with a large sum of money. The Japanese answered that they would use it "for education." This was interpreted as delayed reinforcement. The Hawaiians answered that they would spend the money at once. But this must not be interpreted, in this case, as immediate gratification, since it meant "for the family." Hence it can be seen as a future-oriented accumulation of social credit.

Future time perspective.   Corresponding to the values of Hindu culture, which states that personal effort does not influence life (Karma), Meade (1971) found among Indians, in contrast to Americans, more of an orientation toward the past than toward the future. Nonetheless, within India itself there was considerable variation in future orientation, which corresponded to differences in the strength of the achievement motive and business orientation (Meade, 1972). A low future time perspective, corresponding to cultural values, thus causes (or contributes to) the low need achievement in India. Such a connection would also be plausible according to the theory of causal attribution (Carment, 1974).

The achievement motive is apparently a complex system with very different, relatively isolated elements. Its strength, thematic focus, and the "standards of excellence" depend on many factors, including culture-bound conditions of child rearing and variable value systems. The achievement motive as measured, can indicate a high score/expression of just one component. The scores to be compared between cultures then may be identical in quantity but different in quality. Thus, any indicator of achievement motivation could reflect only one aspect of the construct and should not be used to draw conclusions about the strength of need achievement in general.

On the Question of the Universality of the
Achievement Motive

If Sears (1961) is correct that universality can be based on universal learning processes and experiences, then a basic transcultural motive structure is probable in which person-environment relationships are related to the concept of a standard of excellence. This structure is to be expected if (a) internal maturation processes (cognitive and motoric) meet the necessary requirements, (b) external learning conditions offer incentives for individuals to set their own goals, (c) there is striving for these goals, (d) the effects of individual action are recognized, and (e) the action is evaluated against a standard. Each person starts from this general and undifferentiated motive structure that consists of a motive to be able to reach goals. The more differentiated structure that is culture-specific is the result of additional development. This developmental sequence may be universal.

Thus, in spite of many potential configurations, general characteristics of an achievement motive can be abstracted that are common to all of its components, thus constituting a universal motive. These include (a) the existence of a standard of excellence for an individual's own goal directed behavior; (b) affective reactions to success and failure, such as being proud and happy; or disappointed and sad, respectively; (c) individual feelings of responsibility for the outcome of the act; and (d) incentives based on insecurity about an individual's own capacity or ability to succeed (cf. Maehr, 1974). The culture-bound experiences, cognitive structures, and values of each individual will determine the areas in which standards of excellence will develop and the specific confidence in success in different areas, the causal attribution of success and failure, and the ways of reacting to them. Achievement motivated behavior will thus appear in different cultures in different forms, stimulated by different cues, and directed at different goals (see also Maehr, 1974).

In contrast to Maehr, however, it may be reasonable to assume that different experiences result in the development of different degrees of need achievement in different cultures.

Considering the meaning of behaviors in concrete situations, an analysis of the motive is provided that takes into account the subjective meaning of the pertinent cues, of the situation, of the social conditions, and the norms (Maehr, 1974). Therefore, the achievement motive should be studied only within the context of "subjective culture" (Triandis, 1972).

Aspects of a Universal Motivation Theory: Motive Classification, Development of Universal and Culture-Specific Motives

Some considerations concerning theoretical problems needed to advance a universal theory of motivation will close this chapter.

Need Achievement

There are doubts that the fear of success, reported by Horner (1968, 1972) for women, involves the same construct for men. *Achievement* per se, it can be argued, is synonymous only in name with need achievement but not identical in concept (Hoffman, 1974). It may be that what many females reject is social pressure—a rejection that some researchers may interpret as a fear of success.

Is this ambivalence related to the achievement goal as narrowly interpreted? In fear of failure the relevant goal is achievement itself, which lies at the core of the achievement motive. Fear relates here to missing this central goal, and any ill-effects associated with other motives, like social recognition, are of secondary importance. Even if these secondary effects should prove to initiate the unfavorable self-reinforcement system in part (Heckhausen, 1972), they do not constitute the substantial elements of the motive.

In fear of success, however, fear could result from the incompatibility of different *mutually exclusive goal areas* (components) of the achievement motive, like efficiency in academic settings or in meeting the (requirements of) a female sex role (Alper, 1974; Peplau, 1976).

It is, however, equally plausible that *success* itself is not feared, but instead certain consequences of success (see Veroff, 1973, p. 101). Achievement is desired; what is feared is missing the goal of a *different* motive, e.g., the approval motive. In such circumstances a conflict between two different motives would be present. In any overlapping of two motives (for instance, between power and approval, or attachment and independence) the possibility of such conflicts would be inevitable.

Problems of Motive Classification

The above example begs a more general question: How can a taxonomy of motives be found that transcends mere definitions and is based on *functional* relationships?

The inclusion of social aspects in defining the goal and the areas in which success related to the achievement motive can be experienced (cf. Veroff, 1973, p. 106) is compatible with McClelland et al.'s original definition. An individual may also have a "standard of excellence" in social areas or in fulfilling a mother's role.

But what differences exist between achievement-motivated behaviors and, for example, approval-motivated behaviors? In an early experiment, McClelland et al. (1953) demonstrated the independence of need achievement and need affiliation. The "social form" of the achievement motive could represent the approval motive. For example, the scoring categories and the "standard story" used by Ramirez and Price-Williams (1976) to measure "family achievement" showed that the original clear separation of the approval and achievement motives was abandoned.

How can the *"correct" definition of a motive* be arrived at and an appropriate method to measure it be found? McClelland approached this problem by making his abstract definition more concrete in specific areas of behavior. Corresponding content categories for the TAT then formed the basis for measuring the achievement motive. Many empirical and experimental investigations demonstrate that certain behaviors can be predicted by the motive thus measured.

It may be, however, that the independence of need affiliation and need achievement, found by using the TAT, is artificial. Affiliation learnings could functionally belong to the achievement motive system, and the achievement motive assessed by the TAT may represent only part of this functional system (Veroff, 1973; Ramirez & Price-Williams, 1976). The fact that social goals also should be attained "well" may have led some to infer the presence of an achievement goal. Since each separate motive has as its aim the successful reaching of its goal, interpreting this state of affairs as a unitary achievement motive would render need achievement ineffective as a separate functional system.

The broadening of the need achievement concept, especially through cross-cultural research, would question even further the components of the motive and the way in which different functional units could be recognized as separate motives. In discriminating between need achievement and an aggression motive, for example, the attainment of an achievement goal under competitive conditions may also imply injuring another person, and, while not the goal itself, such behavior could carry aspects of an aggression or power motive.

If motives are understood as "content classes of events" (highly organized, cognitive systems of person-environment relationships), whose realization a person thinks he may influence by his actions (Heckhausen, 1978, p. 2), the specification of classifying the content of such events, or person-environment relationships, is a central problem. Precise specifications are difficult, because one can obtain motive catalogues of various length depending on the level of abstraction (Heckhausen, 1963b, p. 608).

The individual himself organizes cognitively, into a single content class, certain motives from the stream of his developmental experiences. This is accomplished through the abstraction of certain cognitive characteristics of goal systems on the basis of certain affectively toned expectancies, presumably also on the basis of certain characteristics of his or her own instrumental possibilities of action, which leads to goal-attainment. In contrast to a priori classifications, this way would be more fruitful in pinpointing motives because it would permit, through the study of developmental processes, the derivation of hypotheses concerning functional units. A universal theory of motive developmental features could serve as a framework to help the understanding of *universal motives* or basic motivational structures, as well as *culture-specific* motives, the latter being variants of the *common motivational basis*.

Regularities in Motive Development

The human body and its physiological and neurological ways of functioning, its growth, and its rate of growth are common denominators in the development of motives. Other common denominators are the ability to experience different affects, understood as psychophysiological units, having differential experiential components, with (a) energizing and (b) motoric (as in facial expression) aspects, and (c) accentuating (perception, thinking, remembering) aspects. Finally, structuring processes such as learning (by conditioning), the potential to establish cognitive structures, and the way in which these are linked with the conditioning of affects and the formation of complicated affective/cognitive systems must be basic to the species.

Thus a universal hedonistic base would assume a fundamental differentiation of the pleasant and unpleasant quality of emotions. Motives could start with conditions that lead to pleasure and displeasure, emerge in the course of growth and cognitive maturation, and be the result of the activities of an experiencing and cognitively structuring individual. Kagan (1972), with regard to sensory motives, mentioned that pleasant sensations can be aroused by the stimulation of specific receptor areas. Such arousal conditions include warmth, drinking, sex, kinesthesia, and certain tactile stimuli.

The experience of a pleasant state through such stimulation, and perhaps of an unpleasant one if they are absent, and an early primitive learning to approach pleasant and to avoid unpleasant states, must be considered universal. The first reactions evoked in the newborn are certainly not goal directed, but involve the expression of affects (crying, smiling) or of quasi-reflexive movements. In connection with the gradual learning of "associations," babies may wish to return to or to restore the conditions in which they felt well. Breast feeding, and the comforting conditions surrounding it, is but one of untold dozens of such possible wishes. Its gratification is dependent on simultaneously occurring conditions, not on an innate linking. In the course of individual experience, specific and marginal conditions could easily be linked with satisfaction, so as to be included in the cognitive structure of a "genuine" motive that emerges later: not everything edible belongs to the goal of an "eating motive"; some things, like ants, snakes, or spinach, are preferred or rejected depending upon cultural factors.

Considering motives that emerge in the course of growth and development, certain conditions of movement and of strength are dependent upon *motoric maturation*. However, the motive to avoid uncertainty, mentioned by Kagan (1972), already stipulates a *cognitive development*, which enables the recognition of familiar things, the anticipation of events, the formation of expectancies, and so forth. Uncertainty can have many origins. Kagan (1972) assumed that the emergence and persistence of uncertainty probably would lead to strong affective discomfort in the form of fear or anxiety.

People find comfort in the certainty that they attain gradually by creating order in a diffuse stream of events. This, of course, has its basis in recognizing, expecting, and looking forward to similar things (*in the case of something pleasant*), and finding them. Gradually a basis for the general, positive expectation is created so that events can become ordered. Conversely, there is the fear that such order may not be found.

Kagan (1972) posited that the basis of a primary, universal motive is to resolve uncertainty and seek certainty.

In addition, a desire to maintain or approve conditions linked with comfort will certainly arise, which could be a critical source for the development of the attachment motive; it is leaving open to question whether it has an independent genetic component. In her function as a safe base for exploration, the mother offers security. The positive effect this has on further structuring, and on the subsequent certainty it offers, is profound; the negative effects resulting from its absence will be similarly important.

Depending on the preponderance of either positive or negative experience, a generalized conviction and expectation of trust or distrust can develop (Erikson, 1950). Negative experiences can also lead to "subjective techniques for problem solving" in the form of stereotypes, prejudices, neurotic distortions, and mythical practices, all of which enhance aspects of subjective certainty.

Finally, a series of *derived motives* can develop, each with components relating to goals and the means of attaining security. Aside from *attachment*, for example, the *affiliation, approval,* and *dominance* motives can emerge (Kagan, 1972).

Here culture-specific developments are possible. According to the values and learning opportunities offered by a given culture, one or another goal or action area becomes preferable, thus representing one of many possible culture-specific variants of the basic universal motivational pattern.

A culture can offer, additionally, its own form of goal conditions under which an idiosyncratic motive can develop (like, *philotimo* in Greece (Triandis & Vassiliou, 1972; Vassiliou & Vassiliou, 1973) and *amae* in Japan. *Amae*, for instance, indicates a complicated goal and behavior system that (in adults) can hardly be described with Western concepts.[24] The "motive to be free of motives"—dominant in China in the 18th century—is a similar example (Kagan, 1972, p. 56).

The origin of an independent development may have roots in the cognitive sphere. The more children comprehend how much their well being, in the beginning, is dependent on other people (who by no means always fulfill all their wishes) and the more they develop their own abilities and new interests and anticipate possibilities of satisfying them, the more likely is the development of *autonomy*. To attain or defend them become cherished independent goal conditions.

Two kinds of motive systems that have an active-assertive reaction basis: *aggression* and *competence* will be discussed.

Aggressiveness.   Aggressiveness is marked by a specific affective quality upon which this motive is built: rage or anger. (The instigating conditions of "frustration" are experiences of being impeded, hindered, or threatened.) Rage, as a specific aspect, is an inborn tendency to react, but the conditions that evoke it cannot be clearly separated from those that evoke fear. At least a temper tantrum represents a universal form of expression of rage, with probably universal eliciting conditions. (Concerning the transcultural similarity of emotions, in general, see Izard's chapter in this volume of the *Handbook*.)

The development of aggression as a goal-directed motive stipulates additional conditions: (1) the *experience* that anger can be eliminated by behavior directed by rage, characterized by the "discharge of force" (which belongs to the psychophysiological characteristics of affect), and (2) the experience that the *cause* of "frustration" can be attributed to *other human beings*, who can be *influenced*, and not be attributed to natural circumstances that are beyond the individual's control. With the Anggor of New Guinea, even death is supposed to be caused by sorcery, leading to a retaliatory ambush against the supposed causers (cf. Huber, 1972).

The latter stipulates a stage of cognitive development where empathy is possible; the individual must be able to recognize that others can wish him ill, as he himself can wish them ill. A goal, which can be characterized as hostility, can be established with other motives whose gratification is "frustrated." Further stipulations include a certain amount of previous security and confidence. These may influence not only whether an affective reaction receives the characteristic features of anxiety or of rage, but also the expectation to be able to change something by a person's own behavior.

The universal basic motivational pattern of aggression would thus be the specific affectively directed behavioral component (to do something violently or even destructively) with specific goal characteristics, such as elimination of the avoidable and unacceptable frustration caused by others.

In frustration, going beyond the blocking of a goal reaction, the central goal is, as Kagan assumes, the "infliction of physical pain." The two closer concepts are special forms of the intrinsic basic universal pattern.

Quite different partial areas of the goal state, and of actions directed toward it, can develop as culture-specific variants of one universal aggression motive. The complete elimination (killing) of a threatening opponent is supposed to develop universally as a partial goal. How far these goal components become relevant in daily action depends upon cultural factors such as values and life conditions. According to Lonner (see his chapter in Volume 1 of this *Handbook*) aggression has the status of a variform universal, since injurious actions of different kinds appear to be worldwide phenomena.

However this can also include the assumption of a culture-specific minimal strength of aggression. The cultural patterns of interpretation and action may offer little opportunity to activate an anger-affect, and there could be behavior patterns available for the nonviolent, nondestructive coping with frustrations.

Competence.   In competence the concept of one's own efficiency is developed, becoming a goal state to strive for. A motive for competence or for ability to do, as understood in this way, is best expressed by the German word "können." It is not specified by any definite area. McClelland's general term "competition with a standard of excellence" corresponds with this in Heckhausen's German translation: *Auseinandersetzung mit einem Gütemaßstab,* which is literally translated as "comparison with a standard of goodness."

Special areas and kinds of realization—whether intellectual capabilities are emphasized, or endurance or being able to exert efforts—are then variants of one basic motivational theme. Their special distinctness surely depends upon ecological conditions, cultural values, and opportunities. Need achievement, in its narrower sense, would thus be more correctly understood as a Western variant of this more general motive for competence.

"Competition drive," which Sears (1961, p. 453) asserts is universal and which he defines as an "instigation to secure an unsharable goal," has to be considered a motive that results from experience and cognitive structuring. Only after the development of a corresponding processing of experiences can a goal of this kind be set. Consistent with mixed cross-cultural findings related to the achievement motive, we tend to suggest that the "competition drive" cannot be viewed as a universal motive. The experiences that form its basis are not culturally independent to a satisfactory degree. Rather it is a derivation from the competence motive, that is, a special variant in which the competition aspect of competence essentially determines the goal area. From the process of motive development, other motive systems offer similar problems. They are generally developed as independent units, and their universality seems to be plausible at first sight. The "power motive" is given as an example here (Veroff, 1957; McClelland, Davis, Kalin, & Wanner, 1972; Winter, 1973; McClelland, 1975). The goal system as well as instrumental actions include elements that belong to the areas of competence, aggression, and perhaps to affiliation. Therefore the developmental process could hardly be uniform. Thus, doubts are raised as to its universality (different cultures could foster different derivatives producing different forms of "the" one power motive), and also as to whether the power motive concerns a functional unit at all. Perhaps this could help explain the low correlations between the indicators pointed to by Hamilton (1974).

Stipulations for an Integral View of Motives

On the basis of his or her own highly specific learning history, each person develops his own individual package of motives, whose cognitive representation of goal states is idiosyncratically structured. Consequently, discussing a superindividual or even a universal motive such as "aggressiveness" requires considerable abstraction. The formation of such a general concept is, therefore, made possible only at the expense of a doctrine of human uniqueness.

Such abstract and general motives would have to be based on three premises:

1. *One* common human basis for at least the development of very similar motives (similar in relation to instigating conditions and goal states and, within limits, also in regard to instrumental actions) in the basic (neuro-) physiological inventory. This is based on the "sensory" motives, as well as on certain affective qualities, which are crystallization points for the development of motives.
2. Common learning conditions, including relationships based upon biological realities and common experiences[25] and upon common regularities of processing experiences. These factors lead to similar developmental tasks and similar opportunities to solve them. They also would favor the development of similar motives.

3. Human beings grow up in groups,[26] which live under similar ecological conditions and usually in the common tradition of *one* culture. Each individual is thus provided with:
   a. Cognitive structures, classifications and the like for the formation of concepts for certain classes of action and/or experience areas, which can be differentiated from the ones formed in other cultures. These, as well as social evaluations, would be relatively uniform within a single culture.
   b. A socioeconomic structure in which child training techniques, various opportunities for modeling and identification, reinforcement and incentives tend to augment cognitive structures and evaluations.

In cross-cultural research on motivation, hypotheses are to be examined that may justify any abstraction of general motives, i.e., the degree of communality of goal structures and of the emotions and instrumental actions connected with them and associated developmental conditions and processes.

The traditional cross-cultural tactic of simply gathering observations or of applying the same tests in different cultures should now be abandoned as a dead end. Cross-cultural research on motivation could and should be devoted to the goal of contributing to the broadening of our knowledge about the universality of human motives or basic motivational patterns and the functional patterns of motive development. Culture-specific variants and distinctions, while they surely exist, can be best understood and explained within such a general framework.

Notes

1. It was Hartup and Lempers (1973) who made explicit that attachment behavior concerns a "dyadic variable" (see Sears, 1951); i.e., behavior which cannot be attributed to a *single person alone*, but which can be manifested only in *relation to* another person.

2. According to Gewirtz (1961, pp. 219f) it is an *empirical matter* which stimulation in the environment of a child of a given age group can be identified finally as an unconditioned (primary) reinforcer. And according to him the concept of "drive" therefore does not explain more than these empirical facts themselves. He therefore rejects the concept.

3. This extremely compressed summary of the position of ethological theory as well as of learning theory, presents an oversimplified picture. Therefore, it must be noted that on the one hand, Bowlby (1969) does not exclude cognitive aspects from his discussion of "goal corrected attachment plans." He accepts that they can vary in their structure and adds: "the particular degree of complexity of a plan turns partly on the set-goal selected, partly on the subject's *estimate* of the situation obtaining between himself and his attachment fig-

ure. . ." (Bowlby, 1969, p. 351, our italics). On the other hand, Gewirtz (1965) does not explicitly deny the existence of "unlearned behaviours" but he is ". . . open with respect to behaviours that appear to be unlearned, species-specific, and those representing developmental stages" (p. 184). Note, however, that both the statements by Bowlby and Gewirtz do not lead to *principal modifications* of their basic models. This is true for Bowlby (see also, Ainsworth, 1973, p. 6) as well as for Gewirtz (1965) who stated that "the changing capacities of the child in the earliest phase of life through development processes such as those which are indexed by the terms 'organismic maturation,' species-specific behaviors, and the like, would only qualify this model, but would *not change its essential features*" (Gewirtz, 1965, p. 217, our italics).

4. It is interesting in this context that fear of strangers exists in all investigated cultures, but it usually is much more variable. This could be shown for the Hopi and Ganda (cf. Schaffer, 1966), Zhun/Twasi (Konner, 1972) and the !Ko-Bushmen (Eibl-Eibesfeldt, 1972).

5. Similar results were reported for the Wolof in Senegal (Lusk & Lewis, 1972).

6. The distinction between locomotory and manipulatory exploration is but one indicator of the necessity of modifying the original ethological theory. It now does not only refer to locomotory exploration alone (cf. Rheingold, 1969; Ainsworth & Wittig, 1969), a behavior immediately relevant for the survival of a species, but also refers to a general investigatory behavior (cf. Scott, 1971, pp. 231f), which also includes manipulation (cf. Ainsworth & Wittig, 1969) and visual exploration (Konner, 1972; Harlow, 1961).

7. Worchel (1974) classified a multitude of societies on whether they provided structured possibilities for the outlet of aggression. Only restrictive societies (sorcery is not admitted) need an opportunity of that kind. But finally the kinship system (unilineal vs. nonunilineal) proved to be related to restrictiveness and to be a better predictor for structured outlets of aggression (warfare, sports) than the absence of sorcery (taken as an indicator of restrictiveness). Triandis & Lambert (1961) showed that it is verbal aggression that appears spontaneously. The kind of aggression and conditions of its emergence seem to be interdependent.

8. Note here the stronger influence of Chinese culture in developing a certain historical and linguistic (Okinawan) self-sufficiency and that, above all, this concerns farmers on the subsistence level (see Whiting & Whiting, 1975, pp. 11–12).

9. A custom is a "characteristic habit of a typical member of a cultural category of persons" (Whiting & Child, 1953, p. 22).

10. Early anthropological observations by Mead (1935) led to inconsistent results: The Arapesh and Mundugumor did not show any sex differences concerning aggression (in the former both sexes showed little, in the latter much aggression), the women of the Tchambuli were more aggressive than the men. On the other hand statistics show a heavy preponderance of males to females in criminality (Cressey, 1963). Methodical shortcomings do, however, not allow an appropriate evaluation. Mead's writings are poorly documented (Piddington, 1957), and criminality rates are difficult to compare.

11. The term *frustration* is used in the literature with different meanings: (a) in a strict sense of the frustration-aggression hypothesis; (b) in a looser sense as an

antecedent condition for aggression, covering several aversive stimuli, especially threatening the self-esteem, which could be considered as antecedents of aggression; (c) as a term for an inner emotional state, which follows such a situation (Brown & Farber, 1951) and, (d) for certain stereotyped behaviors following such a condition (Maier, 1956). In the following the term *frustration* will be used as an antecedent condition, even though it will not be used in the strict sense of the frustration-aggression hypothesis, unless otherwise expressly indicated.

12. Minturn & Lambert (1964) explored two factors in the mother's reaction to aggression. One concerned her reaction to aggression directed toward her, the other concerned her restrictive and punitive handling of aggression against other children. The second factor showed large differences among societies (see also the synoptical table in LeVine, 1970, p. 593).

13. In Taira, though, this is only the case for the family of the eldest son. Younger sons, in contrast, normally found independent nuclear families (Whiting & Whiting, 1975, pp. 176f). This points to the necessity of considering *intracultural* variance, too; and a clearer analysis that takes such variance into account could perhaps explain the low (r=−.10) value in this culture.

14. Jahoda (1954) found *specific* influences of cultural expectations among the Ashanti. There, the expected aggression is connected with the week day of the birth of a boy. The boys get their names according to the day. This variable allows a prediction of the frequency of offence against people (see Munroe, Munroe & LeVine, 1972).

15. The terms *achievement motive* and *need achievement* are used interchangeably in the literature. Both refer to an enduring disposition.

16. In the same way, Parker (1962) evaluated the mythology of the Ojibwa and Eskimos; he not only found the Ojibwa to be superior to the Eskimos in need achievement, but also he could corroborate the relation between independence training and need achievement.

17. McClelland's report will not be discussed here. According to this report the Yoruba show the highest entrepreneurial activity, which contradicts LeVine's findings. This is, however, not a theoretical, but an empirical contradiction (McClelland, 1964).

18. Morsbach (1969) reported—within a more differentiated system (cf. Rosen, 1956)—his findings from a comparison between English-speaking and Afrikaans-speaking Calvinist high school students. The Calvinist students showed higher achievement value scores, but lower scores in need achievement.

19. Concerning other studies of McClelland's efforts in India see Jahoda's chapter in Volume 1 of this *Handbook*.

20. This was one reason to recognize the necessity of adapting the TAT in cross-cultural research. Several authors, though, think that the TAT is culture-free (Tedeschi & Kian, 1962) or use it in other cultures with no change (cf. Barberio, 1967; Lazarus, Kessel, & Botha, 1969). Other authors choose quite different methods. (See LeVine [1966] as well as Spain's [1969, 1972] use in Nigeria.) Lynn (1969) developed a questionnaire, according to McClelland and Winter (1969), to assess need achievement; it was used cross-culturally (see Melikian, Ginsberg, Cüceloglu, & Lynn, 1971). The questionnaires developed by

Edwards (1954) and Gough (1957) have been used in different cultures (cf. Singh, Chang Huang, & Thompson, 1962; Berrien, 1964; Gough, 1964). It was Maloney (1968) who used the example of Japanese culture, and pointed to the fact that contradictory results in cross-cultural research may in part be caused by different definitions of the achievement motive.

21. Angelini (1959, 1966), constructed his M.P.A.M. measure (Projective Method of Motive Evaluation) in accordance with McClelland et al. (1953). In his studies with male and female Brazilians he employed new pictures for women, where females were depicted in motive inciting situations (e.g., sewing, in a chemistry laboratory) (see also Angelini 1973).

22. Similarly Veroff (1973) explained a high score of fear of success among black males as a fear of losing their black identity.

23. In this distinctive expression of need achievement, religion may be of equal importance, as set forth in McClelland's conception. Whereas Protestantism emphasizes self-realization, the Japanese Tokugawa religion stresses a sense of social purpose (DeVos, 1965, 1968).

24. In the book by Doi (1962) there is no definition of *amae*. It is extremely difficult to express a really culture-specific concept, and motive related to it, in the conceptual language of another culture. One would have to indicate a host of connotations, which stem from a vast array of emotional ties, meanings, experiences, and even from philosophical interpretations (see also Doi 1973).

25. Departing from the study of a definite problem area (the frustration complex) in a *specific* culture (the Kwoma), Whiting (1944) substantiated the transcultural transferability of his results by the facts that (a) all children are helpless, and (b) people everywhere differ in height and strength. Rosenblatt, Jackson, and Walsh (1972), who included a multitude of ethnographic material in their studies, consider the (universal) experience of death of a relative to be a frustration of dependency needs. The reactions of anger and aggression that follow are a problem for every society.

26. The universality of the child's integration into social relations has instigated an extensive research on interpersonal dimensions (cf. Whiting & Whiting, 1975, and Lonner's chapter in Volume 1 of this *Handbook*).

References

ADINOLFI, A. A., WATSON, R. I., JR., & KLEIN, R. E. Aggressive reactions to frustration in urban Guatemalan children: the effects of sex and social class. *Journal of Personality and Social Psychology*, 1973, 25, 227–33.

AINSWORTH, M. D. S. The development of infant-mother–interactions among the Ganda. In B. M. Foss (Ed.), *Determinants of infant behaviour II*. London: Methuen, 1963, pp. 67–104.

———. *Infancy in Uganda: infant care and the growth of love*. Baltimore, Maryland: Johns Hopkins University Press, 1967.

———. Object relations, dependency, and attachment: a theoretical review of the infant-mother relationship. *Child Development*, 1969, 40, 969–1025.

———. The development of infant-mother attachment. In B. M. Caldwell & H. Ricciuti (Eds.), *Review of child development research*, Vol. 3. Chicago: University of Chicago Press, 1973, pp. 1–94.

AINSWORTH, M. D. S., & AINSWORTH, L. H. Acculturation in East Africa II: frustration and aggression. *Journal of Social Psychology*, 1962, *57*, 401–07.

AINSWORTH, M. D. S., & WITTIG, B. A. Attachment and exploratory behaviour of one-year-olds in a strange situation. In B. M. Foss (Ed.), *Determinants of infant behaviour IV*. New York: Wiley, 1969, pp. 111–36.

ALBINO, R. C., & THOMSPON, W. J. The effects of sudden weaning on Zulu children. *British Journal of Medical Psychology*, 1956, *29*, 194–97.

ALLAND, A., JR. *The human imperative*. New York: Columbia University Press, 1972.

ALPER, T. G. Achievement motivation in college women: a now-you-see-it-now-you-don't phenomenon. *American Psychologist*, 1974, *29*, 194–203.

ALPERT, R., & HABER, R. N. Anxiety in academic achievement situations. *Journal of Abnormal and Social Psychology*, 1960, *61*, 207–15.

ANGELINI, A. L. Studies in projective measurement of achievement motivation of Brazilian student males and females. *Acta Psychologica*, 1959, *15*, 359–60.

———. Measuring the achievement motive in Brazil. *Journal of Social Psychology*, 1966, *68*, 35–40.

———. *Motivação humana O motivo de realização*. Coleção psicologia contemporânea. Rio de Janeiro: Livraria José Olympio Editôra, 1973.

ARNOLD, M. B. *Emotion and personality*. Vol. 1: psychological aspects; Vol. 2: neurological and physiological aspects. New York: Columbia University Press, 1960.

ARONOFF, J. *Psychological needs and cultural systems: a case study*. Princeton, N. J.: Van Nostrand, 1967.

ARONSON, E. The need for achievement as measured by graphic expression. In J. W. Atkinson (Ed.), *Motives in fantasy, action, and society*. Princeton, N. J.: Van Nostrand, 1958, pp. 249–65.

ATKINSON, J. W. (Ed.), *Motives in fantasy, action and society*. Princeton, N. J.: Van Nostrand, 1958.

———. *An introduction to motivation*. Princeton, N. J.: Van Nostrand, 1964.

ATKINSON, J. W., & FEATHER, N. T. *A theory of achievement motivation*. New York: Wiley, 1966.

ATKINSON, J. W., & LITWIN, G. H. Achievement motive and test anxiety conceived as motive to approach success and motive to avoid failure. *Journal of Abnormal and Social Psychology*, 1960, *60*, 52–63.

BACON, M. K., CHILD, I., & BARRY, H., III. A cross-cultural study of correlates of crime. *Journal of Abnormal and Social Psychology*, 1963, *66*, 291–300.

BAKWIN, H. Loneliness in infants. *American Journal of Diseases of Children*, 1942, *63*, 30–40.

BALTES, P. B. Longitudinal and cross-sectional sequences in the study of age and generation effects. *Human Development*, 1968, *11*, 145–71.

BALTES, P. B., & NESSELROADE, J. R. Cultural change and adolescent personality development. *Developmental Psychology*, 1972, *7*, 244–56.

BANDURA, A. Social learning through imitation. In M. R. Jones (Ed.), *Nebraska symposium on motivation*. Lincoln, Neb.: University of Nebraska Press, 1962, pp. 211–69.

———. *Aggression: a social learning analysis*. Englewood Cliffs, N. J.: Prentice-Hall, 1973.

BANDURA, A., & WALTERS, R. H. Aggression. In H. Stevenson (Ed.), *Child Psychology*. Chicago: University of Chicago Press, 1963, pp. 364–415.

BARBERIO, R. The relationship between achievement motivation and ethnicity in Anglo-American and Mexican-American junior high school students. *Psychological Record*, 1967, *17*, 263–66.

BARTLETT, E. W., & SMITH, C. P. Childrearing practices, birth order, and the development of achievement-related motive. *Psychological Reports*, 1966, *19*, 1207–16.

BARTLETT, F. G. *Remembering: a study in experimental and social psychology*. London: Cambridge University Press, 1932.

BATESON, G. *The Naven*. Stanford, Calif.: Stanford University Press, 1936.

———. The frustration-aggression hypothesis and culture. *Psychological Review*, 1941, *48*, 350–55.

BAUMRIND, D., & BLACK, A. Socialization practices associated with dimensions of competence in preschool boys and girls. *Child Development*, 1967, *38*, 291–328.

BECKER, W. C. Consequences of different kinds of parental discipline. In M. C. Hoffman & L. W. Hoffman (Eds.), *Review of child development research*. New York: Russell Sage, 1964.

BECKER, W. C., & KRUG, R. S. A circumplex model for social behavior in children. *Child Development*, 1964, *35*, 371–96.

BELL, S. M., & AINSWORTH, M. D. S. Infant crying and maternal responsiveness. *Child Development*, 1972, *41*, 1171–90.

BELLER, E. K. Dependency and independence in young children. *Journal of Genetic Psychology*, 1955, *87*, 25–35.

———. Dependency and autonomous achievement striving related to orality and anality in early childhood. *Child Development*, 1957, *28*, 287–315.

———. Exploratory studies of dependency. *Transactions of New York Academy of Sciences*, 1959, *21*, 414–26.

BENEDICT, R. *Patterns of culture*. Boston: Houghton Mifflin, 1934.

BERKOWITZ, L. *Aggression: a social psychological analysis*. New York: McGraw-Hill, 1962.

———. The concept of aggressive drive: some additional considerations. In W. Berkowitz (Ed.), *Advances in experimental social psychology*, Vol. 2. New York: Academic Press, 1965, pp. 301–29.

———. External determinants of impulsive aggression. In J. DeWit & W. W. Hartup (Eds.), *Determinants and origins of aggressive behavior*. The Hague: Mouton, 1974, pp. 147–65.

BERNDT, R. M. Warfare in the New Guinea highlands. *American Anthropologist*, 1964, *66*, 183–203.

BERRIEN, F. K. Values of Japanese and American students. *Technical Report, 14*, NONR 404 (10). New Brunswick, N. J.: Rutgers University, 1964.

BIJOU, S. W., & BAER, D. M. *Child development*, Vol. II: universal stage of infancy. New York: Appleton-Century-Crofts, 1965.

BIRNEY, R. C., BURDICK, H., & TEEVAN, R. C. Analysis of TAT stories for hostile press thema. Paper read at the annual meeting of the Eastern Psychological Association, 1961.

———. *Fear of failure motivation*. New York: Wiley, 1969.

BLACKWOOD, B. Both sides of Buka passage. Oxford: Clarendon Press, 1935.

BLURTON-JONES, N. Ethological studies of child behavior. Cambridge, Eng.: Cambridge University Press, 1972.

BOESCH, E. E., & ECKENSBERGER, L. H. Methodische Probleme des interkulturellen Vergleichs. In C. F. Graumann (Ed.), Handbuch der Psychologie, Vol. 7: sozialpsychologie, Part 1. Göttingen: Hogrefe, 1969, pp. 515–66.

BOWLBY, J. Maternal care and mental health. Geneva World Health Organization Monographs Series No. 2, 1951.

—————. Attachment and loss, I: attachment. London: Hogarth Press; New York: Basic Books, 1969.

BRADBURN, N. M. The managerial role in Turkey: a psychological study. Unpublished doctoral dissertation, Harvard University, 1960.

—————. Need achievement and father dominance in Turkey. Journal of Abnormal and Social Psychology, 1963, 67, 464–68.

BRAZELTON, T. B. Implications of infant development among the Mayan Indians of Mexico. Human Development, 1972, 15, 90–111.

BRONFENBRENNER, U. Soviet methods of character education: some implications for research. American Psychologist, 1962, 17, 550–64.

BROWN, J. S. Gradients of approach and avoidance responses and their relation to level of motivation. Journal of Comparative and Physiological Psychology, 1948, 41, 450–65.

BROWN, J. S., & FARBER, I. E. Emotions conceptualized as intervening variables— with suggestions toward a theory of frustration. Psychological Bulletin, 1951, 48, 465–95.

BUSS, A. The psychology of aggression. New York: Wiley, 1961.

CAMPBELL, D. T., & FISKE, D. W. Convergent and discriminant validation by the multitrait-multimethod matrix. Psychological Bulletin, 1959, 56, 81–105.

CARMENT, D. W. Internal versus external control in India and Canada. International Journal of Psychology, 1974, 9, 45–50.

CARSTAIRS, G. M. The twice-born: a study of a community of highcaste Hindus. London: The Hogarth Press, 1957.

—————. Cross-cultural psychiatric interviewing. In B. Kaplan (Ed.), Studying personality cross-culturally. New York: Harper & Row, 1961, pp. 533–48.

CASLER, L. Maternal deprivation: a critical review of the literature. Monographs of the Society for Research in Child Development, 1961, 26, No. 2.

CATTELL, J. McK. Mental tests and measurements. Mind, 1890, 15, 375–81.

CAUDILL, W. Japanese-American personality and acculturation. Genetic Psychology Monographs, 1952, 45, 3-102.

CAUDILL, W., & DeVOS, G. A. Achievement, culture and personality: the case of the Japanese Americans. American Anthropologist, 1956, 58, 1102–26.

CHANGNON, N. Yanomamö: the fierce people. New York: Holt, Rinehart and Winston, 1968.

CHANCE, J. E. Independence training and first graders' achievement. Journal of Consulting Psychology, 1961, 25, 149–54.

CHILD, I. L., STORM, T., & VEROFF, J. Achievement themes in folk tales related to socialization practice. In J. W. Atkinson (Ed.), *Motives in fantasy, action, and society.* Princeton, N. J.: Van Nostrand, 1958; pp. 479–82.

CLINARD, R. A., & ABBOTT, D. J. *Crime in developing countries: a comparative perspective.* New York: Wiley, 1973.

COATES, B., ANDERSON, E. P., & HARTUP, W. W. The stability of attachment behaviors in the human infant. *Developmental Psychology,* 1972a, *6,* 231–37.

———. Interrelations in the attachment behavior of human infants. *Developmental Psychology,* 1972b, *6,* 218–30.

CRANDALL, V. J., DEWEY, R., KATKOVSKY, W., & PRESTON, A. Parents' attitudes and behaviors and grade-school children's academic achievement. *Journal of Genetic Psychology,* 1964, *104,* 53–66.

CRESSEY, D. R. Crime and delinqency. In L. Broom & P. Selznick (Eds.), *Sociology: a text with adapted readings,* 3rd ed. New York: Harper & Row, 1963.

DENTAN, R. K. *The Semai: a nonviolent people of Malaya.* New York: Holt, Rinehart and Winston, 1968.

DEVOS, G. A. The relation of guilt towards parents to achievement and arranged marriage among the Japanese. *Psychiatry,* 1960, *23,* 287–301.

———. Symbolic analysis in the cross-cultural study of personality. In B. Kaplan (Ed.), *Studying personality cross-culturally.* New York: Harper & Row, 1961, pp. 599–634.

———. Achievement orientation, social self-identity and Japanese economic development. *Asian Survey,* 1965, *5,* 575–89.

———. Achievement and innovation in culture and personality. In E. Norbeck, D. Price-Williams, & W. M. McCord (Eds.), *The study of personality: an interdisciplinary approach.* New York: Holt, Rinehart and Winston, 1968, pp. 348–70.

———. Deviancy and alienation. In G. A. DeVos, *Socialization for achievement.* Berkeley, Calif.: University of California Press, 1973a, pp. 251–549.

———. *Socialization for achievement: essays on the cultural psychology of the Japanese.* Berkeley, Calif.: University of California Press, 1973b.

DEVOS, G. A., & MIZUSHIMA, K. Delinquency and social change in modern Japan. In G. A. DeVos, *Socialization for Achievement: essays on the cultural psychology of the Japanese.* Berkeley, Calif.: University of California Press, 1973, pp. 327–68.

DE VOS, G. A., & WAGATSUMA, H. Value attitudes toward role behavior of women in two Japanese villages. *American Anthropologist,* 1961, *63,* 1204–30.

DEWEY, J. *Human nature and conduct: an introduction to social psychology.* New York: Henry Holt, 1922.

DOGAN, M., & ROKKAN, S. *Quantitative ecological analysis in the social sciences.* Cambridge, Mass.: MIT Press, 1969.

DOI, L. T. Amae: a key concept for understanding Japanese personality structure. In R. J. Smith & R. K. Beardsley (Eds.), *Japanese culture: its development and characteristics.* Chicago: Aldine, 1962.

———. *The anatomy of dependence.* Tokyo: Kodansha International, 1973.

DOLLARD, J., DOOB, L. W., MILLER, N. E., MOWRER, O. H., & SEARS, R. S. *Frustration and aggression.* New Haven: Yale University Press, 1939.

DOLLARD, J., & MILLER, N. E. *Personality and psychotherapy: an analysis in terms of learning, thinking, and culture.* New York: McGraw-Hill, 1950.

EATON, J. W., & WEIL, R. J. *Culture and mental disorders.* New York: Free Press, 1955.

ECKENSBERGER, L. H. *Methodenprobleme der kulturvergleichenden Psychologie.* (Dissertation, 1969, Sarrbrücken). Saarbrücken: Sozialwissenschaftlicher Studienkreis für Internationale Probleme, 1970.

———. Methodological issues of cross-cultural research in developmental psychology. In J. R. Nesselroade & H. W. Reese (Eds.), *Life-span developmental psychology.* New York: Academic Press, 1973, pp. 43–64.

———. Kulturvergleich als interdisziplinärer sozialwissen-schaftlicher Forschungsansatz. Seine Bedeutung und methodischen Probleme aus psychologischer Sicht. In K. M. Boltz (Ed.), *Materialien aus der soziologischen Forschung.* Luchterhand: München, 1978, pp. 351–99.

ECKENSBERGER, L. H., & KORNADT, H.-J. Ecology and culture: cross-cultural studies of ecological variables in relation to socialization and cognitive development. Introduction: the mutual relevance of the cross-cultural and the ecological perspective in psychology. In H. McGurk (Ed.), *Ecological factors in human development.* Amsterdam: North Holland Publishing Co., 1977, pp. 119–227.

EDWARDS, A. L. *Manual for Edwards Personal Preference Schedule.* New York: Psychological Corporation, 1954.

EGGAN, D. The general problem of Hopi adjustment. *American Anthropologist,* 1943, *51,* 177–98.

EIBL-EIBESFELDT, I. Die !Ko-Buschmanngesellschaft: Aggressionskontrolle und Gruppenbildung. *Monograph of Human Ethology 1.* Munich: Piper, 1972.

———. Phylogenetic adaptation as determinants of aggressive behavior in man. In J. DeWit & W. W. Hartup (Eds.), *Determinants and origins of aggressive behavior.* The Hague: Mouton, 1974, pp. 29–57.

———. *Menschenforschung auf neuen Wegen. Die naturwissenschaftliche Betrachtung kultureller Verhaltensweisen.* Wien-München-Zürich: Molden, 1976.

EMMERICH, W. Continuity and stability in early social development. *Child Development,* 1964, *35,* 311–32.

———. Continuity and stability in early social development, II: teacher's ratings. *Child Development,* 1966, *37,* 17–27.

EPSTEIN, S. The measurement of drive and conflict in humans: theory and experiment. In M. R. Jones (Ed.), *Nebraska symposium on motivation.* Lincoln: University of Nebraska Press, 1962, pp. 127–206.

ERIKSON, E. H. *Childhood and society,* 2nd ed. New York: Norton, 1963. (First edition published, 1950.)

FESHBACH, S. The function of aggression and the regulation of aggressive drive. *Psychological Review,* 1964, *71,* 257–72.

———. Aggression. In P. H. Mussen (Ed.), *Carmichael's manual of child psychology,* Vol. 2. New York: Wiley, 1970, pp. 159–259.

———. The development and regulation of aggression: some research gaps and a proposed cognitive approach. In J. DeWit and W. W. Hartup (Eds.), *Determinants and origins of aggressive behavior.* The Hague: Mouton, 1974, pp. 167–91.

FISHER, S. Patterns of personality rigidity and some of their determinants. *Psychological Monographs,* 1950, *64* (1, Whole Issue).

FISKE, D. W. Can a personality construct be validated empirically? *Psychological Bulletin,* 1973, *80,* 89–92.

FRANK, L. K. Projective methods for the study of personality. *Journal of Psychology,* 1939, *8,* 389–413.

FRENCH, E. G. Motivation as a variable in work-partner selection. *Journal of Abnormal and Social Psychology*, 1956, *53*, 96–99.

FRENCH, E. G., & LESSER, G. S. Some characteristics of the achievement motive in women. *Journal of Abnormal and Social Psychology*, 1964, *68*, 119–28.

FREUD, A. *The psycho-analytical treatment of children.* London: Hogarth Press, 1946.

———. Psychoanalysis and education. *Psychoanalytic Study of the Child*, 1954, *9*, 9–15.

FREUD, S. *Drei abhandlungen zur sexualtheorie.* Gesammelte Werke, Vol. 5. London: Imago, 1905. (*Three essays on the theory of sexuality.* Standard Edition, Vol. 7. London: Hogarth Press, 1953, pp. 122–243.)

———. *Totem und Tabu.* Gesammelte Werke, Vol. 9. London: Imago, 1912. (*Totem and taboo: resemblances between the psychic lives of savages and neurotics.* New York: Moffat Yard, 1912.)

———. *Vorlesungen zur Einführung in die Psychoanalyse.* Gesammelte Werke, Vol. 11. London: Imago, 1917. (*Introductory lectures on psychoanalysis,* 2nd ed. London: Allen and Unwin, 1940.)

———. *Jenseits des Lustprinzips.* Gesammelte Werke, Vol. 9. London: Imago, 1920. (*Beyond the pleasure principle.* London: International Psychoanalytic Press, 1922.)

———. *Hemmung, Symptom, und Angst.* Gesammelte Werke, Vol. 14. London: Imago, 1926. (*Inhibitions, symptoms, and anxiety.* Standard Edition, Vol. 20. London: Hogarth Press, 1959, pp. 77–178.)

———. *Neue folge der Vorlesungen zur Einführung in die Psychoanalyse.* Gesammelte Werke, Vol. 15. London: Imago, 1932. (*New introductory lectures on psychoanalysis.* New York: Norton, 1933.)

———. *Abriß der Psychoanalyse.* Gesammelte Werke, Vol. 17. London: Imago, 1938. (*An outline of psychoanalysis.* Standard Edition, Vol. 32. London: Hogarth Press, 1940, pp. 139ff.)

FRIJDA, N., & JAHODA, G. On the scope and methods of cross-cultural research. *International Journal of Psychology*, 1966, *1*, 109–27.

FROST, B. P., IWAWAKI, S., & FOGLIATTO, H. Argentinian, Canadian, Japanese and Puerto Rican norms on the Frost self-description questionnaire. *Journal of Cross-Cultural Psychology*, 1972, *3*, 215–18.

FRY, P. S. The resistance to temptation: inhibitory and disinhibitory effects of models on children from India and the United States. *Journal of Cross-Cultural Psychology*, 1975, *6*, 189–202.

FUCHS, R. Funktionsanalyse der motivation. *Zeitschrift für Experimentelle und Angewandte Psychologie*, 1963, *10*, 626–45.

GALLIMORE, R. *Variations in the motivational antecedents of achievement among Hawaii's ethnic groups.* Paper read at East-West conference on culture and mental health. Social Science Research Institute, Honolulu, Hawaii, 1969.

GALLIMORE, R., WEISS, L. B., & FINNEY, R. Cultural differences in delay of gratification: a problem of behavior classification. *Journal of Personality and Social Psychology*, 1974, *30*, 72–80.

GARDNER, R., & HEIDER, K. G. *Gardens of war: life and death in the New Guinea stone age.* New York: Random House, 1969.

GÉBER, M. The psycho-motor development of African children in the first year, and the influence of maternal behavior. *Journal of Social Psychology*, 1958a, *47*, 185–95.

———. L'enfant africain occidentalisé et de niveau social superieur en Uganda. *Courrier*, 1958b, *8*, 517–23.

GÉBER, M., & DEAN, R. F. A. *Gesell tests on African children.* Pediatrics, 1957, *20*, 1055–65.

GEWIRTZ, J. L. A learning analysis of the effects of normal stimulation, privation, and deprivation on the acquisition of social motivation and attachment. In B. M. Foss (Ed.), *Determinants of infant behaviour.* New York: Wiley, 1961, pp. 213–90.

———. The course of infant smiling in four child-rearing environments in Israel. In B. M. Foss (Ed.), *Determinants of infant behaviour III.* London: Methuen, 1965, pp. 205–48.

———. Mechanisms of social learning: some roots of stimulation and behavior in early human development. In D. A. Goslin (Ed.), *Handbook of socialization theory and research.* Chicago: Rand McNally, 1969, pp. 57–212.

GOLDBERG, S. Infant development in Zambia. Measuring maternal behavior. Paper presented at the University for Social Science Conference, Nairobi, 1969.

———. Infant care and growth in urban Zambia. *Human Development*, 1972, *15*, 77–89.

GOLDFARB, W. Infant rearing and problem behavior. *American Journal of Orthopsychiatry*, 1943a, *13*, 249–66.

———. The effects of early institutional care on adolescent personality. *Child Development*, 1943b, *14*, 213–25.

———. Infant rearing as a factor in foster home replacement. *American Journal of Orthopsychiatry*, 1944a, *14*, 162–66.

———. Effects of early institutional care on adolescent personality: Rorschach data. *American Journal of Orthopsychiatry*, 1944b, *14*, 441–47.

———. Effects of psychological deprivation in infancy and subsequent stimulation. *American Journal of Psychiatry*, 1945a, *102*, 18–33.

———. Psychological deprivation in infancy and subsequent adjustment. *American Journal of Orthopsychiatry*, 1945b, *15*, 247–55.

———. Variations in adolescent adjustment of institutionally reared children. *American Journal of Orthopsychiatry*, 1947, *17*, 449–57.

GOODWIN, C. *The social organization of the Western Apache.* Chicago: University of Chicago Press, 1942.

GORER, G. Some aspects of the psychology of the people of Great Russia. *American Slavic and East European Review*, 1949, *8*, 155–66.

GORER, G., & RICKMAN, J. *The people of Great Russia.* London: Cresset Press, 1949.

GOUGH, H. G. *Manual for the California Psychological Inventory.* Palo Alto, Calif.: Consulting Psychologist Press, 1957.

———. A cross-cultural study of achievement motivation. *Journal of Applied Psychology*, 1964, *48*, 191–96.

GRAY, P. H. Theory and evidence in imprinting in human infants. *Journal of Psychology*, 1958, *46*, 155–66.

GUNDERS, S. M., & WHITING, J. W. M. Mother-infant separation and physical growth. *Ethnology*, 1968, *7*, 196–206.

GURR, T. R., & DUVALL, R. Civil conflicts in the sixties: a reciprocal theoretical system with parameter estimates. *Comparative Political Studies*, 1973, *6*, 135–69.

GUTTMANN, G. *Einführung in die Neuropsychologie*. Bern: Huber, 1972.

HALL, C. S., & LINDZEY, G. The relevance of Freudian psychology and related viewpoints for the social sciences. In G. Lindzey & E. Aronson (Eds.), *The handbook of social psychology*, 2nd ed. Reading, Mass.: Addison-Wesley, 1968.

HAMBURG, D. Recent research on hormonal factors relevant to human aggressiveness. *International Social Science Journal*, 1971, *23*, 36–47.

HAMBURG, D. A., & VAN LAWICK-GOODALL, J. Factors facilitating development of aggressive behavior in chimpanzees and humans. In J. DeWit & W. W. Hartup (Eds.), *Determinants and origins of aggressive behavior*. The Hague: Mouton, 1974, pp. 59–85.

HAMILTON, D. L. More power needed. (Review of D. G. Winter: *The power motive*. New York: Free Press, 1973.) *Contemporary Psychology*, 1974, *19*, 774–76.

HARLOW, H. F. The nature of love. *American Psychologist*, 1958, *13*, 673–85.

———. The development of affectional patterns in infant monkeys. In B. M. Foss (Ed.), *Determinants of infant behaviour*. London: Methuen, 1961, pp. 75–88.

HARLOW, H. F., & HARLOW, M. K. Social deprivation in monkeys. *Scientific American*, 1962, *207*, 136–46.

HARTMANN, H. Comments on the psychoanalytic theory of instinctual drives. *Psychoanalytic Quarterly*, 1948, *17*, 368–88.

HARTUP, W. W. Dependence and independence. In H. W. Stevenson (Ed.), *Child psychology, Part I*. Chicago: University of Chicago Press, 1963, pp. 333–63.

HARTUP, W. W., & DEWIT, J. The development of aggression: problems and perspectives. In J. DeWit & W. W. Hartup (Eds.), *Determinants and origins of aggressive behavior*. The Hague: Mouton, 1974, pp. 595–620.

HARTUP, W. W., & LEMPERS, J. A problem in life-span development: the interactional analysis of family attachments. In P. B. Baltes & K. W. Schaie (Eds.), *Life-span developmental psychology: personality and socialization*. New York: Academic Press, 1973, pp. 235–52.

HAYASHI, T., OKAMOTO, N., & HABU, K. Children's achievement motivation and its relation to intelligence, school achievements, anxiety tendencies, and parent-child relations. *Bulletin Kyoto Gakugei University, Series A*, 1962, *21*, 16–20.

HAYASHI, T., RIM, Y., & LYNN, R. A test of McClelland's theory of achievement motivation in Britain, Japan, Ireland and Israel. *International Journal of Psychology*, 1970, *5*, 275–77.

HAYASHI, T., & YAMAUCHI, K. The relation of children's need for achievement to their parents' home discipline in regard to independence and mastery. *Bulletin Kyoto Gakugei University, Series A*, 1964, *25*, 31–40.

HECKHAUSEN, H. *Hoffnung und Furcht in der Leistungsmotivation*. Meisenheim/Glan: Hain, 1963a.

———. Eine Rahmentheorie der Motivation in zehn Thesen. *Zeitschrift für Experimentelle und Angewandte Psychologie*, 1963b, *10*, 604–26.

———. Einflüsse der Erziehung auf die Motivationsgenese. In T. Herrmann (Ed.), *Psychologie der Erziehungsstile*. Göttingen:Hogrefe, 1966, pp. 131–69.

———. *The anatomy of achievement motivation*. New York: Academic Press, 1967.

———. Achievement motive research: current problems and some contributions towards a general theory of motivation. In W. J. Arnold (Ed.), *Nebraska symposium on motivation.* Lincoln, Neb.: University of Nebraska Press, 1968, pp. 103–74.

———. Trainingskurse zur Erhöhung der Leistungsmotivation und der unternehmerischen Aktivität in einem Entwicklungsland: Eine nachträgliche Analyse des erzielten Motivwandels. *Zeitschrift für Entwicklungspsychologie und Pädagogische Psychologie,* 1971, 3, 253–68.

———. Die interaktion der Sozialisationsvariablen in der Genese des Leistungsmotivs. In C. F. Graumann (Ed.), *Handbuch der Psychologie, Vol. 7, Part 2: sozialpsychologie.* Göttingen: Hogrefe, 1972, pp. 955–1019.

———. Intervening cognitions in motivation. In D. E. Berlyne & K. B. Madsen (Eds.), *Pleasure, reward, preference.* New York: Academic Press, 1973, pp. 217–42.

———. How to improve poor motivation in students. Paper presented for a symposium on "Motivational psychology and its application in education and management" at the 18th International Congress of Applied Psychology. Montreal, August 1, 1974.

———. *Ein kognitives Motivationsmodell und die Verankerung von Motivkonstrukten.* In H. Lenk (Ed.), *Hanellungstheorien interdisziplinär.* München: Fink, (in press).

HECKHAUSEN, H., & KEMMLER, L. Entstehungsbedingungen der kindlichen Selbständigkeit. *Zeitschrift für Experimentelle und Angewandte Psychologie,* 1957, 4, 603–22.

HECKHAUSEN, H., & OSWALD, A. Erziehungspraktiken der Mutter und Leistungsverhalten des normalen und des gliedmaßengeschädigten Kindes. *Archiv für die Gesamte Psychologie,* 1969, 121, 1–30.

HECKHAUSEN, H., & WEINER, B. The emergence of a cognitive psychology of motivation. In P. C. Dodwell (Ed.), *New horizons in psychology 2,* Harmondsworth, England: Penguin Books, 1972, pp. 126–47.

HESS, E. H. Ethology and developmental psychology. In P. H. Mussen (Ed.), *Carmichael's manual of child psychology,* Vol. 1. New York: Wiley, 1970, pp. 1–38.

HÖRMANN, H. Theoretische Grundlagen der projektiven Tests. In R. Heiss (Ed.), *Handbuch der psychologie, Vol. 6: psychodiagnostik.* 1964, pp. 71–112.

HOFFMAN, L. W. Fear of success in males and females, 1965 and 1971. *Journal of Consulting and Clinical Psychology,* 1974, 42, 353–85.

HONIGMANN, J. J. North America. In F. L. K. Hsu (Ed.), *Psychological anthropology.* Cambridge, Mass.: Schenkman, 1972, pp. 121–65.

HORNER, M. S. Sex differences in achievement motivation and performance in competitive and noncompetitive situations. Unpublished dissertation, 1968.

———. Toward an understanding of achievement related conflicts in women. *Journal of Social Issues,* 1972, 28, 157–75.

HOSHINO, A. Japan. In L. Minturn and J. L. Tapp (Eds.), *Authority, rules, and aggression: a cross-national study of children's judgments of justice of aggressive confrontation, Part 2.* Unpublished manuscript, Chicago: University of Chicago Press, 1970.

HOVING, K. L., LAFORME, G. L., & WALLACE, J. R. The development of children's interpersonal aggression in a competitive task. In J. DeWit and W. W. Hartup (Eds.), *Determinants and origins of aggressive behavior.* The Hague: Mouton, 1974, pp. 193–200.

HUBER, P. B. Death and society among the Anggor of New Guinea. *Omega*, 1972, *3*, 233–43.

HULL, C. L. *Principles of behavior.* New York: Appleton-Century-Crofts, 1943.

JAHODA, G. A note on Ashanti names and their relationship to personality. *British Journal of Psychology*, 1954, *45*, 192–95.

JAMES, W. *The principles of psychology.* New York: Henry Holt, 1890.

KAGAN, J. Motives and development. *Journal of Personality and Social Psychology*, 1972, *22*, 51–66.

KAGAN, J., & KLEIN, R. E. Cross-cultural perspectives on early development. *American Psychologist*, 1973, *28*, 947–61.

KAGAN, J., & MOSS, H. A. *Birth to maturity: a study in psychological development.* New York: Wiley, 1962.

KAGAN, S., & MADSEN, M. C. Cooperation and competition of Mexican, Mexican-American and Anglo-American children of two ages under four instructional sets. *Developmental Psychology*, 1971, *5*, 32–39.

———. Experimental analyses of cooperation and competition of Anglo-American and Mexican children. *Developmental Psychology*, 1972a, *6*, 49–59.

———. Rivaling in Anglo-American and Mexican children of two ages. *Journal of Personality and Social Psychology*, 1972b, *24*, 214–20.

KARDINER, A. *The individual and his society: the psychodynamics of primitive social organization.* With a foreword and two ethnological reports by R. Linton. New York: Columbia University Press, 1939.

———. *The psychological frontiers of society.* New York: Columbia University Press, 1945.

KAUFMANN, H. *Aggression and altruism.* New York: Holt, Rinehart and Winston, 1970.

KENDALL, M. G. *Rank correlation methods.* London: Griffin, 1948.

KIKUCHI, A., & GORDON, L. V. Evaluation and cross-cultural application of a Japanese form of the survey of interpersonal values. *Journal of Social Psychology*, 1966, *69*, 185–95.

KILBRIDE, J. E., & KILBRIDE, P. L. Sitting and smiling behavior of culturally constituted experience. *Journal of Cross-Cultural Psychology*, 1975, *6*, 88–107.

KLUCKHOHN, C. Navaho witchcraft. *Papers of the Peabody Museum of American Archaeology and Ethnology.* Harvard University, 1944, *22*, No. 2.

KLUCKHOHN, C., & MURRAY, H. A. *Personality in nature, culture, and society.* New York: Knopf, 1948.

KLUCKHOHN, C., & SCHNEIDER, D. *Personality in nature, culture, and society.* New York: Knopf, 1953.

KOLB, D. A. Achievement motivation training for underachieving high-school boys. *Journal of Personality and Social Psychology*, 1965, *2*, 783–92.

KONNER, M. J. Aspects of the developmental ethology of a foraging people. In N. Blurton Jones (Ed.), *Ethological studies of child behavior.* Cambridge: Cambridge University Press, 1972, pp. 285–304.

KORNADT, H.-J. Thematische Apperzeptionsverfahren. In R. Heiss (Ed.), *Handbuch der Psychologie, Vol. 6. Psychologische Diagnostik.* Göttingen: Hogrefe, 1964, pp. 635–84.

————. Einflüsse der Erziehung auf die Aggressivitätsgenese. In T. Herrmann (Ed.), *Psychologie der Erziehungsstile*. Göttingen: Hogrefe, 1966, pp. 170–80.

————. Toward a motivation theory of aggression and aggression inhibition: some considerations about an aggression motive and its application to TAT and catharsis. In J. DeWit & W. W. Hartup (Eds.), *Determinants and origins of aggressive behavior*. The Hague: Mouton, 1974, pp. 567–77

————. *Aggressionsmotiv und aggressionshemmung*. Bern: Huber, 1979.

KORNADT, H.-J., & VOIGT, E. *Situation und Entwicklungsprobleme des Schulsystems in Kenia*. Teil 2: Empirischer Beitrag zur sozialpsychologischen Funktion der Schule, besonders der Sekundarschule. Wissenschaftliche Schriftenreihe des Bundesministeriums für wirtschaftliche Zusammenarbeit. Stuttgart: Klett, 1970.

KUBANY, E. S. GALLIMORE, R., & BUELL, J. The effects of extrinsic factors on achievement-oriented behavior: a non-Western case. *Journal of Cross-Cultural Psychology*, 1970, *1*, 77–84.

LAMBERT, W. W. Promise and problems of cross-cultural exploration of children's aggressive strategies. In J. DeWit & W. W. Hartup (Eds.), *Determinants and origins of aggressive behavior*, The Hague: Mouton, 1974, pp. 437–60.

LANTIS, M. Alaskan Eskimo cultural values. *Polar Notes*, 1959, *1*, 35–48.

LAZARUS, J. R., KESSEL, F. S., & BOTHA, E. Cultural differences in *n* achievement externality between white and colored South African adolescents. *Journal of Social Psychology*, 1969, *77*, 133–54.

LEIDERMAN, P. H., & LEIDERMAN, G. F. Affective and cognitive consequences of polymatric infant care in the East African Highlands. In A. Pick (Ed.), *Minnesota symposion on child psychology*, Vol. 8. Minneapolis: University of Minnesota Press, 1974, pp. 81–110.

LEIGHTON, A. H., & LEIGHTON, D. C. *The Navaho door: an introduction to Navaho life*. Cambridge, Mass.: Harvard University Press, 1944.

LESSER, G. S., & KANDEL, D. *The Human Context* 1968/69, *1*, 347–97.

LESSER, G. S., KRAWITZ, R. N., & PACKARD, R. Experimental arousal of achievement motivation in adolescent girls. *Journal of Abnormal and Social Psychology*, 1963, *66*, 59–66.

LEVINE, R. A. *Dreams and deeds: achievement motivation in Nigeria*. Chicago: University of Chicago Press, 1966.

LEVINE, R. A. Cross-cultural study in child psychology. In P. H. Mussen (Ed.), *Carmichael's manual of child psychology*, Vol. 1. New York: Wiley, 1970, pp. 559–612.

LEVINE, S. Influence of infantile stimulation on the response to stress during preweaning development. *Developmental Psychobiology*, 1968, *1*, 67–70.

LEVY, R. I. On getting angry in the Society Islands. In W. Caudill & T.-J. Lin (Eds.), *Mental health research in Asia and the Pacific*. Honolulu: East-West Center Press, 1969, pp. 358–80.

————. *Tahitians. Mind and experience in the Society Islands*. Chicago: University of Chicago Press, 1973.

LEWIS, M., & BAN, P. Stability of attachment behavior: a transformational analysis. Paper presented at meetings of the Society for Research in Child Development. Minneapolis, 1971.

LINDZEY, G. *Projective techniques and cross-cultural research.* New York: Appleton-Century-Crofts, 1961.

LINTON, R. The Comanche. In A. Kardiner (Ed.), *The psychological frontiers of society.* New York: Columbia University Press, 1945, pp. 47–80.

LONGABAUGH, R. The structure of interpersonal behavior. *Sociometry*, 1966, *29*, 441–60.

LORENZ, K. Z. Die angeborenen Formen möglicher Erfahrung. *Zeitschrift für Tierpsychology*, 1943, *5*, 235–409.

———. *Das sogenannte Böse.* Wien: Borotha-Schoeler, 1963. (*On aggression.* New York: Harcourt, Brace and World, 1966.)

LUSK, L., & LEWIS, M. Mother-infant interaction and infant development among the Wolof of Senegal. *Human Development*, 1972, *15*, 58–69.

LYNN, R. An achievement motivation questionnaire. *British Journal of Psychology*, 1969, *60*, 529–34.

MACCOBY, E. E., & FELDMAN, S. Mother-attachment and stranger-reactions in the third year of life. *Monographs of the Society for Research in Child Development*, 1972, *37*, No. 146.

MACCOBY, E. E., & MASTERS, J. C. Attachment and dependency. In P. H. Mussen (Ed.), *Carmichael's manual of child psychology*, 3rd ed., Vol. 2. New York: Wiley, 1970, pp. 73–157.

MADSEN, J. C. The expression of aggression in two cultures. Dissertation abstracts 1967b(27), (Order No. 66–12, 974), 1966.

MADSEN, M. C., & KAGAN, S. Mother-directed achievement of children in two cultures. *Journal of Cross-Cultural Psychology*, 1973, *4*, 221–28.

MADSEN, M. C., & SHAPIRA, A. Cooperative and competitive behavior of urban Afro-American, Anglo-American, Mexican-American and Mexican village children. *Developmental Psychology*, 1970, *3*, 16–20.

MAEHR, M. L. Culture and achievement motivation. *American Psychologist*, 1974, *29*, 887–96.

MAIER, N. R. F. Frustration theory: restatement and extension.

MALINOWSKI, B. *Sex and repression in savage society.* New York: Harcourt, Brace, 1927.

———. *A scientific theory of culture.* Chapel Hill: University of North Carolina Press, 1944. (Reprinted in B. Malinowski, *A scientific theory of culture and other essays.* New York: Oxford University Press, 1960.)

MALONEY, M. P. The question of achievement in the Japanese American. A comment on cross-cultural research. *Psychologia*, 1968, *11*, 143–58.

MARVIN, R. S., VAN DERENDER, T. L., IWANAGA, M. O., LeVINE, S., & LeVINE, R. A. Infant-caregiver attachment among the Hausa of Nigeria. In McGurk (Ed.), *Ecological factors in human development.* Amsterdam: Nort Holland, 1977, pp. 247–60.

MARX, M. H. The general nature of theory construction. In M. H. Marx (Ed.), *Theories in contemporary psychology.* New York: MacMillan, 1964, pp. 4–46.

MASLOW, A. H. *Motivation and personality.* New York: Harper, 1954.

McCARY, J. L. Ethnic and cultural reactions to frustration. *Journal of Personality*, 1950, *18*, 321–26.

McCLELLAND, D. C. *Personality.* New York: William Sloane Associates, 1951.

———. Risk-taking in children with high and low need for achievement. In J. W. Atkinson (Ed.), *Motives in fantasy, action, and society.* Princeton, N.J: Van Nostrand, 1958, pp. 306–21.

———. *The achieving society.* Princeton, N.J: Van Nostrand, 1961.

———. *The roots of consciousness.* Princeton, N.J: Van Nostrand, 1964.

———. *Power: the inner experience.* New York: Irvington Press, 1975.

McCLELLAND, D. C., & ATKINSON, J. W., CLARK, R. A., & LOWELL, E. L. *The achievement motive.* New York: Appleton-Century-Crofts, 1953.

McCLELLAND, D. C., CLARK, R. A., ROBY, T. B., & ATKINSON, J. W. The projective expression of needs, IV: the effect of the need for achievement on thematic apperception. *Journal of Experimental Psychology,* 1949, *39,* 242–55.

McCLELLAND, D. C., DAVIS, W. N., KALIN, R., & WANNER, E. *The drinking man.* New York: Free Press, 1972.

McCLELLAND, D.C., & FRIEDMAN, G. A. A cross-cultural study of the relationship between child-training practices and achievement motivation appearing in folk tales. In G. E. Swanson, T. M. Newcomb, & E. L. Hartley (Eds.), *Readings in social psychology.* New York: Holt, Rinehart and Winston, 1952.

McCLELLAND, D. C., & WINTER, D. G. *Motivating economic achievement.* New York: Free Press, 1969.

McDAVID, J. W., & HARARI, H. *Social psychology, individuals, groups, societies.* New York: Harper, 1968.

McDOUGALL, W. *Introduction to social psychology.* London: Methuen, 1908.

McGHEE, P. G., & TEEVAN, R. C. The childhood development of fear of failure motivation. *Technical Reports,* 1965, *15,* Office of Naval Research.

MEAD, M. *From the South Seas.* New York: William Morrow, 1939. (Copyright 1928, 1935, 1938 by M. Mead)

———. *Sex and temperament in three primitive societies.* New York: William Morrow, 1935.

———. Some theoretical considerations on the problem of mother-child separation. *American Journal of Orthopsychiatry,* 1954, *24,* 471–83.

———. Discussion of the cross-cultural approach to child development problems. In J. M. Tanner & B. Inhelder (Eds.), *Discussions of child development proceedings of the meeting of WHO study group on psychobiological development of the child,* Vol. 1. Geneva, 1953. London: Tavistock, 1956, pp. 200–32.

MEADE, R. D. Future time perspectives of college students in America and in India. *Journal of Social Psychology,* 1971, *83,* 175–82.

———. Future time perspectives of Americans and subcultures in India. *Journal of Cross-Cultural Psychology,* 1972, *3,* 93–99.

MELIKIAN, L., GINSBERG, A., CÜCELOGLU, D., & LYNN, R. Achievement motivation in Afghanistan, Brazil, Saudi Arabia and Turkey. *Journal of Social Psychology,* 1971, *83,* 183–84.

MERZ, F. Aggression und aggressionstrieb. In H. Thomae (Ed.), *Motivation. Handbuch der psychologie,* Vol. 2. Göttingen: Hogrefe, 1965, pp. 569–601.

MEYER, W.-U., WACKER, A., HECKHAUSEN, H. , & OSWALD, A. *Die entstehung der er-*

lebten Selbstverantwortlichkeit: (2) in Abhängigkeit von Selbstverantwortlichkeit, leistungs-motivation und Interaktion der Mutter. Bochum, West Germany: Psychologisches Institut Ruhr-Universität, 1969.

MEYER, W.-U., & WACKER, A. Die entstehung der erlebten selbstverantwortlichkeit: (1) in abhängigkeit vom zeitpunkt der selbständigkeitserziehung. *Archiv für Psychologie, 1970, 122,* 24–39.

MILLER, N. E. The frustration-aggression hypothesis. *Psychological Review, 1941, 48,* 337–42.

———. Experimental studies of conflict. In J. McV. Hunt (Ed.), *Personality and the behavior disorders,* Vol. 1. New York: Ronald, 1944, *1,* 431–65.

———. Studies of fear as an acquirable drive, I: fear as motivation and fear-reduction as reinforcement in the learning of new responses. *Journal of Experimental Psychology, 1948, 38,* 89–101.

———. Liberalization of basic S-R concepts: extensions to conflict behavior, motivation, and social learning. In S. Koch (Ed.), *Psychology: a study of a science,* Vol. 2. New York: McGraw-Hill, 1959.

MINGIONE, A. D. Need for achievement in Negro and white children. *Journal of Consulting Psychology, 1965, 29,* 108–11.

MINTURN, L., & LAMBERT, W. W. *Mothers of six cultures: antecedents of child rearing.* New York: Wiley, 1964.

MISCHEL, W. Father-absence and delay of gratification: cross-cultural comparisons. *Journal of Abnormal and Social Psychology, 1961a, 63,* 116–24.

———. Delay of gratification, need for achievement, and acquiescence in another culture. *Journal of Abnormal and Social Psychology, 1961b, 62,* 543–52.

MITSCHERLICH, A., & MUCK, M. Der psychoanalytische Ansatz in der Sozialpsychologie. In C. F. Graumann (Ed.), *Handbuch der Psychologie, Vol. 7, Part 1: Sozialpsychologie.* Göttingen: Hogrefe, 1969, pp. 108–32.

MORROW, W. R., & WILSON, R. C. Family relations of bright high-achieving and under-achieving high school boys. *Child Development, 1961, 32,* 501–10.

MORSBACH, H. A cross-cultural study of achievement motivation and achievement values in two South African groups. *Journal of Social Psychology, 1969, 79,* 267–68.

MOSS, H. A., & KAGAN, J. Stability of achievement and recognition-seeking behaviors from early childhood through adulthood. *Journal of Abnormal and Social Psychology, 1961, 62,* 504–13.

MOULTON, R. W. Notes for a projective measure for fear of failure. In J. W. Atkinson (Ed.), *Motives in fantasy, action, and society.* Princeton, N. J.: Van Nostrand, 1958, pp. 563–71.

MOWRER, O. H. *Learning theory and personality dynamics.* New York: Ronald, 1950.

MOYER, K. E. *The physiology of aggression.* Chicago: Markham Press, 1971.

MUNROE, R. L., MUNROE, R. H., & LeVINE, R. Africa. In F. L. K. Hsu (Ed.), *Psychological anthropology.* Cambridge, Mass.: Schenkman, 1972, pp. 71–120.

MURDOCK, G. P., & PROVOST, C. Measurement of cultural complexity. *Ethnology, 1973, 12,* 379–92.

MURDOCK, G. P., FORD, C. S., HUDSON, A. E., KENNEDY, R., SIMMONS, L. W., & WHITING, J. W. M. *Outline of cultural materials* (3rd ed., revised). New Haven: HRAF, 1950.

MURRAY, H. A. *Explorations in personality.* New York: Oxford University Press, 1938.

MURSTEIN, B. J. *Theory and research in projective techniques (emphasizing the TAT).* New York: Wiley, 1963.

NAKANE, C. *Japanese society.* Harmondsworth: Penguin, 1970.

NEWCOMB, T. M. *Social psychology.* New York: Dryden, 1950.

NUTTALL, R. L. Some correlates of high need for achievement among urban northern Negroes. *Journal of Abnormal and Social Psychology,* 1964, *68,* 593–600.

OLSEN, N. J. Sex differences in child training antecedents of achievement motivation among Chinese children. *Journal of Social Psychology,* 1971, *83,* 303–04.

OLWEUS, D. *Prediction of aggression.* Stockholm: Scandinavian Test Corporation, 1969.

———. Personality and aggression. In J. K. Cole & D. D. Jensen (Eds.), Nebraska symposium on motivation, 1972. Lincoln, Neb.: University of Nebraska Press, 1973, 261–321.

OSTHEIMER, J. M. Measuring achievement motivation among the Chagga of Tanzania. *Journal of Social Psychology,* 1969, *78,* 17–30.

PAREEK, U. N. *Developmental patterns in reactions to frustration.* London: Asia Publishing House, 1964.

PAREEK, U. N., & KUMAR, V. K. Expressed motive of entrepreneurship in an Indian town. *Psychologia,* 1969, *12,* 109–14.

PARKER, S. Motives in Eskimo and Ojibwa mythology. *Ethnology,* 1962, *1,* 516–23.

PARSONS, T. Psychoanalysis and the social structure. *Psychoanalytic Quarterly,* 1950, *19,* 371–94.

———. Social structure and the development of personality. In B. Kaplan (Ed.), *Studying personality cross-culturally.* New York: Harper & Row, 1961, pp. 165–99.

PEPLAU, L. A. Impact of fear of success and sex-role attitudes on women's competitive achievement. *Journal of Personality and Social Psychology,* 1976, *34,* 561–68.

PIDDINGTON, R. *An introduction to social anthropology,* Vol. 2. Edinburgh: Oliver and Boyd, 1957.

PINNEAU, S. R. A critique on the articles by Margaret Ribble. *Child Development,* 1950, *21,* 203–28.

———. The infantile disorders of hospitalism and anaclitic depression. *Psychological Bulletin,* 1955, *52,* 429–62.

PITKÄNEN, L. Nonaggressive patterns of coping with thwarting situations as alternatives to aggression. Paper presented to the first biennial meeting of the International Society for Research on Aggression, Toronto, 1974.

PITKÄNEN-PULKKINEN, L. Self-control as a prerequisite for constructive behavior. Paper presented at the International Conference on Psychological Issues in Changing Aggression, Warsaw, 1976.

PRESCOTT, J. W. Early somatosensory deprivation as an ontogenetic process in the abnormal development of the brain and behavior. *Primates: Medical Primatology,* 1970, 356–75.

———. Body pleasure and the origins of violence. *The Futurist,* April, 1975, 64–74.

RAMIREZ, M., III, & PRICE-WILLIAMS, D. R. Achievement motivation in children of three ethnic groups in the United States. *Journal of Cross-Cultural Psychology,* 1976, *7,* 49–60.

RAYNOR, J. O. Future orientation and motivation of immediate activity: an elaboration of the theory of achievement motivation. *Psychological Review*, 1969, *76*, 606–10.

REUGAMER, W. R., BERNSTEIN, L., & BENJAMIN, J. D. Growth, food utilization, and thyroid activity in the albino rat as a function of handling. *Science*, 1954, *120*, 134.

RHEINGOLD, H. L. The effect of environmental stimulation upon social and exploratory behaviour in the human infant. In B. M. Foss (Ed.), *Determinants of infant behaviour*. London: Methuen, 1961, pp. 143–71.

———. The effect of a strange environment on the behavior of infants. In B. M. Foss (Ed.), *Determinants of infant behaviour IV*. London: Methuen, 1969, pp. 137–66.

RIBBLE, M. Disorganizing factors in infant personality. *American Journal of Psychiatry*, 1941, *98*, 459–63.

———. Infantile experience in relation to personality development. In J. McV. Hunt (Ed.), *Personality and the behavior disorders*, Vol. 2. New York: Ronald, 1944, pp. 621–51.

ROBSON, K. S. The role of eye-to-eye contact in maternal infant attachment. *Journal of Child Psychology and Psychiatry and Allied Disciplines*, 1967, *8*, 13–27.

RÓHEIM, G. Psychoanalysis of primative cultural types. *International Journal of Psychoanalysis*, 1932, *13*, 1–224.

———. Technique of dream analysis and field work in anthropology. *Psychoanalytic Quarterly*, 1949, *18*, 471–79.

ROHNER, R. P. Parental acceptance-rejection and personality development: a universalistic approach to behavioral science. In R. W. Brislin, S. Bochner, & W. J. Lonner (Eds.), *Cross-cultural perspectives on learning*. New York: Wiley, 1975, pp. 251–69.

RORSCHACH, H. *Psychodiagnostik*. Bern: Huber, 1921.

ROSEN, B. C. The achievement syndrome: a psycho-cultural dimension of social stratification (expanded version of a paper read at the annual meeting of the American Sociological Society, September, 1955). *American Sociological Review*, 1956, *21*, 203–11.

———. Race, ethnicity, and the achievement syndrome (revised version of a paper read at the annual meeting of the American Sociological Society, August, 1957). *American Sociological Review*, 1959, *24*, 47–60.

———. Socialization and the achievement motivation in Brazil. *American Sociological Review*, 1962, *27*, 612–24.

———. Family structure and value transmission. *Merrill-Palmer Quarterly*, 1964, *10*, 59–76.

ROSEN, B. C., & D'ANDRADE, R. The psychosocial origins of achievement motivation. *Sociometry*, 1959, *22*, 185–218.

ROSENBLATT, P. C., JACKSON, D. A., & WALSH, R. P. Coping with anger and aggression in mourning. *Omega*, 1972, *3*, 271–84.

ROSENTHAL, M. K. The generalization of dependency behaviors from mother to stranger. Unpublished doctoral dissertation, Stanford University, 1965.

ROSENZWEIG, S. The picture-association method and its application in a study of reactions to frustration. *Journal of Personality*, 1945, *14*, 3–23.

————. Outline of a denotative definition of aggression. Paper presented to the first biennial meeting of the International Society for Research on Aggression, Toronto, 1974.

ROSENZWEIG, S., FLEMING, E. E., & ROSENZWEIG, L. The children's form of the Rosenzweig picture frustration study. *Journal of Psychology*, 1948, *26*, 141–91.

RUSSELL, E. W. Factors of human aggression: a cross-cultural factor analysis of characteristics related to warfare and crime. *Behavior Science Notes*, 1972, *4*, 275–307.

SBRZESNY, H. Die Spiele der !Ko-buschleute unter besonderer Berücksichtigung ihrer Sozialisierenden und Gruppenbindenden Funktionen. Monographien zur Human-ethologie, Bd. 2. München: Piper, 1976.

SCHAEFER, E. S. Converging conceptual models for maternal behavior and child behavior. In J. C. Glidewell (Ed.), *Parental attitudes and child behavior.* Evanston, Ill.: Thomas, 1961.

SCHAFFER, H. R. Some issues for research in the study of attachment behaviour. In B. M. Foss (Ed.), *Determinants of infant behaviour II.* London: Methuen, 1963, pp. 179–96.

————. The onset of fear of strangers and the incongruity hypothesis. *Journal of Child Psychology and Psychiatry*, 1966, *7*, 95–106.

SCHAFFER, H. R., & EMERSON, P. E. The development of social attachments in infancy. *Monographs of the Society for Research in Child Development*, 1964, Whole No. 29.

SCHAIE, K. W. A general model for the study of developmental problems. *Psychological Bulletin*, 1965, *64*, 92–107.

SCOTT, J. P. Attachment and separation in dog and man. In H. R. Schaffer (Ed.), *Origins of human social relations.* London: Academic Press, 1971, pp. 227–46.

SEARS, R. R. A theoretical framework for personality and social behavior. *American Psychologist*, 1951, *6*, 476–83.

————. Transcultural variables and conceptual equivalence. In B. Kaplan (Ed.), *Studying personality cross-culturally.* New York: Harper & Row, 1961, pp. 445–55.

————. Separation in apes and children. (Review of J. Bowlby, *Attachment and loss*, Vol. 2: separation: anxiety and anger. New York: Basic Books, 1973. *Contemporary Psychology*, 1974, *19*, pp. 580–82.

SEARS, R. R., MACCOBY, E. E., & LEVIN, H. *Patterns of child rearing.* Evanston; Ill.: Row Peterson, 1957.

SEARS, R. R., RAU, L., & ALPERT, R. *Identification and child rearing.* Stanford: Stanford University Press, 1965.

SEARS, R. R., WHITING, J. W. M., NOWLIS, V., SEARS, P. S. Some child-rearing antecendents of dependency and aggression in young children. *Genetic Psychological Monographs*, 1953, *47*, 135–234.

SELIGMAN, C. G. Anthropology and psychology: a study of some points of contact (Presidential Address). *Journal of the Royal Anthropological Institute*, 1924, *54*, 13–46.

————. Anthropological perspective and psychological theory. (Huxley memorial lecture for 1932). *Journal of the Royal Anthropological Institute*, 1932, *62*, 193–228.

SERPELL, R. *Culture's influence on behaviour.* London: Methuen, 1976.

SHAPIRA, A., & MADSEN, M. C. Cooperative and competitive behavior of Kibbutz and urban children in Israel. *Child Development,* 1969, *40,* 609–17.

SHAW, M. F., & DUTTON, B. E. The use of the parent attitude research inventory with the parents of bright academic underachievers. *Journal of Educational Psychology,* 1962, *53,* 203–08.

SHIRLEY, M., & POYNTZ, L. The influence of separation from the mother on children's emotional responses. *Journal of Psychology,* 1941, *12,* 251–82.

SINGER, M. A survey of culture and personality: theory and research. In B. Kaplan (Ed.), *Studying personality cross-culturally.* New York: Harper & Row, 1961, pp. 9–90.

SINGH, N. P. nAch among successful-unsuccessful and traditional-progressive agricultural entrepreneurs of Delhi. *Journal of Social Psychology,* 1969, *79,* 271–72.

———. nAch among agricultural and business entrepreneurs of Delhi. *Journal of Social Psychology,* 1970a, *81,* 145–49.

———. nAch, risk-taking, and anxiety as related to age, years of schooling, job-experience, and family—commitment among progressive-traditional, successful-unsuccessful agricltural entrepreneurs of Delhi. *Psychologia,* 1970b, *13,* 113–16.

SINGH, N. P., CHANG HUANG, S., & THOMPSON, G. G. A comparative study of selected attitudes, values, and personality characteristics of American, Chinese, and Indian students. *Journal of Social Psychology,* 1962, *57,* 123–32.

SLOGGETT, B. B., GALLIMORE, R., & KUBANY, E. S. A comparative analysis of fantasy need achievement among high and low achieving male Hawaiian-Americans. *Journal of Cross-Cultural Psychology,* 1970, *1,* 53–61.

SMITH, C. P. The origin and expression of achievement-related motives in children. In C. P. Smith (Ed.), *Achievement-related motives in children.* New York: Russell Sage, 1969, pp. 102–50.

SPAIN, D. H. Achievement motivation and modernization in Bornu. Unpublished doctoral dissertation, Northwestern University, 1969.

———. On the use of projective tests for research in psychological anthropology. In F. L. K. Hsu (Ed.), *Psychological anthropology.* Cambridge, Mass.: Schenkman, 1972, pp. 267–308.

SPIRO, M. Social systems, personality, and functional analysis. In B. Kaplan (Ed.), *Studying personality cross-culturally.* New York: Harper & Row, 1961, pp. 93–127.

SPITZ, R. A. Hospitalism: a follow-up report. *Psychoanalytic Study of the Child,* 1946, *2,* 113–17.

———. The role of ecological factors in emotional development in infancy. *Child Development,* 1949, *10,* 145–55.

———. *No and yes.* New York: International Universities Press; London: Bailey and Swinfen, 1957.

———. *The first year of life: a psychoanalytic study of normal and deviant development of object relations.* New York: International Universities Press, 1965.

SPITZ, R. A., & WOLF, K. M. Anaclitic depression: an inquiry into the genesis of psychiatric conditions in early childhood, II. *The Psychoanalytic Study of the Child,* 1946, *2,* pp. 313–42.

STERN, W. *Die differentielle Psychologie in ihren Grundlagen.* Leipzig: Banth, 1911.

————. *Die psychologischen Methoden der Intelligenzprüfung.* Ber. 5. Kongr. exp. Psychol. in Berlin. Leipzig: Barth, 1912, pp. 1–109.

STEVENS, A. G. Attachment behavior, separation anxiety, and stranger anxiety. In H. R. Schaffer (Ed.), *The origins of human social relations.* New York: Academic Press, 1971, pp. 137–46.

STONNER, D. M. The study of aggression: conditions and prospects for the future. In R. G. Geen & E. C. O'Neal (Eds.), *Perspectives on aggression.* New York: Academic Press, 1976, pp. 235–60.

STRODTBECK, F. L. Family interaction, values, and achievement. In D. C. McClelland, A. L. Baldwin, U. Bronfenbrenner, & F. L. Strodtbeck (Eds.), *Talent and society.* Princeton, N.J.: Van Nostrand, 1958, pp. 259–66.

SUMIDA, K., & HAYASHI, K. Rosenzweig P-F study (form for children). Manual of Japanese adaptation (in Japanese), 1956.

————. Rosenzweig P-F study (form for adults). Manual of Japanese adaptation (in Japanese), 1957.

SZEKELY, C. Biological remarks on fears originating in early infancy. *International Journal of Psychoanalysis,* 1954, *35,* 1–11.

TAKALA, A., & TAKALA, M. Finnish children's reactions to frustration in the Rosenzweig test: an ethnic and cultural comparison. *Acta Psychologica,* 1957, *13,* 43–50.

TEDESCHI, J. T., & KIAN, M. Cross-cultural study of the TAT assessment for achievement motivation: Americans and Persians. *Journal of Social Psychology,* 1962, *58,* 227–34.

TEDESCHI, R. E., SMITH, R. C., & BROWN, R. C. A reinterpretation of research on aggression. *Psychological Bulletin,* 1974, *81,* 540–62.

TEXTOR, R. B. *A cross-cultural summary.* New Haven: HRAF Press, 1967.

THOMPSON, L., & JOSEPH, A. *The Hopi way.* Chicago: University of Chicago Press, 1944.

THOMPSON, W. R. Development and the biophysical basis of personality. In E. Borgatta & W. Lambert (Eds.), *Handbook of personality theory and research.* Chicago: Rand-McNally, 1968, pp. 145–214.

THORNDIKE, E. L. *Animal intelligence.* New York: Macmillan, 1911.

————. *The fundamentals of learning.* New York: Teachers College, Columbia University, 1932.

TIDRICK, K. Skin shade and need for achievement in a multiracial society: Jamaica, West Indies. *Journal of Social Psychology,* 1973, *89,* 25–33.

TINBERGEN, N. The study of instinct. Oxford: Oxford University Press, 1951.

TRIANDIS, H. C. Culture training, cognitive complexity, and interpersonal attitudes. In R. W. Brislin, S. Bochner, & W. J. Lonner (Eds.), *Cross-cultural perspectives on learning.* New York: Wiley, 1975, pp. 39–77.

TRIANDIS, H. C., KILTY, K., SHANMUGAM, A. V., TANAKA, Y., & VASSILIOU, V. Cognitive structures and the analysis of values. In H. C. Triandis (Ed.), *The analysis of subjective culture.* New York: Wiley, 1972, pp. 181–261.

TRIANDIS, H. C., & VASSILIOU, V. A comparative analysis of subjective culture. In H. C. Triandis (Ed.), *The analysis of subjective culture.* New York: Wiley, 1972, pp. 299–338.

TRIANDIS, H. C. (Ed.). *The analysis of subjective culture.* New York: Wiley, 1972.

TRIANDIS, L. M., & LAMBERT, W. W. Sources of frustration and targets of aggression: a cross-cultural study. *Journal of Abnormal and Social Psychology*, 1961, *62*, 640–48.

TROMMSDORFF, G. Möglichkeiten und probleme des kulturvergleichs am beispiel einer aggressionsstudie. *Kölner Zeitschrift für Soziologie und Sozialpsychologie*, 1978, *30*, 361–81.

VASSILIOU, V. G., & VASSILIOU, G. The implicative meaning of the Greek concept of *philotimo. Journal of Cross-Cultural Psychology*, 1973, *4*, 326–41.

———. Challenges to traditional psychology from cross-cultural data and perspectives. Unpublished manuscript, 1976.

VERMA, G. K. A use of thematic apperception to assess achievement motivation. *Japanese Psychological Research*, 1973, *15*, 45–50.

VEROFF, J. The development and validation of a projective measure of power motivation. *Journal of Abnormal and Social Psychology*, 1957, *54*, 1–8.

———. Theoretical background for studying the origins of human motivational dispositions. *Merrill-Palmer Quarterly of Behavior and Development*, 1965, *11*, 3–18.

———. Social comparison and the development of achievement motivation. In C. D. Smith (Ed.), *Achievement-related motives in children.* New York: Russell Sage, 1969.

VEROFF, J. Wie allgemein ist das Leistungsmotiv? In W. Edelstein & D. Hopf (Eds.), *Bedingungen des Bildungsprozesses.* Stuttgart: Klett, 1973, pp. 94–148.

VONTOBEL, J. *Leistungsbedürfnis und soziale Umwelt: Zur soziokulturellen Determination der Leistungsmotivation.* Bern: Verlag Hans Huber, 1970.

WALTERS, R. H., & PARKE, R. D. Social motivation, dependency and susceptibility to social influence. In L. Berkowitz (Ed.), *Advances in experimental social psychology,* Vol. 1. New York: Academic Press, 1964.

WALTERS, R. H., & RAY, E. Anxiety, social isolation, and reinforcer effectiveness. *Journal of Personality*, 1960, *28*, 358–67.

WEINER, B. New conceptions in the study of achievement motivation. In B. A. Maher (Ed.), *Progress in experimental personality research,* Vol. 5. New York: Academic Press, 1970, pp. 67–109.

———. *Theories of motivation: from mechanism to cognition.* Chicago: Rand McNally, 1972.

WEINER, B., & KUKLA, A. An attributional analysis of achievement motivation. *Journal of Personality and Social Psychology*, 1970, *15*, 1–20.

WEININGER, O. The effects of early experience on behavior and growth characteristics. *Journal of Comparative and Physiological Psychology*, 1956, *49*, 1–9.

WERBIK, H. *Theorie der Gewalt.* Eine neue Grundlage für die Aggressionsforschung. Stuttgart: Universitäts Taschenbuch 168, 1974.

WESTON, P. J., & MEDNICK, M. T. Race, social class, and the motive to avoid success in women. *Journal of Cross-Cultural Psychology*, 1970, *1*, 284–91.

WHITING, B. B. *Six cultures: studies of child rearing.* New York: Wiley, 1963.

WHITING, B. B., & WHITING, J. W. M. *Children of six cultures: a psycho-cultural analysis.* Cambridge, Mass.: Harvard University Press, 1975.

WHITING, J. W. M. *The frustration complex in Kwoma society. Man*, 1944, *44*, 140–44.

————. Effects of climate on certain cultural practices. In W. H. Goodenough (Ed.), *Explorations in cultural anthropology.* New York: McGraw-Hill, 1964, pp. 511–44.

————. Methods and problems in cross-cultural research. In G. Lindzey & E. Aronson (Eds.), *The handbook of social psychology,* Vol. 2, 2nd ed. Reading, Mass.: Addison-Wesley, 1968.

————. A model for psycho-cultural research. Distinguished lecture address delivered at the annual meeting of the American Anthropological Association. New Orleans, 1973.

WHITING, J. W. M., & CHILD, I. L. *Child training and personality: a cross-cultural study.* New Haven: Yale University Press, 1953.

WIGGINS, J. S., RENNER, K. E., CLORE, G. C., & ROSE, R. J. *The psychology of personality.* Reading, Mass.: Addison-Wesley, 1971.

WINTER, D. G. *The power motive.* New York: Free Press, 1973.

WINTERBOTTOM, M. R. The relation of childhood training in independence to achievement motivation. Unpublished doctoral dissertation, University of Michigan, 1953.

————. The relation of need for achievement to learning experiences in independence and mastery. In J. W. Atkinson (Ed.), *Motives in fantasy, action, and society: a method of assessment and study.* Princeton, N.J.: Van Nostrand, 1958, pp. 453–78.

WOLFF, P. H. The natural history of crying and other vocalizations in early infancy. In B. M. Foss (Ed.), *Determinants of infant behaviour, IV.* London: Methuen, 1969, pp. 81–109.

WOODWORTH, R. S. *Dynamic psychology.* New York: Columbia University Press, 1918.

WORCHEL, S. Societal restrictiveness and the presence of outlets for the release of aggression. *Journal of Cross-Cultural Psychology,* 1974, 5, 109–23.

WRIGHT, G. O. Projection and displacement: a cross-cultural study of folk-tale aggression. *Journal of Abnormal and Social Psychology,* 1954, 49, 523–28.

7

Psychological Aesthetics

D. E. Berlyne

Contents

Abstract

The general problem of empirical work on aesthetics is discussed. Work of a cross-cultural nature using both aritifical material (the synthetic approach) and genuine art material (the analytic approach) is reviewed.

The Contemporary Vantage Point

Contemporary Western cross-cultural psychologists know that, before they embark on the study of psychological aesthetics, they must adopt a neutral, dispassionate stance. Nevertheless, they can hardly have been left untouched by certain attitudes towards the arts that are characteristic in their own society. They must be aware of those attitudes to prevent them from clouding their judgment. And they must understand that these attitudes, some that are conducive to a scientific point of view and some that are not, are frequently absent from other societies. Some of them are likewise infrequent or unknown in earlier periods of their own society's history. Consequently, vestiges of earlier and different views are always apt, for good or for ill, to reemerge.

The Contemporary Concept of Art

In the mid-twentieth century, the most bewildering variety of human behaviors and man-made objects, from the most commonplace to the most outlandish, is being offered as "art." Nevertheless, certain constant beliefs about art underlie this motley assortment of artistic endeavors. They tend to be so thoroughly taken for granted among artists and critics that they form the unquestioned, implicit starting point for any aesthetic discussion. They include the following:

1. the artist is in some ways an abnormal person or misfit, who is apt to suffer misunderstanding and persecution, but who is entitled to exceptional freedoms and permitted eccentricities,
2. the artist is a source of transcendent, and even supernatural, wisdom and insight, and
3. the principal function of a work of art is the artist's self-expression, the communication of his or her personal emotional experiences, ways of perceiving the world, and personally held beliefs.

These assumptions would seem rather strange in other societies and in other centuries. They represent outgrowths of the early nineteenth century Romantic movement and have been firmly rooted only since the leaders of that movement proclaimed them with vehement eloquence.

This is not to deny, of course, that somewhat similar ideas had previously cropped up from time to time, especially in the Hellenistic and Renaissance periods. The first two assumptions, in particular, have their antecedents in the old notions of the *furor poeticus* and of poetic "genius," in the overweening pretensions of many Renaissance artists, in the view of the poet as the mouthpiece of a divine power (found in Homer's invocations and in Plato's *Ion*), and ultimately perhaps in the role of the shaman, whom Lommel (1968) presented as the ultimate ancestor of poetry and music.

These lofty conceptions of the artist's functions were originally applied to the poet-cum-musician, but were gradually extended to the visual arts. The painter, sculptor, and carver have often had a lower social status than those who have worked in other media. This may very well be because they work with their hands and, as Hauser (1951) pointed out, often get them dirty. The poet, musician, narrator, and even dancer, on the other hand, seem to be doing something akin to pure brain work. Visual artists have frequently, both in non-Western cultures and in earlier periods of Western culture, been regarded simply as skilled craftsmen, comparable to practitioners of other handicrafts. In Europe in the Middle Ages, they, like other tradesmen, had their guild, sometimes being grouped together with saddlers. As Wagner's *Mastersingers of Nüremberg* illustrates, poet-composers were sometimes viewed and treated in the same way. In less economically advanced societies, there are often no full-time artists, unless the priest or shaman is counted as such. Visual arts may be practiced as a part-time occupation by those who have a particular aptitude for them or they may even be activities that everybody is expected to engage in, with some individuals achieving recognition for their special proficiency. The artist is therefore seldom the maladjusted, but prophetically gifted near-outcast of the Western stereotype.

Stylistic Relativism

Contemporary Western art lovers, who no doubt include many cross-cultural psychologists in their spare time, are likely to adopt the standpoint so eloquently advocated by Herder (1769, p. 41). They aspire "to appreciate Beauty untrammeled by any national or personal tastes, wherever it is to be found, in all periods, and in all nations, and in all arts, and in all the varieties of tastes . . ." In contrast to the situation that prevailed even a few decades ago, today there are translated poems, novels, dramatic performances, musical recitals, dance performances, recordings, art exhibitions, and books of art reproductions from all parts of the earth's surface and from all periods of history. Each culture and subculture is assumed to have its appropriate artistic style. People may have their favorites. They may find a particular value in the artistic products of their own society, and we may not expect fully to understand or appreciate the products of remote ages and regions. Nevertheless, they expect to derive some enjoyment from them and to use them as a means of vicariously experiencing the outlooks and flavors of human communities that contrast to their own.

Such attitudes are conducive to the open-mindedness that must characterize the cross-cultural researcher. But it is important, for the sake of proper perspective, to realize that such tolerance became widespread only recently and that traces of earlier and very different attitudes have by no means entirely disappeared. Before the nineteenth century, there was a strong tendency to recognize essentially two kinds of artistic style, namely good and bad or right and wrong. In the Middle Ages, good style meant conformity to the relatively rigid norms of Romanesque and, later, Gothic art. From the Renaissance to the early nineteenth century, good style generally meant approximation to the supposedly unsurpassed achievements of the ancient Greeks.

Many of the terms that now designate artistic styles or schools originated as insults and only later became rallying cries in which their partisans gloried. These include "Gothic," "Baroque," "Romantic," "Impressionist," "Cubist," and "Fauve."

One important starting point in the shift towards a more catholic relativistic view is the work of the eighteenth century Italian philosopher of history, Vico (1725). He protested against the assumption of a fixed human nature. He concentrated on Descartes as the prime representative of this view, but it is, of course, implicit in the writings of many earlier and later thinkers. He maintained that human societies go through stages marked by vastly different ways of feeling and thinking, and he pointed out the errors that can result if the biases of the current age are injected into the study of other ages. Like his contemporary, Hamann, who is responsible for the much quoted statement that "Poetry is the mother-tongue of the human race," Vico believed that poetic and pictorial forms of expression were particularly characteristic of a primitive stage of social development.

Herder, apparently independently of Vico, became the spokesman of a more thoroughgoing relativism. He paid attention to the geographical as well as historical diversity of human life and recognized the arts as vehicles of that diversity. Every human society, he asserted, has its own genius, generated by a variety of influences, but particularly by climate. And each of them has its own forms of artistic expression, equally worthy of appreciation and respect. This line of thought reached its most extreme, and ultimately most influential, development in the aesthetic writings of Hegel (1818), for whom the major varieties of artistic style corresponded to phases through which Absolute Mind must necessarily proceed on its way to self-realization.

The writers who have just been discussed were philosophers or critics aspiring at philosophical breadth. Parallel developments among practicing artists and critics likewise gradually ushered in a greater willingness to accept stylistic heterogeneity. Even the ancients recognized the contrasting poetic styles of "atticism," rigorously upholding classical ideals, and "asianism," distinguished by greater freedom and fantasy. Later on, after the norms of classical antiquity had been reasserted by the Renaissance, the Mannerist and Baroque movements showed that they could be flouted. For example, the three unities of place, time, and action, which were usually attributed to Aristotle but were first formulated by Italian Renaissance critics such as Scaliger and Castelvetro, were flagrantly violated by Shakespeare and other dramatists of his period. Their audacities were defended as early as the year 1628 by such critics as Ogier (1628; translated by Clark, 1965, p. 86), who wrote in anticipation of Herder that "the taste of nations is different, as well in matters pertaining to the mind as in those of the body," and that ". . . the minds of nations have preferences quite different from one another, and altogether dissimilar feelings for the beauty of intellectual things, such as poetry. . . ."

Whereas Vico propounded the importance of historical diversity, Montesquieu, a little later (1748), inaugurated the kind of social theory that starts out from geographical diversity. He indicated the differences among the "spirits" of nations, which depend on various physical (e.g., climate, terrain) and moral (e.g., religion, mores, and customs) causes. Different legal and political institutions are appropriate to different spirits. Montesquieu did not have much to say about the arts, but this way of thinking could only discourage any inclination to regard certain canons of style as universally preferable to others.

By the end of the seventeenth century, the sway of classical rules and standards of taste had regained much of its strength throughout Europe. But the long-standing belief that the ancient Greeks and Romans were unapproachable models in matters of art was shaken by the quarrel between the Ancients and the Moderns that broke out at the beginning of the eighteenth century in France and later spread to England. The Moderns dared to suggest that the centuries of experience and progress separating contemporary writers from their classical predecessors could enable them to surpass the latter in some respects at least. But they, like their opponents, were essentially upholders of classical norms.

More serious challenges came in the latter half of the eighteenth century. A curious but nevertheless key episode in the story was the publication in 1760 of the epic poems ascribed to the ancient Gaelic poet Ossian (Oisin). They later turned out to have been largely forged by James McPherson. But for a long time, the most celebrated literary figures in Europe believed in their authenticity and hailed Ossian as a figure comparable with Homer in stature but diametrically opposed to him in style. In contrast with Homer's clear-cut narrative and description, Ossian produced outpourings of mainly melancholy emotion. The two poets were regarded as the exemplars and originators of two equally legitimate but very different kinds of poetry, one proper to the Latin peoples of the Mediterranean region and the other to the Germanic and Celtic peoples of Northern Europe. This distinction is in line with Schiller's (1795) contrast between "naive" and "sentimental" poetry and Madame de Staël's (1810) differentiation between the "literature of the south" and the "literature of the north."

The Romantic movement, which grew up in the first decades of the nineteenth century, carried the questioning of the universal validity of classical norms into full-scale rejection. It spread from literature to music and the visual arts. Its first manifestations met with violent hostility. As has been noted, it established some aesthetic beliefs that have persisted with too little questioning up to the present day. But it demonstrated once and for all that widely differing artistic styles can have their defenders and practitioners.

Romanticism was in its turn suceeded by other styles, beginning with Realism and culminating in the head-spinning parade of innovations that the twentieth century has known. Consequently, the earlier recognitions of a dichotomy within the arts had to be replaced by a recognition of a vast multiplicity of possible styles. This was further encouraged in the late nineteenth century by increasing access to the artistic works of major non-Western cultures, which helped to shake some long-standing attitudes and practices. For example, the profound influence of Japanese prints on Degas and Gauguin, of African masks on Picasso, and of Indonesian music on Debussy is well known. So, after a long, painful, and turbulent process of liberation from parochial preconceptions, humankind has arrived at the openness towards the art of remote cultures to which Malraux (1952) refers as the "imaginary museum."

Psychological Aesthetics

Problems of Definition

The "aesthetic" label seems to many people to designate a reasonably distinct and self-contained department of life or set of activities. In fact, a tendency to exaggerate the division between the aesthetic and the non-aesthetic and to treat aesthetic phenomena as if they had little or nothing in common with anything else has been a persistent obstacle to progress (Berlyne, 1971, Ch. 2). Nevertheless, the difficulties of formulating even a provisional and sketchy definition of aesthetic phenomena are formidable. Aesthetic behavior is acknowledged to include activities, overt or covert, that figure in the creation, performance, and appreciation of painting, sculpture, music, poetry, story-telling, dance, and drama—in other words, of works of art. But the contemporary Western broad conception of "the arts" leaves plenty of room for uncertainty, and not infrequently heated disputes, over what objects and events merit designation by this term. In other cultures comparable categories do not exist. What Westerners recognize as another culture's artistic productions are frequently representations of magico-religious rituals or objects designed for use in such rituals. Or, they are useful implements that have been decorated or shaped with some regard for satisfying form. In any case, aesthetics is concerned not only with artifacts, but also with natural objects and scenes that occasion particular kinds of appreciative or pleasurable reactions, both in Western culture and in others.

In much Western literature on the subject, aesthetics is identified with the analysis and investigation of "beauty." But the connotations of this term are scarcely precise enough for scientific usage, and once again, many non-European languages have no exact equivalents. Furthermore, it is agreed that aesthetics must cover the arts, whatever they may be and whatever else may be covered in addition. But beauty is not always accepted as the predominant attribute of a work of art. Other attributes, including sublimity, interestingness, and even ugliness, have been held forth at one time or another as at least equally important ingredients.

It has sometimes been suggested that works of art and other stimulus patterns possessed of aesthetic value evoke distinctive "aesthetic experience," "aesthetic pleasure," or "aesthetic emotions." If so, the presence of these could serve as a criterion for the definition of aesthetics. But, although some individuals would no doubt claim the ability to recognize beyond any doubt when they are undergoing an aesthetic experience, there is no assurance that an external observer could tell. Certain distinguishing marks have been repeatedly attributed to aesthetic reactions over the years, but they have not been specified with sufficient precision and unanimity to permit them to be reliably detected through verbal reports. As for overt reactions, exposure to works of art and the beauties of nature often produces a suspension of motor activity and a posture of rapt attention, accompanied by facial expressions indicative of intense pleasure or fascination. But responses that cannot easily be distinguished from these are also produced by many stimulus patterns that would hardly qualify as artistic or aesthetic. They are, in fact, recognizable as manifestations or the orientation reaction, a complex of psychophysiological changes occasioned by virtually any novel, unexpected, or striking stimulus event that is not excessively intense, arousing, or painful (Sokolov, 1958; Lynn, 1966).

So, the only recourse that is left is to adopt a provisional definition based largely on stimulus characteristics. First of all, aesthetic activities are forms of intrinsically motivated stimulus-seeking behavior (Berlyne, 1960, 1963, 1966, 1971). They are aimed at exposure to stimulus patterns and, when they are classifiable as instrumental conditioned responses or operants, they are rewarded or reinforced by exposure to stimulus patterns. The stimulation in question may result from artifacts the subject himself has created, from artifacts created by other human beings, or from naturally occurring objects or events.

Next, we note that the stimulus patterns are sought "for their own sake," i.e., that they are satisfying, pleasurable, or rewarding in themselves and not because they lead to, or guide, subsequent responses that have pleasurable or rewarding consequences of their own.

Lastly, it seems clear that whenever artistic or other aesthetic activities are in progress, the stimulus patterns that are sought or that are pleasurable or rewarding are characterized, possibly among other attributes, by structural or formal attributes.

Structural or formal attributes depend on relations among elements. They may be internal relations obtaining among elements of the pattern in question. Alternatively, they may be external relations between elements of the pattern, or the pattern as a whole, and stimuli that have been encountered during the subject's previous life history. The relations that matter in this way may be ones of similarity or dissimilarity. Otherwise, they may be probabilistic relations—statistical interdependences, interpredictabilities, correlations, associations. These are the relations on which the measures introduced by information theory depend (Berlyne, 1974a). Elsewhere (Berlyne, 1960), the term "collative stimulus property" has been proposed to refer to quantifiable structural or formal relations of these kinds. The collative stimulus properties include variations along familiar-novel, expected-surprising, simple-complex, clear-ambiguous, and stable-variable dimensions.

So, to sum up, aesthetics can be conceived of as the study of reactions to stimulus patterns that are attractive, pleasurable, or rewarding, at least in part, because of their collative properties. Discussions of aesthetics are usually confined to visual and auditory stimulation, with the kinesthesia occasionally coming in when dance and perhaps drama are considered. But other sensory modalities can play their part, provided that collative factors are of importance. For example, a flavor that is agreeable simply because it is sweet is outside the domain of aesthetics. But culinary aesthetics can appropriately be recognized when a meal is appealing because of the combinations or successions of flavors that it presents, the degree of novelty or surprise that arises from comparisons with what has been experienced before, or the relations between gustatory sensations and accompanying visual, olfactory, tactual, and kinesthesia sensations (as when referring to the "setting" and the "texture" of food).

Branches of Aesthetics

The problems of aesthetics have occupied scholars associated with a variety of disciplines and subjected to a variety of kinds of training (Berlyne, 1974b), but they fall into two major categories.

Until about a hundred years ago, aesthetic inquiry was confined to what may be called *speculative aesthetics*. This term includes *philosophical aesthetics, art theory*, and *art criticism*. The boundaries between these three disciplines are not very sharp. Art theory is especially difficult to distinguish from art criticism. It includes *art history*. All these forms of inquiry are speculative, in the sense that their conclusions are based on deduction from what seem to an author to be self-evident or plausible premises and on the author's own subjective reactions to aesthetic stimulus patterns. This author's hope is that members of his audience will recognize similarities between their own subjective reactions and his, or that they will for other reasons find his statements convincing and enlightening.

In contrast with these speculative approaches, the last century has seen the advent of research that can be classed as *empirical aesthetics* or *scientific aesthetics*. These represent the application of scientific method to those questions within the field of aesthetics that are amenable to scientific inquiry. Here, it must be noted that the term "science" is being used in the usual English sense. It covers investigations that derive conclusions from publicly observable data with experimental or statistical controls to segregate the effects of concomitants of specific variables. It uses terms whose applicability or nonapplicability to a particular object or event can be determined through observational criteria. It is important to make this clear because of the confusions that have arisen from differences in meaning between the English word "science" and what are often wrongly thought to be corresponding words in other languages, e.g., the French *science* and the German *Wissenschaft*. These continental European terms are not infrequently applied to speculative scholarship. For example, the term "art theory" is a translation of *sciences de l'art*, *Kunstwissenschaft*, etc., and a great deal of confusion and unnecessary dissension has resulted from linguistic misapprehensions.

Although there are parts of physics and of chemistry with some bearing on aesthetic phenomena, empirical aesthetics is associated primarily with the behavioral sciences. *Empirical psychological aesthetics* (which must be given this rather cumbersome label to exclude philosophical and other speculative aesthetic writings concerned with psychological questions) must necessarily play a uniquely fundamental role. But crucial tasks also devolve on *sociological, anthropological,* and even *economic aesthetics*.

Both the speculative and the empirical parts of aesthetics have their strengths and weaknesses. Empirical aesthetics can alone provide testability through observation and prediction, as well as quantitative precision, which are the hallmarks of scientific method. It provides criteria for validity that maximize the chances of intersubjective agreement and provides, if not a guarantee of truth, at least bases for estimating the probability that an assertion will be correct. On the other hand, empirical aesthetics must confine itself to those questions that are capable of scientific treatment and must steer clear of many tasks that excite wide interest, such as the evaluation of works of art and the generation of enthusiasm for their merits.

The proceeds of empirical aesthetics, especially in its early stages, are apt to seem superficial and pedestrian. Speculative aesthetics is more likely to provide a sense of penetration and deep understanding accompanied by emotional involvement. But the pitfalls of subjective judgment leave one, or should leave one, in some uncertainty regarding the validity of its pronouncements. One must note, for example, the disagreements that are so vividly in evidence when the same questions are answered by different speculative authors.

Techniques Available to Empirical Aesthetics

The methods at the disposal of empirical aesthetics generally, and of empirical psychological aesthetics in particular, fall into two classes. Experiments can be conducted in which subjects are exposed to stimulus patterns and other conditions contrived by an experimenter. The aim is to measure the effects of a specific independent variable while other variables that might have influenced the results are held constant, counterbalanced, or allowed to vary in a random, unbiased fashion. Experimental methods are not often applied to aesthetic problems by behavioral scientists other than psychologists. Consequently, *experimental aesthetics*, as it has come to be called, is identifiable with that part of experimental psychology that deals with aesthetic phenomena.

Although experimentation is to be preferred as the only conclusive means of establishing causal relations, it is frequently impracticable for one reason or another. So, psychologists and other behavioral scientists must make much use of *correlational studies*. These consist of examining naturally occurring fluctuations in observable variables and using statistical procedures to detect correlations or associations among them.

The correlational procedures used by empirical psychological aestheticians are heirs of the "method of application" proposed by Fechner (1876). This method consisted in examining works of art or artifacts with a view to drawing conclusions about psychological processes participating in their creation or in their appreciation. So, there have been several investigations, and there could fruitfully be many more, in which objectively identifiable characteristics of artistic products are connected with characteristics of their producers or of their intended audience through appropriate measures of correlation and tests of their significance. A special case is content analysis, taken over from social psychological studies of mass media and other forms of communication (see Holsti, 1968). This technique, whose scope has been immeasurably expanded by the availability of computers, can be used to compare the frequency distributions of particular kinds of elements in works of literature, music, or (although this has been little done as yet) visual art and to determine how far the presence of one kind of element if predictable from the presence of another kind.

Empirical aestheticians have also been making use of a wider and wider assortment of techniques (Berlyne, 1971, 1974b). As far as dependent variables are concerned, verbal judgments, recorded through ratings, rank-orderings, paired comparisons, and other procedures, have been the principal, and at times the only, resort of experimental aesthetics for much of its history. Ways of gathering such data and ways of analyzing them and constructing mathematical models out of them have become more and more elaborate and sophisticated, largely through the influence of methodological advances in psychophysics and in social psychology. However, the "new experimental aesthetics" (Berlyne, 1971, 1974b) that has arisen since the middle 1950s does not confine itself to verbal measures but uses psychophysiological recordings (especially measures of arousal) and of nonverbal behavioral measures (measures of exploratory behavior, reward value, attention).

With respect to stimulus material, experimental aesthetics has to use two approaches, both initiated by Fechner and each having its unique advantages and drawbacks. First, there is the *synthetic* approach, which uses specially designed artificial stimulus patterns. These are usually far from qualifying as works of art or even as aesthetic objects, but they are such as may be found among the components of works of art. Their function, however, is to enable particular independent variables to be manipulated, so that their effects can be isolated. The other approach, the *analytic* approach, uses genuine works of art or excerpts from them. The bewildering complexity of any real-life work of art and the consequent multiplicity of factors that might affect, singly or in combination, a subject's reactions obviously raise problems. They can now be mitigated with the help of multidimensional nonmetric scaling techniques, applied in conjunction with multivariate scaling and behavioral investigations and with canonical correlational analysis (e.g. Berlyne & Ogilvie, 1974; Berlyne, 1975a).

Cross-Cultural Aesthetics

Both speculative and empirical aestheticians have made contributions to cross-cultural aesthetics. So far the greater part of the literature that has appeared on the subject has come out of speculative approaches. A philosophical aesthetician or art theorist will sooner or later be interested in variations in content, in stylistic features, or in objectives, and will distinguish categories of art accordingly. Such distinctions invariably lead to a search for the causes and concomitants of the variations. And the evident ease with which anybody with a little knowledge can identify the historical period and geographical region from which a work of art comes reveals the powerful impact of cultural differences on aesthetic activities.

Accordingly, innumerable studies have analyzed salient characteristics of specific works of art, or of bodies of art associated with particular artists or particular styles, and related them to social and economic conditions or beliefs and values characterizing the communities to which their creators and their audiences belong.

This kind of literature, which forms a great part of the output of critics and art historians, is enlightening and interesting. It is replete with ideas and data that the scientific cross-cultural aesthetician can hardly afford to ignore. But from his point of view it has its drawbacks. Any work of art or class of works of art, like any society, must have numerous attributes. Many of the attributes that are discussed in speculative aesthetic literature are defined with insufficient precision to permit reliable detection, let alone measurement. Consequently, there is a serious possibility of error in determining whether a particular attribute is present or not, and there is room for disagreement in determining which attributes are of major importance.

Speculative aestheticians commonly support their contentions, including those that relate characteristics of art to characteristics of societies, by citing particular instances and endeavoring to show by detailed examination that they fit the views that the author is propounding. But this method of argument, which is comparable to the practice of citing supportive case histories in psychotherapeutic literature, raises doubts in anybody with scientific training: was due attention paid to problems of sampling, i.e., how far the cited examples are representative of the class to which the assertions apply? Or could alternative hypotheses have been found that would account for the facts just as well as those favored by the writer?

It is worth noting that many behavioral scientists who have been concerned with cross-cultural comparisons in aesthetics have occupied a position midway between the speculative and the empirical. This applies to leading figures in anthropology, from Boas's classical treatise (1928) on "primitive" art to the distinctive pronouncements of Levi-Strauss (1958). It also holds true of many sociologists. Such writers have typically been extremely scrupulous and objective in their descriptions of behavior in the communities under study and of artifacts made by them. But they become highly intuitive and subjective when they come to interpret their observations, e.g., when they single out the supposedly major characteristics of a culture and of its art and elucidate the relations between the two. They are then partial to the case history method with all its pitfalls.

Truly empirical studies of cross-cultural aesthetics, with due regard for sampling, isolation of variables, and consideration of alternative hypotheses, started relatively recently. Consequently, those that have been carried out are not numerous, but this chapter will review them. All the techniques of empirical aesthetics are at the disposal of the cross-cultural aesthetician, and all have been some use.

Correlational Studies

Geographically Defined Cultural Variation

In 1949, Murdock introduced the notion of statistical cross-cultural analysis to anthropologists and others interested in the scientific study of cultural variations. The method entails (a) unbiased sampling of cultures, as far as possible (usually limited by the availability of pertinent data), (b) objective characterization of cultures according to the presence or absence of a particular trait or according to the degree to which a particular trait is present, and (c) the use of statistical measures of correlation, association, or contingency, together with tests of significance, to ascertain whether particular traits occur together more often (or less often), or covary more than could be accounted for by chance. The objective classification of cultures sometimes means recording data that can be ascertained without much room for doubt (e.g., size of settled communities, number of levels of government), sometimes the unbiased use of whatever data happen to be recorded in some data bank, and sometimes ratings made by judges with instructions and criteria made as explicit as possible and with statistical tests of interjudge consistency.

Murdock himself used contingency tables and chi-squared tests to establish relations between kinship terms and social structure, based on information drawn from the Cross-Cultural Survey, which was the forerunner of the Human Relations Area Files (see Barry's chapter and Naroll, Michik, and Naroll's chapter in Volume 2 of this *Handbook*). The method can be extremely vauable as an exploratory or hypothesis-generating procedure for use when an investigator is faced with measures on a large number of variables and has no way of telling which ones might be interrelated. But, as Murdock pointed out it is also well suited for the verification or falsification of precisely framed hypotheses.

The first step towards exploiting the immense potential of this method for aesthetics appears to have been that of Barry (1957). He took ten to twenty works from each of thirty nonliterate societies. Characteristics of the socialization practices of each society had been rated as part of a study by Whiting and Child (1953). Barry derived a measure of overall complexity by combining eleven intercorrelated indices descriptive of the art of a society. Severity of socialization turned out to be significantly correlated with the global complexity measure and with two of its component indices, namely *complexity of design* and *representativeness.* Overall complexity was negatively correlated with the rated degree of oral satisfaction. Barry concluded tentatively that complex art is likely to come from societies in which "the typical individual learns self-reliant behavior to a high degree and is punished or frustrated for overt expression of dependence" (1957, p. 382).

Fischer (1961) set out to test his view that "in expressive aspects of culture, such as visual and other arts, a very important determinant of the art form is social fantasy, that is, the artist's fantasies about social situations which will give him security or pleasure (pp. 79–80). He concentrated on what he called "latent content," opposing it to "overt (representational) content." He divided twenty-nine societies into those that were "egalitarian" and those that were "hierarchical." It was hypothesized that egalitarian societies would be characterized by designs embodying "repetition of a number of rather simple elements," designs "with a large amount of empty or irrelevant space," "symmetry," and "figures without enclosures." The art of hierarchical societies should have the contrary characteristics. All four hypotheses were confirmed at an acceptable significance level by a chi-squared test. It was found, moreover, that complex, nonrepetitive designs and a predominance of straight rather than curved lines tend to coincide with a high degree of male solidarity and with nonsororal polygamy. Fischer's hypotheses have received further corroboration from a comparison of Attic vase painting during periods when ancient Athens had differing degrees of social stratification (Dressler & Robbins, 1975).

In an investigation focusing on fifty-three African societies, Wolfe (1969) set out to answer the question, "why do some societies produce much art of high quality, while others produce less art and art of poorer quality?" Scholars of several disciplines made the requisite ratings, and 39 out of 105 cultural characteristics turned out to be significantly correlated with the amount and quality of art. The author's final conclusion was that artistic accomplishment is fostered by a "nucleated settlement pattern and fixity of settlement." Other correlates were the existence of "voluntary associations of men (sodalities) who are not necessarily related, and economic surpluses."

By far the most ambitious, thoroughgoing and exemplary application of statistical cross-cultural analysis to aesthetic problems so far is the Cantometrics project, directed by Lomax (1968). Data from 233 cultures, covering virtually the whole of the earth's surface were taken from Murdock's *Ethnographic Atlas.* Their folk songs were classified on each of thirty-seven traits according to an extremely elaborate coding system. It was found possible to classify the cultures along a complexity dimension whose main index was degree of economic development, ranging from gathering, hunting, and fishing to agriculture with irrigation. But economic complexity was positively related to several indices of social complexity, viz. (1) size of local community, (2) form of settlement (nomadic bands to stable and compact settlements), (3) number of extralocal hierarchies, (4) degree of class stratification, (5) incidence of complexly organized and variable tasks, and (6) incidence of control of work products by management and ownership. An examination of statistically significant correlations revealed a tendency for more complex forms of folk song to appear in more complex societies. The principal outcome of the project is stated to be (p. 133) that "a culture's favored song style reflects and reinforces the kinds of behavior essential to its main subsistence efforts and to its central and controlling social institutions." A large number of more detailed analogies emerged between ways in which a society organizes its economic activities and ways in which individuals collaborate in musical activity.

The Cantometrics project has spawned the Choreometrics project (Lomax, 1968, Ch. 10–12; Lomax, Bartenieff, & Forrestine, 1969) devoted to cross-cultural comparisons of filmed folk dances. Further progress has also been made towards working out an "evolutionary taxonomy of culture" with the help of computerized statistical techniques (Lomax & Berkowitz, 1972). Factor analysis of seventy-one measures reveals nineteen factors, some of them pertaining to social and economic organization, some to characteristics of music, and some to both. The bulk of information contained in the factors can be further boiled down into two higher-order factors or *vectors*. The first of these, labelled *differentiation*, covers "economic productivity, stability of settlements, and centralization of political and social controls together with measures of the amount of information (musical) performance carries, as indicated by the importance of small intervals, precise enunciation, and non-repeated text" (p. 232). It is said to represent "man's concern with differential control of the environment" (p. 232). The second vector, *integration*, has its highest values in gathering and gardening societies, which are respectively lowest and intermediate in differentiation. It reflects "the part played by women in the principal subsistence activity," the "degree to which groups are intergrated by organization" (p. 235) and the cohesiveness of song. The data on dance point to two factors correlated with the differentiation and integration vectors, respectively. The first is a manipulative factor, involving "frequent peripheral movement, three-dimensional movement, and hand and foot synchrony" (p. 236). The other is a "sinuous" factor, reflecting strong feminine and erotic influences, involving "frequent multipart trunk movement, trunk synchrony, successiveness, and flowing quality, trunk presentation, high synchrony, and curving movement" (p. 236).

In all correlational studies, there is some uncertainty about the directions of causal relations. It seems unlikely that aesthetic activities play a large enough part in life for their characteristics to influence social organization and other aspects of culture, although the possibility should perhaps not be ruled out entirely. But there is always the likelihood that characteristics of art are not determined by cultural characteristics that are found to be statistically associated with them but by others that affect both. For example, when investigators like Barry find correlations between socialization practices and artistic style, it is natural to suppose that child rearing influences personality which, in its turn, affects aesthetic preferences. But Lomax's work suggests a different hypothesis, namely that both artistic style and child-rearing practices are dictated by forms of social organization, particularly social complexity.

Berlyne (1969) set out to test the frequently encountered assertion that principal subdivisions of Western paintings tend to be located so as to divide the major axis according to the golden-section ratio (0.618). The stimuli consisted of eighteen Western paintings, sampled, with some attempt at rigor, from the eighteenth, nineteenth, and twentieth centuries, and eighteen oriental paintings, six Indian miniatures, six Japanese prints, and six post-Sung Chinese paintings. All were in the form of colored reproductions of about postcard size. French students were asked to move a rubber band to the position that seemed to coincide with the principal subdivision of each picture. There was no evidence for a predominance of subdivisions approximating the golden section with either Western or Eastern paintings. But there was significantly less intersubject agreement with regard to the location of the main subdivision in Chinese paintings than in the Indian and the Japanese, indicating that the composition of the Chinese paintings was more unified.

Historically Defined Cultural Variation

As already mentioned, countless studies of individual schools of art, individual artists, and individual works have argued in favor of particular ways in which social conditions are alleged to have influenced the form and content of art. The defects of the case history method, on which such studies depend, have already been pointed out. One of them is the selection of instances to illustrate the validity of an assertion. The selection must be at best arbitrary, but, in most cases, it reflects the natural inclination of researchers to focus on instances that conform to their beliefs most fully and to ignore those that do not.

This disadvantage is somewhat mitigated by attempts to cover the whole history of an artistic medium comprehensively. But other faults of the case history method still remain. The identification of the most important attributes of a body of art and of the most important factors at work in a society, out of the hundreds or thousands that can be found to distinguish any two works or any two societies, introduces all the hazards of subjectivity. And anybody who has had the least practical experience with inferential statistics knows how easy it is to acquire an impression that particular conditions are found together more often than they would be by chance when there is actually no justification for this conclusion.

Three surveys of the kind under discussion stand out for their meticulous scholarship and breadth of scope. Pending the execution of studies answering the same questions with more rigorous methodology, they are irreplaceable as sources of information, hypotheses, and prima facie evidence. The first, Hauser's (1951) *The Social History of Art,* is an acknowledged classic.

Kroeber (1944) took up the question of whether there are "clusterings or spurts of high cultural productivity." This relates to the question of whether isolated geniuses are responsible for peaks of artistic achievement or whether these appear only when social conditions are favorable. His monumental compilation of major accomplishments in all arts and in all major civilizations reveals periods of exceptional productivity varying in duration from thirty years to one thousand years. The conclusion is that isolated geniuses are rare and that, in general, "geniuses are the indicators of the realization of coherent nuclear growths of cultural value" (p. 839).

Even more ambitious than these two contributions is the work of Sorokin (1937). He contrasted "ideational" societies, in which "reality is presented as nonsensate and nonmaterial, everlasting Being" and "needs and ends are mainly spiritual," with "sensate" societies, in which reality is "only that which is presented to sense organs," emphasis is placed on flux and becoming, and physical needs receive priority. Sorokin inferred that ideational societies will produce "symbolic" art, depicting "unchanging, ultimate reality," whereas sensate societies will be inclined toward "illusionary" styles, i.e., realism or impressionism, representing the "sensory-perceptual or empirical aspect of reality." He mustered grandiose documentation for his hypotheses, tracing parallels between fluctuations in intellectual orientation and fluctuations in style through the entire histories of painting, music, sculpture, architecture, literature, and literary criticism. Sorokin's taxonomy certainly seems to embody a valuable dimension, with both rational and empirical support, but it is scarcely adequate to the entire range of variation to be found among cultures and among schools of art.

Two imaginative attempts to apply the quantitative methods of scientific inquiry to the historical development of style have been concerned with poetry. J. Cohen (1966) develops a theory attaching importance to the poet's use of semantic, logical, and grammatical deviations from nonpoetic discourse. The deviations serve to confuse the reader momentarily, so that the kind of message that poetry uniquely conveys can be transmitted more effectively. Quantitative analyses, some of them combined with statistical significance tests, show, in accordance with predictions, progressively greater frequency of anomalous usages as French Classical poets are succeeded by Romantics and these in their turn by Symbolists.

Martindale (1975) concluded from various theoretical considerations that the historical development of poetry should be characterized by a progressive increase in "metaphor distance." This is achieved through an increasing "degree of elaboration," i.e., departure from the formulae of ordinary language and logic, and increasing "depth of regression," which means incongruous juxtaposition of ideas and images, as well as content reflecting infantile concerns (indicative of regression in the Freudian sense). An alternation between resorting to these two kinds of contrasts with everyday language is, in fact, predicted. The predictions receive confirmation from careful computerized content analysis of English and French eighteenth and nineteenth century poetry, using a dictionary of terms associated with "regressive imagery" themes. The *Regressive Imagery Dictionary* was also used in another study (Martindale, 1973b), which showed the amount of regressive imagery content in folk tales to be negatively correlated with sociocultural complexity. Economic complexity and child-rearing practices appeared to be of minor importance. Martindale (1973a) also carried out an experiment intended as a small-scale simulation of historical changes in taste.

Martindale is one of several authors, another being Peckham (1965), who see novelty and violation of expectation as indispensable components of all art, so that artists are trapped on a never-resting treadmill of stylistic innovation. But, as Meyer (1967) and Berlyne (1971) have pointed out, they may have been led to exaggerate this feature by excessive concentration on Western art during the last century or two. Some societies, such as those of ancient Egypt and of premodern China, have produced artistic works for centuries, and even millennia, with relatively little stylistic variation.

The study of statistical and other mathematical properties of literary texts has made considerable progress (see, for example, Kreuzer & Gunzenhäuser, 1965; Marcus, 1970), but, so far, it has been mainly to help with problems of attribution and in methodological exercises. Its potential fruitfulness for cross-cultural aesthetics must be vast, but has so far scarcely been exploited. Some statistical analyses of musical works of various periods have been undertaken, usually as a guide to computer composition (e.g., Barbaud, 1966a, 1966b). Youngblood (1960, summarized in J. E. Cohen, 1962) has calculated relative redundancies for pitch alone, finding them higher in Romantic compositions that in Gregorian chant and higher still in rock and roll.

Experiments Using the Analytic
Approach

Cross-cultural experiments studying reactions to genuine works of art (or reproductions of them) have concentrated chiefly on finding out how far members of different cultures agree in their aesthetic preferences or judgments. Extreme forms of cultural relativism would lead one to expect virtually no agreement, aesthetic reactions being determined solely by cultural tradition and by the learning processes through which it is perpetuated.

Two early studies provided no evidence for consistency across cultures. McElroy (1952) showed ten kinds of visual material (various kinds of Western pictures, colored papers, polygons) to Australian aborigines in Arnhem Land and to white Australian students in Sydney. The material within each category was ranked in order of preference. There was significant intragroup agreement for most categories, but little or no correlation between cultural groups. Lawlor (1955) presented eight West African designs to West African and English subjects, who were to select the two they liked best and the two they liked least. Once again, there was evidence for agreement within groups but not between groups.

Child and his collaborators, have, on the other hand, obtained evidence for cross-cultural consistency in subjects with specialized training. Child and Siroto (1965) prepared photographs of masks made by the BaKwele of Congo-Brazzaville and Gabon. Thirteen American art specialists (advanced art students, etc.) and eight BaKwele subjects, of whom four were carvers and four cult leaders, rank-ordered the photographs according to liking and according to judgments of beauty. Correlations between the two groups were positive and significant. Trios of miscellaneous pictures (abstract paintings, still-life drawings, Bambara headpieces) were arranged in order of preference by American art students and teachers, by Fijian skilled craftsmen, and by craftsmen from the Greek Cycladic Islands (Ford, Prothro, & Child, 1966). Judgments of Fijian and American subjects showed a positive but not significant correlation, although the responses of two Greek artists closely resembled those of the American subjects.

Morris (1956, Ch. 4) found evidence of agreement between subjects of different cultures who were not art specialists. Eleven Western paintings were ranked by American, Chinese, and Indian students. The rankings of the Chinese and Indian groups showed a high correlation. Correlations of both oriental groups with the Americans were markedly lower. Examining the differences in greater detail, Morris attributes them to the fact that "Western man has emphasized individuality, while Oriental man has stressed man's embedment in the cosmos."

Francès and Tamba (1973) extended this kind of research to music. They prepared ten pairs of Japanese musical excerpts. One group of subjects consisted of Japanese musicology students, and there were three French groups, consisting, respectively, of music students, professional musicians, and nonmusic students. Paired comparisons for preference and 7-point ratings for degree of liking were the data. Japanese subjects showed the greatest intragroup agreement, with French expert groups showing somewhat less. But there was no sign of cross-cultural agreement. The judgments of Japanese experts were unrelated to those of French nonmusicians, and there was a tendency for those of Japanese and French experts to be inversely correlated.

A few other investigations have gone beyond the simple comparison of preferences or evaluations among cultural groups and compared more specific psychological processes. American undergraduates were exposed by Voorhees (cited by Pratt, 1961) to folk music from five cultures. Adjectives descriptive of the mood represented by each piece had been selected by musicologists. The undergraduates showed above-chance agreement with the experts when required to match pieces with adjectives in their turn.

Machotka (1963) found similar developmental stages in the reactions to paintings of French and American children ranging in age from six to eighteen. When required to indicate preferences and the reasons for them, subjects of both nationalities emphasized color under the age of seven; realism, harmony, and clarity from seven to twelve; and style, composition, tone, and luminosity after the age of twelve.

Results obtained by Child (1965) on personality correlates of aesthetic judgment among American undergraduates were tested on Japanese undergraduates by Child and Iwao (1968). The subjects were shown eighty pairs of slides, bearing reproductions of miscellaneous art from a variety of cultures. Half of them had to select the preferred member of each and the other half the one judged to be aesthetically superior. The degree of agreement with American experts was taken as a measure of *aesthetic sensitivity*. There were low but significant correlations between the aesthetic-sensitivity scores of the Japanese scores and tests of *independence of judgment, tolerance of ambiguity,* and *regression in the service of the ego*, personality traits that had had high correlations with the aesthetic sensitivity in Americans.

It was mentioned earlier that the various techniques of multidimensional scaling that have been introduced during the last decade would seem to have great potential usefulness for experimental aestheticians adopting the analytic approach. These techniques can guide researchers towards the attributes of works of art that predominantly govern subjects' perceptions or reactions among the multitudinous attributes that every work must possess. In conjunction with other techniques, e.g., rating scales, they can help in the construction of dimensional systems for classifying styles, based on the responses of particular populations of subjects, in contrast with the more usual taxonomies derived from the judgments of specialists in art history and criticism. For the cross-cultural psychological aesthetician, one question of obvious interest is to what extent subjects of different societies react preponderantly to the same characteristics of art. Although multidimensional-scaling procedures can be applied to a wide variety of kinds of data, dimensions indicative of the most decisive attributes of stimuli are usually derived from pairwise ratings of similarity. Consequently, comparison between the similarity judgments of subjects of different cultures faced with the same stimulus material is what will reveal the degree to which their perceptions reflect the same attributes.

An initial investigation of this kind was carried out by Berlyne (1975c) with a collection of ten postcard reproductions of Western paintings, ranging from Leonardo Da Vinci to twentieth century nonrepresentational works. Responses of ten illiterate Indian villagers, ten Indian students, and ten Canadian students were compared. The first finding of interest was the presence of significant intersubject agreement within each of the three groups, showing that even the Indian villagers, who had never had any experience of comparable tasks and had never encountered paintings resembling those presented to them, could record similarity judgments reflecting the characteristics of the paintings. Even more impressive was the fact that all intergroup correlations between mean similarity judgments over pairs of paintings were significant. However, analysis of variance showed a significant Groups x Pairs of Paintings interaction, so that the results indicate some similarity and at the same time some difference among the judgments of the three populations of subjects. The dimensions issuing from a multidimensional (INDSCAL) analysis of the similarity judgments were compared with the mean ratings of the same paintings on various scales by Canadian students. There were some divergences among the three groups with respect to the patterns of correlations. But in every group, the first INDSCAL dimension had a high and significant correlation with the judged degree to which a painting reproduced the appearance of objects or people and with the degree to which mean ratings on a SOMBRE-BRIGHT scale approached the SOMBRE pole.

Experiments Using the Synthetic Approach

The older experimental aestheticians probably spent more time on color preference than on any other topic. Experimenters from Cohn (1894) to Helson and Lansford (1970) have gathered data on evaluative judgments applied to single patches of color, color combinations, and colors on different backgrounds. With Western subjects, similar rank-orderings of hues have repeatedly emerged, with blue generally coming first. Garth (1931) and Eysenck (1941) reviewed studies extending this work to subjects of differing culture and skin pigmentation. The results support Garth's conclusion that "there are no racial differences in color preferences."

Several experimenters, beginning with Fechner (1865), reported evidence that Western subjects tend to prefer the golden-section rectangle, whose longer side is 1.618 times as long as its shorter side, to rectangles whose sides have other ratios. There has, however, been some controversy over this generalization (see Berlyne, 1971, Ch. 14).

An experiment by Berlyne (1970) was designed to find out whether the golden-section rectangle has a special appeal for non-Western subjects. Some theories, invoking inherent characteristics of the nervous system or visual apparatus, suggest that it will. The subjects were seventeen- and eighteen-year-old high school girls from rural areas in Japan and in Canada. An analysis of first choices and mean rankings revealed no salience of the golden-section rectangle in either group. But it turned out that Canadian subjects had a greater liking for rectangles in the general neighborhood of the golden section, whereas Japanese subjects were more inclined to prefer less elongated rectangles, i.e., those nearer to the square. It transpired after the experiment had been completed that two earlier experiments carried out in Japan had indicated that "Japanese tend to prefer rectangles nearer a square than the golden section."

Exponents of the new experimental aesthetics, when they have adopted the synthetic approach, have concentrated their attention on the collative stimulus variables, especially novelty and complexity, since they seem to be indispensable ingredients of aesthetic patterns, whatever other factors may be at work also.

Cross-cultural data illustrating the importance of novelty have been reported by Robbins (1966). He related Barry's (1957) ratings of relative predominance of straight and curved lines in the art of certain societies to information derived from the *Ethnographic Atlas* on the usual shapes of the houses built by those societies. Statistical analysis showed that societies with circular houses tended to produce linear art, while societies with rectangular houses produced curvilinear art. Robbins' conclusion is that "for an art object to be cognitively preferred and aesthetically satisfying, it should contain certain 'properties' *different* from those normally experienced" (pp. 747–48).

Investigators on motivational effects of complexity have often used polygons with varying numbers of randomly located vertices. Many experiments with Western subjects have shown rated complexity to be higher, the more numerous the vertices. Eysenck and Iwawaki (1971) asked British students and Japanese students to rate polygons for degree of liking on a 5-point scale. The correlation over polygons between mean ratings in the two groups was high and positive. A similar experiment was carried out by Soueif and Eysenck (1971) with British and Egyptian art students and nonart students. Polygons were rated on a 7-point scale according to how pleasing they were. Once again, there were high positive intergroup correlations and no significant intergroup differences.

Robbins collaborated with Berlyne (Berlyne, Robbins, & Thompson,

1974) in a study using visual patterns (see Figure 7-1) from a collection that Berlyne and his collaborators have used in numerous experiments on motivational effects of complexity. The patterns form pairs, each having a "less complex" (LC) or "less irregular" and a "more complex" (MC) or "more irregular" member. Different sets of patterns represent distinct variables that are covered by the term "complexity" in everyday usage. The variables also represent differences in amount of information and redundancy in the information-theoretic senses of these terms. Data were gathered from one hundred urban, one hundred rural, and one hundred intermediate Baganda subjects in Uganda. The same procedures, apart from translation of Luganda words into English, were repeated with thirty Canadian students to permit cross-cultural comparison. Measures of Looking Time, ratings on 7-point scales, and paired comparisons for "pleasingness" and "attractiveness" were obtained.

There were, as one would expect, some differences between Ugandan and Canadian subjects and fewer among the three Ugandan populations. But the similarities were greater than the differences and, in the case of the verbal measures, were quite striking. For example, the factor structures derived from intercorrelations of verbal ratings made by Ugandans and Canadians resembled each other quite closely. Moreover, the same three out of seven rating scales, and the same one out of two estimated factor scores, showed high correlations with Looking Time in both nationalities. There was evidence in either culture for the tendency to look longer at more complex patterns that has been found repeatedly with Western subjects. But this tendency was less pronounced in the Ugandans, although it increased from the rural to the intermediate and from the intermediate to the urban population.

The same procedure (apart from paired-comparison judgments of attractiveness) and the same stimulus material were subsequently used in India with thirty illiterate villagers and thirty students (Berlyne, 1975b), with the labels of the scales translated into colloquial Hindi. Not all the findings that had been common to the Ugandans and the Canadians reappeared with the Indians. But there was still abundant evidence for cross-cultural similarities. With regard to Looking Time, the mean scores of the two Indian groups were significantly correlated over patterns, as those of the three Ugandan groups had been. However, the Indian and Ugandan villagers' scores were not. The Indian students, like the urban Ugandans, showed, however, a significant correlation with the Canadians suggesting that relatively urbanized subjects occupy an intermediate position between the Canadians and their rural compatriots. They may reflect learning experiences that life in modern cities imposes on their inhabitants. Once again, the preference paired-comparison procedure showed the LC (less complex) members of certain pairs and the MC (more complex) members of other pairs to be favored. On the whole, the Indian students

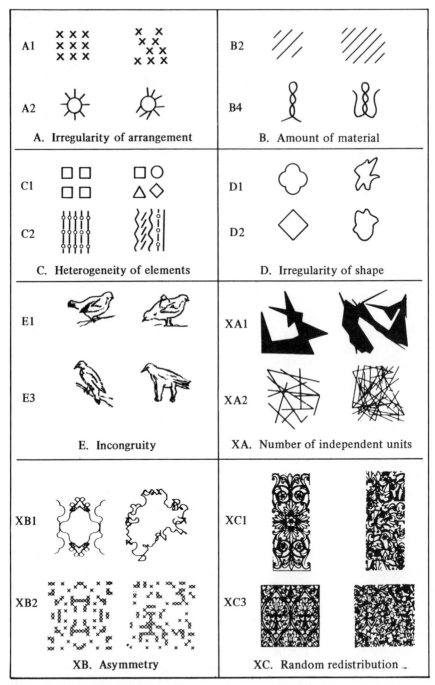

A1

A2

A. Irregularity of arrangement

B2

B4

B. Amount of material

C1

C2

C. Heterogeneity of elements

D1

D2

D. Irregularity of shape

E1

E3

E. Incongruity

XA1

XA2

XA. Number of independent units

XB1

XB2

XB. Asymmetry

XC1

XC3

XC. Random redistribution

Figure 7-1   Patterns Used in Experiments by Berlyne, Robbins, and Thompson, 1974 and by Berlyne, 1975b

tended to make more LC choices than the Indian villagers, just as the Canadian students had made more LC choices than the Ugandans. However, when the number of subjects in each group selecting the LC member of each pair was examined and intercorrelated over pairs among groups, every one of these six groups of subjects was significantly correlated with every other one, indicating some degree of universality in relative degrees of preference for different patterns. The factor analyses derived from the two Indian groups were, again despite translation into yet another language, similar to those derived from the Ugandans and Canadians. Finally, although there were no significant correlations in the Indian villagers between mean Looking Time and scores derived from scaling, the mean Looking Times in the Indian students, like those of the Ugandans and Canadians, were significantly correlated with the Uncertainty factor but not the Hedonic Tone factor.

Similar procedures and patterns from the same collection were used by Francès (1970) to compare the reactions of representatives of two subcultures in France. Two groups of subjects were drawn, respectively, from students and from factory workers of the same age. The students, like student subjects participating in earlier experiments by Berlyne and collaborators, judged more complex patterns more interesting but expressed greater verbal preference for less complex patterns. In the workers, on the other hand, both preference and interestingness judgments favored the less complex patterns. The workers, but not the students, tended to look longer at those members of pairs that they said they preferred and also found more interesting, which were generally the less complex ones. This is contrary to the usual finding with students and other subjects of comparable education, namely longer inspection of more complex material.

A similar experiment was carried out later by Francès (1973) with some improvements in design. That time, both students and workers judged more complex items more interesting but, whereas students were more likely to prefer the more complex items, the workers preferred the less complex items. The apparent discrepancy between this configuration of results and the one reported in the 1970 article is made more intelligible by Francès's examination of what happened with particular pairs of patterns, illustrating different variables commonly covered by the term *complexity*. When the more complex pattern differed from its less complex counterpart in having more numerous elements or more heterogeneous elements, both workers and students tended to prefer it and to judge it more interesting. When, however, the more complex item was characterized by incongruity (i.e., unexpected juxtaposition of elements) or disorderly arrangement of elements, the students were likely to prefer it, but the workers were likely to prefer its less complex counterpart. Both groups, however, judged it more interesting. A subsequent experiment, concerned with the same independent variables but using photographs of arrangements of three-dimensional objects, produced remarkably similar findings.

Vitz (1966) constructed an exceptionally valuable set of auditory stimulus material, permitting investigation of effects of uncertainty in the strict information-theoretic sense on various verbal and nonverbal forms of behavior of interest to experimental aesthetics. The material consists of 20-second sound sequences, each consisting of forty sine-wave tones. Each tone has a frequency, a duration, and a loudness selected randomly and independently from a set of alternatives. There are six levels of uncertainty, depending on the number of alternatives from which each tone is selected. The total number of combinations of a frequency, a loudness, and duration, and thus of possible tones, varies from two (1 bit of uncertainty per tone) at level 1 to 576 (9.17 bits of uncertainty per tone) at level 6. Crozier (1973, 1974) has carried out an extensive series of experiments using Vitz's sequences and others derived from them constructed with the aid of a computer. He found the mean rating on a 7-point SIMPLE-COMPLEX scale to be a remarkably smooth linear function of uncertainty per tone. Several other measures also showed a tendency to increase with uncertainty. They included UNINTERESTING-INTERESTING judgments and Listening Time. Other measures, including DISPLEASING-PLEASING and UGLY-BEAUTIFUL ratings, produced inverted U-shaped curves, when plotted against uncertainty. Exploratory Choice (probability of choosing a particular sequence for further listening when it had been presented together with another) seemed in general to rise and then fall as uncertainty rose. But a more detailed analysis showed individual subjects to differ in the extent to which choices were governed by a factor monotonically related to uncertainty and a factor nonmonotonically related to it.

Bragg and Crozier (1974) used similar sequences in an experiment whose twelve subjects were drawn from among visitors to a science museum, and were thus representative of a somewhat larger segment of the population than the usual undergraduate subject pool. Their sequences differed from those constructed by Vitz in (a) having frequencies whose intervals corresponded to those of the chromatic scale with equal-temperament tuning, and (b) having durations that were integral multiples of one another, producing the impression of a metrical rhythm. The procedures included rating scales and measurement of Exploratory Choice. Since Bragg and Crozier used sequences resembling the original Vitz material for their Listening-Time experiment, data were later gathered, with the modified sequences, from an additional twelve subjects belonging to the same population. Because these data were available to represent a Canadian population, the same sequences, and some of the same procedures, were used with subjects in other parts of the world. Ratings were recorded by thirteen students in the Ivory Coast, thirty Indian students, thirty Indian villagers, and twenty-four Japanese subjects, consisting of twelve nonmusic students and twelve mothers of kindergarten children. The labels for the scales were translated into Hindi, French, and Japanese, respectively for these populations.

Figure 7–2 presents curves for the different groups of subjects showing mean ratings on four of the scales. In what follows, the letters L and Q denote respectively the existence of significant linear and quadratic components of the trend, as revealed by analysis of variance. In the SIMPLE-COMPLEX scale (Fig. 7–2a) there is a tendency for the mean rating to rise with increasing uncertainty in all groups (L in all cases, Q also in the Indian students only). As for the UNINTERESTING-INTERESTING ratings (Fig. 7–2b) there is a predominantly rising trend among the Canadians and among the Indian villagers (L and not Q), whereas, for the other groups the function appears to rise to a peak and then decline (Q and not L). While questions must always arise with regard to the equivalence of translated terms, these questions are particularly acute in the case of the UNINTERESTING-INTERESTING scale in view of the relatively recent date with which the word "interesting" acquired its present connotations in English and other European languages. Except for the Indian villagers (L and not Q), whose mean ratings drop as uncertainty rises, all groups produce inverted U-shaped curves for the DISPLEASING-PLEASING scale (Q and not L in all groups, except the Indian students, for whom L and Q), but the location of the peak varies from group to group (Fig. 7–2c). A similar tendency for intermediate uncertainty levels to receive high scores on the UGLY-BEAUTIFUL scale is in evidence (Fig. 7–2d), although, in the Indian villagers, the Uncertainty main effect is significant but not L or Q. In the other groups, Q is significant, as L also is in the Indian students and the Japanese groups.

Data on the two nonverbal measures are available for Indian and Canadian subjects only (refer to Fig. 7–2e, f). One of these is *Listening Time:* the subjects hear all the sequences in random order and listen to each for as long as they wish. The other is Exploratory Choice: the subjects hear the first half of two sequences and press one of two buttons, thus deciding which of the two sequences they will hear continued. The groups of subjects participating in these last two experiments were distinct from each other and from those carrying out the scaling. In the case of *Exploratory Choice,* there was a slight difference in technique between the Canadian and Indian subjects, because of the limitations imposed on field work. The Canadians actually heard a continuation of whichever sound sequence they selected from each pair, while the Indians simply stated which one they would like to hear continued but did not actually hear any more of it.

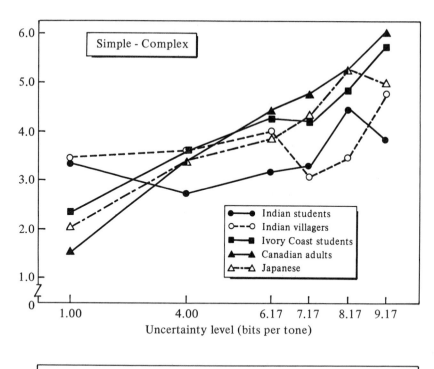

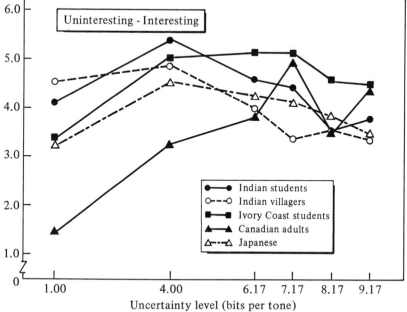

Figure 7-2   Results of Experiments on Verbal and Nonverbal Responses to Random Sound Sequences Varying in Uncertainty Level

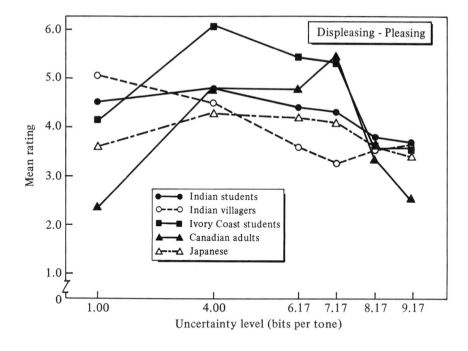

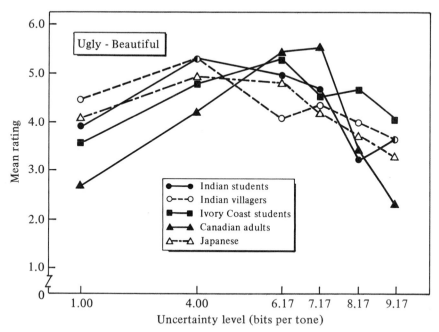

Figure 7-2   (continued)

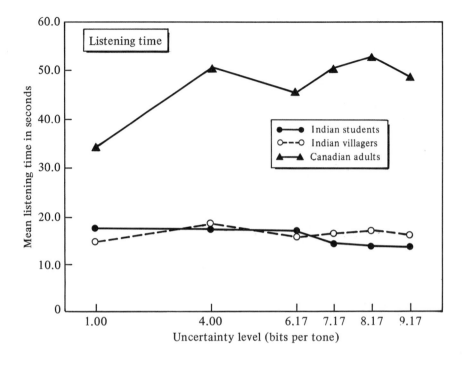

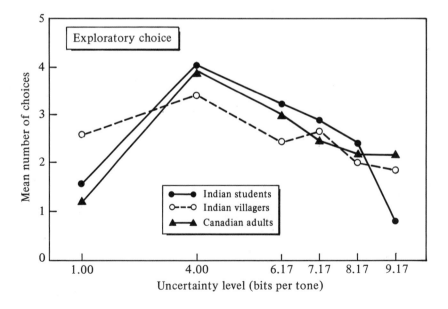

Figure 7-2   (continued)

There is no knowing how much this difference affects choices. So, some caution must be exercised in comparing the findings obtained from the two nationalities. However, the relevant curves for the nonverbal techniques are shown in Figure 7–2e, f. In the case of *Listening Time*, analysis of variance was carried out on logarithmically transformed data, because there was a great variation from subject to subject in mean Listening Time and the proportionate durations allotted to sequences of differing uncertainty level are what matter. As far as the Canadians and the Indian villagers are concerned, the main effect of Uncertainty is significant in both cases, but L and Q are not. The curves suggest that for the Canadians the lowest Uncertainty level produced markedly less Listening Time than the other levels, although other experiments with Western subjects have generally confirmed a tendency for mean Listening Time to increase with uncertainty (and for mean Looking Time to increase with uncertainty level when visual-type patterns are used). In the Indian villagers, there seems to be an irregular pattern that is difficult to interpret. In the students, on the other hand, both L and Q are significant. They have an inverse relation between mean Listening Time and Uncertainty, which although not very steep is confirmed by the statistical test ($p < .01$). This trend is difficult to explain, since no previous experiment with any kind of stimulus material has ever shown a decline in Exploration Time as uncertainty increases. There is usually a rise with an occasional hint of a flattening out or the beginnings of a decline as upper extremes of Uncertainty are approached.

The results are clearer for Exploratory Choice. In the Canadians and the Indian students, there is an inverted U-shaped relation between the mean number of times each level was chosen and the uncertainty level, with a maximum corresponding to level 2 (4.00 bits per tone) in both populations. Nonparametric trend analysis showed significant bitonicity in both groups, with, in addition, a significant monotonic component. The Indian villagers, on the other hand, are less likely to choose a sequence the higher its uncertainty level. Their monotonic component, but not their bitonic component, reaches significance. This is in line with the decline in rated Pleasingness with increasing uncertainty that was evident in the other subjects from the same Indian rural population.

Concluding Comments

The initial phase of cross-cultural empirical aesthetics, which is still in progress, has had one relatively modest objective. This is to ascertain how far findings obtained with subjects from the predominant cultures of Europe and North America can be generalized to other populations or, in other words, to what extent there are universals in the domain of psychological aesthetics. That societies differ in their aesthetic tastes and artistic styles is indisputable. It has been amply confirmed by such cross-cultural investigations as have been carried out.

But many impressive similarities among cultures have also come to light. Evidence is accumulating for the existence of principles of aesthetic reaction that are valid for the human race as a whole. Even when intercultural differences have been discovered, the same independent variables are often found to govern aesthetic behavior. But shapes of curves, slopes, and locations of peaks may differ from one society to another, so that the differences amount to differences in degree. Art all over the world, it appears, exhibits a common dependence on certain dimensions of variation related to collative stimulus properties, even if the preferred segments of these dimensions vary from society to society.

Nevertheless, it has not infrequently been suggested that aesthetic preferences are entirely a matter of cultural relativism, so that there is no hope of discussing aesthetics in relation to human beings in general in any but the most vacuous terms. The contrary view, holding that aesthetic behavior derives from universal and fundamental characteristics of the human nervous system and therefore offers the royal road to the discovery of these characteristics, is incompatible with extreme relativism and would seem to have received appreciable vindication from existing data.

Before long, however, this initial task of probing the generalizability of findings should be near completion, and a second phase should be in full swing. The prime task of the second phase will be to carry further the initial steps towards establishing correlations between cultural characteristics and characteristics of aesthetic preference and seeking the reasons for them. This requires (a) objective ways of measuring preferences, (b) objective ways of classifying artistic styles and measuring their attributes, and (c) objective ways of classifying cultures and measuring their attributes.

With regard to the first of these, the measurement of preferences, we can say that experimental aesthetics and other areas of behavioral science, including social psychology and decision theory, have made substantial progress. Several techniques that can be regarded as means of measuring preferences have come into use. But it has become evident that these techniques are not necessarily measuring the same thing, so that the term *preference* is a treacherous one used at different times to designate several distinct phenomena or variables (Berlyne, 1971, 1973b). Some verbal judgments that could be indicative of preference, such as ratings on GOOD-BAD, DISPLEASING-PLEASING, and UGLY-BEAUTIFUL scales, are generally highly correlated, and it is safe enough to regard them as reflections of one underlying variable called *Hedonic Tone* (Berlyne, 1973a, 1974b). Other forms of verbal evaluation, such as UNINTEREST-ING-INTERESTING ratings, behave differently and are evidently reflecting a different variable or set of variables. Various measures derived from observation of nonverbal behavior, such as Exploration Time, Exploratory Choice, and reward value, might also be thought of as indices of *preference*. But their relations to one another, as well as to verbal evaluative judgments, are complicated. Now a broad and useful armory of measures of *preference* permit the study of *preference* in several senses of the term, which need to be distinguished. An implication is that experimenters purporting to investigate cultural determinants of preference must take care to use several of these measures, as they are likely to give different kinds of information.

With the help of the analytic approach, using multidimensional scaling in conjunction with multivariate techniques, some modest initial advances have been made towards the second goal, that of constructing objective taxonomies of artistic style (e.g., Berlyne & Ogilvie, 1974; Berlyne, 1975a; Hare, 1975; Wedin, 1972). It is encouraging that at least some of the dimensions coming out of this kind of work resemble concepts that have figured for a long time in the writings of art historians. But their nature and purposes are different, and the newer taxonomies, with their greater precision and their origin in the reactions of nonexpert appreciators with tests for interjudge reliability, make them more suitable for scientific cross-cultural comparisons.

Finally, there is the need for an objective taxonomy of cultures. Its lack is an impediment to all branches of cross-cultural research, not only to cross-cultural aesthetics, and it is bound to be discussed in other chapters of this *Handbook*. The categorizations of societies that are found in anthropological and sociological writings are all too often reminiscent of the very early days of personality study. Some of them, even though they have been produced by investigators with a scrupulous concern for objective recording of ethnographic data, belong essentially with the idiographic descriptions of personalities that were favored by the "Understanding" school of psychologists in Germany at the beginning of the century. With their emphasis on the uniquenesses and cohesive unity of a culture pattern, they can have great literary richness and convey the flavor of a society vividly. But they do not have the quantitative precision and interjudge consistency that cross-cultural empirical aesthetics necessitates.

Many classifications consist of typologies. Some of them based on clearly defined criteria of economic or social organization have undoubted value. Others, such as Benedict's (1934) adaption of Nietzsche's Apollonian-Dionysian dichotomy, possess all the shortcomings of early descriptions of personality types, including commitment to debatable theoretical preconceptions.

Cattell (1948, 1949, 1950) has tried to bring the classification of culture into line with up-to-date dimensional or trait approaches to personality by using multivariate techniques to identify continua along which culture patterns or, as he calls them, "syntalities" can vary. He showed how his technique could be applied to the characterization of sixty-nine nationalities. Cattell's example was followed and extended by Sawyer and Levine (1966), who intercorrelated thirty attributes of 565 cultures, with factor analysis yielding nine substantial factors chiefly descriptive of economic and social structure. Rummel's (1972) comparably ambitious analysis of 235 variables characterizing seventy-nine nations revealed fifteen main dimensions descriptive of socioeconomic-political organization and international relations.

Such taxonomies may well prove useful in the search for cultural correlates of aesthetic variables. But other classificatory dimensions with more psychological content are likely to have greater promise for cross-cultural aesthetics, at least initially. First, there are indices of *social complexity*. Variations along simplicity-complexity continua have proved to be important attributes of works of art as far as appreciators' reactions are concerned, and research such as Lomax's (1968), indicates close connections between complexity in artistic style and complexity in social organization and activity. Lomax and Berkowitz's (1972) method, locating societies along *differentiation* and *integration* dimensions, has already been mentioned. Murdock and Provost (1973) introduced another procedure, based on ten descriptive scales, for classifying societies according to their degree of *cultural complexity*.

Then, there were two proposals for scaling societies according to characteristic levels of *anxiety*. What the term *anxiety* denotes here is clearly closely related to the concept of *arousal*. There is an abundance of indications (Berlyne, 1967, 1971) that fluctuations in arousal have a great deal to do with reward value and pleasure, including aesthetic pleasure. There is also plentiful evidence that conditions leading to changes in arousal level can modify the relative appeal of different degrees of novelty, complexity, and other collative variables. Cattell and Scheier (1961) derived their measure of anxiety from questionnaires constructed with the guidance of factor analysis, and showed how it differentiated six nationalities. Lynn (1971) derived his homonymous measure from a number of sociological indices that turn out to be correlated, such as calorie intake, suicide rate, death rate from alcoholism, and hospitalized mental illness. He used it to compare the national characters of eighteen countries.

Some of the cross-cultural studies reviewed have examined artifacts produced by different societies. Others have studied the reactions of subjects to selected stimulus patterns in laboratory conditions or in the nearest approaches to laboratory conditions that are possible in field work. One final kind of information with great potential value for cross-cultural aesthetics has been sought surprisingly seldom. It has received little attention even from behavioral scientists concentrating on Western populations. The information in question concerns the relative frequency of particular kinds of aesthetic patterns among human beings who are not creative artists. A start was made by members of the Institut d'Esthétique et des Sciences de l'Art in Paris (Roubertoux, 1970). These authors have examined the incidence of artistic pursuits, as compared with one another and with other leisure activities, in France. They have also shown how inclinations to engage in particular aesthetic activities are related to personality and demographic factors. It may be thought that this kind of research belongs to the province of the anthropologist or sociologist rather than to that of the psychologist. Be that as it may, the study of how often, and in what circumstances, aesthetic behavior actually occurs in different human societies can surely be enlightening with reference to problems of psychological aesthetics and of psychology in general.

Note

1. The preparation of this chapter and research by the author reviewed in it were supported by research grants A-73 from the National Research Council of Canada and S-72-1405-X2 from the Canada Council.

References

BARBAUD, P. *Initiation à la composition musicale automatique.* Paris: Dunod, 1966.

―――. Structure et simulation de l'harmonie classique et de son evolution. *Sciences de l'Art,* 1966b, *3,* 147–53.

BARRY, H. Relationships between child training and the pictorial arts. *Journal of Abnormal and Social Psychology,* 1957, *54,* 380–83.

BENEDICT, R. *Patterns of culture.* Boston: Houghton Mifflin, 1934.

BERLYNE, D. E. *Conflict, arousal, and curiosity.* New York: McGraw-Hill, 1960.

―――. Motivational problems raised by exploratory and epistemic behavior. In S. Koch (Ed.), *Psychology—a study of a science,* vol. 5. New York: McGraw-Hill, 1963.

―――. Curiosity and exploration. *Science,* 1966, *153,* 25–33.

―――. Arousal and reinforcement. In D. Levine (Ed.), *Nebraska symposium on motivation,* Lincoln, Neb.: University of Nebraska Press, 1967.

―――. La section d'or et la composition picturale occidentale et orientale. *Sciences de l'Art,* 1969, *6,* 1–5.

―――. The golden section and hedonic judgments of rectangles: a cross-cultural study. *Sciences de l'Art/Scientific Aesthetics,* 1970, *7,* 1–6.

―――. *Aesthetics and psychobiology.* New York: Appleton-Century Crofts, 1971.

———. Interrelations of verbal and nonverbal measures used in experimental aesthetics. *Scandinavian Journal of Psychology*, 1973a, *14*, 177–84.

———. The vicissitudes of aplopathematic and thelematoscopic pneumatology (*or* The hydrography of hedonism). In D. E. Berlyne & K. B. Madsen (Eds.), *Pleasure, reward, preference*. New York: Academic Press, 1973.

———. Information and motivation. In A. Silverstein (Ed.), *Human communication: theoretical explorations*. Hillsdale, N. J.: Arlbaum, 1974.

———. The new experimental aesthetics. In D. E. Berlyne (Ed.), *Studies in the new experimental aesthetics: steps toward an objective psychology of aesthetics appreciation*. Washington, D.C.: Hemisphere, 1974b.

———. Dimensions of perception of exotic and pre-Renaissance paintings. Unpublished manuscript, 1975a.

———. Extension to Indian subjects of a cross-cultural study of exploratory and verbal responses to visual patterns. *Journal of Cross-Cultural Psychology*, 1975b, *6*, 316–30.

———. Similarity judgments and preferences of Indian and Canadian subjects exposed to Western paintings. *International Journal of Psychology*, 1976, *11*, 43–55.

BERLYNE, D. E., & OGILVIE, J. C. Dimensions of perception of paintings. In D. E. Berlyne (Ed.), *Studies in the new experimental aesthetics: steps toward an objective psychology of aesthetic appreciation*. Washington, D.C.: Hemisphere, 1974.

BERLYNE, D. E., ROBBINS, M. C., & THOMPSON, R. A cross-cultural study of exploratory and verbal responses to visual patterns varying in complexity. In D. E. Berlyne (Ed.), *Studies in the new experimental aesthetics: steps toward an objective psychology of aesthetic appreciation*. Washington, D.C.: Hemisphere, 1974.

BERNARD, Y. Sex influence in aesthetic behavior. *Perceptual and Motor Skills*, 1972, *34*, 663–66.

BOAS, F. *Primitive art*. Cambridge, Mass.: Harvard University Press, 1928.

BRAGG, B. W. E., & CROZIER, J. B. The development with age of verbal and exploratory responses to sound sequences varying in uncertainty level. In D. E. Berlyne (Ed.), *Studies in the new experimental aesthetics: steps toward an objective psychology of aesthetic appreciation*. Washington, D.C.: Hemisphere, 1974.

CATTELL, R. B. Concepts and methods in the measurement of group syntality. *Psychological Review*, 1948, *55*, 48–63.

———. The dimensions of culture patterns by factorization of national characters. *Journal of Abnormal and Social Psychology*, 1949, *44*, 443–69.

———. The principal culture patterns discoverable in the syntal dimensions of existing nations. *Journal of Social Psychology*, 1950, *32*, 215–53.

CATTELL, R. B., & SCHEIER, I. H. *The meaning and measurement of neuroticism and anxiety*. New York: Ronald, 1961.

CHILD, I. L. Personality correlates of esthetic judgment in college students. *Journal of Personality*, 1965, *33*, 476–511.

CHILD, I. L., & IWAO, S. Personality and esthetic sensitivity: extension of findings to younger age and to different culture. *Journal of Personality and Social Psychology*, 1968, *8*, 308–12.

CHILD, I. L., & SIROTO, L. BaKwele and American esthetic evaluations compared. *Ethnology*, 1965, *4*, 349–60.

COHEN, J. *Structure du langage poétique*. Paris: Flammarion, 1966.

COHEN, J. E. Information theory and music. *Behavioral Science*, 1962, 7, 137–63.

COHN, J. Experimentelle Untersuchungen über die Gefühlsbetonung der Farben, Helligkeiten und ihrer Combinationen, *Philosophische Studien*, 1894, 10, 562–603.

CROZIER, J. B. Verbal and exploratory responses to sound sequences of varying complexity. Unpublished doctoral thesis, University of Toronto, 1973.

———. Verbal and exploratory responses to sound sequences varying in uncertainty level. In D. E. Berlyne (Ed.), *Studies in the new experimental aesthetics: steps toward an objective psychology of aesthetic appreciation*. Washington, D.C.: Hemisphere, 1974.

DRESSLER, W. W., & ROBBINS, M. C. Art styles, social stratification and cognition: an analysis of Greek vase painting. *American Ethnologist*, 1975, 2, 427–34.

EYSENCK, H. J. A critical and experimental study of color preferences. *American Journal of Psychology*, 1941, 54, 385–94.

EYSENCK, H. J., & IWAWAKI, S. Culural relativity in aesthetic judgments: an empirical study. *Perceptual and Motor Skills*, 1971, 32, 817–18.

FECHNER, G. T. Über die frage des goldnen Schnitts. *Archiv für die zeichnenden Künste*, 1865, 11, 100–12.

———. *Vorschule der ästhetik*. Leipzig: Breitkopf & Härtel, 1876.

FISCHER, J. L. Art styles as cultural cognitive maps. *American Anthropologist*, 1961, 63, 79–93.

FORD, C. S., PROTHRO, E. T., & CHILD, I. L. Some transcultural comparisons of esthetic judgment. *Journal of Social Psychology*, 1966, 68, 19–26.

FRANCÈS, R. Intérêt et préférence esthétique pour des stimuli de complexité variable: étude comparative. *Journal de Psychologie*, 1970, 70, 207–24.

———. Effets comparés de six variables collatives sur la préférence et l'intérêt d'étudiants et d'ouvriers. Paper presented at the International Colloquium on Empirical Aesthetics, Leuven, August, 1973.

FRANCÉS, R., & TAMBA, A. Étude interculturelle des préférence et musicales. *International Journal of Psychology*, 1973, 8, 95–108.

GARTH, T. R. *Race psychology*. New York: McGraw-Hill, 1931.

GODKEWITSCH, M. The golden section: an artifact of stimulus range and measure of preference. *American Journal of Psychology*, 1974, 87, 269–77.

HARE, F. G. The identification of dimensions underlying verbal and exploratory responses to music through multidimensional scaling. Unpublished doctoral thesis, University of Toronto, 1975.

HAUSER, A. *The social history of art*, Vols. 1 and 2. New York: Knopf, 1951.

HEGEL, G. F. W. *Vorlesungen über Ästhetik*. Berlin: Duncker & Humblot, 1835. (Posthumous publication of lectures delivered 1818.)

HELSON, J., & LANSFORD, T. The role of spectral energy of source and background color in pleasantness of object colors. *Applied Optics*, 1970, 9, 1513–62.

HERDER, J. G. von. *Kristische Wälder*. Riga: Hartknoch, 1769.

HOLSTI, O. R. Content analysis. In G. Lindzey & E. Aronson (Eds.), *Handbook of social psychology*, 2nd ed. Reading, Mass.: Addison Wesley, 1968.

KREUZER, H., & GUNZENHÄUSER, R. (Eds.), *Mathematik und Dichtung*. Munich: Nymphenburger, 1965.

KROEBER, A. L. *Configurations of culture growth*. Los Angeles: University of California Press, 1944.

LAWLOR, M. Cultural influences on preferences for designs. *Journal of Abnormal and Social Psychology*, 1955, *61*, 690–92.

LEVI-STRAUSS, C. *Anthropologie structurale*. Paris: Plon, 1958.

LOMAX, A. *Folk song style and culture*. Washington, D.C.: American Association for the Advancement of Science, 1968.

LOMAX, A., BARTENIEFF, I., & FORRESTINE, P. Choreometrics: a method for the study of cross-cultural pattern in film. *Research Film*, 1969, *6*, 505–17.

LOMAX, A., & BERKOWITZ, N. The evolutionary taxonomy of culture. *Science*, 1972, *177*, 228–39.

LOMMEL, A. *Shamanism: the beginnings of art*. New York: McGraw-Hill, 1968.

LYNN, R. *Attention, arousal and the orientation reaction*. London: Pergamon, 1966.

———. *Personality and national character*. Oxford: Pergamon, 1971.

MACHOTKA, P. Le développement des critères esthétiques chez l'enfant. *Enfance*, 1963, *16*, 357–79.

MALRAUX, A. *Le musée imaginaire de la sculpture*. Paris: Gallimard, 1952.

MARCUS, S. *Poetica matematica*. Bucharest: Academy, 1970. [*Mathematische Poetik*. Frankfort: Athenaum, 1973.]

MARTINDALE, D. Experimental simulation of literary change. *Journal of Personality and Social Psychology*, 1973a, *25*, 319–26.

———. Primitive mentality and the relationship between art and society. Paper read to 5th International Colloquium on Empirical Aesthetics, Lewen 1973b.

———. *The romantic progression*. Washington, D.C.: Hemisphere, 1975.

McELROY, W. A. Aesthetic appreciation in aborigines of Arnhem Land: a comparative experimental study. *Oceania*, 1952, *23*, 81–94.

MEYER, L. B. *Music, the arts, and ideas*. Chicago: University of Chicago Press, 1967.

MONTESQUIEU, C-L DE SECONDAT, BARON DE. *De l'esprit des lois*. Geneva: Barrillot, 1748.

MORRIS, C. R. *Varieties of human value*. Chicago: University of Chicago Press, 1956.

MURDOCK, G. P. *Social structure*. New York: Macmillan, 1949.

MURDOCK, G. P., & PROVOST, C. Measurement of cultural complexity. *Ethnology*, 1973, *12*, 379–92.

OGIER, F. *Preface au lecteur* to Schélandre, *Tyre et Sidon*, 1628. English translation in B. H. Clark (Ed.), *European theories of the drama*. New York: Crown, 1965. (Originally published by Stewart and Kidd, 1918.)

PECKHAM, M. *Man's rage for chaos: biology, behavior and the arts*. New York: Schocken, 1965.

PRATT, C. C. Aesthetics. *Annual Review of Psychology*, 1961, *12*, 71–92.

ROBBINS, M. C. Material culture and cognition. American Anthropologist, 1966, *68*, 745–48.

ROUBERTOUX, P. Personality variables and interest in art. *Journal of Personality and Social Psychology*, 1970, *16*, 665–68.

RUMMEL, R. J. *The dimensions of nations.* Beverly Hills: Sage, 1972.

SAWYER, J., & LEVINE, R. A. Cultural dimensions: a factor analysis of the world ethnographic sample. *American Anthropologist, 1966, 68,* 708–31.

SCHILLER, J. C. F. Über naive und sentimentale Dichtung. *Die Horen, 1795, 11,* 43–76.

SOKOLOV, E. N. *Vospriiate i uslovny refleks,* Moscow: Moscow University Press, 1958. [*Perception and the conditioned reflex.* New York: Macmillan, 1963.]

SOROKIN, P. A. *Social and cultural dynamics,* Vol. I. *Fluctuations of forms of art.* New York: Bedminster, 1937.

SOUEIF, M., & EYSENCK, J. J. Cultural differences in aesthetic preferences. *International Journal of Psychology, 1971, 6,* 293–98.

STAËL, A-L-M. DE., (NECKER, BARONNE DE). *De l'Allemagne.* Paris: Nicholle, 1810.

VICO, G. B. *Principi di scienza nuova.* Naples: F. Mosca, 1725.

VITZ, P. C. Affect as a function of stimulus variation. *Journal of Experimental Psychology, 1966, 71,* 74–79.

WEDIN, L. A multidimensional study of perceptual-emotional qualities in music. *Scandinavian Journal of Psychology, 1972, 13,* 241–57.

WHITING, J. W. M., & CHILD, I. L. *Child training and personality.* New Haven: Yale University Press, 1953.

WOLFE, A. W. Social structural bases of art. *Current Anthropology, 1969, 10,* 3–44.

YOUNGBLOOD, J. E. Music and language: some related analytical techniques. Unpublished doctoral thesis, Indiana University, 1960.

Name Index

Subject Index

Abilities, as an indicator of intelligence, 135–136
Abstract ability and sorting tasks, 124
Abstract-concrete dichotomy, 172
Achievement motive, 232, 234, 273–289
  approval motive and, 291
  concept of, 273–275
  development of,
    achievement training and, 276
    conditions for, 275–282
    independence training and, 275–276
    kinds of socialization and, 279–280
    role of father in, 280–281
    role of mother in, 281
    self-reliance training and, 276
  differentiation of, 283–289
    fear of failure, 275, 284–285, 290
    fear of success, 285–286, 290
    hope of success, 275, 284
  goal structure of, 286–287
  religious affiliation and, 277
  social and economic consequences of, 282–283
  universality of, 289–290
Achievement orientations
  affective, 287
  future, 287
  definition of success, 287
Acquired drives, theory of, 230
Aesthetic reactions, 329–330
Aesthetic sensitivity, 342
Aesthetic tastes, 17
Aestheticians
  empirical, 333–334
  speculative, 333–334
Aesthetics (see also Psychological aesthetics)
  branches of, 330–332
  cross-cultural, 333–334
    correlation studies in, 335–340
  cultural variations in,
    geographically defined, 335–338
    historically defined, 338–340
  empirical, 331–333
  philosophical, 330
  psychological study of, 16–17
Affect and cognition, division between, 169
Affective components in defining emotions, 198
Affective meaning, 15
Age
  conservation performance and, 130
  independence training and, 276–279
  memory and, 126

Aggression
  anxiety, 266, 269
    displacement of, 261
  concept of, 258
  cultural variations in, 259
  development of,
    as a goal-directed motive, 294–295
  as a dyadic variable, 257
  family structure and, 266
  forms of, 262–263
  retaliation strategy and, 267
  targets, 260, 266–267
    differences in, 263
  types of,
    physical, 256
    symbolic, 257
    verbal, 256
  universality of, 258
Aggression-inhibition conflict, 265
Aggression motive, 256–272
  definition of, 256
  structure of, 270–272
    biological components in, 270–271
    social conditions in, 271–272
Aggressive models
  availability of, 268
  in imitation learning, 268
Aggressiveness
  development of, 263–270
    child-rearing practices and, 263–268
    conditions for, 263–270
  expressive forms of, 259–261
  frustration-aggression theory and, 261
  functional forms of, 261–263
  indicators of, 256–257
  interpretation of, 257
  psychoanalytic projection hypotheses and, 261
  testosterone and, 270
  universality of, 270–272
Amae, 294
Ambiguous communication and test results, 120–121
Ame's rotating window, 54, 60
Analysis of situations in cognitive studies, 166
Analytic approach
  to experimental aesthetics, 33
  experiments using, 340–343
Analytic-relational dyad
  dealing with incompatibility of, 174
    conflict-concrete style, 174
    flexible style, 174